Riad Izhar and Janet Hontoir

ACCOUNTING, COSTING, AND MANAGEMENT

Second Edition

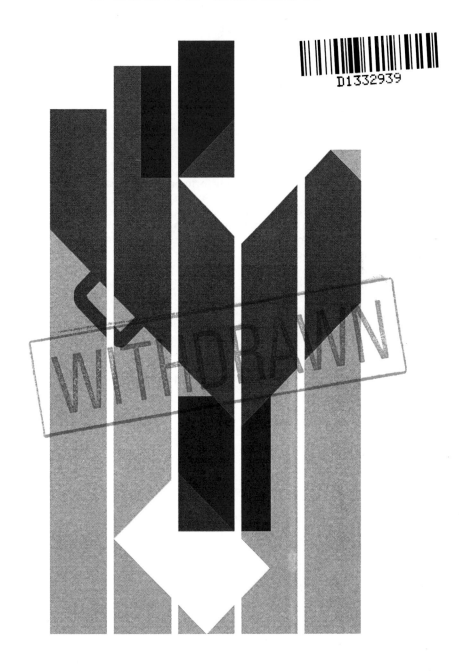

OXFORD

UNIVERSITY PRESS

OXFORD

UNIVERSITY PRESS

Great Clarendon Street, Oxford OX2 6DP

Oxford University Press is a department of the University of Oxford.
It furthers the University's objective of excellence in research, scholarship,
and education by publishing worldwide in

Oxford New York

Athens Auckland Bangkok Bogotá Buenos Aires Calcutta
Cape Town Chennai Dar es Salaam Delhi Florence Hong Kong Istanbul
Karachi Kuala Lumpur Madrid Melbourne Mexico City Mumbai
Nairobi Paris São Paulo Shanghai Singapore Taipei Tokyo Toronto Warsaw

with associated companies in Berlin Ibadan

Oxford is a registered trade mark of Oxford University Press
in the UK and in certain other countries

British Library Cataloguing in Publication Data

Data available

ISBN 0 19 832823 0

Typeset in Times New Roman and Arial
Printed in Hong Kong

Dedication

Riad Izhar dedicates this book to Amma, Abbajan, Angie and Jasmine.

Janet Hontoir dedicates this book to Mum, Dad, Vassilis and Alexandros.

Contents

Introduction

In writing this book, our aims have been twofold. The first has been to produce a text which covers the areas of financial and cost/management accounting in one volume, as most examinations today require students to possess knowledge of both. The second has been to give as much help as possible to students preparing for accounting examinations. We have aimed to provide detailed explanatory text to aid understanding of accounting concepts and have attached importance to illustrating principles and techniques by means of examples. At the end of each chapter is a generous selection of questions, mostly from recent examination papers, which test the work covered in that chapter. Detailed answers, together with workings and explanations, are presented at the end of the book. Students working on their own thus have access to sets of questions which will give them practice in the accounting techniques at the level required by the examination boards and to answers which they can use to check their work and evaluate their progress. These answers will also be of use to tutors as they will not have to spend time working through them. The answers to the questions are our own and have not been produced by the bodies from whose papers they are taken. Examination questions in accounting increasingly require candidates to give written definitions and explanations and to write short reports; we have not answered these formally as the relevant material is covered in the text, but have given some advice on how to handle written answers in the Appendix on Examination Technique.

This second edition has incorporated into the text recent changes in the subject, particularly with regard to accounting standards. It also reflects changes in the specifications of the main examining bodies at 'A' Level and its equivalent. Two new chapters on Computerised Accounting and Social Accounting have been added and we have included an extended introduction to bookkeeping in the belief that a sound grasp of the journal and ledger is an important prerequisite to the understanding of financial statements.

The book is presented in three parts. **Financial Accounting** covers basic bookkeeping and verification of the ledger, the correction of errors, the preparation of financial statements for sole traders (including those who do not keep double entry records), partnerships, limited companies and non-profit-making organisations and a brief outline of computerised accounting systems. It also assesses the financial position of a business through ratio analysis. **Cost Accounting** looks at and classifies the costs of manufacturing firms, goes on to consider material, labour and overhead costs in more detail, distinguishes between job, batch, process and contract costing and compares the absorption and marginal approaches to costing. **Management Accounting** shows how accountants help managers to make decisions by distinguishing between fixed and variable costs, drawing up budgets, setting standards for costs and carrying out variance analysis based on these, calculating break-even points and appraising capital investment projects; it also considers the area of social responsibility in decision-making.

We would like to thank John Saunders for checking selected parts of the second edition. Our appreciation also goes to the following examination bodies for granting their permission to use past questions: The Associated Examining Board (AQA); OCR (UODLE); Welsh Joint Education Committee; Scottish Qualifications Authority; Northern Ireland CCEA; Edexcel International (London Examinations); The Chartered Institute of Bankers (Institute of Financial Services); The Association of Chartered Certified Accountants (CACA); The Association of Accounting Technicians; Institute of Chartered Accountants

Riad Izhar and Janet Hontoir

Examination Technique

When you have mastered the contents of this book you will be in an excellent position to gain a good grade in your accounting examination. The hints which follow are meant to help you maximise your marks.

1. There is always a lot of work to complete in an accounting examination and you must make the best use of your time. You are not usually given much choice of questions and this is an advantage as it saves you having to spend valuable minutes reading through a lot of long questions in order to decide which ones to do. It is a good idea to attempt first those questions which you understand well and which you feel you can do best, as you make sure of the marks early on – this also gives you increased confidence for the rest of the paper.

2. Read each question well before starting it. Several minutes of concentration will ensure that you understand the structure of the question and that you do not leave out items.

3. Work through the sub-sections of the question in the order of presentation as they probably form a logical sequence. For example, you cannot do a balance sheet until you have calculated the profit or loss in the profit and loss account. If, when you come to the end of a question, you find that you have omitted an item or made an error, correct it within the body of your existing answer and **do not** begin all over again. For example, if you finish a final accounts question and then discover that you have left out accrued wages, go back and squeeze the item into the list of expenses in the profit and loss account and into the current liabilities in the balance sheet. Adjust the profit or loss and balance sheet totals accordingly.

4. If making corrections such as the one in (3) above, make sure that your new figures can be read clearly. Do not write over previous figures and do not use correcting fluid (many examination boards forbid the use of this) but just cross out the incorrect figure and insert the correct one on top or at the side. As long as the examiner can read it, you will be given marks for it.

5. If your balance sheet does not balance, do not spend too much time looking for the error. Find the difference between the two sides of your balance sheet and see if this figure appears in the question; also look for half the amount as the effect of some errors is to double the eventual imbalance. Check your figures with the question, check your arithmetic quickly and, if you still cannot find the difference, leave it and move on to the next question. You may have made only one or two errors and spending twenty minutes finding them will gain you only a couple of extra marks, but the time you will have lost could have gained you at least half the marks on another question.

6. Be assured that you will lose marks for any error once only. For example, if you make a mistake in the trading account so that your gross profit is wrong, your net profit and balance sheet will also be wrong. However examiners mark according to the 'own figure' rule which means that you will lose a mark in the trading account where the error occurred but will be awarded all subsequent marks as long as you use your own figure correctly.

7. Accounting examiners use another rule which you must beware of – that of 'duplication'. Where an item should have been used once but the candidate puts it in two places (perhaps on account of not being sure where to put it), the mark will not be given even for the entry which is correct. For example, if you do not know what to do with drawings in a final accounts question and, just to be on the safe side, you include it with the expense in the profit and loss account and also deduct it from capital in the balance sheet, you will gain no marks for it at all. You receive no credit for hedging your bets.

8. Follow the instructions in the question carefully. If you are asked to prepare a journal only, do not do ledger accounts. If you are asked to draw up a table and fill it in, do it in the way laid down in the question.

9. Always show your workings – you can do this as we have done in the answers to the questions in this book i.e. by presenting them before or after the answer. If you make calculations in your head or on your calculator and simply write down the answer without any explanation, it must be right to gain you marks. If it is wrong and you have not shown how you arrived at it, you will score no marks at all whereas if you had shown your workings, you would have gained marks for that part of the calculation which was correct.

10. Accounting questions are increasingly requiring candidates to do written answers, explaining concepts or commenting on accounts just prepared. You can learn definitions by heart but you are often asked to go further than this and analyse the concept or show how it relates to another one. You can get a good idea of how much to write by looking at the number of marks allocated to the section. If it is worth only 3 marks, do not write more than half a page as the most brilliant essay in the world will score only 3 marks; but equally make sure that you write enough as a quick phrase will score 1 mark at most. If asked to comment on the case study in the question, use the information given and make your answer relevant to the case.

11. If you are asked to write a report, use the correct format as this will gain you a couple of marks. Reread the section on report writing in Chapter 12.

12. You are allowed to use noiseless, non-programmable calculators in accounting examinations so be sure that yours works. Take a spare one with you or at least take a spare battery if it is not solar-powered.

13. Try to allocate your time well over the questions you have to do. For example, if a question carries 25 marks out of 100, you should spend around one-quarter of the time allowed on that question.

14. Be very careful that you read the general instructions carefully and that you know how many questions to answer. **Never** answer more than the required number. If the paper asks you to answer four questions and you answer five, you will be marked on four and will have wasted precious time on the fifth.

15. The more questions you have practised before the examination, the better prepared you will be as you will be familiar with the various formats which examiners use. If, on the day, you are faced with an unfamiliar format, read the question carefully and try to get into its meaning so that you know what to do.

16. And finally, good luck!

Part I
Financial Accounting

1

Double-Entry Bookkeeping, the Journal, the Ledger and the Trial Balance

1.1 Introduction

The recording of business transactions is known as bookkeeping. It is essential that owners and managers of businesses keep records of all financial dealings so that they always know their position with regard to their bank balance, debtors, creditors etc. and so that they can calculate their profit or loss at the end of the year. There are various parties who are interested in receiving information regarding the financial position of a business:

- the owner or owners
- the tax authorities (Inland Revenue and HM Customs and Excise)
- the bank manager if the business is seeking a loan or overdraft
- potential investors

The accepted system used today is that of **double-entry bookkeeping**, whereby each transaction is seen as having a two-fold effect on the business – something enters or is gained by the business and something leaves or is lost. For example, if goods are purchased for cash, the business gains the goods and loses the cash. The double-entry system involves opening accounts in ledgers for each type of transaction and showing in each case what has been gained and what has been lost. In this chapter we shall look at the system of bookkeeping used in a typical firm.

1.2 Source Documents

These are pieces of paper which accompany transactions and which form the basis for entries in the accounts. The main source documents a firm is likely to handle are:

- **purchase invoices** received by the firm from suppliers when buying goods or services on credit.
- **sales invoices** sent by the firm to customers when selling goods or services on credit.
- **credit notes** received by the firm from suppliers when goods purchased by the firm are returned as wrong or faulty. The credit notes received partly offset the purchases invoices.
- **credit notes** sent by the firm to customers who have returned goods – these partly offset the sales invoices.
- **cheque counterfoils** which are evidence of cheques paid out by the firm.
- **paying-in slip counterfoils** which are evidence of cheques received and banked by the firm.
- **receipts** issued by the firm for cash received from customers or received by the firm for cash paid out.
- **till rolls** which are the evidence of cash taken by a shop, for example.

- **petty cash vouchers** to back up small amounts of cash paid out by the firm's office.
- **bank statements** received from the firm's bank give information on amounts paid out and deposited as well as on items such as standing orders, direct debits, credit transfers, bank charges etc.

1.3 Subsidiary Books of Account

The information contained in the source documents is transferred to subsidiary books of account, also known as **books of original entry** as they are the first place where transactions are entered. They are also called **journals** as they are kept on a day-to-day basis. These books are not part of the ledger and entries in them do not constitute part of the double-entry system. The main subsidiary books are:

- **day books**. There are four – the purchases, sales, purchase returns and sales returns day books. These books contain details of purchases and sales made on credit (i.e. not for cash) and of returns which have arisen from them.
- **the main cash book** (and its subsidiary the petty cash book) which contains details of all transactions involving cash or cheques.
- **the general or main journal** which contains details of all transactions which do not go into the day books or the cash book.

Information from the source documents is entered straight into the appropriate subsidiary book so that at the end of the month the bookkeeper can calculate totals for the month for purchases, sales, returns, cash received and so on.

1.4 The Ledger

All the information entered in the subsidiary books must be transferred (posted) to the ledger, which is the main book of account and where the double entry takes place. Where appropriate, totals can be extracted from the day books but certain transactions are posted on an individual basis. In large businesses, it is not possible to keep all the accounts in one ledger because of the large volume of entries so the ledger is usually divided into sub-sections. This division is usually done in terms of function as follows:

- **the purchases ledger** contains the accounts of all the suppliers from whom the firm has bought goods and services on credit.
- **the sales ledger** contains the accounts of all the customers to whom the firm has sold goods and services on credit.
- **the cash book** contains the bank and the cash accounts. Notice that this was also cited as a subsidiary book – it is the only book which acts as both a journal and ledger. Many firms keep a columnar cash book, with separate columns for the cash and bank accounts and may even have a third column in which they show discounts (see section on discounts below). The petty cash book is an offshoot of the main cash book. An amount is given to the petty cashier every week or month with which to make small payments, such as for postage, cleaning materials etc. The petty cashier makes out a voucher every time money is paid for something and the amount is recorded in the appropriate column in an analytical book. At the end of each period the petty cashier is reimbursed by the chief cashier for the money spent so that each period begins with the same amount. This is known as the **imprest system**.
- **the general ledger** contains the remaining asset, capital and liability accounts and all the income and expense accounts.

The ledger is divided into two sides – debit and credit. The traditional method splits the page down the middle with debits on the left-hand side and credits on the right-hand side, but many firms today keep ledgers which look like bank statements, with a debit column next to a credit column and a running balance. The method of setting up the page is not important. What matters is that there are two distinct sections for debit and credit and that all transactions are posted to the correct side in the correct accounts. The rules to remember are:

1) Whatever comes into the firm is placed on the debit side and whatever goes out is placed on the credit side. For example, if cash enters the firm we debit the cash account; if goods go out of the firm because we sold them, we credit the sales account (never call an account a 'goods account' as this is vague).
2) For every transaction there must be a debit in the account gaining value and an equal and opposite credit in the account losing value.

The ledger is divided into accounts and each account contains the entries for a particular type of transaction. It is important to classify transactions so that all those of the same type go together e.g. all the purchases, all the transactions made with a particular supplier, all the wages paid etc. In the traditional ledger we keep what we call 'T' accounts where the shape of each account looks like a large letter 'T', as you will see below.

Most accounts will have entries on both the debit and the credit sides and they must be balanced at the end of the period to see the overall position. If the debit side is larger than the credit, we say the account has a debit balance, and vice versa. (Where the total of debits is exactly equal to the total of credits, the account has a nil balance and there is no need to carry or bring down balance.) For example, if we have paid more into our bank account than we have taken out, we have a debit balance but if we are overdrawn we have a credit balance. If you think this sounds the wrong way round, remember that your bank is describing the situation from its own point of view. When you have a positive amount of money in your account, the bank calls this a credit balance because it owes the money to you, but you will call it a debit balance. Your account is the mirror image of that kept at the bank.

1.5 Purchases, Sales, Stock and Fixed Assets

It is important to distinguish between several different types of transaction and to know which accounts are used in each case:

*   goods bought are '**purchases**' and goods sold are '**sales**'. Do not use 'goods' as this is not specific.
*   between purchases of goods bought for stock and resale and the purchase of items known as fixed assets, i.e. buildings, equipment, vehicles, tools etc which will be used in the business over a period of time. Goods bought for stock are entered in the **purchases account** whereas fixed assets go into special accounts of their own eg **land and buildings account, fixtures and fittings account, office equipment account** etc. The money spent on purchases of stock is deducted from profit at the end of the year whereas that spent on purchases of fixed assets is not (with the exception of the depreciation on them, as we shall see in Chapter 5).
*   between **purchases** and **stock**. The purchases account is used during the year to record goods bought for resale. The stock account is opened at the end of the year to show how much of the goods bought remain unsold at the year-end.

1.6 Personal Accounts

The customers' accounts in the sales ledger and the suppliers' accounts in the purchases ledger deserve special treatment. Not only are they some of the most important accounts kept by a business as they show the outstanding amounts owing to and owing by the business but they are also easy to confuse. Here are typical examples of these accounts. When preparing personal accounts, always look at the transactions from the point of view of the business whose books you are keeping, not from the other person's.

Example

Debbie Debtor's Account in the Sales Ledger for June

Debits	£	Credits	£
Balance b/d (a)	250	Returns inwards (c)	170
Credit sales (b)	2 600	Cheques received (d)	2 150
Dishonoured cheques (f)	36	Discounts allowed (e)	220
		Balance c/d (g)	346
	2 886		2 886
Balance b/d (h)	346		

(a) At the beginning of June, Debbie owes us £250 which is outstanding from last month; this is a debit balance because it is an asset to us.
(b) During the month we sell her goods worth £2 600 on credit. This is a debit entry because she owes us the amount. The credit entry is in the sales account, which has lost goods.
(c) Of the goods we have sold her, Debbie returns £170 worth as being unsuitable in some way. We credit her account to cancel part of what she owes. The debit entry goes in the returns inwards account.
(d) During the month Debbie pays us £2 150 of the amount she owes. We credit her account to cancel part of her debt and we debit the bank account as it has received value.
(e) We allowed Debbie £220 in cash discount as a reward for prompt payment and we credit this to her account. The debit is in the discounts allowed account.
(f) Debbie paid us a cheque for £36 during the month which was returned by the bank as she did not have enough funds in her account to cover it. This £36 was part of the £2 150 she had paid us and so we debit her account to reactivate the debt. The credit entry will be in our bank account.
(g) At the end of the month we balance off the account. The debit side is £346 greater than the credit side so we place this difference on the credit side as the balance carried down, to even up the two sides.
(h) The corresponding entry for the balance c/d is the balance brought down which now starts off next month. At this point Debbie owes us £346.

Chris Creditor's Account in the Purchases Ledger for June

Debits	£	Credits	£
Returns outwards (c)	270	Balance b/d (a)	1 300
Cheques paid (d)	2 800	Credit purchases (b)	3 600
Discounts received (e)	140		
Balance c/d (f)	1 690		
	4 900		4 900
		Balance b/d (g)	1 690

(a) The balance we owe Chris from last month is £1 300. This is on the credit side of his account because it is a liability to us.

(b) During the month we bought goods from Chris for £3 600. We credit his account because we owe him this amount and we debit the purchases account, which has gained goods.

(c) We returned goods to Chris to the value of £270. We debit his account to cancel part of what we owe him and credit the returns outwards account.

(d) We have paid Chris a total of £2 800 during the month. This satisfies part of our debt to him so we debit the account. The credit entry is in the bank account.

(e) We received discounts from Chris worth £140 and this cancels part of the debt. The credit entry is in the discounts received account.

(f) Total credits exceed total debits by £1 690. We still owe Chris this amount and it becomes the balance carried down on the debit side to equal up the two sides of the account.

(g) The balance brought down is on the credit side and we start off the next month owing Chris £1 690.

1.7 Discounts

It is important to distinguish between two types of discount allowed by a supplier and received by a customer.

1) **Trade Discount**: This is allowed by a supplier to regular customers or as a reward for buying in bulk. It is typically between 10% and 25%. Trade discount is deducted from the catalogue price of the goods at the start of the transaction and may not even be shown on the invoice, i.e. it is built into the price charged. It is not shown in any ledger account and the price of a purchase or sale is entered after the trade discount has been deducted. Some firms enter the amount of the trade discount in the day book but this is not necessary.

2) **Cash Discount**: This is allowed by a supplier to a customer who pays an invoice by the due date. It is used as an incentive to the purchaser to settle the bill promptly. Since neither the purchaser nor the seller knows whether the discount will apply until the bill has been paid, cash discount is shown in the books at the time of payment. When a firm is paying a supplier for goods purchased, it debits the discount to the supplier's account and credits it to the discount received account. When the firm is receiving money from a customer and allows a discount, it credits the customer's account and debits the discount allowed account. Cash discount is also shown by many firms in the cash book in the discount column, although this is for information only and does not constitute part of the double entry.

1.8 Value-Added Tax

Value-added tax (VAT) is the sales tax used in the UK and in many other countries; in the UK it is administered and collected by HM Customs and Excise. Although some goods and services and small traders are exempt from VAT, most are taxed at a standard rate, which may differ for various classes of products. In the UK the standard rate is the same for all products which are liable to the tax – this is 17.5% at the time of writing.

VAT is collected by all firms involved in bringing a product to the point of sale. Each firm adds the VAT onto the price it charges on its outputs and claims back the VAT it has paid on its inputs, in effect paying the Customs and Excise 17.5% on the value it has added to the product. VAT is added to the price at each stage of production until it

reaches the final consumer, who has nobody to pass it on to and who thus bears the burden of the tax.

Here is an example. The total of a firm's sales invoices for May comes to £20 000, after trade and cash discounts have been allowed but before VAT has been added. The firm will be liable to pay 17.5% of £20 000 i.e. £3 500. The total of the firm's purchases invoices for the same month comes to £17 000 after discounts but before VAT. The suppliers will have charged 17.5% of £17 000 = £2 975. The firm's VAT Return will be:

VAT Return

	£
VAT due on sales	3 500
Less VAT reclaimed on purchases	(2 975)
Amount of VAT payable	525

A firm with a turnover of more than a certain set amount is obliged to be registered for VAT and to make such Returns periodically. It must account for the VAT it charges on all its sales and for that paid by it on all its purchases. The ledger account treatment is as follows.

The main principle to remember is that the net values of goods purchased and sold must be kept separate from the amounts of VAT but the gross amounts must also be shown because these are the amounts actually paid to suppliers and received from customers. To do this we enter the whole amount of the invoice in the supplier's or customer's account (including the VAT) but the double entry is to be found in two accounts. The value of the goods goes in the purchases or sales account and the tax is entered in a separate VAT account.

When returns are made on purchases or sales, the procedure is the same. The personal account will show the whole amount, including the tax, but the returns and VAT accounts will show the items separately.

Example

Big Bang Ltd purchases goods costing £3 000 from Asteroid Warehouses and sells goods for £5 000 to Meteor Stores. Both figures are net of VAT at a standard rate of 17.5%. Subsequently, Big Bang returns £600 worth of goods to Asteroid Warehouses and Meteor Stores returns £800 worth of goods to Big Bang, both figures being net of VAT.

Purchases

	£		£
Asteroid Warehouses	3 000		

Sales

	£		£
		Meteor Stores	5 000

Returns Inwards

	£		£
Meteor Stores	800		

Returns Outwards

	£		£
		Asteroid Warehouses	600

Asteroid Warehouses

	£		£
Returns	600	Purchases	3 000
VAT	105	VAT	525

Meteor Stores

	£		£
Sales	5 000	Returns	800
VAT	875	VAT	140

VAT

	£		£
Asteroid Warehouses	525	Meteor Stores	875
Meteor Stores	140	Asteroid Warehouses	105

1.9 The Trial Balance

At the end of a financial period (this may be a week, a month or a year), those responsible for keeping the firm's books need to check the arithmetical accuracy of the accounts by preparing a trial balance. This is important because the accounts will now be the basis of a profit calculation and of a balance sheet, and no firm wants errors in its end-of-year financial statements.

All the accounts are balanced off and a summary of the balances is drawn up. All debit balances are entered in one column and all credit balances in another. Since every transaction has been entered once on the debit side and once on the credit side, total debits must equal total credits if everything has been done correctly. Going one step further, when there are no errors in the books, total debit balances must equal total credit balances. The final stage in the bookkeeper's work is thus to produce a trial balance which balances. If it does not, the office staff must go through the books to find the error or errors.

The trial balance, however, is not foolproof and there are certain errors which it does not detect. These are treated in Chapter 6.

Example

On 1 January, William set up in a business as a retailer. His transactions for the first two weeks in January are as follows:

Jan 1   Started business by putting £10 000 in a bank account
Jan 2   Withdrew £2 000 cash from the bank
Jan 3   Bought goods for cash, £1 000
Jan 4   Bought a second-hand van on credit from Sun Motors for £400
Jan 5   Sold goods for cash, £200
Jan 7   Paid wages £60, in cash
Jan 9   Bought goods on credit from A Supplier for £400
Jan 11   Sold goods on credit to B Customer for £500
Jan 12   Sent Sun Motors a cheque for £100

Jan 13 Sent A Supplier a cheque for £390 in full settlement for the goods bought
        on 9 January. Discount received for prompt payment, £10
Jan 14 Paid wages £60, in cash
Jan 14 Received a cheque for £200 from B Customer

Record the above transactions in double-entry form, balance the accounts at
14 January and extract a trial balance at the close of business on that date.

Answer

William
Ledger
Bank (Cash Book)

Debit		£	Credit		£
1 Jan	Capital	10 000	2 Jan	Cash	2 000
14 Jan	B Customer	200	12 Jan	Sun Motors	100
			13 Jan	A Supplier	390
			14 Jan	Balance c/d	7 710
		10 200			10 200
15 Jan	Balance b/d	7 710			

Cash (Cash Book)

Debit		£	Credit		£
2 Jan	Bank	2 000	3 Jan	Purchases	1 000
5 Jan	Sales	200	7 Jan	Wages	60
			14 Jan	Wages	60
			14 Jan	Balance c/d	1 080
		2 200			2 200
15 Jan	Balance b/d	1 080			

Capital (General Ledger)

Debit		£	Credit		£
			1 Jan	Bank	10 000

Purchases (General Ledger)

Debit		£	Credit		£
3 Jan	Cash	1 000	14 Jan	Balance c/d	1 400
9 Jan	A Supplier	400			
		1 400			1 400
15 Jan	Balance b/d	1 400			

Motor Van (General Ledger)

Debit		£	Credit		£
4 Jan	Sun Motors	400	14 Jan	Balance c/d	400
15 Jan	Balance b/d	400			

Sales (General Ledger)

Debit		£	Credit		£
14 Jan	Balance c/d	700	5 Jan	Cash	200
			11 Jan	B Customer	500
		700			700
			15 Jan	Balance b/d	700

Wages (General Ledger)

Debit	£	Credit	£
7 Jan Cash	60	14 Jan Balance c/d	120
14 Jan Cash	60		
	120		120
15 Jan Balance b/d	120		

Discount received (General Ledger)

Debit	£	Credit	£
14 Jan Balance c/d	10	13 Jan A Supplier	10
		15 Jan Balance b/d	10

A Supplier (Purchases Ledger)

Debit	£	Credit	£
13 Jan Bank	390	9 Jan Purchases	400
13 Jan Discount received	10		
	400		400

Sun Motors (Purchases Ledger)

Debit	£	Credit	£
12 Jan Bank	100	4 Jan Motor van	400
14 Jan Balance c/d	300		
	400		400
		15 Jan Balance b/d	300

B Customer (Sales Ledger)

Debit	£	Credit	£
11 Jan Sales	500	14 Jan Bank	200
		14 Jan Balance c/d	300
	500		500
15 Jan Balance b/d	300		

William
Trial Balance as at 14 January

	Debit £	Credit £
Capital		10 000
Bank	7 710	
Cash	1 080	
Purchases	1 400	
Motor van	400	
Sun Motors		300
Sales		700
Wages	120	
B Customer	300	
Discount received		10
	£11 010	£11 010

Notes

1) The balance is obtained by adding up both sides of the account on the last day of the period and subtracting one side from the other. Enter this as the balance c/d (done for arithmetical purposes) on the side which has less. Complete the double entry by bringing this down to the other side to begin the next period.

2) Note the difference between buying goods for resale (purchases) and buying fixed assets, eg the motor van, which will be used over a long period in the business. Each fixed asset has its own account whereas goods for resale are all grouped together in the purchases account.

3) Accounts have been grouped above according to which ledger they go in. The account of Sun Motors has been placed in the purchases ledger because Sun Motors is a creditor, even though the goods bought were not stock for resale.

1.10 Assets and Liabilities and the Accounting Equation

An asset is an item which is **owned** by the business and it always has a debit balance in its own account. Examples are buildings, equipment, unsold stock, trade debtors (people who owe money to the business for goods sold to them on credit) and a positive bank balance. A liability is an item **owed** by the business and it always has a credit balance in its own account. Examples are trade creditors (people to whom the business owes money for goods purchased by it from them on credit), loans, overdrafts and capital.

Capital is the amount of money introduced by the owner into the business. It is a liability because the business owes it to the owner. (In accounts the owner is always seen as being a separate entity from the business, even if in law they are one and the same person.)

Just as total debit balances equal total credit balances, total assets must equal total liabilities. All the money which the business has spent on its assets has come from the money borrowed, either from the owner or from outsiders. Equally, all the money borrowed has found a use somewhere.

The accounting equation is based on the above theory and is stated thus:

Assets = Liabilities

Since the liability of capital is different from other liabilities because it is owed to the owners and not to outsiders, the equation can be restated thus:

Assets = Liabilities + Capital

Questions

Question 1.1

Record Muriel's transactions for the month of May, balance off all accounts, and extract a trial balance as at 31 May.

1 May	Started business with £5 000 in the bank and £2 000 cash
2 May	Bought goods for cash £400 on credit from L Jones £200 and from A Smith £300
4 May	Bought fixtures on credit from Desk Ltd £600
7 May	Sold goods for cash £250; sold goods on credit to B Black £350 and to K White £450
9 May	Paid L Jones
10 May	Received a loan from A Friend by cheque £1 000
12 May	Returned some fixtures, invoiced at £100, to Desk Ltd
14 May	Paid Desk Ltd a cheque for £500
14 May	Paid rent by cheque £175
17 May	Bought goods for cash £500; bought goods on credit from L Jones £400
23 May	Sold goods for cash £275; sold goods on credit to B Black £375 and to K White £475
29 May	Received a cheque from B Black £725
29 May	Paid monthly salary by cheque for £450. Paid rent by cheque £175

Author's Question

Question 1.2

The following transactions took place within a small firm:

1) the purchase of goods on credit from suppliers
2) the sale of goods on credit
3) cheques received from credit customers
4) payments to suppliers by cheque for goods previously supplied
5) allowances to credit customers upon return of faulty goods
6) daily cash takings paid into the bank
7) monthly salaries paid to employees
8) the year-end stock valuation

For each of the above types of transactions identify:

(a) the source document from which the data were taken
(b) the book of original entry for the transaction and
(c) the double entry for each transaction in the ledger

Association of Accounting Technicians, Preliminary

Question 1.3

You are responsible for maintaining the journals and ledger accounts for your organisation. Sales are currently all for cash but the managers plan to offer credit to customers in the future in order to increase business activity.

At 1 October 1998, these are the following balances on creditors' accounts:

P Blunt £1 250
J Hall   £150

During the month of October 1998 you compile the following journals:

Purchases Day Book

Date	Name	Net	VAT	Gross
1998		£	£	£
4 Oct	P Blunt	6 000	1 050	7 050
11 Oct	J Bolton	30 000	5 250	35 250
13 Oct	Z Rhawandala	5 000	875	5 875
15 Oct	P Blunt	12 000	2 100	14 100
31 Oct	Totals	53 000	9 275	62 275

Returns Outwards Day Book

Date	Name	Net	VAT	Gross
1998		£	£	£
3 Oct	J Bolton	2 000	350	2 350
28 Oct	P Blunt	600	105	705
31 Oct	Totals	2 600	455	3 055

Petty Cash Book

Date	Debit £	Details	Total £	Postage £	Travel £	Ledger £
1 Oct	600	Balance b/fwd				
6 Oct		Parcel post	65	65		
10 Oct		Bus fares	20		20	
12 Oct		G Hall (train ticket)	125		125	
14 Oct		Post Office Counters	24	24		
16 Oct		Travel reimbursed	85		85	
18 Oct		Post Office Counters	27	27		
21 Oct		J Hall	150			150
			496	116	230	150
31 Oct	496	Bank				
		Balance c/fwd	600			
	1 096		1 096			
1 Nov	600	Balance b/fwd				

You have extracted the following details from the Cash Book for October:

Cash sales in the month were £61 100 including VAT at 17.5%.

Paid to P Blunt on 4 October his opening balance less cash discount of 2%.

REQUIRED

(a) Write up the ledger accounts for all creditors and nominal ledger accounts relevant to the above transactions.
   (Note: You are NOT required to prepare cash, bank or control accounts; you are NOT required to balance the accounts off.)   **(11 marks)**

(b) You later realise that the purchase from Z Rhawandala is for office equipment. Describe the correct treatment for this item in the ledger accounts and explain the effect on profits for the month of the incorrect treatment.   **(3 marks)**

(c) Suggest a simple accounting coding system which might be suitable if your organisation decided to computerise its ledger accounting to accommodate the proposed increase in business activity.   **(6 marks)**

Chartered Institute of Management Accountants

Case Study – Kilburn Tandoori
Part I Bookkeeping

On 1 February 2000 Mr and Mrs Shah bought an existing eating house to convert it to an Indian restaurant. The initial capital of £50 000 banked on 1 February was used the next day to make the following payments: £40 000 for purchase of premises, £4 000 for furniture and fittings and £6 000 for conversion costs.

Customers were required to settle bills by cash or cheque after the meal, and weekly credit accounts were opened for two nearby offices who entertained their guests at the restaurant on a regular basis. A 3 per cent cash discount was offered for payment within one week. All cash and cheques were banked daily. All payments, except petty cash expenditures, were made by cheque. Mr Shah paid his suppliers a week following delivery, thereby obtaining a 2 per cent cash discount from each.

The following is a week-by-week summary of the first month's trading:

	Week			
	1	2	3	4
	£	£	£	£
Credit purchases from suppliers				
Williams Farms		500	450	550
T Green & Sons	80	100	110	100
Hakim Meat	300	350	350	350
Robinson Wines	50	110	175	150
Other Payments				
Cook's wages	100	100	110	100
Waiters' wages	180	180	200	200
Cash register machine		200		
Rates				270
Drawings		55	10	70
For petty cash expenditure	30	30	30	30
Cash Receipts	625	830	1 055	1 210
Cheques Received	810	1 050	1 100	1 175
Invoiced to credit customers				
Sun Finance Co		110	155	150
Chrome Metals plc		60	80	100
Cheques received from credit customers				
Sun Finance plc			107	150
Chrome Metals plc				138
Summary of petty cash expenditure				
Cleaning materials	5	7	7	8
Fresh flowers	10	4	5	6
Napkins	12	14	15	15

The owners employ you to maintain a full double-entry bookkeeping system.
Write up the books for the first month's trading.

Notes

1) Since the information given is on a week-by-week basis it is best to write up the books also on a weekly basis.
2) Classify the £6 000 conversion costs as premises and the £200 cash register as fixtures and fittings.
3) The petty cash expenditures for cleaning materials, fresh flowers and napkins should be grouped into one account called general expenses.
4) In your discount calculations, round off to the nearest whole £.

This Case Study continues in Chapter 4. The solution to the whole exercise is also in Chapter 4.

2

Verification of the Ledger

2.1 Introduction

Since it is human to make errors and omissions, it is necessary for a bookkeeping system to have a means of verifying the accuracy of the double-entry records. We saw in Chapter 1 the role played by the trial balance although, as we have noted, it does not show up all possible errors (see Chapter 6 for more on this). In this chapter we are going to deal with bank reconciliation statements and control accounts.

2.2 Bank Reconciliation Statements

Every firm keeps a record of its bank current account. The bank also keeps a record of this account and sends a statement to the firm at the end of each period, normally every month. For various reasons the latest balance on the bank statement is unlikely to be the same as the latest balance in the firm's cash book, the main reason being that the firm and the bank have access to different information at different times; errors and omissions can also occur.

The following are items which the firm will know of but the bank will not:

- cheques drawn by the firm on its account which have not yet been presented to the bank by the recipients
- cheques received by the firm and deposited into the account but not yet cleared by the banking system
- cheques returned to drawer, i.e. cheques paid to the firm which were not covered by sufficient funds in the drawer's account and which the bank has returned to him, cancelling the credit in the firm's account

There are also items which the bank will know of but the firm will not:

- bank charges debited by the bank to the firm's account
- credit transfers received by the bank on behalf of the firm which the firm has not yet been notified of
- standing orders and direct debits which the bank pays automatically but which the firm has forgotten to enter into its account

On receiving the bank statement each month, the person in charge of the bank account should prepare a bank reconciliation statement which will explain in detail the difference between the bank's balance and the firm's own balance. The procedure is as follows.

The cashier should carefully go through the entries on the bank statement and in the firm's bank account and cross off those which appear correctly in both. Any items which appear in one but not the other should be noted and any errors or unexplained items in the statement should be checked.

16

The bank account in the cash book must now be brought up to date by entering those items on the bank statement which had not been included in the firm's bank account. The bank account will now be correct and up to date.

The final balance on the corrected bank account must now be reconciled with the final balance on the bank statement. The easiest way to do this is to begin with the statement balance (which is wrong), add on any uncleared cheques and deduct any unpresented ones. The balance which results should now equal the balance in the corrected bank account.

Example

The following question is taken from the Chartered Institute of Management Accountants.

From the following information, prepare a statement reconciling the present bank balance as shown in the cash book with that shown on the bank statement at 16 November 1996:

Cash Book

Date		£	Date		£
10 Nov	Balance b/fwd	5 327	11 Nov	Purchase ledger	1 406
12 Nov	Sales ledger	2 804	12 Nov	PAYE	603
13 Nov	Cash sales	543	14 Nov	VAT	435
15 Nov	Sales ledger	1 480	16 Nov	Cheques cashed	1 342
				Balance c/fwd	6 368
		10 154			10 154

Bank Statement

Date		Debit £	Credit £	Balance £
10 Nov	Balance			6 049
11 Nov	Cheque 101204	420		5 629
12 Nov	Cheque 101206	1 406		4 223
13 Nov	Cheque 101205	302		
	Rates DD	844		3 077
14 Nov	Paid in – cheques		2 804	
	Paid in – cash		543	6 424
15 Nov	Credit transfer		685	7 109
	Bank charges	130		
	Dishonoured cheque	425		
	Cheque 101207	603		5 951
16 Nov	Cheque 101209	1 342		4 609

Solution

The first step is to study the two records and cross off those items which are common to both. Then bring the cash book up to date by starting off with the final balance of £6 368 and adjusting it for those items which are in the statement but not in the cash book. Be careful of cheques no 101204 and 101206 which appear in the bank statement but not in the cash book. Since they were cleared on 11 and 12 November, they must have been paid in several days before these dates and before the first item we have been given in the cash book. We can thus assume that these cheques have already been entered in the cash book.

Updated Cash Book on 16 November

	£		£
Balance b/fwd	6 368	Rates (Direct Debit)	844
Credit transfer	685	Bank charges	130
		Dishonoured cheque	425
		Balance c/d	5 654
	7 053		7 053
Balance b/d	5 654		

Now we reconcile the final cash book balance, which is now correct, with the final balance on the bank statement. It is more logical to begin the bank reconciliation statement with the wrong balance (i.e. that on the bank statement) and finish up with the correct one (i.e. that in the updated cash book).

Add to the final bank statement balance all cheques which had been paid in but which have not been cleared. Then deduct all cheques which were paid to others but which have not yet been presented for payment.

Bank Reconciliation Statement at 16 November

	£
Balance as per bank statement	4 609
Add uncleared cheque from sales ledger	1 480
Less unpresented cheque from VAT payment	(435)
Balance as per cash book	5 654

2.3 Control Accounts

Businesses maintain separate accounts for each credit customer and supplier in sales and purchase ledgers to ascertain the amounts owing from and to each at any one time. Where there is a large number it is possible for the sales and purchase clerks to make an occasional error. At the end of the month, before sending statements of accounts to debtors and cheques to creditors it is advisable to perform a check on the figures. This is done by the maintenance of control accounts.

Every time entries are made in, for example, the sales ledger (usually monthly, from the sales day book and cash book) the total of these entries are recorded in an independent account called the sales ledger control account (SLCA), which is kept in the general ledger. If this is done for all entries, the total of the individual balances in the sales ledgers at any one time should equal the single balance on the control account. If it does not, the bookkeeper is alerted to errors. It is useful to have such an alarm system before sending out the monthly cheques and statements of accounts.

Control accounts are used in a wide variety of accounting situations. Their main use in financial accounting is in respect to debtors and creditors, but they are also used in cost accounting e.g. cost ledger control, wages control, production overhead control etc. In this chapter we will look at their application to financial accounting but the principles when using them in cost accounting are the same. At the end of the year, once the individual debtor and creditor accounts have been checked against their respective controls, the single balance on the control is the one that appears in the trial balance. This is a better option than including all the many individual balances in it. Consider the length of the trial balance of a large company with thousands of individual debtors and creditors prepared without control accounts! The balances on the control accounts are also the figures that appear in the balance sheet as trade debtors and trade creditors.

The practice of treating control accounts as part of the double entry varies from firm to firm. In some the individual accounts are regarded as the double entry, with the control being a checking account, not part of the double entry. In others the control account assumes the responsibility of being part of the double-entry system, the individual accounts in this case being regarded as back-up. In such cases the control account is more properly thought of as being a total debtors or total creditors account.

2.4 The Usefulness of Control Accounts

While control accounts are not strictly necessary to operate a double-entry accounting system, businesses with a large number of credit customers and suppliers take the trouble of maintaining them because, in addition to the above function, they offer a number of other advantages. These are as follows:

1) If the trial balance fails to balance, the only books that need to be checked are the general ledger and cash book. The possibility of errors in the sales ledger and purchasers ledger can be ruled out since they have already been reconciled before inclusion in the trial balance. In the absence of control accounts and in the event of the trial balance not balancing, the bookkeeper would have no clue as to which book or books the errors are in. All would need checking. In this way, control accounts can, and in practice do, lead to a considerable saving in time and effort.

2) In the absence of control accounts, if it is desired to check entries in the debtors and creditors accounts, a trial balance for the whole business involving all books has to be extracted; a lengthy and time-consuming exercise which is done only once or twice a year. By building an independent check on debtors and creditors into the recording system, their entries can now be checked without the need to involve all books. Since the process is quicker and cheaper, checks can be performed more regularly.

3) It is possible to find the figure for total debtors or total creditors simply by balancing one account. This is quicker and easier than having to balance all the individual accounts.

4) Control accounts are usually kept by a person other than the sales and purchase ledger clerks. In this way the chance of deliberate fraud is reduced.

Example

The items in the control accounts are exactly those which appear in the individual accounts. The only difference is in the amounts, the control containing the *total* of the individual accounts.

The following are typical sales ledger and purchases ledger control accounts:

Sales Ledger Control Account

Debits	£	Credits	£
Balances b/d	14 000	Returns inwards (RIDB)	2 000
Credit sales (SDB)	256 000	Cheques received (CB)	210 000
Dishonoured cheques	2 000	Discounts allowed (CB)	8 000
		Bad debts	1 000
		Purchase Ledger contra entry	3 000
		Balances c/d	48 000
	272 000		272 000

Purchases Ledger Control Account

Debits	£	Credits	£
Returns outwards (RODB)	4 000	Balances b/d	12 000
Cheques paid (CB)	165 000	Credit purchases (PDB)	190 000
Discounts received (CB)	6 000	Dishonoured cheques	1 500
Sales ledger contra entry	3 000		
Balances c/d	25 500		
	203 500		203 500

SDB   = Sales day book
PDB . = Purchases day book
RIDB = Return inwards day book
RODB = Returns outwards day book
CB   = Cash book

Notice how the control accounts look like larger versions of the personal accounts we studied in Chapter 1. The initial balances b/d is the total of all the balances b/d in the particular ledger. The total credit sales is the total of all the individual sales made on credit, the total returns inward is the total of all returns made to us by customers etc. If everything is correct, the total of the final balances c/d will automatically balance off the account.

Notes:

1) Items that increase the amount receivable from debtors are debited, whilst those that decrease the amount are credited.
2) Items that increase the amount payable to creditors are credited, whilst those that decrease the amount are debited.
3) Cash sales and cash purchases are not included in control accounts.
4) A sales ledger control account may have a small credit balance in addition to the main debit balance. This will arise when goods have been returned by a customer for which we have not sent a refund or credit note or when an account has been overpaid in error.
5) A purchase ledger control account may have a small debit balance in addition to the main credit balance. This will arise when we have not yet received a refund or credit note for goods returned to suppliers or when we have overpaid an account in error.

2.5 Contra Entries

Sometimes a business both sells goods to, and purchases from, another business. Suppose that one of our customers, Mr K, also supplies some materials to us. There will therefore be an account for Mr K in both our sales ledger and purchase ledger. If Mr K is owed £400 for materials supplied but also owes us £1 000, it would be silly of us to pay him £400 and then receive £1000 from him. It makes more sense to 'set off' his indebtedness against ours, with the following book entry:

> Dr K Ltd Creditor (PL) £400
> Cr K Ltd Debtor (SL) £400

The net result is that Mr K now owes us £600. Such a set off is known as a **contra entry**. Of course, the entries made in the individual accounts should be repeated in the control accounts.

2.6 Large firms

In large firms, the sheer number of individual debtors or creditors may make it impossible to keep them all in a single book. The individual ledgers then have to be split up. How this is done will vary according to the nature of the business. Common divisions are by geographical area, type of product and alphabetically. There will be a separate control account for each sub-division of the ledger.

2.7 Examination questions

Questions on control accounts tend to be of two types.

1) A list of balances regarding debtors and creditors is given. From this you have to construct control accounts. These questions are straightforward. Look out for information supplied but not needed, such as cash sales and provision for doubtful debts.

2) A control account balance is given which differs from the total of individual balances. A number of errors are listed. You have to reconcile the control account to the individual accounts by adjusting them for the errors. These questions can be tricky. To answer them, a proper understanding of the bookkeeping for purchases and sales is required. A common difficulty is in recognising whether an error affects the individual account, control account, neither, or both. Proceed as follows. Prepare the control account for the relevant ledger by opening the control account from the opening balance, adding the total transactions and then balancing it off. This balance will not agree with the total balances taken from the ledger because of the errors. Some of these errors will have affected the control account, some the list of debtors and some both. You must sort them out accordingly and then correct both the control account and the debtors' list for the errors which affect them. The two balances should now be the same.

You could be asked to do the process in reverse. You would be given the total of the balances taken from the ledger, told that this does not agree with the control account balance (but not what the balance was) and given various errors which had been made. You would be required to prepare a statement showing the corrected total of the ledger balances after the adjustments and then to prepare the control account, showing the original incorrect balance. In this type of question you have to work backwards.

Illustration

Sales day book

		£
June 4	Green & Co	50
11	Mr Brown	100
13	Hart & Sons	75
25	XYZ Co	25
		250

From this book of original entry the double entry takes place at the end of the month. We debit the individual debtors' accounts in the sales ledger with £50, £100, £75 and £25 respectively and credit the sales account in the general ledger with the total of £250. The debit in the sales ledger control should agree with the total of £250.

From this you should be able to see that:

1) if there is a casting error in the sales or purchases total, only the control account needs to be adjusted. The individual accounts in the sales ledger are not affected.
2) if there is an error of entry in an individual debtor's account (e.g. transposition posting to wrong side) only that individual account should be adjusted. The control account is unaffected.
3) if a transaction has been completely omitted from the books, it will need entering belatedly in both the individual and total account.
4) if the entry in the individual account has been made but the additional entry to control forgotten (eg a contra entry) then only the control account needs updating.
5) if the balance of a debtor's account has been omitted from the list of sales ledger balances this will affect neither the individual nor the total account. The omitted balance should simply be included in the revised list of individual balances.

Questions

Question 2.1

The sales ledger control account of Workitt Ltd for the year ended 31 December 2000 has been prepared from the following information.

	£
Debit balance b/d 1 January 2000	56 000
Totals for the year 1 January 2000 to 31 December 2000	
Credit sales	800 000
Cheques received from debtors	676 000
Cash received from debtors	1 000
Discount allowed	20 000
Dishonoured cheques	2 000
Contra purchase ledger	4 000

The control account debtors balance failed to agree with the total debtors of £156 125 shown by the schedule of debtors. The following errors were subsequently discovered.

i) Workitt Ltd had sent goods on a sale-or-return basis to a customer with a selling price of £1 000. The customer had not signified his intention to purchase the goods sold and Workitt had not made the relevant accounting entries.
ii) No contra entry had been made in a debtors account in the sale ledger in respect of purchases by Workitt Ltd of goods with a list price of £500, trade discount 15%. This entry had been correctly dealt with in the control account.
iii) The discount allowed total shown in the cash book had been undercast by £700.
iv) A customer had returned goods to Workitt Ltd at the selling price of £2 000. These goods had been bought on credit by the customer. No entries had been made to record the return of goods in the accounts of Workitt Ltd.
v) During the year 2000, Workitt Ltd received a cheque drawn by a customer for goods sold on credit for £600. The correct double entry was made in the accounts. The cheque was subsequently returned by the bank marked 'Refer to Drawer'. Workitt Ltd credited the bank account. The amount was included in the total of dishonoured cheques but there was no further entry. The company expects the account will be settled in February 2001.

REQUIRED

(a) A corrected sales ledger account for the year ended 31 December 2000 and a reconciliation statement of the debtors schedule showing the correct total for the schedule of debtors.   **(21 marks)**

(b) Discuss two advantages of operating a control accounts system.   **(8 marks)**

OCR Advanced Subsidiary Specimen Paper

Question 2.2

The following balances have been included in a sales ledger control account for the year ended 31 January 1996.

	£
Balance at 1 February 1995	12 087
Sales (note 1)	117 635
Receipts from customers (note 2)	90 019
Discounts allowed (note 3)	3 000
Goods returned by customers	4 200
Bad debts written off (note 4)	1 550

Balances extracted from the sales ledger at 31 January 1996 were

	£
Debit	35 588
Credit (note 5)	185

Notes:

1) It was discovered that a batch of sales invoices totalling £3 400 had been omitted from the accounting records.

2) Cash sales of £600 had been included in this total.

3) Discounts allowed of £350, included in this total, had been omitted from the personal ledger.

4) The personal ledger accounts of the 'bad debtors' had been debited with £1 550, whilst the correct entry had been made into the control account.

5) Credit balances in the sales ledger of £400 had been transferred during the year into the purchases ledger. No record of this transfer had been made in the control account, although the personal accounts had been correctly adjusted.

REQUIRED

(a) Prepare the sales ledger control account for the year ended 31 January 1996.   **(9 marks)**

(b) Prepare a statement reconciling the sales ledger balances with the control account balance.   **(4 marks)**

(c) Under which balance sheet heading should credit balances contained within a limited company's sales ledger be shown?   **(2 marks)**

London Examinations Advanced Level

Question 2.3

The Sales ledger control account of a trading business for the month of November 1993 was prepared by the accountant, as shown below:

Sales Ledger Control Account

Debits	£	Credits	£
Opening debit balance b/d	27 684.07	Opening credit balance b/d	210.74
Credit sales	31 220.86	Allowances to customers	1 984.18
Purchase ledger contras	763.70	Cash received	1 030.62
Discounts allowed	1 414.28	Cheques received	28 456.07
Closing credit balances c/d	171.08	Cash received (on an account previously written off as a bad debt)	161.20
		Closing debit balance c/d (balancing figure)	30 416.18
	61 253.99		61 258.99
Opening debit balance b/d	30 416.18	Opening credit balance b/d	171.08

The bookkeeper balanced the individual customers' accounts and prepared a Debtors' Schedule of the closing balances which totalled £25 586.83 (net of credit balances).

Unfortunately both the accountant and the bookkeeper had been careless, and in addition to the errors which the accountant had made in the control account above, it was subsequently discovered that:

1) in an individual debtor's account, a debt previously written off but now recovered (£161.20) had been correctly credited and redebited but the corresponding debit had not been posted in the control account;
2) discounts allowed had been correctly posted to individual debtors' accounts but had been under-added by £100 in the memorandum column in the combined bank and cash book;
3) allowances to customers shown in the control account included sums totalling £341.27 which had not been posted to individual debtors' accounts;
4) a cheque for £2 567.10 received from a customer had been posted to his account as £2 576.10;
5) the credit side of one debtor's account had been over-added by £10 prior to the derivation of the closing balance;
6) a closing credit balance of £63.27 on one debtor's account had been included in the Debtors' Schedule among the debit balances;
7) the purchase ledger contras, representing the settlement by contra transfer of amounts owed to credit suppliers, had not been posted to individual debtors' accounts at all;
8) the balance on one debtor's account, £571.02, had been completely omitted from the Debtors' Schedule.

REQUIRED

Identify and effect the adjustments to the Sales ledger control account and Debtors' Schedule, as appropriate, so that the net balances agree at 30 November 1993. **(16 marks)**

Chartered Association of Certified Accountants

3

Final Accounts

3.1 Introduction

At the end of a trading period, normally a year, a firm needs to know its financial position. The owner will ask three main questions:

- How much profit has the business made over the year?
- What is the business worth?
- What is the cash position like?

In order for these questions to be answered, the firm must draw up a set of final accounts. This comprises:
(a) a trading and profit and loss account
(b) a balance sheet
(c) a cash flow statement

In this chapter we will consider the first two of these from the point of view of a sole trader; it is usually only companies which prepare cash flow statements and we shall deal with these in Chapter 11.

The financial statements of a business are drawn up in accordance with certain accounting conventions.

3.2 Accounting Concepts and Conventions

Accounting statements are based on a number of concepts and conventions which are generally accepted by accountants and which dictate certain procedures. These concepts underlie the whole field of accounting and they achieve a degree of standardisation in the way firms prepare their financial statements. The concepts you are about to meet are not, however, to be regarded as laws, nor should they be seen as being immune to criticism and change. They have evolved over time as the best way of doing things in the light of past experience and changes in conditions, attitudes and experiences may well cause a concept to be modified or even abandoned.

The Accruals Concept

This is also known as the **matching** concept. It states that costs and revenues should be recognised when the benefit from them is incurred or earned and not when they are paid or received; in other words the costs for a period should be matched against the revenues for that period. For example, we should charge against profit all those expenses which belong to the year in question but should exclude those which belong to any other year. If at the end of the year a firm has paid rent in advance for next year, this should be charged against next year's profit as the services from the buildings rented will be gained next year even though the money has been paid now. Equally if a firm pays this year a bill which it should have paid last year, this amount belongs in

last year's accounts. We shall consider the treatment of accruals and prepayments in Chapter 4.

The Prudence Concept

This is also known as the concept of conservatism. It states that a firm should not assume profits until they have actually been earned but that losses should be provided for as soon as they are anticipated. It is preferable to understate rather than to overstate profits and assets. The purpose is to avoid overvaluing the assets or the performance of the business as this could lead to wrong decisions being taken. In our final accounts this concept means that we cannot include in this year's accounts profits on unsold goods which we expect to sell next year. (See the realisation concept below.)

The Realisation Concept

This states that profit is regarded as being earned when goods are delivered to the customer. By definition therefore, profit does not happen when the goods are purchased (this would contravene the prudence concept) nor when the buyer pays for them. It is possible to purchase goods in Year 1, sell them in Year 2 and receive payment in Year 3. The profit from these goods should go into the final accounts of Year 2.

The Money Measurement Concept

All business transactions are expressed in the common denominator of money. The sale of ten units of a good at £5 each is recorded in the accounts not as the sale of ten physical units but as £50 earned from sales. While this enables us to add many diverse business activities together, it suffers from the limitation that not all events can be quantified in money terms. Financial statements cannot record in money terms a firms good reputation, the 'know-how' possessed by the business, human assets such as the quality of its workforce etc, although the intangible asset of goodwill is an attempt to record such benefits. A firm's accounts therefore do not tell the full story of a business. Another problem with measurement in money terms is that money is not a stable unit but its value changes over time with inflation or deflation.

The Business Entity Concept

The accounts show the financial affairs of the business and not the private affairs of the owner or owners. The business is regarded as a separate entity from the owner, even if in law they are the same person as is the case with a sole trader and a partner. The owner must distinguish personal finances from those of the business and any overlap must be accounted for. For example, the owner may take physical stocks of goods from the business for personal use but these must be counted as drawings.

The Going Concern Concept

Accounts are prepared on the assumption that the business is a going concern i.e. that it will continue to operate in the foreseeable future. It does not record asset values at the price they would fetch if the business were sold. Assets are stated at cost less accumulated depreciation and this figure is often different from market value if the business is wound up. Departure from this concept is justifiable only if a business is in difficulty and liquidation is a distinct possibility. In this case the assets should be valued at the prices they are expected to obtain on liquidation. The departure from the concept should be stated in the accounts and reasons for doing so should be given.

The Cost Concept

This is the practice of showing assets at cost. Accountants do not like subjectivity in their figures. The advantage of following the simple rule of recording everything at historic cost is that it is objective – immediately verifiable by reference to facts. A limitation of historic cost, however, is that it fails to represent the state of a business realistically in a period of rising prices. True asset values can exceed historic cost and the gap between the two becomes increasingly large as time passes. The accounting profession has developed alternative systems to deal with the problem of rapidly rising prices, the best known being **current cost accounting** and **current purchasing power**. But these systems are complex and the profession is not united on which system to adopt. Neither system has been chosen, although the accounting bodies encourage companies to prepare current cost statements. Financial statements in the UK are thus prepared under historic cost, although some large companies also publish current cost or alternative inflation accounting statements.

The Consistency Concept

There are some matters in accounts for which there is more than one acceptable treatment. Examples include the different possible methods for depreciation and stock valuation, and the treatment of research and development expenditure. But different methods often lead to significantly different profit and balance sheet figures. To overcome the problem, the principle of consistency states that 'like items should be treated in a like manner within one accounting period and from one period to the next'. If this were not done, it would be possible for management to choose the profit figure for a year by selecting those methods of treatment and interpretation of events which suited them best. Profit and other figures would then not be directly comparable between years. A departure from consistency is allowed only if it leads to a truer and fairer representation of the affairs of the business. The change must be disclosed in a note to the financial statements.

The Concept of Materiality

The accountant should be concerned only with items which are material in relation to the size of the business. For example, the purchase of a stapler which lasts for three years should, according to the accruals concept, be charged against income over three years. Since the cost of a stapler is minimal, however, it would not be worth maintaining separate accounts for the stapler at cost and for provision for depreciation of the stapler. The principle of materiality allows the firm to write off the whole of the cost in the year of purchase. What amount is considered to be material and what is not depends on the cost of recording and the size of the business. A figure of £1 000 may be material for a small sole trader but it would not be for a multinational company where the final accounts are expressed in millions of pounds.

3.3 The Trading and Profit and Loss Account

The profit and loss account is an income statement the purpose of which is to calculate how much profit or loss the business has made for the owner over the last financial year. This account refers to the whole of the year or period in question. Calculating profit is an essential exercise for all businesses because profit is

- the business's income and the basis on which the owner makes drawings.
- a source of finance for a firm which wants to expand.
- a key indicator of the health of a business.

- the basis on which the owner pays income tax (or corporation tax in the case of a limited company).

In accounting terms profit is an increase in the firm's capital over the year. It increases the amount owed to the owner by the firm. In economic terms, profit is seen in an opportunity cost sense as the financial reward to the entrepreneur in return for risk-taking and decision-taking and for giving up his time to the business when he could have been earning money in some other way.

The profit and loss account is divided into two sections:

1) the **trading account** which measures **gross profit**; this is the gain on buying and selling goods before taking overhead expenses into account;
2) the **profit and loss account** which measures the **net profit** by deducting the overhead expenses from the gross profit in order to reveal the true and final profit of the business.

The type of income statement prepared depends on the nature of the business. Since the trading account is concerned with the buying and selling of goods, it is prepared only by trading firms such as wholesalers, retailers and manufacturers. Firms in the service industry such as hairdressers, lawyers and mini-cab drivers do not prepare a trading account since they are not dealing in goods. They need to prepare only a profit and loss account, showing fee income less business expenses. The income statement of a manufacturing firm includes a trading and profit and loss account but starts with a **manufacturing account** which calculates the cost of production of goods in the factory. We shall meet manufacturing accounts in Chapter 14.

We shall study the various parts of the profit and loss account in detail by using a worked example.

3.4 The Balance Sheet

The balance sheet is a statement of the financial position of the business on the last day of the year and relates only to the day on which it is prepared. It shows details of the accounting equation which we met in Chapter 1 and consists of two main sections:

1) **Assets**, which are presented in two sub-sections: **fixed assets** used over a long period; and **current assets**, which are the firm's more liquid funds, i.e. those which can be turned into cash easily and quickly without significant capital loss.
2) **Liabilities**, which are presented in three sub-sections: the firm's **capital**; **long-term liabilities** repayable after one year or more; and the **current liabilities** repayable within less than one year.

The balance sheet is not part of the double-entry system of accounts. We shall study how to prepare it in the worked example below.

3.5 Capital and Revenue Expenditure

In order to prepare final accounts correctly, it is important to understand the difference between these two types of expenditure.

Revenue expenditure is money spent on transactions whose influence on the business is short-term i.e. less than one financial year. They are the current expenses of the business – examples are wages, rent, repairs to machinery etc. Revenue expenses are deducted from the year's profit and are included in the profit and loss account.

Capital expenditure is money spent on items which have a long-lasting effect on the business, i.e. on the purchase of fixed assets. This expenditure is not deducted from the year's profit since the fixed assets benefit the firm for more than one financial year, and they are included not in the profit and loss account but in the balance sheet. (Depreciation on fixed assets, which is an estimate of the benefit from those assets attributable to the current year, is deducted from profit. We shall study it in Chapter 5.)

Owning and using an asset incurs several costs, both of a capital and revenue nature. Since depreciation is the writing off of the capital cost of a fixed asset, it is important that the capital element be accurately separated from the revenue element. Examination questions often pick up on this point. The purchase price of an asset is clearly capital and the day-to-day running expenses are clearly revenue. Thus for a lorry the initial purchase price is capital expenditure; petrol, insurance and drivers' wages are revenue expenditure. There are a number of other costs where the distinction is not so obvious however.

- Delivery charge – while transport costs are usually revenue, they are capitalised where they are incurred in connection with the acquisition of a capital item. The general rule is that capital expenditure includes all costs incurred in acquiring an asset and preparing it to be in a state ready for use. Thus the capital cost of a piece of machinery includes delivery and installation charges in addition to the purchase price.
- The legal costs of purchasing property are capitalised.
- Repairs – examples of these are servicing a car or giving a machine an overhaul. This form of expenditure seeks to maintain the value of an asset and not to add to its original value. It is therefore treated as revenue and written off wholly to the profit and loss account in the year in which it is incurred.
- Improvement – an example of this is adding an extension to a building. Here the effect of the expenditure is to add to original value, so the cost should be capitalised and written off over the remaining life of the asset.

3.6 Preparing Final Accounts from a Trial Balance

To prepare the final accounts of a firm, we work from the firm's trial balance. (Some small business owners do not keep double entry records and so there is no trial balance to work from; it is still possible, although a little more difficult, to draw up the final accounts – we shall study this in Chapter 7 on incomplete records.)

Traditionally the final accounts were prepared in double-entry, T-account or horizontal format. This practice has in recent years been replaced by the vertical or statement style of presentation and we have adopted this style throughout the book. Notice that the financial statements are presented in columns. These columns do not represent debits and credits but are used to calculate sub-totals which are then added together to produce main totals. You should set out your accounts logically with first-level sums being done in a left-hand column and proceeding towards the right. Final totals should appear in the right-hand column.

Before we proceed to preparing the final accounts, there are a few points to note about this type of question:

- The trial balance balances i.e. total debits equal total credits. This means that the balance sheet we are going to produce will also balance if we do everything correctly.
- The items in the trial balance are not given in the order in which you will use them so you must go through them carefully and sort them out.

- Everything included in the trial balance will go into the final accounts once only – in either the profit and loss account or the balance sheet.
- In examination questions you are asked to make adjustments to the figures in the trial balance. These adjustments are given underneath the trial balance and, since they have not been through the double entry system, we have to enter them twice in the final accounts – once in the profit and loss account and once in the balance sheet. In this chapter we shall deal with only one adjustment – that of closing stock; the other common adjustments are the subject matter of Chapter 4.
- The trading and profit and loss account should be headed with the phrase 'for the year ending' followed by the year-end date. The balance sheet should be headed with the phrase 'as at' followed by the year-end date.
- Since we are presenting the accounts in the vertical or statement format, we make subtractions as we go. To make it clear which amounts are being added and which subtracted, we present negative figures in brackets ( ).

A Worked Example

If you follow through this example, its answer and explanation carefully, you will understand the basic 'formula' for preparing final accounts.

Charles is a wholesaler of accounting stationery. He conducts his business from a small warehouse which he owns. Part of the building is sub-let to another trader at an annual rent of £2 600. The following year-end trial balance has been extracted from his books at the close of business on 30 June 2001.

Trial Balance as at 30 June 2001

	Debit £	Credit £
Bad debts	500	
Bank	4 400	
Capital		45 000
Debtors	10 000	
Drawings	13 000	
10-year bank loan		10 000
Creditors		9 500
Heating and lighting	1 600	
Motor vehicles at cost	22 000	
Returns outwards		7 000
Interest on bank loan	1 000	
Motor vehicle expenses	3 000	
Carriage inwards	1 000	
Carriage outwards	600	
Purchases	66 000	
Rent and rates	8 000	
Rent received		2 000
Returns inwards	5 000	
Salaries and wages	11 500	
Sales		115 000
Stock at 1 July 2000	16 000	
Warehouse (land and buildings)	25 000	
Discounts allowed	100	
Discounts received		200
	£188 700	£188 700

Additional information:

Stock at 30 June 2001 is valued at £20 000.

REQUIRED

Prepare Charles' trading and profit and loss account for the year ended 30 June 2001
and a balance sheet as at that date.

Solution

Charles

Trading and Profit and Loss Account for the year ended 30 June 2001

	£	£	£
Sales		115 000	
Less returns inwards		(5 000)	
			110 000
Opening stock		16 000	
Purchases	66 000		
Less returns outwards	(7 000)		
		59 000	
Carriage inwards		1 000	
Less closing stock		(20 000)	
Cost of sales			(56 000)
Gross profit			54 000
Add miscellaneous revenue receipts			
Rent received		2 000	
Discounts received		200	
			2 200
			56 200
Less revenue expenses			
Bad debts		500	
Heating and lighting		1 600	
Motor vehicle expenses		3 000	
Interest on bank loan		1 000	
Carriage outwards		600	
Rent and rates		8 000	
Salaries and wages		11 500	
Discounts allowed		100	
			(26 300)
Net profit			£29 900

Balance Sheet as at 30 June 2001

	£	£	£
Fixed Assets			
Land and buildings		25 000	
Motor vehicles		22 000	
			47 000
Current Assets			
Stock	20 000		
Debtors	10 000		
Bank	4 400		
		34 400	
Less Current Liabilities			
Creditors		(9 500)	
Working capital			24 900
Net assets			£71 900
Financed by			
Capital		45 000	
Add net profit		29 900	
Less drawings		(13 000)	
			£61 900
Long-term Liabilities			
10-year bank loan			10 000
Capital Employed			£71 900

Explanation

1. The trading section of the account

The aim of this section is to find the gross profit. The following identities will help you.

- **Gross profit = income from net sales − cost of sales**
- **Income from net sales = sales − sales returns** i.e. what we sold minus what customers sent back.
- **Cost of sales** (sometimes expressed as 'cost of goods sold' = **Opening stock + net purchases (purchases − purchases returns) + carriage inwards + any other trading expense − closing stock.** This requires some explanation.

The main component of cost of sales is purchases but this figure is adjusted, in accordance with the accruals concept, to arrive at the cost of goods chargeable to this year i.e. we want to deduct from sales what it cost us to buy the goods which we sold. The stock left over from last year becomes this year's opening stock and, assuming that it was sold during this year, we charge it to this year's account; opening stock is almost always to be found in the trial balance. The closing stock left over at the end of this year will be sold next year and should not be charged against this year's profit, and so we deduct it from purchases; it will become next year's opening stock. Closing stock is almost always to be found in the adjustments underneath the trial balance. We add on to purchases any expenses which have increased the cost of the goods sold. The main one you will come across is carriage inwards, which is the cost of delivering the goods bought by the firm and which is counted as part of cost of sales. Also include against gross profit any expenses described in the question as 'trading expenses'.

The procedure for the trading account is thus as follows:

i) Deduct returns inwards from sales to find net sales.

ii) Find cost of sales by adding together opening stock, net purchases (first deduct purchases returns from purchases) and carriage inwards and deducting closing stock.

iii) Deduct cost of sales from net sales to find gross profit.

2. The profit and loss section of the account

The aim of this section is to find the net profit.

Net profit = gross profit + total miscellaneous revenue incomes – total revenue expenses

The procedure is as follows:

i) Add any miscellaneous revenue receipts to the gross profit. The main ones you will come across are rent received, discounts received and commission received although certain adjustments also go into this section, as we shall see in Chapter 4. The resulting figure is not gross profit any more but gross revenue income.

ii) Add up all the revenue expenses (be careful not to include any fixed assets here).

iii) Deduct total revenue expenses from gross revenue income. The result is the net profit.

3. The balance sheet

The purpose of the balance sheet is to present the firm's assets and liabilities and show the book value of the business.

i) Include all the fixed assets such as buildings, machinery, furniture, vehicles etc and add them up to show a sub-total. Only items of capital expenditure go in this section.

ii) Now include the current assets. The main items at this stage are closing stock, debtors, bank balance and cash balance. Show a sub-total for current assets.

iii) Although we have now finished the assets section, we make an adjustment for current liabilities. From a bookkeeping point of view, we would include the current liabilities in the liabilities section but deducting current liabilities from current assets gives us a very useful figure – the firm's **working capital**. This shows the amount of cash or near-cash (liquid funds) which are left over at the firm's disposal after the short-term obligations have been met. The working capital must be sufficient to prevent the firm from getting into cash problems and it is good practice to show it clearly. (We shall study working capital and other methods of assessing a firm's performance in Chapter 12.) The main current liabilities are creditors and bank overdraft. There is no overdraft in this question but they can come up so you should check the bank balance carefully to see which side of the trial balance it appears on; if it is a debit it is a current asset but if it is a credit it is an overdraft and thus a liability. Show the sub-total for current liabilities and deduct it from current assets to arrive at the working capital. Place the working capital figure underneath the fixed assets sub-total.

iv) Add the fixed assets total to the working capital to arrive at the firm's net assets.

v) Now present the liabilities section. We often introduce it by the phrase 'financed by' which means that the items to be shown are the sources of the funds which financed the assets. The capital section comes first and it shows the owner's position with the business. Remember that the business entity concept distinguishes the owner from his business. Any money he brings into it is owed by the firm to him and this is why capital is a liability. By the same reasoning, profit is also a liability. Add the net profit to the capital and deduct the drawings – these are amounts which the owner has taken out of the business for his own use and they reduce the firm's liability to him.

vi) Finally, we present any long-term liabilities such as bank loans. These are debts which do not have to be repaid within the next twelve-month period.

vii) Add the long-term liabilities to the capital and we arrive at the capital employed. This must balance with net assets.

The balance sheet balances because it is prepared from a trial balance which balances. In preparing the final accounts, we have simply switched around the information in the trial balance. You will sometimes find, however, when practising these exercises, that your balance sheet does not balance; if this happens you should investigate to find out why and to correct it. Check that you have entered all the figures correctly and also check your arithmetic. Each item in the trial balance should have gone in once, either in the trading and profit and loss account or in the balance sheet; each adjusted item outside the trial balance should have gone in twice – once in each statement.

A word of warning. In an examination your time is short and there is a lot of work to do. If your balance sheet does not balance, do not spend long looking for the error. A quick check of the entries, particularly of the net profit figure, is sufficient. Your balance sheet may fail to balance because you have made one or two small errors which will result in your losing at most two or three marks. You will probably be able to earn more marks by using your time to do another question than in finding the error in your final accounts. You will be awarded marks for each correct entry that you make.

Questions

Question 3.1

Victor Chan runs a small food provisions shop. The following is his trial balance as at 30 September 2004.

Trial Balance as at 30 September 2004

	Debit	Credit
	£	£
Stock on 1 October 2003	2 368	
Carriage outwards	200	
Carriage inwards	310	
Returns inwards	205	
Returns outwards		322
Purchases	11 874	
Sales		18 600
Salaries and wages	3 862	
Rent	304	
Insurance	78	
Motor expenses	664	
Office expenses	216	
Light and heat	166	
General expenses	314	
Premises	5 000	
Motor vehicles	1 800	
Fixtures and fittings	350	
Debtors	3 896	
Creditors		1 731
Cash at bank	482	
Drawings	1 200	
Capital		12 636
	£33 289	£33 289

Stock at 30 September 2004 was £2 592.

REQUIRED

Prepare Victor Chan's trading and profit and loss account for the year ending
30 September 2004 and a balance sheet as at that date.

Author's Question

Question 3.2

The following trial balance was extracted from the books of Marian Eliott on
31 December 2000:

Trial Balance as at 31 December 2000

	Debit £	Credit £
Loan from F Holt		10 000
Capital		52 810
Drawings	16 840	
Cash at bank	6 230	
Cash in hand	590	
Debtors and creditors	24 600	18 740
Stock at 1 January 2000	47 720	
Motor van	8 200	
Office equipment	12 500	
Purchases and sales	184 200	261 800
Returns	1 100	614
Carriage inwards	430	
Carriage outwards	618	
Motor expenses	3 260	
Rent	5 940	
Telephone	810	
Wages and salaries	26 620	
Insurance	984	
Office expenses	2 754	
Interest on loan	568	
Totals	£343 964	£343 964

The closing stock on 31 December 2000 was valued at £39 220.

REQUIRED

Prepare Marian Eliott's trading and profit and loss account for the year ending
31 December 2000 and a balance sheet as at that date.

Author's Question

Question 3.3

'The exclusion of the accounting concepts from a set of final accounts would not make
any significant difference to the overall financial position of a business.'

REQUIRED

(a) Briefly explain:
    i) the accruals concept;   **(5 marks)**
    ii) the consistency concept.   **(5 marks)**

(b) With reference to **each** of these two concepts illustrate, using numerical examples, how their exclusion from a profit and loss account and balance sheet would affect:
   i) the net profit or loss for the year;   **(12 marks)**
   ii) the net current assets.   **(12 marks)**

Associated Examining Board Advanced Level

Question 3.4

The practice of accounting is firmly based upon the application of the following concepts:

going concern;

accruals;

consistency;

prudence;

materiality.

REQUIRED

State clearly your understanding of **each** of these concepts and illustrate the manner in which **each** concept influences the accounts of a business.   **(5 × 6 marks)**

Associated Examining Board Advanced Level

4

Adjustments to Final Accounts

4.1 Introduction

In Chapter 3 we looked at the final accounts of a sole trader prepared from a trial balance with an adjustment for closing stock. In this chapter we will consider the treatment of other adjustments, both in the final accounts and in the ledger.

There is one rule which was mentioned in Chapter 3 but which is worthwhile repeating here. The items included in the trial balance go into the final accounts once only, either in the trading, profit and loss account or balance sheet. Adjustments made after the trial balance go into the final accounts twice – once in the trading and profit and loss account and once in the balance sheet.

4.2 Accrued and Prepaid Expenses and Receipts

The payment of expenses and the receipt of income do not always coincide neatly with the end of the firm's financial year and, when the books are closed, there may be outstanding balances. This is an extension of the fact that we include the opening stock but not the closing stock in the cost of sales for the year.

For example, the year may end on 31 December but the electricity bill may be timed for the quarter including November, December and January and will not arrive until the end of January, i.e. next year. On 31 December, however, the firm owes electricity for two months and this must be reflected in the profit and loss account. Equally, there may be amounts paid in advance for next year. The firm may pay its rent three months in advance and at the year-end may have prepaid up to the first month of next year.

Expenses owing: In order to comply with the accruals concept, the expenses which are deducted from profit are those which belong to this year, whether they have been paid or not. The accountant must match all revenues attributable to a financial period with all expenses attributable to that period. So any amount outstanding (also known as accrued) must be added in the profit and loss account on to the amount actually paid as if it had been paid; the fact that it is still owing is shown in the balance sheet, where it appears as a current liability.

Expenses prepaid: Since these have been paid for next year they must appear in next year's accounts and are deducted from the amount of the expense actually paid in the profit and loss account. The amount of the prepayment is then included in the balance sheet as a current asset.

Receipts owing: The same principle applies to any miscellaneous receipts eg rent received from property let to a tenant. If the tenant owes rent at the end of the year, the amount owing is added to profit just as if it had been paid and it then becomes a current asset in the balance sheet.

Receipts prepaid: If the tenant has paid us rent in advance for next year, the prepayment must not be added on to profit and must be deducted from the rent actually received. It then becomes a current liability in the balance sheet, as we owe the tenant use of the property which he has not yet received.

The ledger accounts for receipts and expenses must show any accruals or prepayments at the end of the year. Here is an example of each.

Example

Donald rents business premises at a cost of £1 000 per month, payable quarterly. His financial year corresponds to the calendar year. Cheques for £3 000 are paid on 3 April, 3 July and 3 October 2001. At 31 December the amount due for the final quarter is still outstanding as it is payable on 3 January 2002. The ledger account will look as follows:

Rent

2001		£	2001		£
3 April	Bank	3 000			
3 July	Bank	3 000			
3 Oct	Bank	3 000			
31 Dec	Balance c/d	3 000	31 Dec	Profit and Loss	12 000
		12 000			12 000
2002			2002		
			1 Jan	Balance b/d	3 000

By adjusting the expense account for the accrual, we have achieved two things:

1) The charge for rent in the profit and loss account is now correct.
2) The account has a credit balance of £3 000, reflecting the obligation existing at the year-end. This will be shown in the balance sheet under current liabilities.

Suppose that on 1 December Donald pays the rent for the last quarter of 2001 and for the first quarter of 2002. The account will look like this.

Rent

2001		£	2001		£
3 April	Bank	3 000	31 Dec	Profit and Loss	12 000
3 July	Bank	3 000			
3 Oct	Bank	3 000			
1 Dec	Bank	6 000	31 Dec	Balance c/d	3 000
		15 000			15 000
2002			2002		
1 Jan	Balance b/d	3 000			

Here the amount paid for the year is too much and the account has a debit balance of £3 000, the amount of the prepayment. The trick to remember is always to transfer to the profit and loss account the exact amount which belongs to the year, in this case twelve payments of £1 000.

Here is a summary of the procedure to follow when constructing a ledger account with an accrual or prepayment.

1) Bring forward any accrual or prepayment from last year.
2) Debit the account with cash and cheques paid.
3) Credit the account with the amount incurred, i.e. which should have been paid. This is the transfer to the profit and loss account.
4) Balance the account. The balancing figure is the accrual or prepayment.

The procedure for revenue is the same except that cash received is credited to the account and the transfer to profit and loss account debited.

4.3 Bad Debts

A bad debt is one which the firm does not expect to collect, probably because the debtor has gone bankrupt or has disappeared. The bad debt must be written off by crediting the debtor's account and debiting a bad debts account. This now becomes an expense which is deducted from profit at the end of the year – after all, it would not be fair to pay tax on profit which included sales which had not been paid for. Here is what it looks like in the ledger if Stoneybroke Ltd goes bankrupt owing us £500.

Stoneybroke

2001		£	2001		£
1 March	Sales	500	31 March	Bad debt	500

Bad Debts

2001		£	2001		£
31 March	Stoneybroke	500			

Bad debts usually feature in final accounts questions and there are two ways in which they can be presented to you.

1) They may be in the trial balance as a debit item – this means that the figure for debtors has already been adjusted for them. In this case, treat them like any other expense in the profit and loss account and deduct them from profit.

2) They may be given as an adjustment after the trial balance which will tell you that, after the books had been closed, it was discovered that a particular debt had become bad. The debtors figure has not been adjusted for this and the figure must appear twice in the final accounts. It is deducted from profit in the normal way (as above) and it is deducted from the debtors in the balance sheet.

4.4 Provision for Doubtful Debts

Many firms which grant credit know from experience that a certain number of debtors will fail to pay each year and they do not wait for these debts to become bad. They create a provision for doubtful debts. This is in line with the concept of prudence which states that a loss should be provided for as soon as it is anticipated and that it is preferable to understate rather than overstate profits and assets.

To create a provision for doubtful debts, no entry is made in any individual debtor's account. A special provision for doubtful debts account is credited and this is deducted from the total of debtors at the end of the year to give a more realistic value of the amount of money the firm expects to collect. Provisions for doubtful debts are much liked by examiners and are commonly found in a final accounts question. The provision can be presented in one of two ways:

1) It may appear in the trial balance as a credit balance. (Bad debts may also appear in the same question but they will have a debit balance.) The fact that the provision is in the trial balance means that it was created previously and that profit has been adjusted in a previous year. All we have to do is to deduct the provision from debtors in the balance sheet.

2) It may be given to you after the trial balance. In this case there are three different possibilities:
   - You may be told to create a new provision. You would either be given the amount or told that it is a particular percentage of the debtors. This figure

must now appear twice in the final accounts – it will be deducted from debtors as above but it must also be shown as an expense in the profit and loss account.

- You may be told to adjust a provision which already exists in the trial balance. If you are told to increase it, show the increase only in the profit and loss account and deduct the whole of the new provision from the debtors in the balance sheet.

- If you are told to decrease the provision, show the amount of the decrease as a miscellaneous receipt in the profit and loss account and deduct the new lower provision from the debtors.

Example

On 1 January 2002 the balance on a provision for doubtful debts account stands at £70. At 31 December 2002 it is decided to set the year's provision at 3% of debtors, which total £3 000. Show the provision for doubtful debts account.

Provision for Bad Debts

2001		£	2001		£
			1 Jan Balance b/d		70
31 Dec Balance c/d		90	31 Dec Profit and loss		20
		90			90
			1 Jan Balance b/d		90

This is an example of an increase in the provision. The £20 will be deducted from profit and the £90 will be deducted from debtors.

4.5 Depreciation

We shall deal with this topic in more detail in Chapter 5 and consider it here from the point of view of the final accounts only.

Depreciation is the amount deducted annually from the book value of the fixed assets. The money paid for a fixed asset cannot be deducted in its entirety from profit in the year of purchase but must be spread over the number of years during which the asset will be used. A business has to decide how to split the value of the asset over these years. Here we shall consider two ways.

1) **The straight line method** whereby the original cost of the asset, minus any value it is expected to have at the end of its life, is spread equally over its life. For example, if a machine costs £1 100 and is expected to last for four years with a resale value of £100 at the end of that period, the firm will divide £1 000 equally over the four years, i.e. it will depreciate the asset by £250 every year.

2) **The reducing balance method** whereby the firm chooses a percentage and deducts this from the net book value of the asset at the end of each year. For example, if a vehicle costs £10 000 and is depreciated by 40% each year, the first year's depreciation will be 40% of £10 000 i.e. £4 000, the second year's will be 40% of (£10 000 – £4 000), i.e. £2 400 and so on. Here the amount of depreciation deducted each year gets smaller over time.

The amount of depreciation increases over the years just as the book value of the asset decreases. The depreciation is credited to a provision for depreciation account and the double entry for this is in the profit and loss account.

In a final accounts question you will be given the instructions concerning depreciation in a note after the trial balance; it will of course need two entries. You calculate the amount of depreciation and include this in the profit and loss account with the other expenses to be deducted from net profit. Then you deduct it from the value of the asset in the balance sheet.

If the asset is a new one then you deduct the depreciation from its cost price. But if it has already been held for more than one year, depreciation will already have been deducted from it. You will see the old depreciation in the provision for depreciation account on the credit side of the trial balance. Add the new depreciation for this year onto this figure and deduct the whole amount from the asset in the balance sheet.

4.6 Stock Drawings

All sole traders make drawings from their businesses. This is usually in the form of cash but sometimes you will be told that the owner withdrew goods from stock for private use. In this case you must do the following:

1) Deduct the amount from the purchases in the trading account. The purchases figure represents the cost price of the goods sold by the business, but in this case the goods were not sold and therefore must be taken off the cost of sales.
2) Add the value of the stock drawings to the money drawings figure and include this in the capital section of the balance sheet.

A Worked Example

The question which follows contains most of the basic adjustments you might be asked to deal with for a sole trader.

Ann Teak's Second-Hand Shop
Trial Balance as at 31 December 2000

	Debit £	Credit £
Capital		56 920
Drawings	2 960	
Plant and machinery at cost	35 000	
Motor vehicles at cost	15 000	
Debtors	34 000	
Creditors		21 000
Bank	14 000	
Cash	505	
10-year bank loan		9 000
Stock (1 January 2000)	25 200	
General expenses	11 020	
Purchases and Sales	164 764	233 384
Bad debts	2 400	
Interest on loan	900	
Discounts allowed and received	325	640
Wages and salaries	34 000	
Insurance	300	
Returns inwards	210	
Returns outwards		170
Provisions for depreciation:		
Plant and machinery		17 000
Motor vehicles		10 240

Electricity and telephone	7 000	
Carriage inwards	320	
Carriage outwards	980	
Provision for doubtful debts (1 January 2000)		530
	£348 884	£348 884

You are given the following additional information:

(a) The closing stock at 31 December 2000 was estimated at £28 247.
(b) Depreciation is to be charged on Plant and Machinery at 10% of cost and on Motor Vehicles at 20% of cost.
(c) Insurance prepaid on 31 December 2000 came to £60.
(d) General expenses outstanding were £110 on 31 December 2000.
(e) The provision for doubtful debts is to be increased to £750.
(f) Ann Teak took £500 worth of stock for personal use.

REQUIRED

Prepare a Trading and Profit and Loss Account for the year ended 31 December 2000 and a Balance Sheet as at that date, taking into account the above adjustments.

Author's Question

Solution

Ann Teak
Trading and Profit and Loss Account for the year ended 31 December 2000

	£	£
Sales (233 384 – 210)		233 174
Opening stock	25 200	
Purchases (164 764 – 170)	164 594	
Carriage inwards	320	
Less stock drawings	(500)	
Less closing stock	(28 247)	
Cost of sales		(161 367)
Gross profit		71 807
Add discounts received		640
		72 447
Less expenses		
General expenses (11 020 + 110)	11 130	
Bad debts	2 400	
Interest on loan	900	
Discounts allowed	325	
Wages and salaries	34 000	
Insurance (300 – 60)	240	
Electricity and telephone	7 000	
Carriage outwards	980	
Increase in provision for bad debts	220	
Provision for depreciation on plant and machinery	3 500	
Provision for depreciation on motor vehicles	3 000	
		(63 695)
Net profit		£8752

Balance Sheet as at 31 December 2000

	£	£	£
Fixed Assets			
Plant and machinery at cost		35 000	
Less accumulated depreciation (17 000 + 3 500)		(20 500)	
			14 500
Motor vehicles at cost		15 000	
Less accumulated depreciation (10 240 + 3 000)		(13 240)	
			1 760
			16 260
Current Assets			
Stock		28 247	
Debtors	34 000		
Less provision for doubtful debts	(750)		
		33 250	
Insurance prepaid		60	
Cash at bank		14 000	
Cash on hand		505	
		76 062	
Less Current Liabilities			
Creditors	21 000		
General expenses accrued	110		
		(21 110)	
Working Capital			54 952
Net Assets			£71 212
Financed by			
Capital		56 920	
Add net profit		8 752	
Less drawings (2 960 + 500)		(3 460)	
			62 212
Long-term liabilities			
10-year bank loan			9000
Capital Employed			£71 212

Questions

Question 4.1

Claire Voyant is the owner of a shop selling beauty products and cosmetics for women. At 31 December 2000, the end of her financial year, the following balances have been extracted from the books:

Trial Balance as at 31 December 2000

	Debit	Credit
	£	£
Bank balance	4 900	
Capital		14 500
Cash	2 000	
Discounts allowed	560	
Discounts received		500
Drawings	2 500	
Fixtures and fittings at cost	14 000	
Provision for depreciation on fixtures		3 500
Light and heat	900	
Provision for doubtful debts		60
Purchases	13 000	
Rent and rates	1 700	
Sales		20 000
Stock at 1 January 2000	2 000	
Trade creditors		6 850
Trade debtors	2 000	
Wages	1 850	
	£47 150	£47 150

The following matters are to be taken into account before preparation of the final accounts:

1) The stock-take on 31 December 2000 valued the shop's stock at £3 000 at cost.
2) At 31 December 2000, rent and rates were prepaid by £200 and there was an outstanding bill of £150 for wages.
3) The fixtures and fittings are to be depreciated by £500.
4) The provision for doubtful debts is to be 5% of the debtors at the year-end.

REQUIRED

Prepare Claire Voyant's trading and profit and loss account for the year ended 31 December 2000 and a balance sheet as at that date.

Author's Question

Question 4.2

The following trial balance has been extracted from the ledger of Mr Yousef, a sole trader.

Trial Balance as at 31 May 1996

	Debit £	Credit £
Sales		138 078
Purchases	82 350	
Carriage	5 144	
Drawings	7 800	
Rent, rates and insurance	6 622	
Postage and stationery	3 001	
Advertising	1 300	
Salaries and wages	26 420	
Bad debts	877	
Provision for bad debts		130
Debtors	12 120	
Creditors		6 471
Cash on hand	177	
Cash at bank	1 002	
Stocks as 1 June 1995	11 927	
Equipment		
at cost	58 000	
accumulated depreciation		19 000
Capital		53 091
	216 770	216 770

The following additional information as at 31 May 1996 is available:

(a) Rent is accrued by £210.
(b) Rates have been prepaid by £880.
(c) £2 211 of carriage represents carriage inwards on purchases.
(d) Equipment is to be depreciated at 15% per annum using the straight line method.
(e) The provision for bad debts is to be increased by £40.
(f) Stock at the close of business has been valued at £13 551.

REQUIRED

Prepare a Trading and Profit and Loss Account for the year ended 31 May 1996 and a Balance Sheet as at that date.   **(20 marks)**

Association of Accounting Technicians, Preliminary

Question 4.3

PLJ has been in business for some years and has kept her drawings slightly below the level of profits each year. She has never made a loss, and therefore feels that her business is growing steadily. You act as her accountant and she has passed you the following list of balances at 30 April 1997:

	£000
Capital at 1 May 1996	228
Drawings	14
Plant at cost	83
Plant depreciation at 1 May 1996	13
Office equipment at cost	31
Office equipment depreciation at 1 May 1996	8
Debtors	198
Creditors	52
Sales	813
Purchases	516
Returns inwards	47
Discounts allowed	4
Provision for doubtful debts at 1 May 1996	23
Administration costs	38
Salaries	44
Research costs	26
Loan to a friend, repayable in 6 months	25
Bank	50
Bad debts written off	77

You ascertain that stock at 1 May 1996 was £84 000 and stock at 30 April 1997 was £74 000. On 1 November 1996, she brought her personal computer, valued at £2 000, from home into the office; no entries have been made for this.

You are also given the following information at 30 April 1997:

i) Depreciation on plant is charged at 10% per annum on cost. Depreciation on office equipment is charged at 20% per annum on the net book value at the year end.
ii) Administration costs includes insurance prepaid of £3 000.
iii) Salaries accrued amount to £2 000.
iv) The research costs are all in relation to pure research.
v) It is agreed that the provision for doubtful debts is to remain at £23 000.

REQUIRED

(a) Prepare a trial balance at 30 April 1997 after adjusting for the computer which PLJ has brought from home, but prior to making any other adjustments. **(6 marks)**
(b) Prepare a trading and profit and loss account for the year ended 30 April 1997. **(7 marks)**
(c) Prepare a balance sheet at 30 April 1997. **(10 marks)**

Chartered Institute of Management Accountants

Question 4.4

Alan Watson owns a sportswear business. The following trial balance was drawn up for Alan Watson at 31 March 1998.

Trial Balance at 31 March 1998

	£	£
Capital		80 000
Premises	236 000	
Fixtures	90 000	
Motor vans at cost	84 000	
Provision for depreciation:		
fixtures		36 000
motor vans		48 000
Debtors and creditors	10 000	6 000
Stock (1 April 1997)	94 000	
Bank		56 000
Sales		580 000
Purchases	220 000	
Wages	30 000	
General expenses	38 000	
Rent received		26 000
Discount received		2 000
Drawings	32 000	
	£834 000	£834 000

The following information is also relevant.

  i) Closing stock of goods for resale £51 000.
 ii) Rent is still owed for the accommodation above the premises. The occupier owes Alan Watson £3 000 for year ended 31 March 1998. This will be paid in April 1998.
iii) Depreciation is to be provided on fixtures at 20% per annum on cost. Motor vans are to be depreciated at 25% per annum on cost. No fixed assets were bought or sold during the year.
 iv) General expenses include prepaid electricity of £600 at 31 March 1998.
  v) During the year Alan Watson paid £2 000 for a personal holiday in America. This had been paid through the business and entered as a general expense.
 vi) During the year Alan Watson has withdrawn, for his own personal use, goods costing £1 500.

REQUIRED

(a) A trading and profit and loss account for Alan Watson for the year ended 31 March 1998 and a balance sheet as at that date. **(17 marks)**

(b) Alan expects that, in the future, credit sales will have to increase, and the business will have to create a provision for bad debts. Identify and explain the accounting concepts being applied when making a provision for bad debts. **(4 marks)**

(c) Why is it important that Alan monitors and debtors in his business? What steps could Alan take to prevent a customer from becoming a bad debt? **(6 marks)**

(d) State the reasons why Alan should employ an accountant to prepare his year end accounts. **(2 marks)**

UODLE Advanced Level

Case Study – Kilburn Tandoori
Part II Final Accounts

On completion of writing up the books, the following matters are brought to your attention:

(a) Stocks of food and drink at 28 February 2001 are valued at £250.
(b) Mr Shah owes a waiter £20 in respect of overtime worked in Week 4.
(c) The rates payment covers the period 1 February to 31 April.
(d) Electricity consumed in the month is estimated to be £100.
(e) Being a prudent man, Mr Shah instructs you to create a provision for doubtful debts of 4% of debtors.
(f) It is decided to write off fixtures and fittings by equal instalments over 10 years.

You are required to:

1) Adjust the books for the above.
2) Prepare the restaurant's trading and profit and loss account for the first month and a balance sheet as at 28 February 2001.

5

Depreciation

5.1 Introduction

Fixed assets have been defined as long-term assets held, not with a view to resale, but for permanent use in the business. They represent investment in the business, known as **capital expenditure**, rather than revenue expenditure which is the necessary day-to-day expenses to keep the business working.

Such investments in assets have a finite life. The fall in value of fixed assets over time is known as **depreciation**. This has been defined in SSAP 12 (Accounting for Depreciation) as 'a measure of the wearing out, consumption or other loss of value of a fixed asset whether arising from use, effluxion of time or obsolescence through technology and market changes'. Let us examine these causes:

1) Use. There are two aspects to depreciation through use. Firstly, the mere fact that an asset becomes second-hand reduces its value. Secondly, use leads to loss of value from wear and tear (eg with machinery and vehicles) and exposure to the elements (eg rust with vehicles, weathering with buildings).
2) Time. The simple passage of time also reduces the value of an asset, even if it is not used. This is especially so for assets with a definite finite life such as leasehold property.
3) Obsolescence. Another cause of depreciation is an asset becoming out-of-date or obsolete, either through technological advances or a change in tastes and fashions. Thus the typewriter has virtually been replaced by the technically superior word-processor and the market value of a fleet of company cars drops on the day a new model comes onto the market.

5.2 Benefits of Depreciation

Depreciation is a method by which a business spreads the cost of a fixed asset over the years of its useful life. Take the following example. A firm buys a lorry for £20 000 and it estimates its useful life at 5 years. The benefits derived by the firm from the lorry are as follows:

Year	1	2	3	4	5
Benefit (£)	4 000	4 000	4 000	4 000	4 000

The firm should charge £4 000 provision for depreciation against its profit for each of the five years or for as long as it keeps the lorry.

Charging the full cost of the lorry to the profit and loss account in year 1 with no charge in subsequent years would be wrong for several reasons:

- It would be unrealistic as it would look from the accounts as if the lorry were fully used up in the first year.
- It would contravene the accruals or matching concept which states that expenditure should be charged against profit in the year or years in which the benefit of the expenditure is received. Profit would be understated by too much in

the first year and overstated in the years that follow. The cost of a fixed asset, which gives benefits over several years, should be divided up between those years. That division does not have to be done equally as we shall see below.

- It would be unacceptable to the tax authorities. For income tax and corporation tax purposes, the cost of a fixed asset cannot be charged against profit when purchased but must be spread out by what are called capital allowances.

Equally, charging the full cost of a fixed asset in the final year of its life would be unrealistic. In this case the firm would overstate its profits for the first four years (and perhaps take out too much money in drawings based on these figures) and would understate its profit by a large amount in the final year.

5.3 What Depreciation is not – Common Misconceptions

Firstly, depreciation is not a fund for replacement. The effect of a provision for depreciation is to reduce reported profit so reducing the outflow of cash from the business in the form of drawings taken by the owner or dividends paid to the shareholders. The amount of depreciation is not specifically set aside in, for example, a sinking fund which is designed to mature at the end of the expected life of the asset and thus finance its replacement. The amount not taken out by the owner is used to finance the business in general, e.g. it may boost the working capital or it can be held as a general reserve.

Secondly, depreciation is not an attempt to value an asset at the end of each financial year but is, as we have seen, a process of allocating the cost of the asset to the years which have benefited from its use. Valuing an asset is fraught with difficulties because there are several different possible bases of valuation, each providing different figures. The reason for the misconception is that balance sheets often use the term 'net book value' for fixed assets. Readers of accounts, being mostly non-accountants, interpret this as an attempt to value the asset at that moment in time. This it is not. What the accountant means by 'book value' is historic cost less accumulated depreciation, i.e. that portion of the original cost which has still to be written off to the profit and loss account.

Thirdly, a provision for depreciation does not involve a cash outflow from the business, unlike other charges in the profit and loss account such as wages, rent and rates etc. In making a provision for depreciation there is no double-entry with cash or bank. Look at the following example. A lorry is bought for £20 000 with an expected life of 5 years. The annual provisions for depreciation are £4 000.

Year	1	2	3	4	5
Depreciation	4 000	4 000	4 000	4 000	4 000
Cash flow (£)	(20 000)				

We can see from the above table that the provisions in years 2 to 5 do not involve any cash outflow. The whole of the cash outflow is in year 1. By year 2 the lorry has been paid for, so the firm does not have to pay for it again in years 2 – 5.The annual provisions for depreciation are a mere internal book adjustment not involving any financial transactions with the outside world. (This point has particular significance for cash flow statements which we look at in Chapter 11.)

5.4 Methods of Depreciation

How should the total cost of a fixed asset be divided up between the years of its existence? Should it be simply a function of time and, if so, should an equal amount be written off each year? Or should an attempt be made to reflect usage? Can the risk of obsolescence be built into the charge?

There are four main methods of calculating depreciation:

- the straight line or equal instalment method
- the reducing (or diminishing) balance method
- the revaluation method
- the usage method

Of these, the first two are the most commonly used and examined.

5.5 The Straight Line Method

This is also known as the Equal Instalment Method. Here the asset is deemed to lose value by an equal amount each year, as in the lorry example above. The annual transfers to the profit and loss account are given by

$$\frac{\text{Cost} - \text{Residual value}}{\text{Years of useful life}}$$

Residual value means how much the firm can expect the asset to be worth at the end of the period for which it is expected to be kept. Some firms keep assets until they are virtually worthless while others prefer to replace them while they are relatively new.

While the cost is known with certainty, residual value and years of useful life have to be estimated and are subjective. All methods of depreciation (except the revaluation method) suffer from the weakness of having to forecast. The assumption implicit in this method is that depreciation is a function of time and no account is taken of possible variations in use from year to year. The risk of obsolescence can be incorporated into the calculation by varying the estimate of useful life. The straight line method assumes that the asset loses value at a constant rate. While this may not always be the case, it is not the object of the exercise to find the market value at the end of each year and it has the great advantage of being simple to calculate and understand.

Sometimes an examination question will tell you to depreciate an asset at a certain percentage 'on cost'. If you see this phrase, use the straight line method.

Worked Example

Horace sets up in business offering a removal service with the purchase of a van for £10 000 on 1 January 2000. He expects to use it for 3 years and then sell it for £4 000. Show the annual depreciation charges and relevant balance sheet figures over the life of the van if Horace uses the straight line method.

Solution

Annual depreciation charge = (£10 000 – £4 000) ÷ 3 years = £2 000

			Balance Sheet	
Year	Charge to P&L A/c	Cost	Accumulated Depreciation	Net Book Value
	£	£	£	£
2000	2 000	10 000	(2 000)	8 000
2001	2 000	10 000	(4 000)	6 000
2002	2 000	10 000	(6 000)	4 000

Notice the £4 000 residual value which had been provided for in the calculation.

5.6 The Reducing Balance Method

You will also see this referred to as the Diminishing Balance Method. Under this method the asset is deemed to lose a greater part of its value in the early years of its use compared with later years. The charge is calculated as a given percentage of the previous year's net book value (under the straight line method the change is based on cost.) The percentage which should be used is given by:

$$1 - \sqrt[n]{\frac{\text{Residual value}}{\text{Cost}}}$$

where n = number of years.

In examinations at this level you will not be asked to calculate the annual percentage rate. You will be given it and merely have to apply it in depreciating the asset.

Worked Example

Using Horace's van, show the annual depreciation charges and relevant balance sheet figures if he uses the reducing balance method at 26%.

Solution

			Balance Sheet	
Year	Charge to P&L A/c*	Cost	Accumulated Depreciation	Net Book Value
	£	£	£	£
2000	2 600	10 000	(2 600)	7 400
2001	1 924	10 000	(4 524)	5 476
2002	1 424	10 000	(5 948)	4 052

* Year 1: 10 000 × 26% = 2 600

   Year 2: 7 400 × 26% = 1 924

   Year 3: 5 476 × 26% = 1 424

Note that: (i) the annual percentage rate that reduces the value of the van to exactly £4 000 in 3 years' time is over 26% but under 27%

        (ii) in year 1 the reducing balance charge is greater than the straight line charge whereas in years 2 and 3 the reverse is true.

5.7 A Comparison Between the Two Methods

- The straight line method is simpler to calculate, it is therefore cheaper to operate and there is less chance of making errors.
- The reducing balance method is more realistic as, in practice, assets tend to lose market value faster in the early years compared with later years.
- The reducing balance method is more appropriate where the risk of obsolescence is high; since most of the cost is written off in the early years, the loss suffered is small should the asset become obsolete.
- As assets get older the burden of repairs and maintenance gets progressively higher. The reducing balance method results in a more even total charge for use of the asset. In the early years when repair expenses are low, depreciation is high; in later years repairs are high and depreciation is low.

5.8 The Revaluation Method

This is the only method that attempts to relate the charge to the actual fall in value of the asset during the year. For this, the asset has to be valued at the end of each year.

Worked Example

Let us take the example of a factory and its stock of loose tools.

		£
Valuation	1 January	10 000
Purchases	During year	2 000
Valuation	31 December	8 500

The depreciation is worked out as a balancing figure in the ledger account.

Loose Tools – Net

		£			£
1 January	Balance b/d	10 000	31 December	Profit and loss	3 500
	Bank	2 000	31 December	Balance c/d	8 500
		12 000			12 000

The amount of depreciation is calculated by deducting the final valuation of £8 500 from the total of the debit side of the account. This method is conveniently applied to asscts which are individually so small that it is not worth identifying for each the cost, estimated useful life and residual value.

5.9 The Accounting Entries Necessary for Depreciation

A fixed asset is shown in its own account at cost. Depreciation is not shown here but in a separate provision for depreciation account. The net book value of the asset is found by deducting the last balance on the provision for depreciation account from the last balance on the fixed asset account. (Some small businesses probably still deduct depreciation from the asset cost in the asset account but you would be expected in an examination to handle it in the way shown here.)

The double entry for depreciation is made at the end of the year, just before preparation of the final accounts. The entry is the same regardless of the method used. It is:

Debit profit and loss account
Credit provision for depreciation account

There is a provision for depreciation account for each category of fixed assets. The balance on this account represents the total amount of the cost of the asset written off to date. Be careful about the distinction between the charge for the year and balance on the account. The annual charge is written off to the profit and loss account while the balance is shown in the balance sheet.

Worked Example

Let us take for our example Horace's van bought by cheque on 1 January 2000 at a cost of £10 000 which is expected to last for 3 years, when it can be sold for £4 000. Horace has decided to use the straight line method. The accounts would be as follows:

Motor Van

		£			£
1.1.2000	Bank	10 000	31.12.2000	Balance c/d	10 000
1.1.2001	Balance b/d	10 000	31.12.2001	Balance c/d	10 000
1.1.2002	Balance b/d	10 000	31.12.2002	Balance c/d	10 000
1.1.2003	Balance b/d	10 000			

Horace brings down the value of the van at cost at the end of each year to start off the next year.

Provision for Depreciation

		£			£
31.12.2000	Balance c/d (B)	2 000	31.12.2000	Profit and Loss (A)	2 000
			1.1.2001	Balance b/d (C)	2 000
31.12.2001	Balance c/d (E)	4 000	31.12.2001	Profit and Loss (D)	2 000
		4 000			4 000
			1.1.2002	Balance b/d (F)	4 000
31.12.2002	Balance c/d (H)	6 000	31.12.2002	Profit and Loss (G)	2 000
		6 000			6 000
			1.1.2003	Balance b/d (I)	6 000

The entries in the provision for deprecation account are lettered in sequence. Only (A), (D) and (G) represent double entries with the profit and loss account; the rest are for computation of the balance on the account.

At the beginning of 2003, the van's net book value is its cost minus the total accumulated depreciation, i.e. £10 000 – £6 000 = £4 000. This was the expected residual value.

5.10 Fixed Assets Register

Fixed assets of a similar type are normally grouped into one account. For example, a company with fifty pieces of machinery would not keep a separate account for each one but would show them all in one account, probably calling it 'plant and machinery'. This would have its related provision for depreciation account. It would however maintain a fixed assets register which shows details for each machine such as the make and model, serial number, date of purchase, cost and accumulated

depreciation. You will see an examination question containing a fixed asset register at the end of this chapter.

5.11 The Disposal of Assets

With the exception of freehold land, assets have a finite life and the entries made have to be written out of the books when an asset is either scrapped, sold or part-exchanged for another asset. The main task is to remove the cost of the asset from the asset account and the amount of accumulated depreciation which belongs to that asset from the provision for depreciation account; the double entries for these go into a special asset disposal account. The procedure is as follows.

1) Transfer the asset at cost from the asset account into the asset disposal account:
     Debit the disposal account
     Credit the asset account at cost
2) Transfer the depreciation which has accumulated to the asset over its life:
     Debit the provision for depreciation account
     Credit the disposal account
   You will usually have to calculate this depreciation from the information given in a question.
3) Now complete the double entry for the amount received for the asset. If the purchaser paid by cash or cheque:
     Debit the bank account
     Credit the disposal account
    If the asset is being exchanged for another item:
     Debit the asset account with the value of the new asset received
     Credit the disposal account
4) Balance off the disposal account. If the accumulated depreciation and proceeds of the sale exceed the cost of the asset, a profit has been made on the sale and this is shown in the profit and loss account as a miscellaneous gain:
     Debit the disposal account
     Credit the profit and loss account
   If the accumulated depreciation and proceeds of sale are less than the cost of the asset, a loss has been made on the sale and this is deducted from profit:
     Debit the profit and loss account
     Credit the disposal account

Gains and losses on disposal are not really gains and losses but a recognition that the wrong amount of depreciation has been deducted from the asset. A 'gain' means that the asset has been over-depreciated and was worth more than we thought, as evidenced by the selling price; the profit and loss account is credited in order to reduce the total depreciation charged on the asset. Similarly a 'loss' means that the asset has been under-depreciated and was worth less than our records showed and the profit and loss account must be debited in order to increase the total depreciation on the asset.

Gains and losses on disposal are not attributable to the year of sale. Since they represent adjustments to the depreciation charge on the asset, they should be distributed over the profits and losses of the years during which the asset had been owned, i.e. we would have to recalculate the depreciation charges for these years and adjust all the profit figures accordingly. Such an exercise, however, is laborious and impractical and SSAP 12 allows gains and losses to be wholly written off in the year of sale.

5.12 Assets Bought or Sold Part-Way Through the Year

A business whose financial year runs from 1 January to 31 December buys a machine on 1 July. In the year-end accounts, should it charge a full year's depreciation on the asset or only for the time it was used, i.e. for 6 months? Strictly speaking, the charge should be proportional to the number of months of ownership. The first approach is simpler to operate however and large firms tend to charge a full year's depreciation on assets bought during the year as a slightly incorrect depreciation charge does not affect the accounts materially. To compensate for this overcharge, they make no charge for assets sold during the year, even though they were used for part of it. In this way the overcharges and undercharges roughly cancel each other out and the overall charge for depreciation is not materially different from that which would have been obtained from a month-by-month calculation. The firm is, in effect, charging a full year's depreciation on all assets held at the end of the year.

Examination questions should indicate which system the business is applying. If they do not, follow this guideline:

- if no dates are given, it is not possible to apply depreciation on a month-by-month basis;
- if dates are given and no mention is made of the policy followed, apply depreciation on a month-by-month basis. Do not forget to state the assumption made in your answer.

Worked Example

A machine was purchased for £24 000 on 1 May 1997 and was sold on 30 September 2000 for £4 000. Depreciation on the machine was charged at 25% per annum by the equal instalment method. The firm's financial year runs from 1 January to 31 December and its depreciation policy is to charge a full year's depreciation in the year of purchase and nothing in the year of sale. Here are the accounts and calculations.

Disposal at 30 September 2000

	£		£
Machine A/c	24 000	Provision for depreciation	18 000
		Bank	4 000
		Profit and loss account	2 000
	24 000		24 000

Depreciation has been charged on the machine for 1997 (the year of purchase), 1998 and 1999 but not for the year of sale, 2000, i.e. it has been depreciated for 3 years: 75% of £24 000.

5.13 Subjectivity and Manipulation

As we have seen, depreciation is quite a subjective affair. The amount charged is affected by the estimates of useful life and residual value and also by the method used. Given that there is no one correct charge, it can be tempting for a business to manipulate reported profit by varying the amount of the charge from year to year. If higher profits are desired the charge could be lowered and vice versa. SSAP 12, recognising this, forbids a change in the depreciation rate or method unless the change is necessary to represent the affairs of the business more fairly. In any case, changing the rate or method for no good reason contravenes the principle of consistency.

Where an original estimate of useful life has proved to be too optimistic, perhaps due to unforeseen technical obsolescence, a business may make a change in the calculations. The remaining net book value (the amount of cost still to be written off to the profit and loss account) should be written down to the residual value over the remainder of the new estimate of useful life. SSAP 12 recommends that '…businesses do not backdate charge for depreciation when useful lives are revised or any other charge connected with the asset made'.

Freehold land is unique in that it is probably the only asset that does not depreciate with time – in fact it often appreciates when market prices rise. For this reason SSAP 12 allows firms not to depreciate freehold land. Leasehold property however does have to be depreciated, as the value of the land or buildings falls as the lease expires. The straight line basis should be used since the fall in value of the lease is a function of time. Whereas most land has unlimited life, buildings do not and SSAP 12 requires buildings to be depreciated. The rate of depreciation is usually low, 2% per year on the straight line basis being a common provision.

Questions

Question 5.1

Roadcraft Ltd owns a fleet of delivery vans. At 31 March 1995 details of the vans in service were as follows:

Reference Number	VEH 101	VEH 102	VEH 103
Date purchased	June 1991	May 1992	July 1994
Cost	£18 000	£18 600	£19 500

The company's policy up to 31 March 1995 had been to depreciate these vans by 20% per annum using the reducing balance method. Calculations had been made to the nearest £.

After a management discussion, it was agreed to change the method of calculating depreciation from reducing balance to straight line retrospectively to the purchase date of the vehicles. The calculations were to be based on a five-year life for each van with estimated residual values of £500 per van.

It was also agreed to continue the policy of providing depreciation for a full year in the year of purchase and to ignore depreciation in the year of sale. The new policy and the consequent adjustments would take effect from 1 April 1995.

During the financial year ended 31 March 1996, a van (VEH 102) was sold for £6 000 cash and a new van (VEH 104) was purchased for £20 800 from Brownlee Ltd.

REQUIRED

(a) Using the reducing balance method, prepare a statement showing the amount of depreciation calculated to 31 March 1995. **(10 marks)**
(b) Calculate the adjustment required at 1 April 1995 to implement the change in depreciation policy. **(10 marks)**
(c) Write up the following ledger accounts for the year ended 31 March 1996:
    (i) delivery vans (at cost) account **(3 marks)**
    (ii) provision for depreciation on delivery vans account **(5 marks)**
    (iii) disposal of delivery vans account **(2 marks)**
(d) Identify and briefly comment on the causes of depreciation. **(8 marks)**

Associated Examining Board Advanced Level

Question 5.2

Your organisation maintains a fixed asset register which contained the following details at 1 April 1997:

		Cost/Valuation at 1 April 1997	Accumulated depreciation at 1 April 1997
		£	£
Land		120 000	nil
Building		80 000	18 000
Plant:	Machine A	60 000	27 000
	Machine B	40 000	24 000
	Machine C	26 000	11 700
	Machine D	18 000	13 500
Office equipment:	Computer	20 000	7 200
	Scanner	1 000	600
	Printers (2)	600	250
Small tools		1 200	300

Land is revalued every three years. The last revaluation took place on 31 March 1997. Buildings are depreciated at 2.5% per annum on cost. Small tools are revalued annually, the value at 31 March 1998 being £800. Plant is depreciated at 7.5% per annum on cost and office equipment is depreciated at 7.5% per annum on cost.

During the year ended 31 March 1998, the following transactions occurred:

i) Machine E was purchased by cheque for £17 000.
ii) Machine C was sold for £13 000 to A Jones on credit.
iii) The computer memory was upgraded by the manufacturer at a cost of £2 000.
iv) The scanner was repaired at a cost of £300.
v) Machine F was purchased by cheque for £42 300 including VAT at 17.5%. The purchase price included delivery and installation of £1 200 plus VAT and a one-year maintenance contract of £2 000 plus VAT.
vi) The total on the fixed asset register at 1 April 1997 was compared with the ledger accounts, and it was discovered that one of the printers had been passed to a supplier in part-payment of his debt during December 1996 but had never been removed from the fixed asset register. The cost of the printer was £400 and depreciation of £200 had been charged up to 1 April 1996.

Note (1): Ignore VAT on all items except for those in transaction (v).
Note (2): The organisation's policy is to charge a full year's depreciation in the year of purchase.

REQUIRED

(a) Prepare the fixed asset accounts (at cost) and the provision for depreciation accounts for each of the above categories of fixed asset, commencing with the totals in the fixed asset register on 1 April 1997. Make entries for additions, disposals, adjustments and depreciation for the year ended 31 March 1998. **(10 marks)**
(b) Prepare the fixed asset disposals account for the year ended 31 March 1998. **(4 marks)**
(c) Describe the information which could be held on a fixed asset register and discuss the advantages of maintaining a computerised fixed asset register. **(6 marks)**

Chartered Institute of Management Accountants

Question 5.3

At the beginning of the financial year on 1 April 1995, a company had a balance on plant account of £372 000 and on provision for depreciation of plant account of £205 400.

The company's policy is to provide depreciation using the reducing balance method applied to the fixed assets held at the end of the financial year at the rate of 20% per annum.

On 1 September 1995 the company sold for £13 700 some plant which it had acquired on 31 October 1991 at a cost of £36 000. Additionally, installation costs totalled £4 000. During 1993 major repairs costing £6 300 had been carried out on this plant and, in order to increase the capacity of the plant, a new motor had been fitted in December 1993 at a cost of £4 400. A further overhaul costing £2 700 had been carried out during 1994.

The company acquired new replacement plant on 30 November 1995 at a cost of £96 000, inclusive of installation charges of £7 000.

REQUIRED

Calculate

(a) the balance of plant at cost at 31 March 1996   **(3 marks)**
(b) the provision for depreciation of plant at 31 March 1996   **(10 marks)**
(c) the profit or loss on disposal of the plant   **(4 marks)**

Chartered Association of Certified Accountants

Question 5.4

The financial year of AB Manufacturing ends on 31 December.

Depreciation on machinery is charged at 18% per annum by the straight line method. In the year in which a machine is purchased or sold, the depreciation charge is based on the number of months the asset has been owned.

Depreciation of vehicles is charged at 25% per annum, by the reducing balance method. A full year's depreciation is charged in the year of purchase, but none in the year of sale.

The firm began trading on 1 January 1995.

Asset Purchases

		£
Machine 101	1 March 1995	20 000
Machine 102	1 April 1996	30 000
Machine 103	1 September 1997	7 200
Vehicle A	1 July 1995	12 800
Vehicle B	1 October 1997	24 000
Vehicle C	1 December 1998	18 000

Asset Sales

		£
Machine 102	31 May 1998	16 300
Vehicle A	30 November 1998	6 200

(i)

(a) complete the depreciation schedule for 1995 to 1998; **(9 marks)**

(b) calculate the profit or loss on sale of machinery for 1998; **(2½ marks)**

(c) calculate the profit or loss on sale of vehicles for 1998; **(2½ marks)**

(d) complete the balance sheet extract as at 31 December 1998. **(3 marks)**

(ii) State the purposes of providing for depreciation. **(3 marks)**

Scottish Qualifications Authority

Question 5.5

The fixed asset register of Glassware plc showed the following information at 31 March 1998.

Freehold properties which cost £200 000
Plant and Machinery which cost £250 000
Motor vehicles which cost £40 000
Provision for depreciation – freehold premises £36 000
                            – plant and machinery £69 375
                            – motor vehicles £24 000

The accounting policies with regard to the depreciation of fixed assets are as follows:

– Freehold property: 2% per annum on the carrying amounts
– Plant and machinery: 15% per annum on reducing balance
– Motor vehicles: 20% per annum on cost

A full year's depreciation is provided for in the year of acquisition and no depreciation is charged in the year of disposal.

The following transactions occurred in the company's accounting year ended 31 March 1999.

Freehold property which cost £80 000 in May 1989 was sold for £140 000 and following the disposal the remaining property was revalued at £270 000.
Additional machinery was purchased for £120 000.
A motor vehicle which cost £8 000 in July 1995 was sold for £2 500.
A new motor vehicle was purchased for £10 000 in May 1998.

REQUIRED

(a) Prepare:
    i) the fixed asset schedule of Glassware plc at 31 March 1999 in accordance with the Companies Act 1985;
    ii) the Profit and Loss Account entries relating to fixed assets for the year ended 31 March 1999; **(22 marks)**

(b) Discuss the reasons why a company may choose to depreciate some assets using the reducing balance method and others using the straight line method. **(10 marks)**

(c) Identify which information shareholders and creditors would find useful from the statutory notes to published accounts. Explain your answer. **(8 marks)**

Northern Ireland Council for the Curriculum Examinations and Assessment Advanced Level

6

Correction of Errors

6.1 Introduction

Given that in the course of a year thousands, sometimes millions, of separate transactions have to be entered in the books it is perhaps not surprising that some errors are made. A tired bookkeeper, temporary loss of concentration, working in times of extra pressure, a mislaid invoice – all of these can, and in practice do, lead to incorrect entries being made in the books. Bookkeepers can try to be conscientious in trying to prevent errors but no system is foolproof. When an error is located it has to be corrected by first making a note of the adjustment required in the journal and then putting through the double-entry in the ledger.

6.2 Errors not Detected by the Trial Balance

Errors can be of many types but it is possible to classify them into a few groups. Some errors are more difficult to detect than others. A bookkeeper will not be easily alerted to errors which debit and credit accounts with the same amount since the trial balance prepared to 'check' the books will balance. Herein lies a major weakness of the trial balance – if it balances, this does not in itself prove that the books have been correctly written up. There are certain errors which are not picked up by the trial balance.

Type of error	Nature of error	Example
1. Error of Omission	A transaction is completely omitted from the books.	A purchase of goods is not recorded because the purchase invoice has been mislaid.
2. Error of Commission	A purchase or sale is entered in the wrong creditor or debtor account.	A sale of goods to J Tyler is posted to J Taylor's account.
3. Error of Principle	An item is entered in a completely wrong class of account.	A purchase of a fixed asset is posted to the purchases account.
4. Error of Original Entry	A wrong account is entered in a book of original entry and this figure is then used for posting to the ledger.	A sales clerk in a hurry reads an invoice of £10 000 as £1 000 and enters the latter figure in the sales day book.
5. Compensating Errors I	By coincidence, an error on the debit side cancels out a separate and independent error of the same amount on the credit side.	The wages account is overcast by £200 and the creditors are also overstated by £200.

6. Compensating Errors II	Two errors compensate for each other on the same side.	Advertising is understated by £50 and electricity is overstated by £50.
7. Reversal of Entries	The debit entry is written on the credit side and the credit entry is written on the debit side.	A cash sale is debited to the sales account and credited to the cash account.
8. Entries Done Twice	The double entry is correctly completed but two debits and two credits are entered.	A purchase of goods by cheque is debited twice to the purchases account and credited twice to the bank account.

6.3 Errors Detected by the Trial Balance

The following types of errors will cause the trial balance to disagree:

- Entering a transaction as two debits or two credits
- Posting either the debit or the credit to the ledger twice
- Entering the wrong figure one side (transposition error)
- Incorrect totalling of an account
- Incorrect balancing of an account
- Correction made to only one part of a transaction
- Entering an item incorrectly in the trial balance (either the wrong amount or on the wrong side)
- Omitting a transaction entirely from the trial balance

While a difference in trial balance totals alerts the bookkeeper to errors within the books, it does not pinpoint where the errors are nor how many there are. For this the entries made must be checked until the errors are found.

6.4 Suspense Accounts

If the trial balance does not agree, a Suspense Account is opened with the difference. If the total of debits is less than the total of credits, the suspense account is debited with the difference and vice versa. Here is the end of a trial balance:

	Dr £	Cr £
Totals	92 100	92 000
Suspense account		100
	£92 100	£92 100

A suspense account is however only a temporary device and as soon as it has been opened, the errors must be located and the account balanced off in the way shown below. (The object of the exercise is to put the accounts right and get rid of the suspense account.) This is done by using the main journal in order to explain the correcting entries. If the profit has already been calculated, this will have to be corrected too.

6.5 Correction of Errors

Let us suppose that the two sides of the trial balance disagree. The complete correction procedure is as follows:

Open the suspense account with the difference, as shown above.
Go through the books to locate the error or errors.
Make entries in the main journal to correct the errors, i.e. say which accounts you are debiting and crediting and by how much and explain what you are doing. In the case of errors which cause the trial balance to disagree, one of the correcting entries in each case will be in the suspense account; in the case of errors which do not cause trial balance disagreement, the suspense account will not be involved. The desired effect is that things should be put back to what they would have been if no errors had been made.
Now post these entries to the relevant ledger accounts, including the suspense account. If everything is done correctly, the suspense account will balance off.
Redraft the trial balance, inserting the correct balances.
Prepare a statement showing the corrected net profit and rewrite the balance sheet if necessary.

6.6 Effect of Errors on Profit or Loss

Some errors affect the profit while others do not. This distinction does not always coincide with whether or not the trial balance balances.

Errors affecting Profit or Loss

These errors affect those accounts which are included in the Trading and Profit and Loss Account eg purchases, sales, expenses etc. We must ask the following questions:

1) Does the error affect the gross profit, the net profit or both?
   (a) Errors which affect items that go into the trading account affect gross profit **and** net profit to the same extent and in the same direction. Such items are sales, purchases, returns, stocks, carriage inwards etc.
   (b) Errors which affect items that are entered in the profit and loss section of the account, i.e. operating expenses, affect only net profit. Purchases of fixed assets affect profit only indirectly through provisions for depreciation.

2) In what direction is profit affected?
   (a) If sales are overstated or purchases understated, both gross profit and net profit are too big and must be reduced by the relevant amount. The same applies if sales returns are understated or purchases returns overstated.
   (b) If sales are understated or purchases overstated, both gross profit and net profit are too small and must be increased by the relevant amount. The same applies if sales returns are overstated or purchases returns understated.
   (c) If miscellaneous receipts are overstated or if expenses are understated, gross profit is not affected but net profit is too big and must be reduced.
   (d) If miscellaneous receipts are understated or if expenses are overstated, again gross profit is not affected but net profit is too small and must be increased.
   (e) If capital expenditure is wrongly treated as revenue expenditure, eg if the purchase of a fixed asset is treated as an expense, then net profit will be too small and must be increased. The opposite applies if revenue expenditure is treated as capital expenditure.

3) Will errors that affect items in the balance sheet affect profit as well? The answer is only those that were adjusted after the trial balance was prepared. Errors affecting fixed assets, current assets and liabilities do not normally affect profit but if one of these items has changed as a result of an adjustment, then profit **is** affected. For example:

(a) If the closing stock has been overvalued, the stock figure in the balance sheet is too big and so are the gross profit and the net profit. The opposite is true of a closing stock which is undervalued. Remember that closing stock adds on to gross profit and opening stock takes away from it.

(b) If an accrued or prepaid expense is the wrong amount, both profit and the item in the balance sheet are wrong. If an amount owing is overstated or a prepayment is understated, profit is too small and must be increased, and vice versa.

(c) The opposite to (b) applies in the case of accrued or prepaid receipts.

Estimating the effects of errors can be confusing and you must keep a clear mind. Think how the original figure has affected profit and then try to see in which direction the error is affecting the profit.

6.7 Examination Questions

A typical examination question on this topic would give you the difference in the trial balance, tell you what errors were found and ask you to write the journal entries to correct the errors, write up the suspense account and prepare a statement to show the adjusted profit.

Worked Example

This example is taken from the Associated Examining Board Advanced Level

In the trial balance as at 31 October 1995 of Dawdon Ltd, the debit balances total exceeded the credit balances total by £3236. As a result, a suspense account was opened. The annual profit and loss account was then prepared which revealed a net profit of £19 220. The company does not maintain control accounts. A subsequent investigation revealed the following errors.

1) The sales journal had been overcast by £300.
2) The wages account had been undercast by £450 on the debit side.
3) Depreciation on machinery had been overlooked. The company provides for depreciation on the basis of 12½ % on cost. The cost of machinery owned at the end of the year was £48 000.
4) The bank overdraft of £1 842 had been carried forward in the cash book as a debit balance of £1 824.
5) The account of K Smith, a doctor, had been overcast by £200 on the debit side.
6) A payment of £80, by cheque to M James, had been posted twice to her account.
7) A balance of £40 on S David's account had been written off correctly to the bad debts account but had not been entered in the personal account.

REQUIRED

(a) Journal entries to correct the errors which the investigations had revealed. (Narratives are not required.) **(16 marks)**

(b) Write up the suspense account. **(6 marks)**

(c) A statement showing the adjusted profit after taking into consideration the
     appropriate corrections.   **(4 marks)**
(d) In relation to errors in a trial balance explain why a suspense account is opened.   **(6 marks)**

Workings

(a)

Journal

		£ Dr	£ Cr
(1)	Sales	300	
	Suspense		300
(2)	Wages	450	
	Suspense		450
(3)	Profit & loss	6 000	
	Provision for depreciation		6 000
(4)	Suspense	3 666	
	Bank		3 666
(5)	Suspense	200	
	K Smith		200
(6)	Suspense	80	
	M James		80
(7)	Suspense	40	
	S David		40

1) As the sales journal has been overcast, the sales account will also be too big so we
    cancel out the error by debiting sales with £300; the double entry for the
    correction is credited to the suspense account.
2) As the wages account has been undercast, we debit it with the shortfall of £450
    and credit suspense with the same amount as the double entry for the correction.
3) The depreciation which had been omitted is 12½% of £48 000 = £6 000. This does
    not affect the suspense account at all since it is an error of omission. We credit the
    provision for depreciation account and debit profit and loss.
4) The bank balance was entered on the debit side instead of the credit side and in
    addition different figures were used. To correct this we credit the bank account
    with £1 824 to cancel out the incorrect debit and then we credit it again with the
    correct amount of £1 842. The overall credit is thus the total of these two figures
    i.e. £3 666 and we debit suspense with this amount.
5) To cancel out the excess £200 debited to the debtor, we credit K Smith's account
    and complete the double entry on the debit side of the suspense account.
6) The payment is on the debit side of the creditor's account as it cancels out the
    amount owing to her. Here however the payment has been debited twice so we
    credit M James's account with £80 to cancel out the excess and debit suspense.
    We credit S David's account with the bad debt (as should have been done) and
    debit suspense with the same amount.

Narratives in the journal are not required in this question but, if you are asked to
give them, describe briefly after each item the nature of the error you are
correcting.

(b)

Suspense

	£		£
Bank	3 666	Trial balance	3 236
K Smith	200	Sales	300
M James	80	Wages	450
S David	40		
	3 986		3 986

The opening balance in the suspense account is the difference between the trial balance totals, entered on the side which has less i.e. a credit entry of £3 236. We now complete the suspense account by following the instructions we gave ourselves in the journal. Since the suspense account balances off, we can be almost sure that our answer is right; there might be occasions where wrong corrections could result in the suspense account balancing but this is rare.

(c)
Statement of Adjusted Profit

	£	£
Net profit as per P & L account		19 220
– Sales	(300)	
– Wages	(450)	
– Depreciation	(6 000)	
		(6 750)
Adjusted net profit		£12 470

We begin our statement with the incorrect net profit of £19 220 given in the question and adjust it for those items which affect the profit:

1) As sales were too big, profit is also too big and we reduce it by £300.
2) As wages were too small, profit is too big and we reduce it by £450.
3) As depreciation was omitted, profit is too big and we reduce it by £6 000.
4) to 7) None of the remaining errors affect profit as they all concern assets and liabilities i.e. the bank balance, the debtors and creditors balances.

(d) A suspense account is opened as a temporary device to balance the books until the errors are discovered. It must be eliminated by correcting the errors and entering the double entries of the corrections in the suspense account.

Questions

Question 6.1

Jackson Printing Company Limited, a small private company, has produced its unaudited balance sheet as at 31 March 1994.

	£	£	£
Fixed Assets			
Tangible Assets			
Freehold land and buildings			60 000
Plant and machinery		40 000	
Accumulated depreciation		(18 000)	
			22 000
Motor vans		25 000	
Accumulated depreciation		(11 000)	
			14 000
			96 000
Current Assets			
Stocks		10 000	
Debtors		14 000	
Cash		1 200	
		25 200	
Current Liabilities – amounts falling due within one year:			
Creditors	10 000		
Bank	6 000		
		16 000	
Working capital			9 200
			£105 200
Equity and Reserves			
Called-up shares			75 000
Retained profits			30 200
			£105 200

In the course of your audit you find that:

1) During the year a motor van was sold for £1 100. The van was bought four years ago at a cost of £10 000 and had been depreciated to £2 000. Proceeds were included in sales and no other entries had been made.
2) The land and buildings had been revalued by a surveyor at freehold land £20 000 and buildings at £50 000. The directors wish to incorporate these new values in the balance sheet and to depreciate the buildings at 2% per annum.
3) A debtor, owing the company £1 000, is unlikely to pay and should be written off.

REQUIRED

(a) Journal entries to adjust the balance sheet as at 31 March 1994 for items referred to above (supporting narrative is not required).
(b) A balance sheet as at 31 March 1994, after the adjustments as in 1) above.

(16 marks)

Institute of Chartered Accountants, Foundation

Question 6.2

The draft final accounts of RST Ltd for the year ended 30 April 1995 showed a net profit for the year after tax of £78 263.

During the subsequent audit, the following errors and omissions were discovered. At the draft stage a suspense account had been opened to record the net difference.

1) Trade debtors were shown as £55 210. However
    i) bad debts of £610 had not been written off
    ii) the existing provision for doubtful debts, £1 300, should have been adjusted to 2% of debtors
    iii) a provision of 2% for discounts on debtors should have been raised.
2) Rates of £491 which had been prepaid at 30 April 1994 had not been brought down on the rates account as an opening balance.
3) A vehicle held as a fixed asset, which had originally cost £8 100 and for which £5 280 had been provided as depreciation, had been sold for £1 350. The proceeds had been correctly debited to the bank but had been credited to sales. No transfers had been made to the disposals account.
4) Credit purchases of £1 762 had been correctly debited to the purchases account but had been credited to the supplier's account as £1 672.
5) A piece of equipment costing £9 800 and acquired on 1 May 1994 for use in the business had been debited to the purchases account. (The company depreciates equipment at 20% per annum on cost.)
6) Items valued at £2 171 had been completely omitted from the closing stock figure.
7) At 30 April 1995 an accrual of £543 for electricity charges and an insurance prepayment of £162 had been omitted.
8) The credit side of the wages account had been under-added by £100 before the balance on the account had been determined.

REQUIRED

(a) Prepare a statement correcting the draft net profit after tax. **(13 marks)**
(b) Post and balance the suspense account. *(Note: The opening balance of this account has not been given and must be derived.)* **(4 marks)**

Chartered Association of Certified Accountants

Question 6.3

Kathleen Mason owns a small grocery store. The following balances remained in her ledgers on 30 April 1998 after the draft profit and loss account had been prepared.

Trial Balance as at 30 April 1998

	£	£
Fixed assets	31 200	
Stock	1 250	
Trade debtors	1 130	
Bank	610	
Trade creditors		2 720
Net profit for the year		3 100
Drawings	1 180	
Capital as at 1 May 1997		29 200
Suspense		?

She subsequently discovered the following errors.

1) An unpaid invoice for electricity for £192 had been correctly recorded in the heating account, but no other entry had been made for this item.
2) The part-time assistant receives £40 per week in wages, which is paid out of takings. One payment had been omitted from the wages account. The other entry in respect of this item was correct.
3) New shelving costing £320 had been recorded incorrectly in the purchases account.
4) Sales on credit to a local hospital amounting to £160 had been correctly entered in the personal ledger account but had been omitted from the sales account.
5) An invoice for £124 for telephone calls had been posted to the expense account as £142.
6) A supplier of groceries had been sent a cheque for £240 in March 1998. This was in full settlement of an invoice after Kathleen had deducted a 4% cash discount. The cash discount had been recorded on the debit side of the discounts allowed account.

REQUIRED

(a) Explain the use and limitations of a trial balance.   **(4 marks)**
(b) Name the **two** types of errors made in (3) and (5) above.   **(2 marks)**
(c) Show the journal entries required to adjust the errors (1) to (6). (Narratives
    are **not** required.)   **(12 marks)**
(d) Write up the corrected suspense account clearly showing the balance originally
    arising as a result of the errors.   **(7 marks)**
(e) Prepare a statement showing the corrected net profit for the year ended 30 April 1998.   **(8 marks)**

Associated Examining Board Advanced Level

Question 6.4

The following draft balance sheet as at 31 December 1996 has been prepared for the partnership of R Black and B Brown, who share profits and losses equally.

	£ Cost	£ Depreciation	£ Net book value
Fixed Assets			
Premises	50 000		50 000
Plant and machinery	40 000	(25 000)	15 000
Fixtures and fittings	30 000	(10 000)	20 000
	120 000	(35 000)	85 000
Current Assets			
Stock	26 000		
Debtors	24 000		
Bank	10 000		
		60 000	
Current Liabilities			
Creditors		25 000	
Net current assets			35 000
Net book value of assets			£120 000

Financed by		
Capital accounts		
R Black	60 000	
B Brown	30 000	
		90 000
Current accounts		
R Black	5 000	
B Brown	4 000	
		9 000
		99 000
Long-term Liabilities		
Bank loan		21 000
Capital Employed		£120 000

After the preparation of the above draft balance sheet, the following discoveries have been made.

- The valuation of the stock at 31 December 1996 had been incorrectly shown in the accounts as £26 000 instead of the correct amount of £30 000.
- No entry has been made in the accounts to record the sale of an item of fixtures and fittings on credit to James Sainsbury for £4 500 on 31 October 1996. The fixtures and fittings were purchased on 1 January 1990 for £10 000. It is company policy to depreciate fixtures and fittings by 10% per annum on cost. No depreciation is charged in the year of disposal and depreciation has not been provided on this asset for the year to 31 December 1996.
- A provision for doubtful debts equal to 5% of the trade debtors should be created.
- No entries had been made in the accounts for goods costing £1 000 taken by R Black for his own use.
- Interest at the rate of 8% per annum is to be provided on the long-term bank loan.
- A rates bill of £1 500 relating to B Brown's home was paid by the partnership and charged to the profit and loss account.

Required

(a) Prepare a corrected balance sheet of the partnership at 31 December 1996.   **(15 marks)**

(b) Discuss the firm's policy of not providing for depreciation on premises.   **(5 marks)**

Northern Ireland Council for the Curriculum Examinations and Assessment

Question 6.5

At the year end of TD, an imbalance in the trial balance was revealed which resulted in the creation of a suspense account with a credit balance of £1 040.

Investigations revealed the following errors:

(i) A sale of goods on credit for £1 000 had been omitted from the sales account.

(ii) Delivery and installation costs of £240 on a new item of plant had been recorded as a revenue expense.

(iii) Cash discount of £150 on paying a creditor, JW, had been taken, even though the payment was made outside the time limit.

(iv) Stock of stationery at the end of the period of £240 had been ignored.

(v) A purchase of raw materials of £350 had been recorded in the purchases account as £850.

(vi) The purchase returns day book included a sales credit note for £230 which had been entered correctly in the account of the debtor concerned, but included with purchase returns in the nominal ledger

REQUIREMENTS

(a) Prepare journal entries to correct EACH of the above errors. Narratives are NOT required.   **(22 marks)**

(b) Open a suspense account and show the corrections to be made.   **(3 marks)**

(c) Prior to the discovery of the errors, TD's gross profit for the year was calculated at £35 750 and the net profit for the year at £18 500.
Calculate the revised gross and net profits after the correction of the errors.   **(5 marks)**

Chartered Institute of Management Accountants

7

Incomplete Records

7.1 Introduction

While most large and medium-sized businesses maintain a separate clerical function which operates a full double-entry system, a lot of small businesses do not. With most sole traders, for example, the books are kept by the owner. Employing an independent bookkeeper may not be justified by the size of the business, nor may the owner be able to afford one. The task has to be somehow fitted in with all the countless other tasks involved in running a business. As a result, the recording is incomplete because the owner has not devoted sufficient time to it and may not be conversant with the techniques of double-entry. At the end of the financial year, the owner will take the records to an accountant. The accountant has to play the role of a detective, working out missing items by logical deductions from information supplied. The techniques used are looked at in this chapter. The final accounts can be prepared from these deductions and from information supplied.

Jobs on incomplete records tend to be of two types:

1) those where the client has maintained records but in **single-entry** form, often in just a cash book. In these cases what is incomplete is not so much the records as the **system of recording.** The accountant posts the items from the cash book to ledger accounts, thereby converting the single-entry to double-entry. The year-end adjustments are then put through in respect of accruals, prepayments, and provisions. These are then used as the basis on which to prepare the year-end final accounts.

2) jobs in which the client has not followed even single-entry. The recording has probably not been based on any system at all and is patchy. Here the accountant has very little to go on and is not able to prepare a normal set of final accounts; profit for the year must be estimated as the **difference between the opening and closing capital values** of the business.

Examination questions tend to be of type 1, mainly because they are a good test of double-entry principles and involve application of several key accounting concepts. The only principle tested in type 2 in the above list is the accounting equation Assets = Capital – Liabilities. We shall look first at the approach and techniques required to answer each type of question in turn.

7.2 Single-entry Systems

Questions provide information on:

* assets and liabilities at the start of the financial year
* receipts and payments during the year
* some of the assets and liabilities at the end of the year

From this you are required to prepare a set of year-end final accounts. In examinations it is not necessary to construct a full set of ledger accounts before preparing the final

accounts. There is not enough time for this nor does it indicate knowledge of additional principles. Your main aim is to prepare the final accounts. For this, the following techniques can be used:

1) Accounting ratios can be used to find sales or cost of goods sold.
2) The balancing figures in ledger accounts can be used to find purchases, sales and expenses.
3) The cash book can be reconstructed to find cash drawings.
4) The accounting equation can be applied to find opening capital, profit and drawings.

Let us look at each in turn.

7.3 Accounting Ratios

A clue to the figure for sales or cost of goods sold is often given in the form of the **mark-up** applied to cost of goods or the **margin** achieved on sales. Mark-up is the amount of profit added to cost, while margin is profit in relation to the selling price.

Question	Answer
Take this cost structure:	(a) $\text{Mark up} = \dfrac{\text{Profit}}{\text{Cost}} = \dfrac{1}{4}$ or 25%
Cost + Profit = Selling price	
£4 + £1 = £5	(b) $\text{Mark up} = \dfrac{\text{Profit}}{\text{Price}} = \dfrac{1}{5}$ or 20%

Being both measurements of profitability we can expect them to be linked. They are. This is how:

$$\text{When mark-up is } \frac{1}{4}, \text{margin is } \frac{1}{4+1} = \frac{1}{5}$$

$$\text{When mark-up is } \frac{2}{7}, \text{margin is } \frac{2}{7+2} = \frac{2}{9}$$

You should know and be able to apply this relationship in questions because examiners often give the cost of goods sold and the profit margin. The mark-up can be deduced from the margin. Since cost is given and mark-up is now known, profit can be found. This simple technique has helped many a student unlock the trading account.

Question

Cost of goods sold = £1 000
Gross profit on sales = 20%
Prepare a trading account.

Solution

Since the margin is $\frac{1}{5}$, the mark-up must be $\frac{1}{4}$.

i.e. Cost + Profit = Selling price

$\quad$ 4 $\quad$ + $\quad$ 1 $\quad$ = 5

Trading Account

	Relationship		£	£
Sales	5	$\frac{5}{4}$ of 1 000	1 250	
Less cost of goods sold	4	Given	(1 000)	
Gross profit	1	$\frac{1}{4}$ of 1 000	250	

This technique can also be used to prepare the trading account when sales and mark-up is given.

7.4 Balancing Figures in Ledger Accounts

If no information is given on mark-up or margin, purchases and sales will have to be calculated through the change in creditors and debtors position. Taking debtors as the example, a business will know the value of debtors at the start of the financial year (from last year's balance sheet), debtors at the year-end and amounts received from debtors during the year (from the cash book or bank statements). From this it is possible to deduce the value of sales during the year as follows:

	£
Total received during the year	9 600
Less amounts received in respect of sales made last year	1 000
	8 600
Add sales made this year for which payment has not yet been received	1 400
Credit sales made this year	10 000

Total Debtors

	£		£
1 Jan 2002 Bal b/f	1 000	Bank – cheques received	9 600
Sales (bal. fig.)	10 000	31 Dec. 2002 Bal c/f	1 400
	11 000		11 000

The second approach is better because examiners often prefer workings to be shown in the form of accounts.

Be careful!

(a) The figure deduced in this way represents credit sales only. If a business has also made cash sales during the year these have to be added to credit sales to arrive at total sales.

(b) If there are any discounts allowed, bad debts, or contras (set-offs) in the question, these have to be included in the account before arriving at the balancing figure.

We know that the figure of cash paid for an expense is not necessarily the charge for the year. It has to be adjusted for any accruals or prepayments. This is best done by constructing the ledger account and finding the charge as a balancing figure.

Example

Wages paid during the year:	£4 850
Outstanding at beginning of the year 1.1.2002:	£200
Outstanding at end of the year 31.12.2002:	£350
Charge for the year:	?

Wages

	£			£
Bank – wages paid	4 850	1.1.2002	Balance b/f	200
		31.12..2002	Profit and loss	
31.12.2002 Bal c/f	350		(balancing figure)	5 000
	5 200			5 200

7.5 Reconstructing the Cash Book

If a Cash Book has not been maintained by the client, the accountant prepares one from bank statements and cheque stubs retained. In questions you may have to construct a cash book from information on receipts and payments during the year. The figure for cash drawings is sometimes not given. This is because proprietors of small businesses do not always record the amount of cash withdrawn for private purposes. You have to deduce the amount as a balancing figure in the cash column of the Cash Book. Examiners sometimes do not give the closing bank or cash figure but you can find it by counting the amount of cash and looking at the bank statement.

Example

	£
Opening balances at 1 January 2002:	
Cash	100
Bank	2 000
Cash sales during the year	1 400
Cheques received from debtors	7 500
Cheques paid to suppliers	6 000
Cash paid to suppliers	50
Cash paid for expenses	300
Cheques paid for expenses	2 500
Closing balances, 31 December 2002:	
Cash	150
Bank	not given
Required:	
Cash drawings	?
Closing bank balance	?

Solution

Cash Book

	Cash £	*Bank* £		*Cash* £	*Bank* £
1 Jan 2002 Bals b/f	100	2 000	Creditors	50	6 000
Cash sales	1 400		Expenses	300	2 500
Debtors		7 500	Drawings	1 000	
			31 Dec 2002 Bals c/f	150	1 000
	1 500	9 500		1 500	9 500

Be careful with drawings. The cash book reveals the amount of cash drawings only. If the proprietor used some business stock for personal purposes during the year this has to be reflected in the final accounts – by adding to the figure for drawings (Dr) and subtracting from purchases (Cr).

A common difficulty with questions on incomplete records is that in the mass of information supplied one does not know just where to start. You might find it helpful to follow the steps laid out below.

1) Put down on paper the format of the trading account and insert the figures given (easy).

2) Deduce the missing figures, using techniques 1 and/or 2 (not as easy, workings needed).

3) Determine gross profit.

4) Perform workings for profit and loss account using technique 2 (not difficult). Be sure to leave some space below the trading account for the profit and loss account.

5) Prepare the profit and loss account.

6) Deduce the figure for drawings using technique 3, if required.

7) Calculate opening capital using technique 4, described below.

8) Finally, prepare the year-end balance sheet.

If no records of transactions have been maintained, it is not possible to construct ledger accounts and thus not possible to close them off to a trading and profit and loss account. All that can be estimated is profit made during the year, using technique 4.

7.6 Using the Accounting Equation

By looking at the various assets and liabilities at the start and end of the year, it is possible to prepare a statement of affairs or balance sheet at the start and end of the year. The increase in capital represents profit less drawings for the year. A decrease represents a loss, or drawings which are in excess of profit.
The principle is this:

Capital at end of year = Capital at start + Additional capital introduced during the year + Profit (– Loss) – Drawings.

Example

	1 Jan 2002	31 Dec 2002
	£000	£000
Fixed assets	50	50
Current assets	25	30
Current liabilities	20	20
During the year		
Drawings		10
Additional capital introduced		7
Required:		
Opening capital		?
Profit for the year		?
Closing capital		?

Solution

First find opening capital, by drawing up a statement of affairs.

Statement of affairs as at 1 January 2002

	£000	£000
Fixed assets		50
Current assets	25	
Less current liabilities	(20)	
Net assets (= capital)		5
		55

Next prepare a similar statement of affairs for the end of year.

Statement of affairs as at 31 December 2002

	£000	£000
Fixed assets		50
Current assets	30	
Less current liabilities	(20)	10
Net assets		60
Financed by:		
Capital, 1 Jan 2002 (from above)		55
Add additional capital introduced		7
		62
Add profit (balancing figure 70 – 62)		8
		70
Less drawings		(10)
Capital 31 Dec 2002 (= Net assets)		60

Having found the closing capital of £60 000 we work backwards to find the amount of profit for the year.

A limitation of deducing missing figures as balancing items is that its correctness depends on the rest of the account or statement being correct. Thus if in the above example we had forgotten to include the additional capital introduced of £7 000, our profit figure would have been out by £7 000. It is advisable therefore to read any question very carefully and make sure that you have included all items relevant to an account or statement before calculating the balancing item.

7.7 A Final Word

Although incomplete records are not an easy topic, successfully writing the answers to a question can be most satisfying as you will no doubt experience for yourself when, starting with a mass of haphazard information, you manage to deduce missing items one by one to finish with a complete set of final accounts and a balance sheet that balances. The techniques required do need a lot of practice, perhaps more so than for other topics, and we have included a generous selection of past examination questions for you to attempt. Remember that the more you do at home the quicker you will be able to do them in an examination.

If a question seems too difficult because of the amount of information or the manner in which the information is presented, make things easier for yourself by drawing up a pro-forma trading and profit and loss account, putting in the figures already given, then tackling each missing figure one by one as you work your way down the account – in other words, follow steps 1– 8 outlined above. Apart from helping to organise your thoughts on paper it will show the examiner that you have approached the question in a systematic manner and this in itself will earn you some marks. Finally, remember to reference your workings to their place in the final accounts.

Questions

Question 7.1

Jean Smith, who retails wooden ornaments, has been so busy since she commenced business on April 1995 that she has neglected to keep adequate accounting records. Jean's opening capital consisted of her life savings of £15 000 which she used to open a business bank account. The transactions in this bank account during the year ended 31 March 1996 are summarised from the bank account which follows.

Receipts	£
Loan from John Peacock, uncle	10 000
Takings	42 000
Payments	
Purchases of goods for resale	26 400
Electricity for period to 31 December 1995	760
Rent of premises for 15 months to 30 June 1996	3 500
Rates of premises for the year ended 31 March 1996	1 200
Wages of assistants	14 700
Purchase of van, 1 October 1995	7 600
Purchase of holiday caravan for Jean Smith's private use	8 500
Van licence and insurance, payments covering a year	250

According to the bank account, the balance in hand on 31 March 1996 was £4 090 in Jean Smith's favour.

Whilst the intention was to bank all takings intact, it now transpires that, in addition to cash drawings, the following payments were made out of takings before bankings:

	£
Van running expenses	890
Postage, stationery and other sundry expenses	355

On 31 March 1996, takings of £640 awaited banking: this was done on 1 April 1996. It has been discovered that amounts paid into the bank of £340 on 29 March 1996 were not credited to Jean's account until 2 April 1996 and a cheque of £120, drawn on 28 March 1996 for purchases, was not paid until 10 April 1996. The normal rate of gross profit on the goods sold by Jean Smith is 50% on sales. However, during the year a purchase of ornamental goldfish costing £600 proved to be unpopular with customers and therefore the entire stock bought had to be sold at cost price.

Interest at the rate of 5% per annum is payable on each anniversary of the loan from John Peacock on 1 January 1996.

Depreciation is to be provided on the van on the straight line basis: it is estimated that the van will be disposed of after five years' use for £100.

The stock of goods for resale at 31 March 1996 has been valued at cost at £ 1 900.

Creditors for purchases at 31 March 1996 amounted to £880 and electricity charges accrued due to that date were £180.

Trade debtors at 31 March 1996 totalled £2 300.

REQUIRED

Prepare a trading and profit and loss account for the year ended 31 March 1996 and a balance sheet as at that date.

(25 marks)

Association of Accounting Technicians, Intermediate

Question 7.2

Linda Bernt has owned an ironing parlour, Press-Out, for four years. During this time her books have been maintained by a part-time bookkeeper, Thomas Bord. Unfortunately, for the last three months of the year ended 31 October 1997, Thomas has been absent from work due to illness. Linda is now experiencing difficulty in compiling a set of accounts.

A summary of the bank account transactions for the year is as follows.

Receipts	£
Ironing fees banked	19 650

Payments	£
Staff wages	9 000
Rent	2 250
New iron press	190
Electricity	1 350
Telephone	620
Delivery van running costs and maintenance	2 200
Part-time secretary	450
Bookkeeper	2 477
Advertising	800

Linda has a copy of the previous year's accounts which show that her assets and liabilities at 1 November 1996 were as follows.

	£
Ironing equipment at net book value	910
Fixtures and fittings at net book value	210
Ironing fees due	1 710
Cash at bank	2 150
Wages owing	750
Telephone unpaid	190
Delivery van at net book value	4 100
Capital	8140

Additional information

1) Linda collects and irons 480 bags of clothing per month at a charge of £6 per bag.

2) She employs two staff to do the ironing, each of whom is paid £5 500 per year, and one part-time secretary who is paid £50 per month.

3) The rent of the premises is £250 per month. The last payment for rent was made in July 1997.

4) Linda had paid for several items out of fees received prior to banking. These included staff and secretarial wages for the last three months of the year, delivery van running costs of £640 and personal drawings. However, she had not kept a record of the amount taken as drawings.

5) There were accrued expenses as at 31 October 1997 in respect of electricity £450, telephone £280 and advertising £240.

6) At 31 October 1997 customers owed Linda £1 920 for work done.

7) An old iron press which had a net book value of £60 at 1 November 1996 was sold for £50 cash. Linda kept this money for her own use.

8) All fixed assets are depreciated at the rate of 10% per annum of the net book value. A full year's depreciation is charged in the year of acquisition but none is charged in the year of disposal.

9) Linda has agreed that if the business is profitable she will pay a bonus to her two ironing staff. The bonus will be calculated as 2.5% of the ironing fees less their wages.

REQUIRED

(a) Prepare the profit and loss account for Linda Bernt for the year ended 31 October 1997.   **(20 marks)**

(b) (i) Calculate Linda Bernt's drawings for the year ended 31 October 1997.   **(9 marks)**
    (ii) Prepare a balance sheet as at 31 October 1997.   **(13 marks)**

(c) Write a memorandum addressed to Linda Bernt advising her as to why she should keep better records of the amounts taken out as drawings.

(Memorandum format: 2 marks)

(6 marks)

Associated Examining Board Advanced Level

Question 7.3

Ben is an ex-regular soldier who retired from the army on 1 October 1988 and started a car-hire firm with a gratuity of £2 500 and no other assets or liabilities.

On 30 September 1991 he borrowed £20 000 from his brother-in-law so that he could expand his business. Just before the receipt of the money from his brother-in-law, Ben owed a fleet of cars valued at £35 000 and stocks of spares of £470. His customers owed him £1 860 and his bank balance was £2 190. Deposits received in advance from prospective hirers amounted to £250 and he owed £2 110 to various suppliers.

On 30 September 1993 the Inland Revenue became aware of the existence of the business and required to be informed of the profits or losses from the date of Ben's discharge from the army.

At 30 September 1993 the fleet of cars was valued at £55 000 and stocks at £2 100 while debtors stood at £5 630. There was a bank overdraft of £1 190, deposits of £350 and creditors of £6 300.

Ben has kept no books of account but estimates that his drawings from the business were £80 per week from 1 October 1988 to 30 September 1991 and £250 per week from 1 October 1991 to 30 September 1993.

REQUIRED

(a) Calculate the apparent profit up to 30 September 1991.

(b) Calculate the profit or loss from 1 October 1991 to 30 September 1993.

(c) State whether it would have made any difference if Ben claimed to have won £10 000 at a race-track during 1992 and used it in the business.

(13 marks)

Institute of Chartered Accountants, Foundation

Question 7.4

Julie Ross has been in business for several years without keeping complete accounting records. The following information relates to the year ended 31 December 1997:

(i)   Summarised bank account for the year ended 31 December 1997 as extracted from bank statements:

	£		£
Cash banked	52 000	Opening balance	3 500
Sale of machinery	4 300	Rent and rates	4 200
Bank loan	12 000	Bank loan repaid	3 600
		Telephone and electricity	2 400
		Plant and machinery	15 000
		New car	10 000
		Paid to suppliers	22 000
		Drawings	5 200
		Closing balance	2 400
	68 300		68 300

(ii)   Trade debtors at 31 December 1996 were £4 600 and a year later £6 000.

(iii) Trade creditors at 31 December 1996 were £1 800 and a year later £2 400.

(iv) The gross profit for the year was 60% of sales.

(v)   The selling price of stock in trade at 31 December 1997 was £12 000.

(vi) A car which had a book value of £5 500 at 31 December 1996 was sold for £4 600 on 1 January 1997. The proceeds were paid into the business bank account. The rate of depreciation on cars is 25% per annum on a straight line basis.

(vii) All takings from customers were banked with the exception of £800, which was used to pay a supplier's invoice, and £1 200 which was used to pay for motor running expenses.

(viii) £500 was owing by the business for rent and rates on 31 December 1996, and £600 was owing on 31 December 1997.

(ix) Julie had paid £80 from her private funds for business stationery during the year.

(x)   Plant and machinery at 31 December 1996 had cost £18 000, accumulated depreciation at that date being £4 000. Machinery costing £6 500 on 10 June 1996 was sold on 10 March 1997.
      Depreciation is provided on machinery at 20% on the reducing balance basis. A full year's depreciation is provided in the year of purchase, but no provision is made in the year of sale.

(xi) To assist in the purchase of additional fixed assets, Julie borrowed money from her bank on 1 July 1997. The loan was repayable in quarterly instalments of £1 800 over a two year period commencing 30 September 1997. Each instalment contained an equal amount of interest.

(xii) A provision was to be made at 5% for doubtful debts at 31 December 1997; the provision at 31 December 1996 was £250.

REQUIRED

(a) Prepare Julie's trading and profit and loss account for the year ended
    31 December 1997.   **(24 marks)**

(b) Calculate the balance on Julie's capital account at 1 January 1997.   **(10 marks)**

(c) Prepare Julie's balance sheet as at 31 December 1997.   **(10 marks)**

(d) Give an explanation of the application of accounting concepts to the provision of depreciation on fixed assets.   **(6 marks)**

(e) Write brief notes to Julie setting out the ways in which her accounting system could be improved.   **(7 marks)**

Welsh Joint Education Committee

Question 7.5

Bhupesh Chaughan runs a small retail shop selling costume jewellery. He does not keep a full set of accounting records, but is able to give the following information about the financial position of the business at 1 May 1994 and 30 April 1995.

The business assets and liabilities were:

	1 May 1994	30 April 1995
	£	£
Fixtures and fittings (cost £10 000)	9 000	8 100
Van (E742 XBA)	7 000	
Van (M217 PFQ)		6 750
Stock	6 000	7 000
Debtors	1 750	1 160
Creditors	850	700
Insurance prepaid	340	400
Rent accrued due	250	200
Balance at bank	1 480	
Bank overdraft		9 170
Cash in hand	140	160

He has also provided the following summary of the business bank account for the year ended 30 April 1995.

	£		£
Balance 1 May 1994	1 480	Purchases	35 670
Receipts from debtors for sales	6 170	Rent and rates	4 170
Proceeds from sale of van		Lighting and heating	2 140
(E742 XBA)	4500	Advertising	850
Cash banked		Insurance	1 200
Balance 30 April 1995	41 120	Motor expenses	2 110
	9 170	General expenses	3 180
		Van (M217 PFQ)	9 000
		Payments to creditors for	
		purchases	4 120
	£62 440		£62 440

All the takings from cash sales were banked after the following payments were made:

	£
Purchases	1 360
Wages	15 240
Drawings	14 150

Bhupesh now knows that a part-time assistant who left his employment in October 1994 was systematically stealing cash from the shop; he is uncertain of the exact amount. He was not insured against this loss.

The shop normally earns a uniform gross profit on sales of 50%.

REQUIRED

(a) A computation showing how much cash has been stolen from Bhupesh Chaughan's shop. **(8 marks)**

(b) A trading and profit and loss account for the year ended 30 April 1995 and a balance sheet as at that date. **(32 marks)**

(c) A memorandum addressed to Bhupesh indicating the measures that he could take to prevent cash being stolen in future. Include advice on how Bhupesh could improve his financial record keeping. **(10 marks)**

Associated Examining Board Advanced Level

8

The Accounts of Non-profit-making Organisations

8.1 Introduction

Non-trading, non-profit-making organisations such as clubs and societies have to keep accounts but probably in a less informal way than a business. The accounting function of a club is often performed on a voluntary basis by the person elected as treasurer, who is unlikely to be versed in the principles of double-entry bookkeeping. Many club treasurers keep their financial records in single entry, i.e. they simply jot down receipts and payments in one place. This means that in effect their accounts are examples of incomplete records, and in this chapter you will see similarities to what you learned in the last lesson.

In practice club treasurers often confine themselves to a cash book. They enter all receipts and payments as they happen and prepare a summary of cash movements at the end of the year in the form of a receipts and payments account.

8.2 The Receipts and Payments Account

This is the name which most clubs call what you know as the cash book. The debit side shows cash and cheques received by the club and the credit side shows cash and cheques paid out by it. At the end of the year the account is balanced and the members can see

- the overall cash position;
- what amounts were received from what sources;
- what amounts were paid out and to whom.

Example

The Amateur Musical Society

Receipts and Payments Account for the year ended 31 December 2005

Receipts	£	Payments	£
1 Jan Balance b/d	300	Committee members' expenses	300
Subscriptions received	2 000	Rent of hall	800
Donations received	300	Light and heat	200
Sale of concert tickets	400	Concert expenses	300
		Purchase of piano	1 000
		31 Dec Balance c/d	400
	3 000		3 000
1 Jan Balance b/d	400		

In this example the club began the year with a debit (i.e. positive) bank balance of £300. It received subscriptions from members, donations and it sold concert tickets. It spent money on general expenses, rent, electricity and concert expenses and it bought a piano. At the end of the year it had a debit bank balance of £400 and this was brought down to start off the next year.

A lot of small clubs present their final accounts in this simple format due to the limitations of the treasurer and also because the members do not demand anything more formal or detailed. There are however two main disadvantages of presenting accounts in this way:

- The receipts and payments account does not take account of non-cash items such as depreciation, accruals and prepayments, neither does it distinguish between capital and revenue items.
- There is too little information to allow a balance sheet to be prepared from it.

In the above example, for instance:

- Some of the subscriptions received might have been for last year or for next year and there might also have been subscriptions owing from certain members. Some of the rent might have been prepaid and there might still be electricity owing.
- The concert tickets were purchased by the club for £300 but were sold for £400, i.e. a surplus of £100 was made, but this is not emphasised.
- The general expenses, rent and electricity are items of revenue expenditure while the purchase of the piano is capital expenditure but this distinction is not recognised in the receipts and payments account. The club may own other musical instruments which need to be depreciated.

8.3 The Income and Expenditure Account

If the receipts and payments account is adjusted to incorporate the above items, we end up with an income statement. Larger clubs, and those with treasurers with accounting knowledge, do this and prepare an income and expenditure account. This is the equivalent of a profit and loss account for a business. It lists revenue receipts and revenue expenses for the year, taking account of prepayments and accruals, and then deducts total expenses from total receipts. If receipts are greater than expenses, the club has made a surplus – we do not call it a profit as the club's main objective is to provide a service to its members and not to make a profit, but there is no reason why it should not have something left over at the end of the year which can be spent to benefit the members, e.g. buying new equipment. (As we shall see later in this book in the case of businesses, the fact that an organisation makes a profit or surplus is no guarantee that there is cash in the bank.)

The conversion of the receipts and payments account into an income and expenditure account is commonly asked for in questions. There are several points to note here.

Subscriptions receivable must be calculated and are credited to the income and expenditure account. This is a test of the accruals concept as it is unlikely that all members will pay their dues on time, and at the same time some people may pay in advance. You could be given several figures from which to calculate the amount of subscriptions which belong to this year:

- the amount of money actually received for subscriptions;
- the opening balances of subscriptions owing and prepaid from last year;
- the closing balances of subscriptions owing and prepaid for this year.

The calculation is as follows:

1) Subscriptions received this year
2) minus the opening balance of subscriptions owing (paid this year for last year)
3) plus the opening balance of subscriptions prepaid (paid last year for this year)
4) plus the closing balance of subscriptions owing (to be paid next year for this year.
5) minus the opening balance of subscriptions prepaid (paid this year for next year)

The object of the exercise is to include in the income and expenditure account a figure equal to the number of members in the club multiplied by the annual subscription.

Expenses also have to be adjusted for opening and closing balances of owing and prepaid amounts. We have already seen how to do this in the chapter on incomplete records and in fact the formula will be like the one stated above for subscriptions.

Distinguish between items of revenue and capital expenditure Most of the money spent out of the receipts and payments account will be for running costs (i.e. revenue expenditure) but there is usually at least one capital item, eg the purchase of equipment. This is not included in the income and expenditure account but is added to fixed assets in the balance sheet. You could however be asked to provide for depreciation on fixed assets, including new ones purchased, and the relevant amount for the year should be included in the income and expenditure account just as in a profit and loss account.

Showing a surplus or deficit on an individual event Sometimes the receipts and payments account will contain both a receipt and an expense for the same item or event, eg raffle proceeds and expenses, dance ticket sales and dance expenses etc. An overall surplus or deficit on the event can be shown by grouping these figures together on the appropriate side of the account. Doing this gives clearer information to the members about the event.

8.4 The Bar Trading Account

Although a club is a non-profit-making organisation, it might nevertheless try to make a profit on some activities. The most common of these is running a bar or canteen service. How formally this is organised depends on the size of the club. A small social club might meet in a premises where there is a kitchen and members of the club might sell teas and coffees to members for a small profit. A large sports club on the other hand might have its own premises with a permanent licensed bar and might even employ a part-time bartender.

Since the bar aims to make a profit to boost club finances, it is good practice to prepare a separate bar trading account. This should include all incomes, expenditures and stocks relating to the bar and is set out like a normal business trading account.

8.5 Balance Sheet

Larger clubs which have assets to their name, such as property, equipment and a bank balance, would probably want to prepare a balance sheet. The structure of this is no different from the balance sheet of a sole trader. Fixed assets are shown at cost and their accumulated depreciation is deducted to give the current net value. Current liabilities are deducted from current assets to obtain the working capital (remembering to include unpaid subscriptions receivable as a current asset and subscriptions received in advance as a current liability). Any long-term loans are also shown. The owner's equity section is the same as for a small business except that a club's capital is called its **accumulated fund**.

You are normally asked to calculate the accumulated fund from the opening balances, i.e. deduct total liabilities from total assets (remember to include the opening cash balance in this calculation as it is usually shown in the receipts and payments account and not in the list of assets and liabilities). A surplus of income over expenditure is added to the accumulated fund and a deficit is deducted. Changes in the accumulated fund figure over time show changes in the monetary value of the club.

8.6 Examination Questions

Examination questions on this topic usually give a summary of cash movements during the year (these are contained within the receipts and payments account) with additional information on accruals, prepayments and depreciation. From this you have to prepare the income and expenditure account and balance sheet. Some figures are often not given and you have to deduce them as balancing figures by constructing the appropriate ledger accounts. Thus, if the figure of bar purchases is omitted it can be found by preparing the bar creditors control account. The opening value of the accumulated fund is not usually given either and you have to calculate it by preparing a summary balance sheet at the beginning of the year.

Let us now look at a worked example of a typical question. The question selected is from an examination paper of the GCE Advanced Level in Accounting of the Associated Examining Board (AEB).

Worked Example

The Greenfields Tennis Club has been established for many years but recently its financial position has declined. The treasurer of the club has prepared the following:

The Greenfields Tennis Club
Receipts and Payments Account for the year ended 30 September 1994

1993	*Receipts*	£	1994	*Payments*	£
1 Oct	Balance b/d	6 740	30 Sept	Affiliation to CTA	250
1994				Purchase of balls	180
30 Sept	Sales of balls	260		Dance expenses	650
	Dance receipts	390		Wages	2 400
	Sale of fixtures	180		General expenses	2 680
	Subscriptions	4 310		Balance c/d	5 720
		11 880			11 880
1994					
1 Oct	Balance b/d	5 720			

The following information is also available:

	30 Sept 1993	30 Sept 1994
	£	£
Pavilion	6 000	6 000
Stock of tennis balls	30	20
Fixtures and equipment	2 400	2 000
Subscriptions in advance	40	60
General expenses owing	70	110

REQUIRED:

(a) The income and expenditure account for the year ended 30 September 1994 of the Greenfields Tennis Club.

(b) A balance sheet as at 30 September 1994 of the Greenfields Tennis Club.

Solution to (a)

Greenfields Tennis Club

Tennis Balls Trading Account for the year ended 30 September 1994

	£	£
Sales		260
Less cost of balls sold:		
Opening stock	30	
Purchases	180	
	210	
Less closing stock	(20)	
		(190)
Profit to income and expenditure account		£70

Income and Expenditure Account for the year ended 30 September 1994

	£	£	£
Income			
Subscriptions (W_1)			4 290
Profit on sale of balls			70
			4 360
Less Expenditure			
Affiliation to CTA		250	
Dance receipts	390		
Less dance expenses	(650)		
Loss on dance		260	
Wages		2 400	
General expenses (W_2)		2 720	
Depreciation on fixtures and equipment (W_3)		220	
			5 850
Deficit of income over expenditure			£(1 490)

Workings

W_1

Subs received + Opening subs prepaid − Closing subs prepaid
£4 310 + 40 − 60 = £4 290

W_2

General expenses paid − Opening expenses owing + Closing expenses owing
£2 680 − 70 + 110 = £2 720

W_3

We find the depreciation on fixtures as a balancing figure. The net value of fixtures has decreased by £400 over the year (from £2 400 to £2 000) but £180 of this was accounted for by some fixtures sold. Depreciation must therefore be £400 − £180 = £220. It is assumed that fixtures were sold at net book value.

Solution to (b)

Since we are not given the opening value of the accumulated fund as at 1 October 1993, we must derive it as a balancing item, i.e. as total assets − total liabilities.

Total assets = £6 000 + 30 + 2 400 + 6 740 (don't forget opening cash) = £15 170
Total liabilities = £40 + 70 = £110
Opening accumulated fund = £15 170 – 110 = £15 060

Balance Sheet as at 30 September 1994

	£	£	£
Fixed Assets			
Pavilion			6 000
Fixtures and equipment			2 000
			8 000
Current Assets			
Stock of tennis balls		20	
Bank		5 720	
		5 740	
Less Current Liabilities			
Subscriptions prepaid	60		
General expenses owing	110		
		(170)	
			5 570
Net Assets			£13 570
Financed by:			
Accumulated fund (derived)			15 060
Less deficit for the year			(1 490)
			£13 570

8.7 Life Membership

Some clubs offer life membership for one large lump sum payment. Let us take the example of a club which offers permanent membership for £200. When a member takes up the offer the income is received all in one year but the consideration is to be discharged over several years. Should we credit all of the £200 to that year's income and expenditure account? No – that would contravene the accruals (matching) concept. An accountant would estimate for how many years on average a life member is likely to use the club. Ten years seems to be a reasonable length of time and if we assume that the life member uses the club for that period, the £200 should first be credited to a life membership account. Annual transfers of £20
(i.e. £200 ÷ 10 years) should be made from this to the income and expenditure account. The account would look like this:

Life Membership

		£			£
31 Dec 2001	I & E	20	1 Jan 2001	Cash	200
31 Dec 2001	Bal c/f	180			
		200			200
31 Dec 2002	I & E	20	1 Jan 2002	Bal b/f	180
31 Dec 2002	Bal c/f	160			
		180			180
31 Dec 2003	I & E	20	1 Jan 2003	Bal b/f	160
31 Dec 2003	Bal c/f	140			
		160			160

... and so on for 10 years, by which time the balance on the account is reduced to nil.

While there is a credit balance on the life membership account it is shown in the balance sheet as a **long-term liability**, i.e. the club owes the member the provision of amenities paid for but not yet received. It is rather like a payment received in advance.

There is no correct figure for the number of years assumed for life membership and this in practice varies with the experience of the individual club. Examination questions usually state the number of years used by the club.

Questions

Question 8.1

The Treasurer of Bourne Ladies Hockey Club has fallen ill and is unable to complete the accounting records for the impending Annual General Meeting in respect of the year ended 31 May 1998. She has, however, prepared a receipts and payments account for the year, which is as follows:

Receipts	£	Payments	£
Balance b/f	410	New hockey sticks	1 260
Membership subscriptions	4 740	Ground maintenance	2 800
Fundraising evening	630	Bar staff wages	900
Bar sales	2 850	Bar purchases	1 200
Christmas raffle	250	Raffle prizes	150
		Fundraising costs	590
Balance c/f	510	Club house running costs	2 490
	9 390		9 390

Other information available is as follows:

	1997	1998
	£	£
Club house	120 000	120 000
Equipment (excluding hockey sticks)	4 860	3 240
Bar stock	600	810
Club house running costs owing	150	280
Membership subscriptions owing	240	630
Membership subscriptions in advance	60	40
Creditors for bar stock	130	170

The new hockey sticks are to be depreciated at the same rate as the other equipment.

REQUIRED

(a) Prepare an income and expenditure account for the year ended 31 May 1998 for the Bourne Ladies Hockey Club, showing clearly the profit or loss on bar trading. **(22 marks)**

(b) Prepare a balance sheet as at 31 May 1998. **(17 marks)**

(c) Write a memorandum to the Treasurer suggesting ways of improving the club's cash resources. **(Memorandum format: 2 marks)**
(9 marks)

Associated Examining Board Advanced Level

Question 8.2

The Happy Wanderers Rambling Club is a non-profit-making organisation catering for the leisure pursuits of those interested in walking, hiking and rambling, each admitted member agreeing to pay a membership fee of £10 per annum on 1 January each year. In addition, fees are also charged for each outing or excursion. The club has a small clubhouse which serves as headquarters and also houses a bar and kitchen for light refreshments and snacks.

Below is a summary of the cash/bank book as maintained by the treasurer:

Cash/Bank Book details – Year ended 31 December 1992

	£		£
Balance at 1/1/92	300	Wages – bar staff	200
Receipts from members:		Rent and rates	400
annual fees for 1992	450	Insurance	80
annual fees for 1991	30	Lighting and heating	110
annual fees for 1993	10	Equipment and fittings:	
outings and excursions	490	purchase and repairs	140
Bar and snack takings	1 030	Creditors - bar & snack purchases	500
		Telephone, postage and stationery	85
		Magazines and periodicals	76
		Balance at 31 December 1992	719
	2 310		2 310

The above details represent the only accounting records which have been maintained apart from the following information:

1) The following sundry balances were applicable as at the start and end of the year:

		1.1.1992	31.12.1992
Creditors for bar and snack purchases		40	110
Prepayments: rent and rates		100	
insurance			20
Accruals:	rent and rates		75
	insurance	15	
	telephone, postage and stationery		15
	lighting and heating		15
	wages – bar staff	20	25

2) The record of members' annual fees revealed the following:
   - as at 1 January 1992, four members had not paid their fees for 1991
   - as at 31 December 1992, five members had not paid their fees for 1992, whilst one member had paid in advance for 1993.

   The annual fee had been set in 1989 and had not changed since that date. It is the policy of the Club to write off as bad debts any annual fees outstanding for two years or over.
3) Certain members owed a total of £15 for outings and excursions as at 31 December 1992.
4) Equipment and fittings had a book value at 1 January 1992 of £1 200 with £800 depreciation having been provided to that date. All equipment and fittings are depreciated at a rate of 10% per annum on cost.
5) The £140 spent on purchases and repairs of equipment and fittings included £40 for repairs. It is Club policy to charge a full year's depreciation in the year of acquisition.

6) Bar stock held at 1 January 1992 had all been purchased on 1 December 1991 at a cost of £30. At 31 December 1992 stock on hand had cost £60.

Using the information and details above, you are required to prepare:

(a) a Statement showing the Club's Accumulated Fund at 1 January 1992
(b) an Income and Expenditure Account for the year ended 31 December 1992, and
(c) a Balance Sheet as at 31 December 1992.

(25 marks)

Institute of Chartered Accountants, Foundation

Question 8.3

As treasurer of your local tennis club you have just prepared a draft receipts and payments account, which is reproduced below.

The club committee decides, however, that it wishes its financial statements for 1993 and subsequent years to be in the form of an income and expenditure account accompanied by a balance sheet and requests you to amend the 1993 account accordingly.

Receipts and Payments Account for the year ended 31 December 1993

		£
Receipts		
Cash in hand at 1 January 1993		100
Cash at bank at 1 January 1993:	Current account	1 160
	Deposit account	2 000
Members' subscriptions: 1992		620
1993		8 220
1994		125
Interest on deposit account		85
Entry fees for club championship		210
Tickets sold for annual dinner/dance		420
Bank overdraft at 31 December 1993		4 000
		£16 940

	£
Payments	
Groundsman's wages	4 000
Purchase of equipment (on 30 June 1993)	8 000
Rent for year to 30 September 1993	2 000
Rates for year to 31 March 1994	1 800
Cost of annual dinner/dance	500
Secretarial expenses	400
Prizes for club championship	90
Miscellaneous expenses	100
Cash in hand at 31 December 1993	50
	£16 940

Additional information:

1) At 31 December 1993, £700 was outstanding for members' subscriptions for 1993.
2) During 1992, £230 was received in respect of members' subscriptions for 1993.

3) The cost of equipment purchased in previous years was:

	£
30 June 1982	5 000
1 January 1987	1 000
30 September 1991	1 000

4) The committee decides that equipment should be depreciated at the rate of 10% per annum on cost.
5) Rent has been at the rate of £2 000 per annum for the last two years and is not expected to change in the immediate future.
6) Rates of £750 for the six months to 31 March 1993 were paid on 2 November 1992.
7) Interest of £250 on the bank overdraft had accrued at 31 December 1993.
8) Taxation is to be ignored.

You are required to prepare:

(a) the club's income and expenditure account for the year ended 31 December 1993; and
(b) its balance sheets as at 31 December 1992 and as at 31 December 1993.

(35 marks)

Chartered Institute of Management Accountants

Question 8.4

The treasurer of the Players Sports and Social Club prepared the following receipts and payments account for the year ended 31 December 1998.

	£	£
Opening bank balance 1 January 1998		1 470
Add receipts		
Subscriptions re 1997	620	
re 1998 and 1999	14 080	
Competition fees	2 590	
Proceeds from sale of van (1 January 1998)	1 000	
Sales of dance tickets	1 778	
		20 068
		21 538
Less payments		
Wages	8 450	
Printing and advertising	2 070	
Repairs to sports equipment	800	
Competition prizes	2 200	
Dance expenses	2 060	
Purchase of new van (1 January 1998)	6 300	
Motor expenses	1 200	
Sundry expenses	1 180	
		(24 260)
Bank overdraft at 31 December 1998		£(2 722)

It was felt by many members that this information was inadequate to give a full picture of the club's financial situation and the treasurer subsequently produced the following additional information:

1. The assets and liabilities at the start and end of 1998 were:

	1 Jan	31 Dec
	£	£
Subscriptions due from members	1 440	1 620
Subscriptions received in advance		720
Stock of competition prizes	850	450
Value of computer (cost £2 000)	1 600	1 400
Sport equipment (depreciated value)	6 200	5 400
Van (see below)		

2. The van sold during the year had originally cost £4 000 in 1996 and had been
    depreciated at 25% on the reducing balance method for exactly two years up to the
    date of sale. The new van is to be depreciated on the same basis as the previous
    one

REQUIRED

(a) An income and expenditure account for the year ended 31 December 1998.   **(12 marks)**

(b) Comment on a suggestion from one of the club's members that future club
    dances should be cancelled because they 'always make a loss'.   **(3 marks)**

London Examinations Advanced Level

9

Partnership Accounts

9.1 Introduction

A partnership exists when two or more persons carry on business with a common view to profit. It is the natural extension to the simple sole trader type of business. The agreement between partners is usually written down in a formal **deed of partnership** and this helps to resolve and even prevent disputes. The document covers, among others, the following matters:

1) The amount of capital to be contributed by each partner.
2) The profit and loss sharing ratio.
3) Interest on capital. The reward for risk-taking is profit and the greater the amount of capital risked by each partner (partnerships do not have the safeguard of limited liability) the greater is the return to them.
4) Salaries. Where a partner works harder or puts in more hours than the others, this partner may be allowed a salary for the additional investment in time.
5) Interest to be charged on drawings. This is to discourage partners from taking out more from the business than they really need.

After the net profit has been calculated, each partner receives the agreed interest on capital and any salary and is charged interest on drawings. If any profit is left over after these amounts have been allocated, it is shared amongst them in the agreed ratio.

An oral agreement may also be upheld in a court of law in the event of a dispute between the partners over the way the profit should be shared out. This would normally have to be substantiated by figures from past final accounts. An implied agreement may also be held to exist, again by looking at past accounts eg the profit-sharing ratio may be gauged by looking at past distributions of profit. If no agreement can be found to exist, whether written, oral or implied, the terms of the Partnership Act of 1890 apply. Section 24 of this Act provides that, in the absence of any agreement, profits and losses are to be shared equally between the partners, no interest is to be allowed on capitals nor charged on drawings, no salaries are payable to any partner and loans made to the business by a partner are to receive interest at 5 per cent a year.

All the techniques of bookkeeping and accounting relevant to a sole trader apply equally to a partnership, but the latter has one added complication. In the case of a sole trader the business is owned by one person who has invested all the capital and takes all the profits and losses. In the case of a partnership, we need accounts to show the financial relationship between one partner and the other partners and between each partner and the business as a whole. This is done with the use of capital, current and appropriation accounts. We shall look at each in turn.

9.2 Partners' Capital Accounts

Each partner has a capital account which shows on the credit side the amount of long-term resources invested in the business and which is owed to them by the business. Usually there is little movement in the account and it needs to be adjusted only if:

- a partner brings in more long-term resources or withdraws some existing capital. For example, if Brian decides to hand over to the partnership his motor car which is valued at £10 000, the firm's motor vehicles account will be debited and Brian's capital account credited with £10 000.

- an existing partner retires or a new partner is admitted. This situation is looked at later in the chapter.

9.3 Partners' Current Accounts

Each partner also has a current account which shows the amount of short-term funds contributed. The current accounts are credited with the various amounts due to the partners from the year-to-year profits and are debited with their drawings and interest on drawings, the former of which may be in money or in goods. The current account of each partner should be kept separate from the capital account and, although some firms combine them in one account, it is better accounting practice to distinguish between the long-term and short-term position.

Example

Here are the capital and current accounts of Andrew, who is in partnership with two other people.

Andrew's Capital Account

	£		£
31 Dec 2000 Balance c/d	20 000	1 Jan 2000 Balance b/d	20 000
		1 Jan 2001 Balance b/d	20 000

Andrew's Current Account

	£		£
Drawings	8 000	1 Jan 2000 Balance b/d	350
Interest on drawings	80	Interest on capital	2 000
31 Dec 2000 Balance c/d	10 270	Salary	9 000
		Share of profit	7 000
	18 350		18 350
		1 Jan 2001 Balance b/d	10 270

From this we can see that Andrew has invested long-term capital of £20 000 into the partnership and this balance is brought down from year to year. His current account had a credit balance of £350 at the beginning of this year (i.e. the business owed him £350 which he had not withdrawn). He has been allocated interest on capital, a salary and a share of profit. He has taken out drawings and has been charged interest on these. At the year-end his current account has a credit balance of £10 270 which is owed to him and which is brought down to start next year's current account.

A debit balance on a partner's account indicates that the partner has withdrawn more than her entitlement. This may happen when, for example, profits are lower than was expected or where the business had suffered a loss.

9.4 Loans by Partners

If a partner wishes to lend money to the partnership, this is a liability not capital since the partner does not intend to leave the money in the business indefinitely. A time for repayment may have been set. In addition the partner will be paid interest on the loan and, since this is a mandatory business expense, it is charged against profits in the profit and loss account. This contrasts with interest on partners' capitals which is an appropriation of profit.

9.5 Appropriation of Profit

The appropriation account is prepared after the business's profit and loss account. Its purpose is to share out the profit made between the partners in accordance with their agreement. The account is normally set out in vertical format. Proceed as follows.

1) Bring down the net profit from the profit and loss account.
2) To this add any interest on drawings charged to the partners (usually a percentage of their drawings), being careful to include also any stock drawings which might have been made.
3) Deduct interest on partners' capitals and salaries paid to any of the partners.
4) The remainder is the amount to be shared amongst the partners in accordance with the agreed ratio. Ensure that the whole of this amount is shared out, i.e. the appropriation account must not have a remaining balance.

In all of the above steps, show clearly how much of each type of payment or receipt belongs to which partner.

Example

Jack and Jill are in partnership sharing profits and losses equally after receiving 10% interest on their capitals and after paying Jack a salary of £10 000. Jack's capital is £50 000 and Jill's is £40 000. The partners pay interest on their drawings of 5%. Drawings for the year were: Jack £4 000 and Jill £8 000. The net profit was £100 000. At the beginning of the year, Jack's current account had a debit balance of £2 500 and Jill's current account had a credit balance of £6 000.

Appropriation Account for the year ending 31 December 2000

	£	£
Net profit b/d		100 000
Interest on drawings:		
Jack	200	
Jill	400	
		600
		100 600
Interest on capital:		
Jack	5 000	
Jill	4 000	
		(9 000)
Salary: Jack		(10 000)
Remainder		£81 600
Share of profits:		
Jack (50%)		40 800
Jill (50%)		40 800
		£81 600

97

Note

Partners' drawings do **not** go in the appropriation account but in their current accounts, although interest on drawings goes in both.

The partners' current accounts can be prepared at the end of the year by transferring the amount paid by and owing to each partner from the appropriation account.

Jack's Current Account

	£		£
Balance b/d	2 500	Interest on capital	5 000
Drawings	4 000	Salary	10 000
Interest on drawings	200	Share of profit	40 800
Balance c/d	49 100		
	55 800		55 800
		Balance b/d	49 100

Jill's Current Account

	£		£
Drawings	8 000	Balance b/d	6 000
Interest on drawings	400	Interest on capital	4 000
Balance c/d	42 400	Share of profit	40 800
	50 800		50 800
		Balance b/d	42 400

9.6 Changes in Partnership Structure

Partnerships are an inherently unstable form of business organisation. Differences in opinion, a loss of trust, desire for change, need for new capital, the death of a partner, retirement – all of these can lead to changes in the structure of a partnership. Such changes could be:

(a) a change in the profit-sharing ratio among the same partners (an arithmetical exercise);
(b) the admission of a new partner;
(c) the retirement of an existing partner.

In (b) and (c) there are two complications – goodwill and revaluation of assets.

9.7 Goodwill

Successful businesses have a reputation linked to their name. They also have an established group of loyal customers or the location of the business may be such as to attract a lot of custom eg a tourist shop at an airport. These desirable features create an intangible asset known as **goodwill**. Goodwill is different from tangible assets in that:

1) it has been acquired over time and not specifically bought like other assets;
2) it is difficult to quantify in money terms.

Goodwill can be valued by taking an indicator of business performance and multiplying it by a chosen figure. The indicator may be:

(a) average weekly sales;
(b) average annual net profit over the past few years;
(c) gross annual fees.

The **super-profits method** can also be used to value goodwill.

Super-profits are the firm's net profit minus the economic cost to the owner of being in business, namely:

(a) the salary which could be earned by working for an employer
(b) the interest which could be earned by investing the capital elsewhere.

Super-profits are multiplied by an agreed number. This might be the number of years it took the owner to build the business up to its present level.

9.8 Revaluation of Assets

Historic cost accounting requires assets to be stated at cost less accumulated depreciation. In practice the underlying market value of an asset often does not correspond to its book value. Take the following examples:

(a) Fixed assets may be revalued to reflect their current market values. Premises and land are often revalued upwards, especially if property prices have been rising, while assets such as machinery, vehicles etc are often devalued to reflect wear and tear and obsolescence.
(b) Stock may be devalued if some items are found to be damaged or out of date.
(c) Debtors may be changed in either direction by making adjustments to the provision for doubtful debts.
(d) Creditors can also be revalued eg if a provision had been made for the payment of damages in an outstanding lawsuit or if a creditor agrees to accept less in full payment.

Example

Revaluation Account

	£		£
Assets decreased in value		*Assets increased in value*	
Furniture and fittings	2 000	Freehold land	20 000
Motor vehicles	5 000		
Stock	6 000		
Increase in provisions	3 000		
Surplus to capital accounts:			
A (½)	2 000		
B (½)	2 000		
	20 000		20 000

It is the amount of the increase or decrease in each case that we credit or debit to the revaluation account. The double entry for each change in value is found in the relevant asset account.

For example, if we increase the value of the buildings by £10 000, we debit the buildings account and credit the revaluation account with £10 000. The opposite applies to a decrease in value.

9.9 Admission of a New Partner

When a person wants to join a partnership, some money has to be paid for the benefit of sharing in the profit and part-owning the business assets. Since goodwill almost certainly exists, the new partner can expect to have to pay a certain amount for this as well – after all, it has been built up by the existing partners with the hard work they

have put into the business. In addition existing partners often use the admission of a new partner as an opportunity to revalue some of the firm's assets, as described above. The net change in asset values (i.e. total increases minus total decreases) is added to the goodwill for the initial share out between the existing partners but it is not written off again. Only the goodwill is written off and the new asset values are shown in the partnership books and balance sheet.

Bookkeeping Entries

Goodwill and revaluation of assets is dealt with in the following way.

1) Create the goodwill by opening and debiting a goodwill account.
2) Open the revaluation account. Debit it with any decreases in asset values and credit it with any increases. Share out the balance between the old partners in their original profit-sharing ratio.
3) Credit the goodwill and any increase in asset values to the capital accounts of the original partners in their original profit-sharing ratio. (If there is a net decrease in asset values, debit the capital accounts in the same ratio.) The accounts of the existing partners now reflect the work they have put into the business over the years and changes in value of their assets. The goodwill account is usually opened just for the day of admission or retirement (examination questions will often say that the firm does not maintain a goodwill account).
4) Debit the capital accounts of all partners (including the new one) with the goodwill figure in the new profit-sharing ratio. Do not include changes in asset values here.
5) Now eliminate the goodwill by crediting the goodwill account.

Example

A and B are in partnership sharing profits and losses equally, the balance on the capital accounts being £20 000 each. C is admitted as a partner, all three partners now having an equal one-third share. The goodwill of the business at the time of C's admission is valued at £30 000. C introduces £20 000 cash into the firm. The way this would be recorded in the capital accounts is shown below.

Capital Accounts

	A	B	C		A	B	C
	£	£	£		£	£	£
Goodwill out	10 000	10 000	10 000	Balances b/d	20 000	20 000	
Balances c/d	25 000	25 000	10 000	Goodwill in	15 000	15 000	
				Cash			20 000
	35 000	35 000	20 000		35 000	35 000	20 000
				Balances b/d	25 000	25 000	10 000

The goodwill is initially credited one-half each to A and B. At the end it is written off by A, B and C, each being debited with one-third of the same amount.

The existing partners' balance has increased by £5 000 each, even though they have not introduced any additional capital. At the same time C's balance is £10 000 less than the amount of cash introduced by him. Since C is acquiring one-third of the business, he has to pay for one-third of the goodwill. This amounts to one-third of £30 000 i.e. £10 000. Since the original partners are giving up a share of the business, they need to be compensated by the new partner. A and B share profits equally, so the £10 000 goodwill payment is split equally between them. The end result is as follows:

A's capital increases by £5 000
B's capital increases by £5 000
C's capital decreases by £10 000.

An alternative method of accounting for goodwill is to enter only the consideration payable by the new partner to the existing partners in the ledger. The amount of goodwill payable is calculated first. Then the amount receivable by each existing partner is determined by looking at the profit-sharing ratio. The capital accounts under this approach would look as follows.

Capital Accounts

	A £	B £	C £		A £	B £	C £
Goodwill paid			10 000	Balances b/d	20 000	20 000	
				Goodwill received	5 000	5 000	
Balances c/d	25 000	25 000	10 000	Cash			20 000
	25 000	25 000	20 000		25 000	25 000	20 000
				Balances b/d	25 000	25 000	10 000

The two methods produce the same final result.

9.10 Retirement of an Existing Partner

An outgoing partner is usually paid the share of the business owing on the day of leaving. The assets and liabilities should therefore be revalued to their true values on that date so that this person may be paid a fair sum. This is done, as above, in a revaluation account. Assets which are worth more than book value are brought up to current value by debiting the asset account and crediting revaluation with the amount of the increase. For assets worth less than book value, the opposite entry takes place. A surplus on revaluation is credited to the original partners in the original profit-sharing ratio. In this way the outgoing partner is credited with his share of any increase in asset values. Conversely a deficit is debited to capital so that a share of the reduction in values is paid for.

If the remaining partners do not wish to adopt the revalued amounts for their books, they may continue using historic costs by writing back the revaluation surplus. For this they would:

Debit the capital accounts of the remaining partners in the new profit-sharing ratio
Credit the asset accounts with the amounts of the increase or decrease.

The outgoing partner may also need to be compensated for the contribution to the growth of the business during the time spent with the firm. Goodwill therefore needs to be created (in the same way as we saw previously in the case of admission of a new partner). The goodwill is divided between the partners in their normal profit-sharing ratio and this amount is credited to each partner's account.

It is sometimes the case that the outgoing partner takes away a business asset eg a motor car. The double-entry for this is:

Debit the capital account
Credit the asset account
with the revalued amount. The increase or decrease from book value of the asset taken over should be included in the revaluation account.

Outgoing partners do not usually demand full payment of the amount owing to them on the date of leaving. The balance owing is transferred from capital to a loan account – this is shown in the balance sheet of the remaining partners as a liability.

9.11 Purchase of a Partnership by a Limited Company

A company taking over a partnership may pay the owners of the business:

- in cash
- in company shares
- in company debentures
- in some combination of the above.

The partnership's assets are revalued at the time of sale. If the purchase price exceeds the total value of the assets taken over, the difference is goodwill and if it is less, then the difference goes into a capital reserve. The accounting procedure is as follows:

(a) Draw up a realisation account to show the difference between the value of the assets taken over and the purchase price.
(b) Share the profit or loss on sale amongst the partners in their profit-sharing ratio.
(c) Balance off each partner's current account and transfer the difference to his or her capital account; also credit each account with the amount of profit apportioned to each partner (or debit the capital account if the partners have sustained a loss on the sale). Debit each capital account with the amount being received by each partner.
(d) Add the assets and liabilities being taken over by the purchasing company to its balance sheet.
(e) If the company is buying the partnership by paying cash, reduce its bank balance. If it is issuing new shares, increase the share capital.

See Question 9.2.

Questions

Question 9.1

Philip, Simon and Ann have been in partnership for many years as bottlers and canners of non-alcoholic drinks. Their partnership agreement provided for:

- interest on capital to be paid at 10% per annum
- salaries per annum to be as follows: Philip £10 000; Simon £6 000; and Ann £5 000
- balance of profits to be shared between Philip, Simon and Ann in the ratio 2:1:1.

The trial balance of the firm as at 31 December 1996, after the net profit for 1996 had been calculated but before the appropriation of profits between the partners, was as follows:

	Dr £000	Cr £000
Plant and equipment at cost	25	
Motor vehicles at cost	22	
Provision for depreciation at 31 December 1996:		
Plant and equipment		15
Motor vehicles		16
Stock	14	

Debtors	28	
Bank	3	
Creditors		10
Capital accounts at 1 January 1996:		
Philip		8
Simon		8
Ann		4
Current accounts at 1 January 1996:		
Philip	5	
Simon		2
Ann		3
Profit for the year		31
	£97	£97

On 1 January 1997, Kate is admitted as a partner on payment of £10 000 to the partnership. It is agreed to revise the sharing of profit between Philip, Simon, Ann and Kate in the ratio of 4:3:2:1 respectively.

Goodwill as at 31 December 1996 is valued at £20 000. No account for goodwill is to be maintained in the partnership books. In addition, it is agreed that the following revaluations are made:

	£000
Motor vehicles	4
Debtors	25
Stock	15

REQUIREMENT

(a) (i) Prepare the profit and loss appropriation account for the year ended 31 December 1996.
   (ii) Prepare the partners' current accounts for the year ended 31 December 1996.
  (iii) Prepare the revaluation account.
  (iv) Prepare the partners' capital accounts to record the treatment of both goodwill and any profit or loss on revaluation arising from the admission of Kate as a partner.

(14 marks)

(b) Discuss whether goodwill arising on the admission of a new partner should be eliminated from the accounts or retained as an intangible asset.

(6 marks)

Northern Ireland Council for the Curriculum Examinations and Assessment
Advanced Level Accounting

Question 9.2

The summarised balance sheet of Scotby and Wetheral, who are trading in partnership, is given below.

Scotby and Wetheral
Balance Sheet as at 30 November 1996

	£	£
Fixed assets		102 000
Current assets:		
Stock	28 500	
Debtors	10 500	
Bank balance	7 500	
	46 500	
Less current liabilities		
Trade creditors	(3 000)	
Working capital		43 500
		£145 500
Capital accounts:		
Scotby	75 000	
Wetheral	45 000	
		120 000
Current accounts:		
Scotby	(1 700)	
Wetheral	7 200	
		5 500
Loan account – Scotby		20 000
		£145 500

The partnership agreement includes the following provisions.

1) Wetheral is to be credited with a partnership salary of £6 000 per annum.
2) Interest is to be paid on partners' capital account balances at the rate of 10% per annum.
3) The balance of profits and losses is to be shared between Scotby and Wetheral in the ratio of 2/3rds and 1/3rd respectively.
4) Interest is to be paid on any loans made by the partners to the partnership at a rate of 6% per annum.

The loan from Scotby, together with the accrued interest, was repaid by cheque on 28 February 1997.

The partnership's net profit for the year ended 30 November 1997, before taking into account the interest on Scotby's loan to the partnership, was £37 500.

Partners' drawings during the year ended 30 November 1997 were:

	£
Scotby	15 600
Wetheral	18 400

On 30 November 1997 Scotby and Wetheral sold their business to Warwick, Bridge and Co Ltd for £230 000. The company took over the partnership's net assets as at 30 November 1997 with the exception of the partnership's bank balance of £10 000.

The purchase consideration was satisfied by the issue of the following shares by Warwick, Bridge and Co Ltd:

    80 000 7½ % preference shares of £1 each fully paid at par;
    100 000 ordinary shares of £1 each fully paid

The partnership was dissolved on 30 November 1997. The partners agreed to divide the shares in Warwick, Bridge and Co Ltd as follows:

    Preference shares in proportion to the capital account balances as at
    30 November 1996;
    Ordinary shares in accordance with the partnership's profit-sharing ratios.

Scotby and Wetheral agreed to pay into, or withdraw from, the partnership's bank account any amounts that may be necessary to close the accounts in the partnership's books.

REQUIRED

(a) Prepare the partnership profit and loss appropriation account for the year ended
    30 November 1997. **(8 marks)**

(b) Prepare the partners' current accounts for the year ended 30 November 1997. **(12 marks)**

(c) Prepare the partners' capital accounts for the year ended 30 November 1997. **(16 marks)**

(d) Explain why a partnership agreement might include provisions to credit partners with
    (i) salaries **(2 marks)**
    (ii) interest on capital. **(2 marks)**

(e) From an investor's point of view, outline **two** differences between preference shares
    and ordinary shares. **(6 marks)**

(f) Shares are sometimes issued 'at par' or 'at a premium'.
    Explain clearly the meaning of the terms:
    (i) at par **(2 marks)**
    (ii) at a premium. **(2 marks)**

Associated Examining Board Advanced Level

Question 9.3

Parks, Langridge and Sheppard were in partnership sharing profits and losses: Parks one-half, Langridge one-third and Sheppard one-sixth.

The firm's summarised Balance Sheet as on 31 March 1995 was as follows:

	£	£		£	£
Capital:			Freehold land and buildings		16 000
Parks	24 000		Plant and machinery		6 000
Langridge	12 000		Motor car		2 400
Sheppard	8 000		Stock		11 200
		44 000	Debtors	12 000	
Loan – Parks		4 000	Less provision for doubtful debts	(1 200)	
Creditors		8 000			10 800
			Balance at bank		9 600
		£56 000			£56 000

Parks retired on 31 March 1995 to commence business on his own account and Langridge and Sheppard continued in partnership, sharing profits in the ratio: Langridge two-thirds and Sheppard one-third.

It was agreed that Parks should take over certain plant and machinery valued at £1 500 and one of the firm's cars at its book value of £1 000.

It was further agreed that the following adjustments should be made in the balance sheet as on 31 March 1995:

1) Freehold land and buildings should be revalued at £20 000 and plant and machinery, inclusive of that taken over by Parks, at £5 000.
2) The provision for doubtful debts should be increased by £300.
3) A provision of £500 included in creditors for a possible claim for damages was no longer required.
4) The stock should be reduced by £800 for obsolete and damaged items.

In accordance with the terms of the partnership agreement, the total value of goodwill on 31 March 1995 was agreed at £30 000. Since Parks intended to retain certain of the customers it was agreed that the value of the proportion of the goodwill to be purchased by him was £6 000. Langridge and Sheppard decided that goodwill should not appear in the books of the new partnership as an asset, the necessary adjustments being made through the partners' Capital Accounts. Pending the introduction of further cash capital by the continuing partners, the amount owing to Parks was agreed to be left on loan account.

REQUIRED

(a) the Revaluation Account;
(b) the partners' Capital Accounts in columnar form of the old and new firm, recording these transactions;
(c) the opening Balance Sheet of the new firm.   **(21 marks)**
(d) What is the reasoning behind the adjustments made for goodwill?   **(4 marks)**

Institute of Chartered Accountants, Foundation

10

Limited Company Accounts

10.1 Introduction

Companies differ from sole traders and partnerships in three main respects:

1) There is no limit to their membership and number of owners – they are therefore larger in size.
2) They are a separate legal entity – their owners therefore enjoy the protection of **limited liability**. This means that the company's liability for debts is limited to the amount of its share capital and that, in the event of the company failing and being wound up, the most its shareholders can lose is the value of their shares; they would not be liable to sell their personal property to pay company debts.
3) There is a separation of ownership from control.

From an accounting standpoint the principles you learnt in bookkeeping and the preparation of accounts of sole traders and partnerships also apply to companies. The differences lie in:

1) the presentation of the final accounts – these have to conform to statutory requirements and Statements of Standard Accounting Practice (SSAPs) and Financial Reporting Standards (FRSs)
2) how profit is appropriated
3) the capital and reserves section of the balance sheet, reflecting the different sources of finance.

One of the features of sole traders and partnerships is that the owners have day-to-day control over their business. Companies are owned by their shareholders, the people who provide the capital, of which there may be many and, in some cases, millions. It would be impractical for all of them to attempt to run the company. Fortunately they do not want to. Most shareholders invest in order to share in a company's profits and are happy to leave its running to the 'experts'. A Board of Directors is appointed for this. It is composed of specialists in marketing, production, finance etc who are given the responsibility of running the company in return for a salary. The profits of the company, calculated after payment of these, are distributed as **dividends** to the shareholders.

The directors therefore have **stewardship** of the company on behalf of the members. To ensure that they are carrying out their duties honestly and in the interests of the members whom they serve, the law requires them to make public the financial affairs of the company once a year in an Annual Report. The minimum information to be contained in this Report is set out in the provisions of the Companies Acts in the UK. In this way the law affords protection not only to the shareholders but also to potential creditors and investors who have an interest in knowing whether their debts and capital are likely to be repaid. This is particularly necessary in view of the fact that companies have limited liability, which can leave creditors unpaid in the event of bankruptcy. Anyone considering lending money or selling goods on credit to a

company needs to have access to the company's published accounts in order to assess its creditworthiness.

There are various groups of people who have an interest in knowing the financial position of a company. These are known as **stakeholders**:

- Shareholders want to know the profit prospects as this affects their dividend return. They like to be assured that the company's general position is sound so that the market value of their shares remains at a healthy level. The same applies to prospective shareholders who are deciding whether or not to buy shares in the company.

- Loan stockholders and prospective lenders need to know that the company is creditworthy and that they will be repaid both principal and interest on time. They need to be assured that the company's long-term prospects are good.

- Trade creditors want to see the company's short-term liquidity position as they are interested mainly in its ability to pay its short-term debts on time.

- The company's employees and their trade unions want to be assured that the company is making enough profit to continue to pay their wages and salaries and to award pay increases. They also need to know the company's longer-term prospects so as to assess the security of their jobs.

- The company's Board of Directors and management team have a similar interest as they are employees but further than this, because they are the people who make decisions concerning the company's future, they need to know its financial position in detail.

- A potential purchaser would study the details of the accounts of the past few years before deciding whether or not to put in a bid for the company.

- Financial analysts and journalists study the accounts of companies so as to comment on the performance of their specialist sector or of the economy as a whole. Financial advisors need to be well informed on the performance and positions of a wide range of companies so as to recommend purchases and sales of shares to their clients.

Examination questions on limited company accounts often ask for preparation of the final accounts in a form suitable for publication to shareholders and a knowledge of the main aspects of the presentation and disclosure requirements of the Companies Acts is required. Detailed provisions of the Acts is not required until professional levels of study.

10.2 Private and Public Limited Companies

Limited companies may be either private or public. Both are owned by private individuals and not by the public sector but the difference is that public companies can sell their shares to the public at large, through national advertising, whereas private companies can do so only by finding private buyers. Private companies tend to be small family businesses which have been incorporated into a company in order to enjoy the benefit of limited liability. Many companies consist of two shareholders who act as director and secretary respectively. It is now possible in the UK for one person to form a single-member company, although he or she would have to find another person to act as director or secretary. If the owners of a private limited company wish to expand, they must personally find additional people willing to invest in their business, such as friends and relatives. In contrast, public companies can advertise to the public at large for finance. As a result they find it easier to expand and become large organisations. The shares of the larger public companies are quoted (listed) on the Stock Exchange, a market-place for second-hand securities. A lot of these companies are multi-nationals, i.e. they operate in more than one country.

A further difference between the two types of company is in their name. Private companies must include the word 'limited' in their name, or 'Ltd' for short. Public companies must use the letters 'plc', which is an abbreviation of 'public limited company'.

10.3 Setting up a Limited Company

The Registrar of Companies requires those setting up a company to prepare and present certain documentation before it will issue a Certificate of Incorporation. At this point the company comes into existence as a separate legal entity. The main documents are described below.

1) The Memorandum of Association states the name of the company, its objectives, the amount of the authorised share capital and its division into fixed units.

2) The Articles of Association regulate the internal affairs and management of the company and lay down provisions governing the rights of shareholders, the issue of new shares, procedures for general meetings, the powers and duties of the directors including their borrowing powers and how dividends are to be paid and reserves held.

10.4 Sources of Company Finance

Share Capital

A limited company issues shares which are purchased by people who then become part-owners or shareholders of the company. Although the company can borrow money from external sources, a large part of the liability section of its balance sheet represents the funds owing to these shareholders.

There are several different types of shares which a company may issue:

(a) **Preference shares**: as their name suggests, these shares receive the first share of the profit made by the company and they are also the first shares to be reimbursed in the event of the company being wound up, if any money is left over after paying off the creditors. Preference shares are thus safer to own but they receive a fixed percentage of dividend which is the maximum they can receive even if the company makes a very large profit.

(b) **Cumulative preference shares**: if a company makes little or no profit during a year, then even the preference shareholders will receive no dividend. But if the shares are cumulative, their holders may carry their dividend forward to future years if profits allow, i.e. the dividend owing can accumulate and be paid later.

(c) **Ordinary shares**: these are the most common form of shares and are also known as **equities**. They are paid dividend out of profits after the preference shareholders have received theirs. The amount they receive depends on the amount of profit made by the company that year. Their holders run a greater risk of receiving nothing but they may be paid a very high rate in a good year. The directors decide on and declare the dividend on the ordinary shares after the profit and loss account has been prepared.

Every company has an **authorised share capital**, which is the maximum it is allowed to issue to the public. This is stated in the **Memorandum and Articles of Association**, the official documents which incorporate the company. The company

may issue up to its authorised share capital but not beyond. The **issued share capital** is the amount that has actually been sold to the shareholders. If all of the authorised capital has been issued, then the authorised and issued capital are the same.

When new shares are taken up by shareholders, the company will ask them to pay cash but may not require the full value of each share to be paid immediately. For example, a company may require purchasers of new £1 shares to pay 50p on application followed by two further instalments of 25p. The **called-up capital** is the amount which the company has actually asked shareholders to pay on the shares they have purchased. The **uncalled capital** is that amount which has not yet been asked for. **Calls in arrears** are amounts which new shareholders still owe to the company in respect of monies they have been asked to pay for shares. At any time the company's **paid-up capital** is the amount the company has actually received from shareholders.

Be careful to distinguish between the purchase of a newly issued share and that of an existing share. When shares are first issued and people buy them, the money they pay goes to the company and becomes part of the paid-up capital. The shares are then traded on the second-hand market known as the Stock Exchange. When this happens the purchaser pays the agreed price to the holder of the shares and the company is not involved at all in this exchange.

We must also distinguish between the **nominal value** and **market value** of a share. Nominal value is the fixed official value of the share recorded in the company's balance sheet and is the amount the company is obliged to pay back to the shareholder in the event of a liquidation. The market value of the share is the current value of the share on the Stock Exchange (its second-hand value) and is determined by the interaction of the demand for and the supply of that particular share. Market price changes frequently based on recent company performance and the investment community's perception of expected future performance.

When a company issues new shares it may charge only the nominal value of the shares (in this case we say that the shares have been issued **'at par'**) or, if it is well known and successful, it may issue the shares at a **premium**. For example, a company may issue shares with a nominal value of £1 for £1.50. The 50p is the premium and investors are happy to pay this if they believe that the market value of the shares will soon rise above nominal value and perhaps even beyond nominal value plus the premium.

Sometimes a company makes a **rights issue**, which means that it gives the right to existing shareholders to buy new shares, often at a discount. Again a **bonus issue** may be made whereby existing shareholders are allotted new shares without paying any money. Shares may also be **redeemed** by the company. These transactions will be dealt with in section 10.9 later in this chapter.

Debentures

In addition to attracting investment from shareholders, a company can borrow money long-term by issuing debentures. Interest is paid to the debenture holders (who are creditors and not shareholders) and is fixed for the term of the loan. The annual interest is shown in the 'interest payable' section of the profit and loss account, as shown below.

Since debenture holders are assured of their interest even if the company makes a loss (as long as the company does not go into liquidation), they are a safer investment than shares but they represent a greater burden on the company, which is obliged to pay the interest on them whatever the profit and loss situation.

In the event of the company being liquidated, debenture holders would be reimbursed before shareholders. Some debentures are secured against specific company assets;

these are known as **mortgage debentures** and if the company fails, the specified assets are sold to raise money to repay the holders. Others have no charge on any specific asset and are called **simple** or **naked** debentures.

Debentures may be **redeemable**, i.e. they must be repaid by or on a set date, or they may be **irredeemable** and continue in existence, like shares, as long as the company is in existence.

Loans

Companies are also able to borrow long-term loans from banks, merchant banks, venture capital companies and other financial institutions. These could be anything from a year or two to ten or more years and would be used to finance expansion, new projects and capital expenditure. The lender normally asks for security in the form of a charge on a specific asset.

Retained Profits

As we shall see later in this chapter, companies do not distribute all their profits to the shareholders but retain some as reserves. This money is invested in assets such as shares in other companies etc and can be used in the future to finance expansion without the necessity of raising loans. Internal financing is especially important to small companies who find it difficult to raise capital because they are not well known and cannot offer security.

Government Grants

Governments in some countries make money available to companies as low interest loans or grants, especially if the companies generate economic activity and provide employment in less-developed regions.

10.5 Final Accounts – the Profit and Loss Account

A limited company prepares a profit and loss account and balance sheet just like a sole trader and partnership but these statements are more complex. In addition in the UK, the Companies Acts of 1981, 1985 and 1989 require limited companies to disclose certain information and also lay down how the financial statements are to be presented. This is seen to be necessary because company accounts are published for general information and should be presented in a way that is satisfactory and understandable for interested parties.

The law requires that the accounts presented to shareholders give a 'true and fair' view of the financial affairs of the company. It also requires that the fundamental concepts of accounting are followed, i.e. going concern, accruals, consistency, and prudence. Any departure from a concept should be mentioned in the accounts and the reasons for doing this should be stated.

Disclosure requirements are very specific and concern many items and it is beyond the scope of this book to consider briefly more than just a few of them or to give much detail on them.

The law lays down four alternative formats in which the profit and loss account is to be presented but it is sufficient for you to know only one. The natural choice is to use the one most frequently used in practice and expected by examiners. This is known as Format 1 and it is presented below. The letters on the left-hand side refer to the

explanations of the items which follow after the account. The figures are fictitious and have been inserted to make the account easier to understand.

Sample Company Profit and Loss Account for the year ending 31 December 2001

		£	£
A)	Turnover		350 000
B)	Cost of sales		(210 000)
C)	Gross profit		140 000
D)	Distribution costs	20 000	
D)	Administration expenses	40 000	
			(60 000)
E)	Trading profit		80 000
F)	Other operating income		40 000
			120 000
G)	Income from shares in group companies	15 000	
G)	Income from shares in related companies	10 000	
G)	Income from other fixed asset investments	5 000	
H)	Other interest receivable and similar income	7 000	
			37 000
I)	Amounts written off investments	(6 000)	
J)	Interest payable and similar charges	(8 000)	
			(14 000)
K)	Profit or loss on ordinary activities before taxation		143 000
K)	Tax on profit or loss on ordinary activities		(43 000)
K)	Profit or loss on ordinary activities after taxation		100 000
L)	Extraordinary income	18 000	
L)	Extraordinary charges	(11 000)	
L)	Extraordinary profit or loss	7 000	
L)	Tax on extraordinary profit or loss	(2 000)	
			5 000
			105 000
M)	Other taxes not shown under the above items		(2 000)
M)	Profit or loss for the financial year		103 000
N)	Transfers to reserves	(35 000)	
O)	Dividends paid and proposed	(55 000)	
			(90 000)
P)	Retained profit for the year		£13 000

Explanation of the Items

A) **Turnover**: This is net sales and is to be shown exclusive of value-added tax (VAT). An analysis of turnover and profit is required for substantially different classes of business and for substantially different geographical areas, e.g. Europe, Asia, North America etc.

B) **Cost of sales**: This is found in the usual way, i.e.
opening stock + net purchases – closing stock – purchasing expenses.
Manufacturing concerns are not required to disclose details of production costs.

C) **Gross profit**: This is found by deducting cost of sales from turnover.

D) **Distribution and administration costs**: It is not necessary to show the amounts of all the many different types of expenses; instead they are grouped into two broad classes – distribution costs and administration expenses. The totals of these

are shown in the account. In questions it is advisable to calculate the totals separately in workings and then reference them to the entry in the account. The net figure of discounts allowed and discounts received should be shown as an administration expense.

E) **Trading profit**: The law requires the amount charged in respect of certain items to be disclosed. These are depreciation, hire of plant and machinery, directors' remuneration and auditors' remuneration. In practice companies usually include this information in notes to the accounts.

F) **Other operating income**: This consists of income arising outside the normal trading activity, such as rents receivable from the sub-letting of premises and any profit on sale of fixed assets.

G) **Income from shares receivable**: It is common for public limited companies to acquire holdings in other companies for a wide variety of reasons. In later studies you will meet the topic of group accounts or consolidated accounts which deal with the aggregation of the results of a holding company with subsidiaries into one set of group accounts. For our purposes we need to know the distinction between income from group companies, related companies and fixed asset investments. The income in question is dividends. Companies in which the holding or parent company has a controlling interest, i.e. over 50% of the equity shares, are known as group companies. If the holding is less than 50% but over 20%, it is a related company. Holdings of less than 20% are known as fixed asset investments. Dividends can also be receivable from short-term holdings of shares purchased in times of excess liquidity.

H) **Other interest receivable and similar income**: At times of excessive cash, companies not only buy shares but also lend some of the surplus, for example to the government by acquiring treasury bills. These short-term loans attract interest. Details of the loans made have to be disclosed.

I) **Amounts written off investments**: These represent reductions in the market value of the above investments.

J) **Interest payable and similar charges**: This represents interest on bank loans and overdrafts and debenture interest. Details are required.

K) **Profit or loss on ordinary activities before and after taxation**: This is trading profit or loss plus other operating income plus the net figure resulting from net dividends and interest minus amounts written off investments. It is the overall profit or loss made by the company in the course of the activities it normally undertakes. Corporation tax is levied on this figure and the profit or loss net of tax is shown. Any tax owing but not paid at the end of the year is shown as a current liability in the balance sheet.

L) **Extraordinary items**: As the name suggests, this represents gains or losses arising from events outside the ordinary trading activities of the company. They are one-off items which are not expected to recur. An example would be the loss sustained by a multi-national company by the nationalisation of a branch in a foreign country. Examination questions at this level usually state when an item is to be treated as extraordinary. The nature of an extraordinary item has to be disclosed.

M) **Other taxes and profit and loss for the financial year**: Any other taxes are deducted here and the result is the company's final profit or loss for the year.

N) **Transfers to reserves**: Companies do not distribute all of their profits but put some away into reserves which may be either general or specific. This is undistributed profit that belongs to the shareholders.

O) **Dividends paid and proposed**: Dividends are paid to the shareholders depending on the number and type of shares held and on the amount of profit made by the company, as we saw in section 10.4 above. Total figures shown include both preference and ordinary dividends and both interim dividend paid and final dividend proposed. Proposed dividends which have not yet been paid are shown as current liabilities in the balance sheet.

P) **Retained profit for the year**: This figure, representing undistributed profits for the year, is added to the retained profit at the beginning of the year to arrive at the final balance to be carried forward to next year; this is shown in the balance sheet.

10.6 Final Accounts – the Balance Sheet

There are two allowable formats for the balance sheet, one horizontal and one vertical. Most companies in the UK now use Format I, which is the vertical style of presentation, and this is also the one preferred by examiners. It is presented below. Again the letters on the left-hand side will be used to explain the items after the balance sheet.

Sample Balance Sheet as at 31 December 2001

		£	£
A)	Called-up share capital not paid		20 000
B)	*Fixed Assets*		
C)	Intangible assets	250 000	
D)	Tangible assets	450 000	
E)	Investments	80 000	
			780 000
F)	*Current Assets*		
G)	Stock	75 000	
H)	Debtors	130 000	
I)	Investments	35 000	
J)	Cash at bank and in hand	15 000	
		255 000	
K)	Creditors: amounts falling due within one year	(110 000)	
L)	Net current assets (liabilities)		145 000
M)	Total assets less current liabilities		945 000
N)	Creditors: amounts falling due after more than one year	(125 000)	
O)	Provisions for liabilities and charges	(20 000)	
			(145 000)
P)	Net Assets		£800 000
	Capital and Reserves		
Q)	Called-up share capital		600 000
R)	Share premium		100 000
S)	Revaluation reserve		30 000
T)	Other reserves		15 000
U)	Profit and Loss Account		55 000
V)	Capital Employed		£800 000

The total of capital and reserves is known as Shareholders' Funds or Owners' Equity. To find capital employed we need to add to this long-term liabilities (item N). The upper half of the balance sheet minus item N represents Net Assets. Of course, capital employed is equal to net assets.

Explanation of the Items

A) **Called-up share capital not paid**: This represents monies owing from shareholders for shares issued and called for but still unpaid. In effect they represent debtors. It is permissible for the item to be aggregated with the figure for debtors under current assets.

B) **Fixed assets**: These are assets held not primarily for resale but for long-term use in the business. Usually only the aggregates of the three different classes of asset are shown in the balance sheet. Details are shown in the Notes. These must contain, for each type of asset within each class:
   - the cost of the asset at the beginning and end of the financial year
   - acquisitions and disposals during the year
   - details of any depreciation, including charge for the year, the effect of disposals on depreciation and accumulated depreciation to date
   - the method of depreciation used and useful lives and depreciation rates adopted.

The last point is usually shown in the Statement of Accounting Policies, to be found at the beginning of the notes to the accounts.

C) **Intangible assets**: These are non-physical assets which cannot be seen or touched, such as goodwill and patents. The concept of historic cost dictates that only those assets which have been bought at a cost may be shown in the accounts at the cost of purchase. Therefore goodwill may be included in the balance sheet only when it has been paid for in acquiring a business. The 'real' goodwill of a company, which has been built up through trading is not shown, as it has not been paid for. It can be seen then that the balance sheet figure of net assets may not represent a company's true value.

D) **Tangible assets**: These are physical assets such as land and buildings, plant and machinery and motor vehicles.

E) **Investments**: These represent shares in group companies held on a long-term basis. They are to be stated at the lower of cost and market value. Details are required.

F) **Current assets**: These are short-term liquid assets expected to be converted into cash within the next twelve months.

G) **Stocks**: Most companies show the aggregate figure for stock on the face of the balance sheet. The split between the different categories, i.e. raw materials, work-in-progress, and finished goods, is shown by way of note. The policy of valuing stock at the lower of cost and net realisable value should be mentioned in the statement of accounting policies.

H) **Debtors**: Again only the aggregate figure is shown on the balance sheet itself. The individual amounts of trade debtors and prepayments are disclosed in the Notes. Debtors are split between amounts due within one year and amounts due after more than one year.

I) **Investments**: These are short-term investments such as treasury bills. The disclosure requirements are similar to those for long-term investments.

J) **Cash in hand and at bank**: This is the most liquid of all assets. Both balances are shown together.

K) **Creditors: amounts falling due within one year**: These consist of trade creditors, bank overdraft, taxes owing, dividends payable, and other current liabilities.

L) **Net current assets**: This represents the working capital of the company at the balance sheet date.

M) **Total assets less current liabilities**: This is unpaid share capital owing plus fixed assets plus working capital.

N) **Creditors: amounts falling due after more than one year**: These consist of debentures, bank loans, and other long-term obligations.

O) **Provisions for liabilities and charges**: The concept of prudence requires companies to make provision for possible losses as soon as they become foreseeable. The provision is to be deducted from assets. The reason for making a provision should be stated.

P) **Net assets**: This is total assets minus all liabilities owing to external third parties.

Q) **Called-up share capital**:. The authorised share capital of a company represents the maximum it can issue to the public, divided into the different classes of shares – ordinary, preference and cumulative preference. That part of the authorised capital which has actually been issued is known as the issued share capital. Only the amount of issued share capital which has been paid for is shown in the balance sheet. The notes disclose the authorised share capital and the amounts issued by type of share, number issued and nominal value.

R) **Share premium**: When a company first sets up, each share is given a nominal or par value – this is usually the issue price of the new shares. If the company does well and wishes to expand later, it may, if it has acquired goodwill and the shares are in demand, be able to sell at a price higher than nominal value. Monies received in excess of the nominal price are shown in a separate account, called share premium. The figure for share capital (item Q) then represents the nominal value of shares issued.

S) **Revaluation reserve**: Freehold land is one fixed asset that is not often subject to depreciation. Fixity of supply combined with an ever-increasing demand causes the value of most land to rise with time. If current market values move completely out of touch with historic cost as stated in the accounts such that the balance sheet ceases to give a true and fair view of asset values, then it is permissible to depart from historic cost. The figure for land can be updated by the creation of a revaluation reserve, the double-entry being:
    Dr Freehold land
    Cr Revaluation reserve

Since the gain benefits the owners of the company, the shareholders, the reserve is shown as part of shareholders' funds.

Both share premium and revaluation reserve are known as capital reserves, because they are non-distributable. Reserves that can be distributed as future dividend to shareholders are known as revenue reserves. Capital reserves can be utilised in only a limited number of ways, as stated in the Companies Acts, for example in financing a bonus issue of shares.

T) **Other reserves**: These may be either revenue reserves such as the general reserve or capital reserves such as the capital redemption reserve, which is used when a company buys back its own shares or when it issues bonus shares.

U) **Profit and loss account**: This represents the retained, undistributed profits from this and previous years to be carried forward to next year. It can be used to pay part of next year's dividend, and is therefore a revenue reserve.

V) **Capital employed**: This is the total of the shareholders' funds and is equal to net assets.

In the Notes it is necessary to show, for each reserve, the balance at the start of the year, additions during the year and balance at end of the year. Note that capital reserves are shown before revenue reserves.

10.7 Statement of Accounting Policies

The law requires companies to disclose in their Annual Report the accounting policies used in subjective areas where there is more than one basis of treatment. These include:

1) the basis of accounting, i.e. whether historic cost, current cost, or current purchasing power
2) the method of depreciation i.e. whether straight-line, reducing-balance, or other method
3) stock valuation, whether at cost, market value, or net realisable value
4) research and development
5) goodwill
6) basis of consolidation (for group companies)
7) any other policies relevant to the nature of the business

The statement is usually to be found as the first item in the Notes to the Accounts.

The law lays down only the minimum amount of information that a company must disclose. It is free to disclose more than this if it so wishes. In fact, with the development of social responsibility accounting, the trend is towards the disclosure of more and more information to the public, both of a financial and non-financial nature.

10.8 The Annual Report

In addition to the profit and loss account and balance sheet, the Report contains six other items:

*   Notes to the Accounts
*   the Directors' Report
*   the Auditors' Report
*   the Chairman's Statement
*   a Cash Flow Statement
*   a Statistical section.

117

A brief description of each follows.

Notes to the Accounts

The disclosure requirements of the Companies Acts may be shown either on the face of the accounts or in the form of Notes appended thereto. Most companies present only aggregates of figures on the face of the accounts. Details and breakdowns are shown in the Notes. For example, while the balance sheet contains just one figure for tangible fixed assets, a breakdown of this total figure by types of asset, their historic cost, depreciation and acquisitions and disposals during the year are contained in the Notes. In this way the main accounts are kept short and simple, and the reader who is interested in detail is directed to the Notes.

The Directors' Report

This must contain the following information:

1) a fair review of the development of the company during the financial year and of its position at the year end;
2) proposed dividends for the year and transfers to reserves;
3) particulars of the Directors such as their names, remuneration, holdings in the company's shares, and changes in composition of the Board during the year;
4) significant post-balance sheet events, progress in the field of research and development, and likely future development of the company.

Companies with over 250 employees must include staff details such as the number of employees, total bill for wages and salaries, social security, and other pension costs. This is usually presented in the Director's Report or Notes.

Auditors' Report

Once the accounts have been prepared internally they must be checked or audited by an independent firm of professional accountants. This is to assure shareholders that their trustees are not conspiring to present a false picture of the company or perhaps covering up a misappropriation of funds diverted for personal use. It is the duty of the auditors to check that the accounts give a 'true and fair' view of the affairs of the company. Figures they are not happy with are discussed with the company's own accountants and directors and often changed. If they are unable to persuade the directors to change the figures in dispute and feel that as a result of this the accounts fail to give a true and fair view, they may qualify their report, i.e. not certify that the accounts give a true and fair view while explaining their reasons for doing this.

The legal requirement of the annual audit is a powerful deterrent against fraud by directors and an effective safeguard to shareholders' interests.

The Chairman's Statement

Companies tend to include a statement from the Chairman in their Annual Report, although this is not legally required. The statement is a light-hearted general comment on the performance of the business over the year, both as a whole and by product group and geographical area. It is also a place to make comments on non-financial factors not covered in the accounts, such as changes in the environment in which the company is operating and the state of industrial and customer relations.

Cash Flow Statement

This statement seeks to reconcile the profit position with the change in the cash position since last year. Under FRS (Financial Reporting Standard) 1 companies are obliged to prepare this statement. They often appear in examinations and the whole of Chapter 11 is devoted to them.

Statistical Section

Most companies present a statistical section in their report, although this again is not a legal requirement. In this, they take the opportunity to:

1) present recent trends (typically over the past 5 years) in sales, profits and other key variables by means of graphs
2) analyse the performance of the year under review by means of presentation devices like pie-charts and bar-charts. A common feature of annual reports is a pie-chart to show distribution of the trading profit as between taxation, dividend to shareholders, retention, and other claimants (if any). Bar-charts are often used to show a breakdown of turnover by class of business and geographical area.

The reason for the popularity of this section is that most shareholders are non-accountants who are happier at looking at charts and diagrams than at tables of figures and accounts.

You will not be asked to prepare directors' reports, auditors' reports, chairman's statements or statistical sections in examination questions.

10.9 Miscellaneous Company Matters

Rights Issue

Public limited companies usually raise additional capital by offering shares to the public at large. The costs of a new share issue can be quite high as these include professional fees to the merchant bank handling the issue, publicity, advertising etc. One way to reduce these costs is to make a rights issue. Under this, existing shareholders are given the right to buy so many shares, for example one for every five held. The offer price is usually pitched slightly below the existing market price, a discount the company can afford to make in view of the cost savings on the issue. If the current market price is much higher than the nominal value of the shares, the company may in fact be issuing the new shares at a premium. Of course, an existing shareholder does not have to take up his rights to buy the additional shares – he can sell them to a third party, at a profit.

If you are asked to handle a rights issue in the examination, add the nominal value of the issue to the existing share capital. If the shares have been issued at a premium, then the amount in excess of the nominal value is entered in the share premium account.

Bonus Issue

Reserves represent monies attributable to shareholders but retained within the company to finance future activities and growth. If reserves increase beyond the level thought to be needed by the directors, they can be **capitalised**. This means that additional shares are issued to existing shareholders free of charge, on a pro-rata basis. Unlike a rights issue no additional money is received. This distribution is also known as a **scrip issue**.

If you are asked to deal with a bonus issue, increase the share capital by the nominal amount of the issue and decrease the reserves by the same amount. Any revenue or capital reserve can be used for this purpose and an examination question would tell you which to use.

Share Redemption

Monies received from issuing debentures and redeemable shares have to be repaid by a certain date, which is stated at the time of issue. This act of repayment is known as redemption. The Companies Act requires that, when shares are redeemed, an equal amount is transferred from revenue reserves to a **capital redemption reserve** which is not distributable to shareholders. The reason for this requirement is to maintain the capital of the company. Companies are not allowed to reduce the amount of capital except in certain special cases (you will meet the topic of reduction of capital at professional level). The maintenance of capital is for the protection of the company's creditors. It would be wrong for a company which is in difficulties to repay capital to the shareholders since creditors have first claim on the assets in the event of a winding-up. The transfer to capital redemption reserve is usually made in the appropriation account. The double-entry is:

Dr profit and loss account
Cr capital redemption reserve

The redemption reserve is then included under 'other reserves' in the balance sheet and details of it shown in the notes to the accounts. This requirement does not apply to the redemption of debentures as they are long-term loans and not part of a company's capital.

10.10 Examination Questions

If a question does not specifically ask for preparation of the accounts in accordance with statute, you do not need to follow the precise rules on presentation and disclosure requirements. The examiner is testing merely whether you can prepare a set of final accounts from a list of balances with additional information and adjustments. If a question specifically mentions the Companies Acts, then you need to present the accounts as required by law and prepare a full set of Notes to the Accounts. Failure to do this will lose you marks, even if the figures in the accounts are all correct. In addition to the figures, examiners look out for what you have and have not disclosed, and how you have disclosed it.

You are unlikely in questions to be given all the information that is required to be disclosed. In such cases show what you can from the information – you can do no more than this. Some questions accept this limitation by asking for presentation 'in so far as the available information permits'. For some strange reason questions often fail to give information on the split between administration and distribution of common expenses such as wages and general expenses. In such cases it is usually best to assume that they are to be apportioned equally, stating the assumption made in your answer.

It is a requirement that companies show the previous year's figures for all items in the Annual Report. This is to help the reader get an idea of the trend of events over the past year. The two years' results are usually shown in column form; the current year's figures are often shown to the left of the previous year's, but do read the column headings carefully to see which is which.

Questions

Question 10.1

The following are some of the balances taken from the books of R R Hood plc at 31 December 1998.

	£
Purchases	426 000
Sales	981 000
Stock 1 January 1998	69 800
Purchase returns	8 700
Sales returns	13 400
Discount allowed	7 200
Discount received	5 500
General distribution costs	110 200
General administrative expenses	93 000
Rent receivable	8 700
Interest payable	13 100
Plant and equipment at cost	682 000
Motor vehicles at cost	146 600
Provision for depreciation of plant and equipment	298 000
Provision for Depreciation of motor vehicles	53 800
Income from investments	14 700
Provision for bad debts	3 700
Debtors	158 200
Profit and loss credit balance b/f	78 300

Additional information as at 31 December 1998:

1) The closing stock was valued at £74 300.

2) Rent receivable of £1 200 is outstanding.

3) £400 is owing for general distribution costs, and the general administrative expenses include a prepayment of £900.

4) Provision for bad debts is to be provided as £400 for a specific debt plus 2.5% on the remainder of debtors. This is to be treated as an administrative expense.

5) Deprecation is to be provided as follows:
   (a) Plant and equipment 20% per annum using the reducing balance method.
   (b) Motor vehicles 15% per annum using the reducing balance method.

   Depreciation on plant and equipment is attributable 75% to administrative expenses and 25% to distribution costs. Depreciation on motor vehicles is fully attributable to distribution costs. It is company policy to charge a full year's depreciation on all assets held at the year end.

6) During the year the company acquired its own premises at a cost of £130 000. This cost included £2 000 relating to the legal costs involved, and this amount has been included in the general administrative expenses. Premises are not depreciated.

7) Corporation tax for the year on profit from ordinary activities is estimated to be £81 000.

8) The directors recommend a transfer to general reserves of £70 000 and an ordinary share dividend of £85 000.

REQUIRED

(a) A Profit and Loss Account for the year ended 31 December 1998 (to be in accordance with the minimum required by the Companies Act 1985). **(20 marks)**

(b) Name three users of accounting statements of a public limited company, stating in each case the information they would be interested in. **(6 marks)**

OCR Advanced Level

Question 10.2

The following summarised draft balance sheet of Salutin plc as at 31 May 1998 has just been drawn up after completion of the profit and loss account.

Balance Sheet as at 31 May 1998

	£000	£000	£000
Fixed Assets			
	Cost	*Aggregate depreciation*	*Net book value*
Land and buildings	620		620
Machinery	430	272	158
Vehicles	550	300	250
	1 600	572	1 028
Current Assets		168	
Creditors: amounts falling due within one year			
Trade creditors and accrued expenses		(46)	
Net Current Assets			122
			1 150
Creditors: amounts falling due after more than one year			
9% Debentures (2009)			(200)
Net assets			£950
Capital and Reserves			
Ordinary shares of 25 pence each			560
Share premium		140	
Capital redemption reserve		10	
Profit and loss account		240	
			390
Capital employed			£950

Additional information

After the draft balance sheet had been prepared, the following information became available, none of which had been incorporated into the draft accounts.

1) On 8 May 1990 the land and buildings were revalued at £750 000.

2) On 23 May 1998 a vehicle which had cost £35 000 was destroyed in a fire. The vehicle had been depreciated by £28 000 by 31 May 1998 (including £7 000 for the current year). The insurance company has agreed to pay Salutin plc £9 000.

3) A bonus issue of shares of one ordinary share for every two held was made on 25 May 1998. It is company policy to maintain reserves in their most flexible form.

4) The Directors have proposed a dividend of 2.5 pence per share. The bonus shares do not qualify for a dividend in the year ended 31 May 1998.

REQUIRED

(a) Prepare journal entries to record the adjustments to Salutin plc's final accounts. (Narratives **are** required.) **(21 marks)**

(b) Prepare a redrafted summarised balance sheet as at 31 May 1998 after taking into account items 1 to 4 above. **(11 marks)**

(c) Explain the following terms used in the balance sheet of Salutin plc:

   (i)   share premium; **(2 marks)**
   (ii) capital redemption reserve; **(2 marks)**
   (iii) aggregate depreciation; **(2 marks)**
   (iv) trade creditors and accrued expenses. **(2 marks)**

(d) Explain **one** difference between **each** of the following:

   (i)   ordinary shares and preference shares;
   (ii) capital reserves and revenue reserves;
   (iii) a bonus issue of shares and a rights issue of shares.

                                          (10 marks)

Associated Examining Board Advanced Level

Question 10.3

Brampton Ltd has an authorised share capital of 100 000 ordinary shares of £1 each and 16 000 8% redeemable preference shares of £1 each. The company's trial balance as at 30 April 1996 was as follows:

	£	£
Ordinary share capital, fully paid		80 000
Share premium account		20 000
Plant and machinery at cost	76 000	
Motor lorries at cost	114 000	
Debtors and creditors	88 960	50 740
10% debentures		18 000
Purchases and sales	326 978	466 668
General expenses	17 040	
Bad debts	4 800	

Stock at 1 May 1995	15 400	
Debenture interest for half-year to 31 October 1995	900	
Discounts received		3 280
Bank	72 170	
Salaries	31 420	
Insurance	2 600	
Directors' fees	32 000	
Provisions for depreciation:		
Plant and machinery		60 000
Motor lorries		52 400
Interim preference dividend (see note 4)	640	
Profit and loss account, 1 May 1995		30 760
Provision for doubtful debts, 1 May 1995		1 060
	£782 908	£782 908

Notes:

1) At 30 April 1996:
   (a) Insurance of £420 was prepaid.
   (b) Doubtful debts totalled £900.
   (c) Stock totalled £16 500
   (d) A corporation tax provision of £7 000 is to be made.
   (e) The directors propose to pay dividend of 10% to the ordinary shareholders.

2) Depreciation is to be calculated on fixed assets at 20% on the reducing balance basis.

3) The debenture interest for the second half of the year is to be accrued.

4) 16 000 8% redeemable preference shares were redeemed at par value on 1 November 1995. No new shares were issued by the company during the year.

REQUIRED

A trading and profit and loss account for the year to 30 April 1996 and a balance sheet as at that date, prepared in a vertical style. **(25 marks)**

London Examinations Advanced Level

Question 10.4

Brighton Ltd produced a set of draft accounts for the year ended 31 March 1998. The trial balance at that date includes the following balances:

Trial Balance as at 31 March 1998

	Dr	Cr
	£	£
Net profit for the year		565 000
Profit and loss account, 1 April 1997		400 000
8% preference shares of £1 each, fully paid		120 000
Ordinary shares of £1 each, fully paid		600 000
Share premium account		100 000
9% debentures		20 000
Debtors and creditors	120 000	80 000
Cash at bank	60 000	
Stock at 31 March 1998	310 000	
Preference dividend, 6 months to 30 September 197	4 800	

The authorised share capital of the company at 31 March 1998 was

8% preference shares of £1 each	£200 000
Ordinary shares of £1 each	£800 000

The directors made the following decisions which affect the draft accounts:

(i)   A bonus of £20 000 was to be paid to the directors (the amount relates to the year ended 31 March 1998, but will not be paid until June 1998).

(ii)   Taxation of £160,000 was to be provided on the profit for the year.

(iii) A dividend of 5% on the ordinary shares was to be proposed. No interim dividend was paid in the year.

(iv)   A transfer to a general reserve of £30 000 was to be made.

(v)   The balance of the preference dividend was to be accrued.

Note:

An adjustment is required for the interest on the debentures which had been omitted from the draft accounts in error. The payment for the year had been made in full on 31 March 1998 from the bank account.

REQUIRED

(a) Prepare the profit and loss account of Brighton Ltd for the year ended 31 March 1998.   **(12 marks)**

(b) Prepare relevant balance sheet extracts as at 31 March 1998.   **(18 marks)**

(In both (a) and (b), present as much detail as is possible from the above information.)

Welsh Joint Education Committee

Question 10.5

The summarised draft balance sheet of Gupta plc as at 31 March 1999 was as follows:

	£000
Fixed assets	10 000
Net current assets	1 160
	£11 160

Capital and reserves:	
9 000 000 ordinary shares of £1 each	9 000
400 000 8% preference shares of £1 each	400
Share premium account	250
Profit and loss account	1 510
	£11 160

Since the preparation of the draft balance sheet, the following additional information has become available.

(1) Closing stock which was valued at cost price of £428 000 at 31 March 1999 should have been valued at £482 000.

(2) Plant costing £48 000 with accumulated depreciation of £23 000 was sold during the
     year for £9 000. The only entries made in the company's books of account were:

Debit Bank £9 000   Credit Sales £9 000

The directors of Gupta plc had also carried out the following transactions but had not
recorded them in the company's books of account.

(3) Included in the figure for fixed assets were premises which cost £3 400 000.
     These were revalued at £4 000 000 on 31 December 1998.

(4) On 31 January 1999 an issue of 1 bonus share for each 10 ordinary shares held
     was made. The directors wish to retain the company reserves in the most flexible form.

(5) On 1 March 1999 a rights issue of ordinary shares on a 1 for 5 basis was made at
     £2.50 per share. The issue was completed on 20 March 1999. (The bonus shares
     issued at the end of January 1999 were eligible for the rights issue.)

(6) The directors had proposed:

  (i) a final ordinary dividend of 5 pence per ordinary share;

  (ii) a half year's dividend on the preference shares.

  (All shares issued at 31 March 1999 were eligible for dividends.)

REQUIRED

(a) Prepare the journal entries necessary to take account of notes (1) to (6).
     (Narratives are not required).   **(22 marks)**

(b) Prepare the summarised balance sheet of Gupta plc as at 31 March 1999
     after any amendments due to notes (1) to (6) have been taken into account.   **(8 marks)**

(c) Explain **one** benefit a company might gain through a rights issue of shares rather
     than by issuing bonus shares.   **(4 marks)**

(d) (i) State **one** advantage and **one** disadvantage to a company of raising funds by
         issuing ordinary shares.   **(4 marks)**

  (ii) Evaluate **one** alternative way that Gupta plc could have used to raise further
         long term funds.   **(4 marks)**

(e) Explain the terms

  (i) provision;

  (ii) capital reserve;

  (iii) revenue reserve.   **(8 marks)**

Associated Examining Board Advanced Level

11

Cash Flow Statements

11.1 Introduction

Financial Reporting Standard 1 (FRS 1) obliges all companies to prepare a cash flow statement at the end of the financial year in addition to the profit and loss account and balance sheet. In this chapter we shall look at the contents of this statement, how it is prepared and what can be learnt from it.

A lot of the figures in a firm's year-end balance sheet are quite different from those of the previous year. The profit and loss account cannot explain many of these changes and it is the cash flow statement which is the link between two successive balance sheets.

It is also important to realise that profit and cash are not the same thing. Profits made by the firm do not always find their way into the cash and bank accounts and equally the cash and bank balances are affected by items other than profit. The cash flow statement reconciles the profit position of a firm with its cash position.

Since the profit and loss account focuses on profit, and matches revenues receivable and costs attributable to the period in question, it does not compare revenues actually received to costs actually incurred. There are several aspects of this:

(a) Adjustments are made in the profit and loss account for expenses and revenues accrued and prepaid. The account shows the amounts which belong to the year but these are not necessarily the amounts actually paid and received eg money could still be owing to the firm for sales made on credit and by the firm for purchases made on credit, expenses may still be owing and amounts may have been paid in respect of next year.

(b) The profit and loss account does not include transactions of a capital nature since these are attributable to the income and expenditure of several accounting periods. Thus the purchase and sale of fixed assets and the raising and repayment of long-term finance are left out.

(c) Conversely the profit and loss account contains book items which do not involve cash flows. Items such as depreciation on fixed assets (representing the share of capital costs allocated to a period) and the profit or loss on sale of fixed assets affect profit but not cash.

Producing a cash flow statement thus allows a firm to understand, for example, why it has made a healthy profit but has no cash in the bank, or conversely why it has a good bank balance but has made no profit. Since it is vital for a firm to perform well on both fronts, i.e. to make a satisfactory profit and to keep solvent, it is useful for it to be able to understand the relationship between its profit and cash positions. In Chapter 12 we shall consider ways in which the firm can assess its profitability and liquidity.

Cash flow statements are drawn up to show all the reasons, under various set headings, why cash flowed in and out of the company. The statement will show how the firm is doing on both the cash and profit fronts. The firm may have raised a long-term loan which has boosted its bank account but which is disguising the fact that the profits were low and that drawings or share dividends were greater than the profit made.

Alternatively the firm may be making a wonderful profit on paper but have a serious liquidity problem. This can happen when the demand for the product is growing fast. The firm is obliged to invest large amounts in capital equipment to allow it to cope with this demand and it is existing on extended credit with suppliers while at the same time allowing long credit periods to customers so as not to lose them. This situation is known as **overtrading** and it can lead to bankruptcy, despite the buoyancy of the firm's demand and profits. Preparing and analysing a cash flow statement can help managers to see the problem coming and take action to restore liquidity before its creditors force it into bankruptcy.

11.2 Financial Reporting Standard 1 (FRS 1)

FRS 1 applies to all companies apart from those which are exempt on account of their small size or because their accounts are not published in the UK. It requires those reporting entities which are within its scope to prepare a cash flow statement in the manner set out (see below). Cash flows are increases or decreases in amounts of cash, and cash means cash in hand and deposits repayable on demand at any qualifying institution less overdrafts from any qualifying institution repayable on demand.

Cash flow statements portray the financial position, performance and financial adaptability of a firm (in particular by indicating the relationship between profitability and cash-generating ability) and thus of the quality of the profit earned.

A firm's cash flow statement should list its cash flows for the period classified under the following standard headings:

- Operating activities
- Returns on investments and servicing of finance
- Taxation
- Capital expenditure and financial investment
- Acquisitions and disposals
- Equity dividends paid
- Financing
- Management of liquid resources (changes in cash)

FRS 1, which was revised in 1996, replaced the original FRS 1 which was issued in September 1991 to replace SSAP 10 'Statements of source and application of funds'.

11.3 Preparing a Cash Flow Statement

In order to prepare the statement we must have before us two successive balance sheets along with the latest profit and loss account. The information we need is extracted from these sources. Here is the format prescribed by FRS 1 for a cash flow statement, which is divided into specific sections.

1. Operating activities

The main source of cash inflow comes from the firm's operating (or trading) activities. There are two ways of presenting these operating cash flows:

(a) **on a net basis** using the indirect method. This can be used when the profit and loss account is available. The layout is as follows:

> Operating profit
> Add depreciation
> Add loss / deduct profit on sale of tangible fixed assets
> Add decrease in stocks / deduct increase in stocks
> Add decrease in debtors / deduct increase in debtors
> Add increase in creditors / deduct decrease in creditors
> Net cash inflow/outflow from operating activities

The first step is to find the operating profit, assuming it has not been provided in the question. Find the difference between this year's and last year's profit and loss account (be careful to retain the positive and negative signs) and add to this figure the tax and dividends attributable to this year and the difference between this year's and last year's general reserve. This will give us the operating profit before tax.

The amount of depreciation can be found either from the profit and loss account or by deducting this year's net book value of the fixed assets from last year's. Be careful to adjust this figure for any new fixed assets purchased during the year; such purchases will be shown in a later section of the cash flow statement. Depreciation is a non-cash cost, i.e. no money has been paid out on behalf of depreciation in the year in question; cash was paid for the asset at the time of purchase but the asset is depreciated over several subsequent years. Since depreciation has been deducted from profit, it must be added back again.

A 'loss' on the sale of a fixed asset means that the amount for which it was sold was less than its book value at that time. In other words, too much depreciation has been deducted so this is added back. The opposite applies to a profit on the sale of a fixed asset and this is deducted from profit. In an examination, be prepared to calculate the profit or loss on sale if it is not provided in the question.

The next sections of this calculation concern changes in the current assets (except for the bank balance) since last year. The relevant figures are found by subtracting this year's balance sheet figure from last year's. The changes in the bank and cash balances are left to the end of the cash flow statement as it is these changes that we wish to explain.

A decrease in stocks since last year means that more goods have been sold than have been replaced; this has caused a net cash inflow into the business and this is added. (Conversely an increase in stocks is deducted.)

A decrease in debtors means that the amount of money being paid by debtors was more than the amount of new debtors created, the effect being a net cash inflow – this is added to the calculation. Conversely an increase in debtors is equivalent to a net cash outflow and is deducted.

A decrease in creditors means that more cash was paid out to creditors than new creditors created, the net effect being a cash outflow, and this is deducted; an increase in creditors is added.

It is vital for you to sort out the pluses and minuses and to know what to add and what to subtract. You can learn the formula off by heart but it is better to understand it by studying the above section carefully.

(b) **on a gross basis**, using the direct method. This is used when a question provides us with the cash account instead of the profit and loss account. The layout is as follows:

Add cash received from customers
Deduct cash paid to suppliers
Deduct cash paid in wages
Deduct other cash payments
Net cash inflow/outflow from operating activities

Both the net and gross methods result in the same figure for net cash flow from operating activities. If an examination question instructs you to use a particular method, then follow the instruction; otherwise which you use will be dictated by the information given.

2. Returns on investments and servicing of finance

This section shows the cashflows arising from the receipts and payments of interest and dividends on profits. Proceed as follows:

Add interest received from bank accounts or loans / deduct interest paid on bank loans, debentures etc.
Add dividends received / deduct dividends paid (or drawings in the case of a sole trader).

Interest or dividends received are cash inflows while those paid out are outflows.

3. Taxation

This section relates to flows of tax on the firm's income or profit (but it does not include VAT which is included in the 'Operating Activities' section).

Deduct payments of income or profits tax
Add rebates of tax received

Payments of tax take cash out of the business while tax rebates received bring cash in.

4. Capital expenditure and financial investment

This section shows the cashflows arising from the purchase and sale of fixed assets, both tangible and intangible.

Add sale of fixed assets or investments
Deduct purchase of fixed assets or investments

A sale of assets brings cash into the business while a purchase causes cash to flow out

5. Acquisitions and disposals

This section includes purchases and sales of other businesses, subsidiaries etc.

Add the disposal of a business already owned
Deduct the acquisition of a new business

6. Equity dividends paid

Here we include the dividends paid to shareholders of the company. Remember to include in your cash flow statement the dividends payable for last year, since these will have been paid this year.

7. Financing

This section shows cashflows in respect of shares and loans:

Add increases in capital / share capital
Add loans raised
Deduct repayment of capital
Deduct repayment of loans

When a firm raises new capital there is a cash inflow; when it repays capital to the owners, there is a cash outflow.

8. Change in cash

The final figure resulting from the above calculation will be equal to the net increase or decrease in the bank and cash balances (combined) over the past year. If a positive bank balance changes to an overdraft or vice versa, remember to add the two figures together.

Worked Example

The balance sheets of SAF Ltd were as follows:

Balance Sheets as at 31 March

| | 2002 | | 2001 | |
	£	£	£	£
Fixed assets				
Land and buildings	196 000		200 000	
Plant and machinery	925 800		830 700	
Fixtures and equipment	204 600		182 400	
		1 326 400		1 213 000
Investments other than loans		72 000		10 800
Current assets				
Stock	381 000		421 500	
Debtors	110 200		134 600	
Bank and cash	92 400		89 200	
	583 600		645 300	
Creditors: amounts due in less than one year				
Bank loans and overdrafts	77 300			
Trade creditors	9 400		120 900	
Bills of exchange payable	51 900		16 000	
Other creditors:				
Taxation	163 200		157 300	
Proposed dividends	190 500		175 000	
	(492 300)		(469 200)	

Net current assets	91 300	176 100
Total assets less current liabilities	£1 489 700	£1 400 000
Creditors: amounts due in more than one year		
Debenture loans	150 000	400 000
Provisions for liabilities and charges		
Provision for legal damages and costs		56 000
Capital and reserves		
Called up share capital	700 000	700 000
Share premium	5 000	5 000
Profit and loss	634 700	239 000
	£1 489 700	£1 400 000

Note: The amounts shown in 2001 for taxation, proposed dividends and legal damages and costs were paid in the year ended 31 March 2002 at the amounts stated.

During the year ended 31 March 2002 the company had

(a) sold plant with a written down value of £25 800 for £22 400;
(b) made a profit before tax of £749 400 after charging depreciation of the following amounts:

	£
Buildings	4 000
Plant and machinery	110 200
Fixtures and equipment	28 100

REQUIRED

(a) Prepare a cash flow statement for SAF Ltd for the year ended 31 March 2002.
(b) Comment briefly on the financial position of the company.

Solution

Cash Flow Statement for year ending 31 March 2002

	£	£	£
Operating activities			
Operating profit (W_1)		749 400	
Add depreciation (4 000 + 110 200 + 28 100)	142 300		
Add loss on sale of plant (25 800 – 22 400)	3 400		
		145 700	
Add decrease in stock (W_2)	40 500		
Add decrease in debtors (W_2)	24 400		
Less decrease in creditors (W_2)	(111 500)		
Add increase in bills of exchange payable (W_2)	35 900		
		(10 700)	
Net cash inflow from operating activities			884 400
Returns on investments and servicing of finance			
Less dividends paid (W_3)			(175 000)

Taxation			
Tax paid (**W₃**)			(157 300)
Investing activities			
Sale of plant		22 400	
Purchase of plant (**W₄**)		(231 100)	
Purchase of fixtures (**W₅**)		(50 300)	
Acquisition of investments (72 000 – 10 800)		(61 200)	
			(320 200)
Financing			
Less redemption of debentures (400 000 – 150 000)		(250 000)	
Legal damages and costs paid*		(56 000)	
			(306 000)
			£(74 100)
Movement in net liquid funds			
Increase in bank and cash		3 200	
Increase in bank loans and overdrafts		(77 300)	
			£(74 100)

Workings

W₁

The profit figure is given in the question but if it had not been it would be possible to calculate it thus:

	£	£
Increase in retained profit (634 700 – 239 000)		395 700
Add back:		
Tax charge for the year	163 200	
Proposed dividends	190 500	
		353 700
Profit before tax		£749 400

W₂

These figures are found by finding the difference between this year's figure and last year's.

W₃

This represents the tax and dividends owing at the end of last year and paid during this year. The tax and dividends relating to this year will be paid next year.

W₄

The purchase of plant and machinery is found thus:

	£
Balance at end of 2002	925 800
Less balance at end of 2001	(830 700)
Add disposal of plant (book value)	25 800
Add depreciation	110 200
Value of plant purchased	231 100

W₅

The value of fixtures and equipment purchased is found thus:

	£
Balance at end of 2002	204 600
Less balance at end of 2001	(182 400)
Add depreciation	28 100
Value of plant purchased	50 300

* The legal damages and costs paid for last year comes under none of the normal headings of the cash flow statement and we include it in the most appropriate section.

Comments

The cash flow statement reveals that there has been a net outflow of funds of £74 100, caused partly by the redemption of debentures. This has resulted in an equivalent net decrease in working capital.

As a general rule, total applications or outflows of funds should not exceed total sources or inflows. A net outflow of funds will have to financed by depleting reserves of working capital and this can lead to cash flow problems. Management should budget for future business activities in advance to reveal periods of expected cash shortage and surplus. Where finance is needed for a major application such as the purchase of a fixed asset or repayment of a loan, arrangements can be made in advance for the raising of long-term capital. Long-term applications should not be financed by short-term capital.

Questions

Question 11.1

The Cash Flow Statement of Clifton plc for the year ended 31 December 1998 is shown below:

	1998 £000	1997 £000
Net cash inflow from operating activities		
Net cash inflow from continuing operating activities	8 445	6 150
Returns on investment and servicing of finance		
Interest paid	(1 077)	(1 388)
Interest received	207	172
Net cash outflow from returns on investment and servicing of finance	(870)	(1 216)
Taxation		
UK corporation tax paid	(648)	(680)
Capital expenditure and financial investment		
Purchase of tangible fixed assets	(769)	(1 093)
Purchase of intangible fixed assets	(30)	
Proceeds from sale of tangible fixed assets	94	131
Net cash outflow from capital expenditure and financial investment	(705)	(962)
Net cash outflow from the acquisition of subsidiary undertakings	(206)	(992)
Equity dividends paid	(2 291)	(2 100)
Net cash inflow before financing	3 725	200

Financing		
Issue of ordinary share capital	23	238
Proceeds from new borrowings		3
Repayments of loans	(4 294)	(319)
Net cash outflow from financing	(4 271)	(78)
(Decrease) / increase in cash	(546)	122

REQUIRED

(a) An explanation of the following terms found on the statement:
    (i) Purchase of tangible fixed assets
    (ii) Purchase of intangible fixed assets
    (iii) Equity dividends   **(6 marks)**

(b) An identification of *three material* changes in the company's cash flow situation during the year ended 31 December 1998 when compared with 1997. Explain whether you consider them to be positive, negative or 'neutral' from the company's point of view.   **(9 marks)**

(c) An explanation as to why you believe that, overall, Clifton plc's cash flow situation in 1998 was better or worse than in 1997.   **(5 marks)**

London Examinations Advanced Level

Question 11.2

The balance sheets of Tower plc as at 31 May 1997 and 1998 are as follows:

Tower plc
Balance Sheets

	31 May 1997	31 May 1998
	£000s	£000s
Fixed Assets (net book value)	64 000	86 000
Current Assets:		
Stock	36 000	38 000
Debtors	15 000	38 000
Bank	9 600	
	124 600	162 000
Creditors due for payment within one year		
Trade creditors	19 800	12 200
Taxation	8 000	10 000
Proposed dividends	4 000	6 000
Bank overdraft		5 400
	31 800	33 600
Total net assets	£92 800	£128 400
Share Capital		
Ordinary shares of 25p each	32 000	38 000
Preference shares of £1 each	14 000	10 000
Share premium account	400	600
Retained earnings	46 400	79 800
	£92 800	£128 400

The summarised profit and loss accounts for the two years ended 31 May 1998 are:

Profit and Loss Accounts for the two years ended 31 May 1998

	1997	1998
	£000s	£000s
Gross profit	57 800	92 200
Less expenses	24 200	36 400
	33 600	55 800
Loss on sale of fixed assets		6 400
Operating profit	33 600	49 400
Less taxation	8 000	10 000
Operating profit after tax	25 600	39 400
Dividends	4 000	6 000
Retained earnings	21 600	33 400
Retained earnings b/fwd	24 800	46 400
Retained earnings c/fwd	£46 400	£79 800

A summary of the company's fixed assets account for the year ended 31 May 1998 is shown below:

		£000			£000
1 June 1997	Cost b/fwd	152 000	31 May 1998	Disposal account	16 000
31 May 1998	Additions	44 000	31 May 1998	Cost c/fwd	180 000
		196 000			196 000

The assets which were sold realised £3.6 million, which represented a loss on disposal of £6.4 million when compared with their book value.

REQUIRED

(a) Produce a cash flow statement for the year ended 31 May 1998 in accordance with Financial Reporting Standard (FRS) 1: cash flow statements. Notes should be provided showing:
  (i) A reconciliation of the operating profit to the net cash flow from operating activities.
  (ii) An analysis of changes in cash during the year.   **(37 marks)**

(b) Suggest **three** reasons why a company might invest more in its fixed assets than it pays to its shareholders in dividends.   **(10 marks)**

(c) The managing director is concerned about the high level of investment in fixed assets and the increase in debtors during the year. Explain ways in which cash flow relating to these areas can be improved.   **(10 marks)**

Welsh Joint Education Committee Advanced Level

Question 11.3

The following are the summarised Balance Sheets for B B Wolf plc at 31 December:

	1997 £	1997 £	1998 £	1998 £
Fixed Assets				
Premises		1 760 000		1 960 000
Machinery		540 000		579 600
Office Equipment		138 000		110 000
		2 438 000		2 649 600
Current Assets				
Stock	83 000		71 200	
Debtors	51 600		44 700	
Bank	42 300		64 100	
	176 900		180 000	
Creditors due in less than one year				
Creditors	53 400		62 100	
Corporation Tax	41 000		48 000	
Proposed Dividend	80 000		65 000	
	174 400		175 100	
Net Current Assets		2 500		4 900
Total Assets less Current Liabilities		£2 440 500		£2 654 500
Capital and Reserves				
£1 Ordinary Shares		1 700 000		2 040 000
Share Premium		480 000		140 000
Revaluation Reserve				200 000
General Reserve		78 500		128 500
Profit and Loss		182 000		146 000
		£2 440 500		£2 654 500

(i) During 1998 machinery costing £195 000 had been purchased. There were no disposals of machinery.

(ii) Office equipment with a book value of £8 000 had been sold during 1998 for £6 500. This had been replaced by new office equipment costing £19 000.

(iii) During 1998 there was a bonus issue of one ordinary share for every five already held; this was effected by using part of the share premium.

REQUIRED

(a) A Cash Flow Statement in accordance with good accounting practice for the year ended 31 December 1998.   **(22 marks)**

(b) Explain your treatment of the bonus issue of shares.   **(3 marks)**

(c) Explain the purposes of a Cash Flow Statement.   **(4 marks)**

OCR Advanced Level

Question 11.4

Jayne Smart has just received a telephone message from her boss, Brenda O'Flynn, who has just started a fortnight's holiday in Southern Ireland and cannot now be contacted. Brenda should have taken a copy of the current year's final accounts to the bank. Brenda has asked Jayne to take the relevant documents to the bank tomorrow. Jayne has found copies of the previous year's balance sheet and the current year's draft profit and loss account and the cash flow statement but she cannot find a copy of the necessary balance sheet. Jayne feels confident that you, as an advanced level accounting student, can draw up the balance sheet for her. She supplies you with the following information.

Brenda O'Flynn Ltd
Balance Sheet as at 31 May 1996

	£000	£000	£000
Fixed assets (net book value)			7 535
Investments (at cost)			780
			8 315
Current assets			
Stock		587	
Debtors		828	
Bank balance		374	
		1 789	
Creditors – amounts falling due within one year			
Creditors	761		
Proposed ordinary dividend	467		
Taxation	200		
		(1 428)	
Net current assets			361
			£8 676
Capital and reserves			
Ordinary share capital (£1 shares)			6 400
Share premium account			1 008
Retained earnings			1 268
			£8 676

Brenda O'Flynn Ltd
Cash Flow Statement for the year ended 31 May 1997

	£000	£000
Net cash flow from operating activities		1 788
Returns on investments and servicing of finance		
Dividends paid – final ordinary	(467)	
interim ordinary	(210)	
Net cash outflow from returns on investments and servicing of finance		(677)
Taxation		
Corporation tax paid		(200)
Investing activities		
Payments made to acquire tangible fixed assets	(638)	
Payments to acquire investments	(240)	

Net cash outflow from investing activities		(878)
Net cash inflow before financing		33

Financing

Issue of ordinary share capital	500	
Net cash inflow from financing		500
Increase in cash and cash equivalents		533

Reconciliation of Operating Profit to Net Cash Flow from Operating Activities

	£000	£000
Operating profit:		
Retained profit	495	
Provision for corporation tax	140	
Dividends: interim (paid)	210	
final (proposed)	801	
		1 646
Depreciation		423
Increase in stocks		(54)
Increase in debtors		(153)
Decrease in creditors		(74)
		1 788

Analysis of Cash and Cash Equivalents

	£000
Balance 1 June 1996	374
Net cash inflow	533
Balance 31 May 1997	907

Jayne provides the following additional information:

(1) On 1 December 1996 the freehold land and buildings (included in the fixed assets at cost £4 800 000) were revalued at £8 000 000. The revaluation reserve created by this transaction was used to provide a bonus issue of ordinary shares on the basis of one share for every two shares previously held.

(2) No fixed assets were disposed of during the year.

(3) On 31 January 1997 a rights issue of 400 000 £1 ordinary shares was made at a price of £1.25 per share. The issue was fully taken up and paid for.

REQUIRED

(a) Prepare a draft balance sheet as at 31 May 1997 for Brenda O'Flynn to replace the missing copy. **(26 marks)**

(b) Prepare a memorandum addressed to Jayne Smart explaining why, in the 'Reconciliation of Operating Profit to Net Cash Flow from Operating Activities'.

(Memorandum format: 2 marks)

(i)   depreciation is added to the operating profit;

(ii)   the increase in stocks is deducted from the operating profit;

(iii) the increase in debtors is deducted from the operating profit;

(iv)   the decrease in creditors is deducted from the operating profit.   **(12 marks)**

(c) Explain **two** reasons why a cash flow statement may be helpful to users of
     accounting information.   **(10 marks)**

Associated Examining Board Advanced Level

12

Ratio Analysis

12.1 Introduction

So far we have been concerned mainly with the role of accounting as a technique of recording the performance of a business and on reporting this to its owners. While these are important functions they are not the only ones. In practice accountants are also expected to evaluate performance, inform management of underlying trends, and give advice on how unfavourable trends can be arrested and favourable trends further encouraged.

Useful though a set of accounts is, the figures in themselves do not tell the full story of a business. A key element in analysing performance is to study relationships between key variables that may be expected to be linked to one another, such as profit to sales, and sales to net assets. The chief tool for such analysis is ratios. A ratio is simply the relationship between two variables. While telling us something additional about a business, a ratio, if it is to have real significance, has to be compared with a yardstick to determine whether it is good or bad. This yardstick is provided by comparison to previous years, competitors (inter-firm comparison), and budgets (expected performance). A few words on each follow.

12.2 Inter-firm Comparison

Consider this information:

A Ltd made a net profit of £10 000

B Ltd made a net profit of £10 000

If you had to buy shares in one of the companies, which would you choose? At first sight it does not seem to matter – they are making equal profits. This is not to say however that they are equally profitable. What is really important is not the absolute amount of profit each is making so much as the amount of **profit in relation to capital employed**. We need information on this. You are told:

A Ltd's capital employed is   £50 000

B Ltd's capital employed is £100 000

We can now compute a measure of profitability through a ratio.

$$\text{Return on capital employed} = \frac{\text{Net profit}}{\text{Capital}} \times 100$$

$$\text{For A Ltd} = \frac{10\,000}{50\,000} \times 100 = 20\%$$

For B Ltd $= \dfrac{10\,000}{100\,000} \times 100 = 10\%$

This simple calculation shows A to be the better investment. Investors in A are earning twice as much on their money as investors in B.

Because ratios are relationships between two variables within the same business, they enable comparisons to be made between businesses, even though they may be of different sizes. Such comparisons are possible even between different countries. Thus a large multinational company can make a direct comparison of the return on capital of its operations in the USA with operations in Europe, since both figures are expressed in a like manner – as a percentage.

12.3 Comparison with Previous Years

It is also of interest to learn how a business has performed compared to previous years. Thus if A Ltd achieved a return on capital of 15% last year, shareholders will be pleased with this year's 20% return and management will concentrate on those policies which brought about the improvement. When comparing with previous periods, we should always take into account the external economic, political and social environment which can affect the demand for a firm's product, and we should make comparisons at the same time with other firms who have sustained the same problems; the results of a firm which has suffered a 10% fall in sales in a period of recession do not look so bad when compared with other firms whose sales have fallen by 20%.

Comparison over a longer time period, e.g. the past 5 years, reveals trends of the direction a business is moving. These trends can be used to forecast future performance, in an exercise known as budgeting.

12.4 Comparison with a Budget

A third yardstick is provided by comparing actual performance with expected or budgeted performance, revealing variances of both under- and over-achievement. Knowledge of significant unfavourable variances can help management focus on those aspects of the business in most need of attention. A consideration of budgeting, variance analysis and performance evaluation is deferred to Chapters 22 and 23.

Different parties will be interested in different aspects of a business performance. While the owners are most interested in profitability, bankers and creditors are interested in liquidity, potential shareholders in gearing and investment ratios. For this reason analysis is usually separated into ratios which measure:

* profitability
* liquidity
* working capital management
* gearing
* investment ratios.

We shall look at each in turn.

12.5 Profitability

It is the aim of all private sector firms to make a profit. Profit provides an income for the owner or owners, enables the firm to put away reserves in case of future need, is a source of funding for investment projects and is an indicator of the health of the business. It is the hope of making a profit which attracts investors and creditors. It is vital that a firm's managers, shareholders and potential investors have a reliable measure of the ability of the firm to generate satisfactory profits and to be able to compare these with profits made by the same firm in previous years, by other firms in the same industry and with the firm's own budget and expectations. The following are the main indicators used to assess a firm's profitability.

a) Return on Capital Employed

The ultimate test of profitability is the amount of profit a business is earning for every £ of capital invested in it. This Return on Capital Employed, or ROCE, should be compared with other returns in the same risk category, e.g. returns achieved by other firms in the same industry, to determine adequacy. The formula used is

$$\frac{\text{Profit}}{\text{Capital Employed}} \times 100$$

The profit figure taken to determine ROCE is usually **net profit before interest and tax**. Interest payable is excluded because its level is determined by the mix of finance between equity and debt, and not by the operating profitability of the business. Taxation is excluded because the amount of tax payable is felt to be determined by factors outside management's control – the rate of tax and levels of allowances are set by government. Not all accountants agree with this definition of profit. Some argue that good management will choose that mix of finance which minimises the cost of capital to the company and will arrange their financial affairs so as to minimise the tax liability to the government. The amount of these charges should therefore be included in the determination of ROCE for a more complete picture of efficiency.

The capital employed also needs to be defined and in practice there are different interpretations of this identity. The main distinction is between the capital invested by ordinary shareholders and that invested by long-term suppliers of capital, including preference shareholders, debenture holders and lenders of long-term loans. Since all long-term sources of capital are in effect employed by the firm, it is more realistic to include them and to let capital employed be equal to net assets, i.e. total assets minus creditors falling due within one year (or total assets minus current liabilities in the case of sole traders and partnerships). So it is best to assume that 'capital employed' means net assets unless otherwise instructed. (Profit as a percentage of ordinary share capital plus reserves is known as **Return on Owners' Equity.**)

b) Net Profit to Sales Ratio

What factors make for a high ROCE? Clearly the amount of profit on sales is important. This can be expressed as

$$\frac{\text{Net profit}}{\text{Sales}} \times 100$$

The higher the figure the better. A high profit margin will not on its own, however, lead to a high ROCE.

c) Gross Profit to Sales Ratio

This is also known as the sales margin and shows how much gross profit on average the firm is making on every £ of sales. The higher the margin the greater the profit per unit sold but the less competitive the product will be on the market.

d) Gross Profit to Cost of Sales Ratio

This is also known as the mark-up and shows what percentage the firm adds to its buying cost to arrive at the selling price. For a review of the distinction between mark-up and margin, refer back to Chapter 7.

e) Asset Turnover Ratio

The **level of sales** is also important. A business holds assets not for the sake of it but to use them productively by generating sales. The relationship between sales turnover and the asset base can therefore be expected to influence the ROCE. It can be measured as the Asset Turnover Ratio, given by

$$\frac{\text{Sales}}{\text{Net assets}}$$

Again the higher the figure the better. ROCE is in fact a product of the net profit on sales and asset turnover ratios.

Example

We are given the following information regarding a business:

	£
Net assets	200
Sales	400
Net profit	20

$$\text{Net profit on sales} = \frac{20}{400} \times 100 = 5\%$$

$$\text{Asset turnover} = \frac{400}{200} = 2$$

The above ratios indicate that for every £1 of asset the business is generating £2 of sales, and for every £1 of sales it is earning 5 pence in profit. For every £1 of asset it is therefore earning 5 pence × 2 = 10 pence in profit. The return on net assets should therefore be 10%. Let us see if this is so.

$$\text{ROCE} = \frac{20}{200} \times 100 = 10\%$$

or $5\% \times 2 = 10\%$

An inverse relationship usually exists between profit margin and asset turnover (stemming from the economist's downward-sloping demand curve). A business which

increases price to improve its profit margin will suffer a drop in the volume of sales, especially if demand is price-elastic. In such a case the improvement in the profit margin may be offset by a worsening asset turnover leaving ROCE unchanged, or possibly even causing it to decline. The art of profit maximisation is to operate at that balance between the two ratios that produces the highest overall return on net assets.

Ratios can always be further analysed into their constituent parts. The reason for a decline in ROCE can for example, be analysed into whether it was caused by a reduced profit margin or by a lower asset turnover, or both. If the cause is a reduced profit margin, this can be further investigated into its component parts. An important determinant of the net profit margin is the gross margin, as this reflects the cost of buying stocks and any changes in selling price. Net profit is also a function of the level of expenses and the accountant could compute **expense ratios**, which are calculated as

$$\frac{\text{Item of expense}}{\text{Sales}} \times 100$$

to try and identify which expenses are getting out of hand. Manufacturing concerns can in addition analyse their costs of production by substituting 'Item of expense' with 'Direct materials', 'Direct labour', 'Direct expenses' and 'Production overheads'.

The asset turnover ratio can similarly be further divided into its component parts, namely:

$$\frac{\text{Sales}}{\text{Fixed assets}} \quad \text{and} \quad \frac{\text{Sales}}{\text{Net current assets}}$$

This might reveal for example that fixed assets are being under-utilised because of surplus capacity. Management may then investigate just which assets are being under-utilised by breaking down fixed assets into plant, buildings, vehicles etc and substituting each into the sales to fixed assets ratio.

The question that should be asked is 'Are we using the assets productively and can we reduce the investment in any asset while maintaining the current level of activity?' A low sales to plant ratio could be attributable to machines lying idle because the production level does not warrant their use, or to frequent machine breakdowns. A low sales to buildings ratio could be caused by inefficient arrangement and layout of a factory, warehouse or office or simply by space lying unused. The number of vehicles may also be surplus to requirements.

Where over-investment is detected the surplus should be liquidated into cash and then used profitably by investing in assets really needed by the firm or by using it to finance working capital requirements. The significance of the component parts of the sales to net current assets ratio is considered in the section on working capital management later in this chapter.

Profitability analysis can be represented diagramatically as follows:

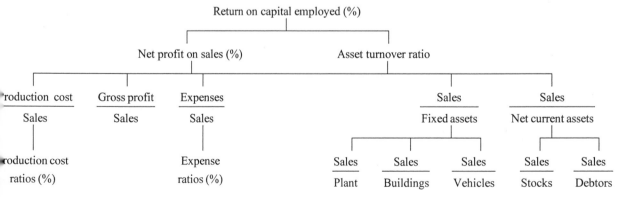

12.6 Liquidity

This shows the ability of a firm to meet commitments as they fall due. A firm should have sufficient liquid resources (cash and assets readily convertible into cash) to meet all current liabilities. Two ratios are commonly used as tests of liquidity: the current ratio and the acid-test ratio.

Current Ratio

This is computed as

Current assets : Current liabilities (Current assets divided by current liabilities). It is expressed as a ratio eg 2 : 1.

The difference between current assets and current liabilities is the firm's working capital but since it is an absolute and not a relative figure, simply stating it gives no idea of how satisfactory the amount is. Consider these two firms:

Singh Brothers have a small corner shop. Their current assets total £50 000 and their current liabilities are £30 000. Their working capital is thus £20 000.

Pancosmic Warehouses plc is a large wholesaling company. Its current assets are £2 020 000 and its current liabilities are £2 000 000. Its working capital is also £20 000.

Although both firms have the same working capital, it is clear that the small firm is in a much better liquidity position than the large one. The position can be more clearly stated if we express the ratio between the current assets and the current liabilities. Singh Brothers have a current ratio of 1.67:1 while that of Pancosmic Warehouses is 1.01:1.

As a general rule current assets should be between 1.5 and 2 times the current liability (a ratio of 2:1 is considered to be safe without tying up too much capital in cash). A firm whose current liabilities exceed liquid resources is not going to be popular with suppliers, bankers, and other creditors. If the ratio stays below 1:1 for long and creditors become increasingly impatient, the firm may have to shut down, forced into closure by insolvency or bankruptcy. This is, unfortunately, not an uncommon occurrence as many new businesses close within one year of setting up. Of these, a large proportion fail not so much because of unprofitability as insolvency. A common cause of a negative working capital is **overtrading**.

Overtrading is an attempt to finance too high a level of sales for the given size of business. The result is that the excessive investment in stock and debtors have to be financed by short-term credit from suppliers and the bank. The danger of doing this is that a point may be reached when creditors are no longer prepared to support the business. The result is bankruptcy. This mistake is often made by inexperienced new businesses, rapidly expanding small businesses and those whose management pay insufficient attention to cash flow and working capital. Profitability alone does not guarantee survival and even a profitable firm can go under if it leaves itself short of liquid resources.

Acid-Test Ratio

In businesses where stock is slow-moving it is wrong to count it as a liquid asset. Stock not only has to be sold but the business also has to wait until the invoice is paid, and this can take months. Consider the following balance sheet extract of Exclusive Ltd, a retailer of quality furniture.

	£000	£000
Current assets		
Stock		20
Debtors		6
Cash		4
		30
Less current liabilities		
Trade creditors	15	
Bank overdraft	5	
		(20)
Working capital		10

The current ratio (sometimes also called the working capital or liquid ratio) suggests a healthy liquidity position. However, assuming that it takes about 3 months on average for the shop to sell an expensive item of furniture and to receive payment, we can see that counting stock as a liquid asset gives a false impression of the firm's ability to raise liquid funds quickly. The acid-test ratio leaves stock out of the calculation thus:

Current assets – stock : Current liabilities

This harsher but more realistic test of liquidity tells us that the firm has left itself short of liquid assets. For every £1 of impending liability it has only 50 pence in liquid assets.

Simply holding stock does not guarantee quick conversion into cash and the acid-test ratio is a better test of solvency for businesses with slow-moving stock and firms suffering a slowdown in sales which might be caught with a large amount of unwanted stock. As a general rule-of-thumb the acid-test ratio should not fall below 1:1. In practice, however, a lot of firms operate dangerously below this level.

A document often used in conjunction with ratios in analysing liquidity is the cash flow statement, the subject of the previous chapter.

The solvency position is determined largely by the quality of management of the working capital of a business. We look at this aspect of performance next.

12.7 Profitability and Liquidity

There is a strong relationship between these two basic financial objectives. The more profitable an asset is, the less liquid it is likely to be for the firm. For example, a manufacturing firm depends on its plant and machinery to make its products and the better and more up-to-date this equipment is, the better the quality and the greater the quantity of what it produces. However, fixed assets are not liquid as they cannot be sold quickly and easily to generate cash, neither does the firm want to sell them. Conversely, liquid assets such as money in the bank, debtors and unsold stock enable the firm to secure short-term funds with which to pay its debts but these assets do not generate a profit. On the whole we can say that the more liquid an asset, the less profitable it is likely to be and vice versa.

While it is important for a firm to be both profitable and liquid, every decision it makes concerning its asset structure will favour one objective at the expense of the other. The overall objective for any firm should thus be to achieve a satisfactory balance between having enough fixed assets which will make possible production, sales and profits and having enough liquid funds to keep the firm solvent. When assessing the performance of a firm in an examination question, it is vital to bear this balance in mind and to weigh up profitability against liquidity.

12.8 Management of Working Capital

The aim here is to manage the various elements of the working capital cycle such that a minimum amount of finance is needed to sustain it. The working capital cycle is the process of converting stocks:

creditors → sales → debtor → cash → stocks → creditors → sales and so on.

The amount of finance needed to support the cycle is determined by

1) the **length** of one complete cycle, and
2) the **time-lag** between one part of the cycle and the next.

Policies should be followed which reduce the cycle. For example, giving preference to cash customers reduces the cycle by the period of credit normally extended to debtors. In a lot of industries, however, it is expected that trade will be carried out on credit terms and in these cases management accepts the need to invest some amount in debtors. Instead it pursues policies to minimise the amount of debt outstanding at any time by speeding up the **debt collection period**. Stocks are not sold instantly. They are held in the warehouse or shop for a length of time before being sold. Some amount of money is then also needed to finance this idle stock. The quicker the rate of selling, the shorter is the period of stockholding and the smaller the amount of capital tied up in stocks.

There are other ways of boosting working capital. One of these is **leasing**. Many firms lease equipment, which means that they pay an annual charge for the use of machinery etc which does not belong to them and for which they do not have to make a large capital outlay. This means that they have access to modern technology while conserving their liquid funds and not having to raise loans.

Factoring has become increasingly popular. This is the process whereby a firm sells its debtors to a factoring agency or other financial institution in exchange for a percentage of the invoices total. For example, a firm with a list of debtors totalling £100 000 might sell it for £90 000, preferring to have the lower figure now rather than wait for the full amount and also taking into account that some of the outstanding debts might become bad. This boosts cash flow and liquidity at the expense of profitability.

Rate of Stock Turnover

This indicates the number of times during one year that a batch of stock is completely sold and replaced with a fresh batch. A figure of 6, for example, indicates 6 complete orders sold, meaning that each consignment was held on average for 2 months before being sold. The formula for the ratio is

$$\frac{\text{Cost of goods sold}}{\text{Average stock}}$$

To find the exact value of average stock, stock levels would have to be recorded at the end of each trading day and added together at the end of the year, this figure then being divided by the number of trading days. Such an exercise is laborious, time-consuming, and expensive. Instead it is common to use a proxy for it by taking the average of opening and closing stocks. Although 'cheating' in this way does not give us the exact figure of average stock, it is probably close enough not to affect the rate of turnover materially. Certainly it is the method you need to apply in examinations. All the information can be obtained from the trading account.

Illustration

	£000	£000
Sales		160
Less cost of goods sold		
Opening stock	15	
Purchases	130	
Less closing stock	(25)	
Cost of goods sold		(120)
Gross profit		40

$$\text{Rate of stock turnover} = \frac{120}{(15+25) \div 2} = 6$$

The answer of 6 means that the average stock has been sold 6 times during the year. It is often useful to express the rate as the average number of days stocks are held before being sold. This is done by dividing 365 (the number of days in the year) by the rate of turnover. In the above case we have

$365 \div 6 = 60.8$ days i.e. two months.

There is no single ideal rate of turnover. It varies from firm to firm and industry to industry. Thus, while our furniture retailer might be happy with a rate of 6, this would never do for a greengrocer. He would need to replace stock every week, giving a rate of over 50. A newsagent would need a rate of 365. From a given position however, a higher rate is preferable since it implies an increase in selling activity, a decrease in average stockholding and hence a reduction in the amount of capital tied up in stock.

The rate of turnover can be increased simply by buying stock in smaller amounts but more frequently, thereby holding less in the warehouse at any one time. In addition to reducing the investment in stock, this also incurs lower storage and insurance costs. The stock controller has to be careful though how far he goes down this road. If a low stock policy is taken too far there is the danger that the firm will be unable to respond to an unexpected increase in demand. Also, with no protection against interruptions from suppliers the risk of being caught out of stock, a stock-out, is increased. In addition, discounts on bulk-buying are lost. The art of stock control is to achieve the optimum balance between the conflicting forces calling for high and low stock levels – to hold that amount at which the total cost of stockholding, including the risk of a stock-out, is at its lowest.

Debtors' Collection Period

This measures the average number of days debtors take to pay by relating debtors at a particular date to the average value of credit sales per day. Alternatively it indicates the number of days of credit sales tied up in debtors. The formula expressed in days, is

$$\frac{\text{Debtors at balance sheet date}}{\text{Credit sales for the year}} \times 365$$

For example, if a firm's total credit sales are £250 000 and its debtors are £75 000, the debt collection period is 75 000 × 365 / 250 000 = 109.5 days, which is about $3\frac{1}{2}$ months.

The period can be shortened by demanding quicker payment but this is often at the expense of reduced sales. The art of debt management is to achieve that balance between debtors and sales that will maximise the return on capital employed. Large firms employ specialist credit controllers to carry out this function. There are several

possible causes of an unsatisfactory collection period. It could be that the procedure for chasing up slow payers is not being followed. A useful tool in this is the **aged debtors list**, which analyses debtors by the number of days each debt is outstanding. In this way the controller is alerted to those balances most in arrears. A second possible reason is that the setting of credit limits on customers has not been properly thought out. Each account in the sales ledger should then be examined and the credit limit revised downwards for those customers most often in arrears. Another possible area of improvement is to review the policy on cash discounts. Offering larger cash discounts for quick payment would shorten the collection period, although this is at the expense of a lower profit margin.

Creditors' Payment Period

While a firm should try to give as little credit to customers as possible, it should take as much credit from suppliers as possible. It is useful to compute the average period of credit taken from the formula:

$$\frac{\text{Trade creditors at balance sheet date}}{\text{Credit purchases over the year}} \times 365$$

Thus, if a supplier gives 30 days to pay it is a good idea to take the full 30 days before paying. But if a cash discount is offered for quick payment the effective rate of interest on this should be computed. If it is above the rate the firm's cash is currently earning, the offer should be taken and the supplier paid early. Some firms consistently pay their creditors only after receiving several reminder letters and, while this policy extends their credit period, they are endangering both the continuation of credit from their suppliers and their general reputation for creditworthiness. Information about the firm's creditors' payment period and the debtors' collection period is most meaningful when considered together – a firm whose debtors are taking 12 weeks to pay is not in a bad position if it has 13 weeks to pay its own creditors.

Cash

A final, and important, aspect of working capital is the management of cash. The idea here is always to have some amount to finance day-to-day expenses such as wages, but not too much since holding cash does not earn interest and therefore incurs an opportunity cost. A formal exercise in cash budgeting is needed to reveal expected balances in the future. Arrangements can then be made in advance for overdraft facilities in times when the business is expected to be short of cash and for short-term investments in times of expected cash surpluses. The nature of cash budgets and their preparation is looked at in Chapter 22, Budgeting and Budgetary Control.

12.9 Gearing

Companies finance their activities by either

1) attracting investment in their equity shares, on which returns are variable depending on the level of profit

or

2) borrowing from banks and the public by issuing debentures, on which they are committed to pay a fixed rate of interest.

The **gearing ratio** is a measure of the proportion of the capital employed to which the company is committed to fixed return payments. The formula is

$$\frac{\text{Long - term liabilities} + \text{Preference shares}}{\text{Total shareholders funds} + \text{Long - term liabilities}} \times 100$$

For the purpose of the ratio, preference shares are included under long-term liabilities since they command a fixed rate of return, though in the form of dividends and not interest.

Illustration

The following information relates to two companies.

	High Ltd	Low Ltd
	£000	£000
Ordinary shares	15	60
10% preference shares	15	
8% debentures	65	20
Reserves	5	20
Capital employed	100	100

The gearing ratio is given as follows:

$$\text{High Ltd} = \frac{80\,000}{100\,000} \times 100 = 80\%$$

$$\text{Low Ltd} = \frac{20\,000}{100\,000} \times 100 = 20\%$$

High Ltd, with a large proportion of debt in its capital structure, is said to be **high-geared**. Low Ltd which has only limited fixed interest commitments is said to be **low-geared**. Just like a car, a company is in a safer position if it is in a lower gear.

The gearing ratio is important because it affects the company's cost of capital, degree of risk in the capital structure, and return to equity. Borrowing is usually a cheaper source of finance than equity, not least because interest payments, being a normal business expense, are tax-deductible whereas dividends are not. Given this, there is a temptation for companies to borrow heavily. Management has got to be careful however because a high proportion of debt introduces risk into the way the business is financed and makes it difficult for the company to raise further loans. After a certain level of borrowing is reached, the benefit of cheap borrowing is more than offset by the cost in terms of increased financial risk in the capital structure, not only to lenders but also to investors (explained below). Just before this point is reached could be said to be the **optimum level of gearing** for a company. Unfortunately there is no single optimum level – this varies from firm to firm and industry to industry. The optimum cost of finance is a complex subject on which there is no unanimous agreement amongst accountants. You will meet the theoretical issues at degree and professional level.

The whole idea of a company borrowing money for, say 8%, is to earn a return greater than this, say 12%. The 4% profit then belongs to the owners of the company – the shareholders. It follows then that the greater the level of borrowing the higher the return to equity. In the above example, if both our companies earn 4% above the cost

of borrowing, the earnings per share and return to equity will be much higher for the high-geared company, High Ltd, because firstly the absolute amount of profit is larger since it has borrowed more, and secondly this larger profit is to be distributed amongst a smaller number of ordinary shareholders.

In bad years, though, when the company makes a loss on borrowed funds, earning say only 6% on the 8% debentures, the earnings per share will fall more dramatically for High Ltd than Low Ltd, because the absolute amount of the loss is larger since it has borrowed more, and also because this larger loss has to be borne by a smaller number of shareholders. Gearing thus works both ways. Returns fluctuate violently for investors in high-geared companies, in line with whether return on capital employed has been above or below the cost of borrowing. For investors in low-geared companies the fluctuations between good and bad years are less exaggerated. This is an important consideration for a potential investor. If they want the chance of large returns with the risk and excitement that goes with this, they should buy ordinary shares in a high-geared company. If they wants security they should look to a low-geared company.

12.10 Investment Ratios

In addition to gearing and profitability ratios, investors will be interested in a number of additional ratios applicable to public limited companies.

Dividend Yield

The dividend yield is the

$$\frac{\text{Ordinary dividend per share}}{\text{Market price per share}} \times 100$$

To the shareholder this represents the immediate return on his investment. The ratio compares the actual dividend paid on each share with the market value of the share at that time. A low dividend yield does not in itself mean that a particular share is a bad investment. Dividend yield should be considered together with the pay-out ratio (dividend cover).

Dividend Cover

This is given by

$$\frac{\text{Profit attributable to equity}}{\text{Dividend}}$$

and is expressed in number of times. Profit attributable to equity is profit after interest, tax and preference dividend have been deducted. The dividend cover shows the relationship between the maximum dividend the directors could have declared and what they did in fact declare. A high dividend cover implies a low dividend yield and substantial re-investment of profit in the company. This will hopefully increase future earnings. Potential shareholders may then look favourably on a low dividend yield and want to invest, to share in the future larger profits. The split of profit between dividends and retention is determined by the amount of dividends declared in the recent past (to which existing shareholders have become accustomed) and the amount of capital the company needs to finance its current and future operations. Retaining profit to finance investment is the cheapest source of finance but management has to be careful not to keep too much, as shareholders may be disappointed and sell their shares which could lead to a fall in the market price. In addition such a policy may backfire in the future when the company needs to issue further shares.

Return on Equity

This ratio relates total equity earnings, whether they are distributed or not, to the amount of the investment by shareholders. It is found by

$$\frac{\text{Profit attributable to equity}}{\text{Investment by equity}} \times 100$$

Earnings per Share

This relates the total equity earnings to the number of shares issued and is a more general ratio.

$$\frac{\text{Profit attributable to equity}}{\text{Number of ordinary shares issued}}$$

It is expressed in pence per share.

The two last ratios are often used by investors and potential investors in deciding whether the return on a particular company is sufficient for the level of risk taken.

Price–Earnings Ratio

A further ratio, often quoted in the financial press, is the price–earnings ratio which is a measure of the relationship between earnings per share and market price.

$$\frac{\text{Market price per share}}{\text{Earnings per share}}$$

It represents the number of times by which current market price exceeds current earnings. Since market price changes every day so does the ratio. The lower the figure the cheaper the company is as an investment in relation to its earnings potential.

Example

This example is a question from University of Oxford Advanced Level.

The following is a list of balances from the books of Vale plc for the year ended 31 December 1997.

	£000
Tax on profit on ordinary activities	85
Turnover	1 250
Distribution costs	200
Investment income	45
Interest payable	30
Cost of sales	470
Administrative expenses	270
Transfer to general reserve	145
Proposed dividend on ordinary shares	30
Undistributed profit from last year	82

The issued share capital of the company is 1 000 000 £1 ordinary shares and the current market price of one ordinary share is £2.40.

REQUIRED

(a) A profit and loss account for the year ended 31 December 1997 in accordance
with the minimum required by the Companies Act 1985. **(10 marks)**

(b) Calculate the following:
    (i) earnings per share;
    (ii) price/earnings ratio;
    (iii) dividend yield;
    (iv) dividend cover. **(8 marks)**

(c) Comment on the dividend policy of the company. **(6 marks)**

Vale plc

(a)

Profit and Loss Account for the year ended 31 December 1997

	£000	£000	£000
Turnover	1 250		
Cost of sales	(470)		
Gross profit		780	
Distribution costs	200		
Administration expenses	270		
		(470)	
Trading profit			310
Income from investments			45
Interest payable and similar charges			(30)
Profit or loss on ordinary activities before taxation			325
Tax on profit or loss on ordinary activities			(85)
Profit or loss on ordinary activities after taxation			240
Transfers to reserves			(145)
Dividends paid and proposed			(30)
Retained profit for the year			65
Profit and loss credit balance b/f			82
Profit and loss account transferred to Balance Sheet			£147

(b)

(i) Earnings per share $= \dfrac{\text{Proft after interest and tax}}{\text{Number of ordinary shares issued}}$

$= \dfrac{240\,000}{1\,000\,000}$

$= £0.24$

(ii) Price/earnings ratio $= \dfrac{\text{Market price per share}}{\text{Earnings per share}}$

$= \dfrac{2.40}{0.24}$

$= 10$

(iii) Dividend yield $= \dfrac{\text{Ordinary dividend per share}}{\text{Market price per share}} \times 100$

$= \dfrac{30\,000\,/\,1\,000\,000}{2.40} \times 100$

$= \dfrac{0.03 \times 100}{2.40}$

$= 1.25\%$

(iv) Dividend cover $= \dfrac{\text{Profit after interest and tax}}{\text{Dividend}}$

$= \dfrac{240\,000}{30\,000}$

$= 8$

(c) Comments: The price-earnings ratio is very low and the share is cheaply priced in relation to earnings potential. The dividend yield is low and the dividend cover is high, showing that the company is distributing to the shareholders only a small proportion of the profits. This indicates management's intention to invest substantial amounts in capital expenditure and expansion in the near future.

12.11 Using Ratios

Although the above represent the more important ratios, they are by no means the only ones. If a firm is interested in the relationship between two items not covered above, it can easily invent a ratio to meet its needs.

Example

Information regarding a major advertising campaign by a firm:

Increase in advertising expenditure	£10 000
Profit on resulting additional sales	£12 000

It is of interest to the firm to calculate the return obtained from the additional advertising. This can be done as:

$\text{Return} = \dfrac{\text{Net benefit}}{\text{Cost}} \times 100$

$= \dfrac{£2\,000}{£10\,000} \times 100 = 20\%$

As stated earlier in this chapter, many different parties are interested in a set of accounts and for different reasons. Potential creditors such as suppliers and banks will examine the liquidity ratios to estimate whether the business will be able to make payments as they fall due, while owners of a business are more interested in profitability. Potential shareholders are likely to be interested most in the gearing and investment ratios. A company considering a take-over bid of another company will probably conduct a detailed analysis of the potential acquisition involving all the ratios mentioned.

In addition, it is not only parties outside the business that are interested in a set of accounts. Insiders too are interested, that is, management and workers. In small single-product businesses, management may be content with calculating ratios for the business as a whole. In larger companies, in addition to ratios for the business as a whole, management will:

1) in decentralised organisations, calculate ratios for each autonomous division, giving top management levels an idea of how each division and divisional manager is doing;

2) in group companies owning subsidiaries and related companies, calculate ratios for each company;

3) in multi-product companies, calculate ratios for each product group;

4) in multinationals, compare ratios for operations in different parts of the world.

Workers and trade union leaders will be interested in the profitability ratios and their comparison to previous years as a guide to their wage claims, and the liquidity ratios to assess the ability of the firm to meet these claims.

12.12 Limitations of Ratio Analysis

Users of ratios should be aware of the limitations of the technique to avoid the possibility of making false conclusions from them. There are several limitations:

1) Ratios focus exclusively on proportions, completely ignoring absolute values. Because of this they are unable to reveal all significant changes in a business. This is easily illustrated with an example. The following figures relate to Expansion Ltd.

	2001	2002
Net assets (capital employed)	£100 000	£200 000
Sales	£200 000	£400 000
Net profit	£20 000	£40 000
Net profit on sales	10%	10%
Asset turnover ratio	2	2
Return on capital employed	20%	20%

Looking at the absolute figures we can see that 2002 was a year of considerable growth. The business experienced a large increase in the amount of capital employed. This was used to generate additional sales, producing increased profits. In contrast, the three ratios show no change. Because the variables have increased in the same proportion (each has doubled) the change has not shown up in the ratios.

2) Without a proper understanding of the constituent elements of a ratio, a false picture may be obtained. A common misconception is that the profit margin and ROCE are the same. An improvement in ROCE is then taken to mean an increase in the profit margin. However, this need not be so. In fact, the profit margin may actually decline. Consider the following change for Expansion Ltd.

	2001	2002
Net profit on sales	10%	8%
Asset turnover	2	3
Return on capital employed	20%	24%

The improved return on capital, from 20% to 24% was caused by a lower profit margin. Price reductions boosted sales, leading to a higher asset turnover ratio. This has more than offset the reduced profit margin, and improved overall ROCE.

3) The novice may also be misled by a ratio where changes take place in its constituent elements but, because these move in opposite directions and compensate one another, do not show up in the ratio. Expansion Ltd again:

	2001	2002
Net profit on sales	10%	5%
Asset turnover	2	4
Return on capital employed	20%	20%

The fact that the ROCE is unchanged from 2001 to 2002 hides the fact that a significant change has taken place in selling strategy – from high margins and moderate sales in 2001 to low margins and volume sales in 2002.

4) While ratio analysis may be usefully conducted to analyse changes in a firm from one year to another, inter-firm comparisons should be made with caution. Only if the two firms follow identical accounting policies in subjective areas like depreciation and stock valuation will the comparison have any meaning.

5) Ratios do not take into account the fact that the value of money changes with time. Comparison with previous years should then be made with care. The user should have an appreciation of the effect of inflation on a set of accounts.

6) Accounts record only those aspects of a business which can be expressed in money terms. Calculating ratios from such accounts will therefore not give a complete picture of the business such as the atmosphere at the place of work, state of industrial relations and amount of goodwill.

For the above reasons ratios should be regarded only as broad indicators bringing to attention those aspects of a business that need further investigation. They do not raise all the questions that need asking. In addition they do not provide answers to all the questions which could be raised – this has to be done by management and accountants.

12.13 Examination Questions

Examination questions on this topic are either
1) closed, asking you to calculate a number of specific ratios followed by their interpretation, or
2) open-ended, asking you to compare two businesses or the same business over time, in general terms.

The second type of question is probably more difficult since you have to decide which ratio to use. Here you should try and structure your answer by first stating that a business may be evaluated from several different standpoints depending on the user, then evaluate it from each standpoint – profitability, liquidity, and so on. You will not normally be given the formulae for the ratios which means that you need to learn them by heart. When using each ratio, always state its formula first so that, even if you make an error in the calculation, you can earn some marks for knowing the correct relationship.

If a question requires you to analyse or interpret a set of accounts, do just that. Do not stop at a mere calculation of the ratios. Comment on the meaning of the figures and of changes in them, what could have brought them about and what management should do about them. If you are told what sector the business is operating in, this can give you a clue to its performance from the point of view of demand, special problems etc. This is proper analysis. Without it the answer is incomplete.

Examinations in accounting increasingly aim to test candidates' ability to use language as well as figures and you may be required to produce a report, with 2 or 3 marks being awarded for format. Here is how you should set out your report:

- Indicate at the top who the report is meant for by writing the name of the person or company to whom you have been instructed to address it.
- Put your name as the writer of the report.
- Put today's date.
- Write the title of the report, i.e. the subject or topic.
- Under the heading of 'Findings' write what you have discovered from the information given and your own computations.
- Under the heading of 'Conclusions' summarise your thoughts and findings.
- Under the heading of 'Recommendations' state what actions you think the business should take to deal with its current problem or situation.

Questions

Question 12.1

Laura Labbatt has some spare funds which she would like to invest in a public limited company. She has obtained some information on two companies which is given below. She would like to use this as a basis for making a decision as to which company may provide the better investment.

Becky plc

Profit and Loss Account for the year ended 28 February 1998

	£000
Sales	28 980
Less cost of sales	15 295
Gross profit	13 685
Less expenses	3 785
Net profit before taxation	9 900
Taxation	3 000
Net profit after taxation	6 900
Proposed ordinary share dividend	3 960
Retained profits for year	2 940
Transfer to general reserve	1 770
Balance retained in profit and loss account	£1 170

Becky plc

Balance Sheet as at 28 February 1998

	£000	£000
Fixed assets (net book value)		49 910
Current assets		
Stock	13 860	
Debtors	8 030	
Bank	1 080	
	22 970	
Creditors: amounts falling due within one year		
Trade creditors	4 650	
Taxation	3 000	
Dividends	3 960	
	11 610	
Net current assets		11 360
Net assets		£61 270
Capital and reserves		
Ordinary shares of £1 each		52 800
General reserve		4 670
Profit and loss account		3 800
Capital employed		£61 270

Additional information

1) The market price of Becky plc's ordinary shares at close of business on 28 February 1998 was £1.25.

2) All Becky plc's purchases and sales are on a credit basis.

3) Credit purchases for the year were £18 515 000.

Charlotte plc

Accounting ratios extracted from recent published accounts

Gross margin	56.72%
Net margin	39.61%
Return on capital employed	21.39%
Current ratio	2.01 : 1
Acid test ratio	0.67 : 1
Debtors' collection period	32 days
Creditors' payment period	43 days
Earnings per share	11.02 pence
Dividend cover	2.95
Dividend yield	4%

REQUIRED

(a) Using the financial information given in the final accounts of Becky plc, calculate, correct to two decimal places, the same ratios as those already given for Charlotte plc. In each case state clearly the formula you have used. **(20 marks)**

(b) Draft a report addressed to Laura Labbatt advising her which company might provide the better investment. In your report you should:

  (i)   select four ratios for Becky plc from those you calculated in (a) and compare them with those of Charlotte plc;
  (ii) explain what each chosen ratio indicates;
  (iii) give possible reasons for any differences in these ratios.

(Report format: 2 marks)
(18 marks)

(c) Explain **two** limitations of using ratio analysis as a business performance indicator.   **(4 marks)**

(d) Explain why profitability and liquidity are important to the survival of a business.   **(6 marks)**

Associated Examining Board Advanced Level

Question 12.2

The balance sheets of London Ltd and Bridge Ltd at 31 March 1998 were as follows:

London Ltd and Bridge Ltd
Balance Sheets as at 31 March 1998

	London Ltd £	Bridge Ltd £
Fixed Assets (net book value)	744 000	628 000
Current Assets		
Stock	266 000	274 000
Debtors	186 000	206 000
Bank	6 000	478 000
Total Assets	1 202 000	1 586 000
Less: Creditors, amounts falling due within one year	472 000	336 000
	730 000	1 250 000
Less: Creditors, amounts falling due after more than one year		520 000
	£730 000	£730 000
Share Capital:		
Ordinary shares of £1 each	400 000	200 000
Reserves	330 000	530 000
	£730 000	£730 000

Note:

The profits of London Ltd have averaged £60 000 per annum whilst the profits of Bridge Ltd have averaged £60 000 per annum before debenture interest.

REQUIRED

(a) Calculate the following ratios for both of the companies and give a brief explanation of their significance:
  (i)   the gearing ratio
  (ii) the working capital ratio
  (iii) the acid-test ratio
  (iv) return on capital employed.   **(16 marks)**

(b) Write a brief report to a potential investor with £100 000 available, to explain which of the two companies represents the better choice of investment.   **(9 marks)**

(c) If the audit report on London Ltd's accounts had stated that the going-concern concept were not applicable, how would that affect the advice given to the potential investor in (b) above?   **(5 marks)**

Welsh Joint Education Committee Advanced Level

Question 12.3

The management of Slipshod Ltd has calculated the following statistics from its results for the year ended 31 December 1998. Equivalent average figures from a relevant trade association are also given.

	Slipshod Ltd	Trade Average
(i) Gross Profit Margin	50%	40%
(ii) Operating Profit Margin	10%	8%
(iii) Return on Capital Employed	16%	12%
(iv) Acid Test	1:1	1.5:1
(v) Gearing Percentage	80%	30%

REQUIRED

(a) Explain the significance of, and the basis of calculation for, each of the five statistics listed above.   **(10 marks)**

(b) If you were informed that Slipshod Ltd's current ratio was 5:1, compared with a trade average of 2:1, explain why this does not necessarily indicate a satisfactory situation.   **(5 marks)**

London Examinations Advanced Level

Question 12.4

Part 1

The following figures apply to the firm of North-East Traders Ltd for the year ending 31 December 1997.

	£
Turnover (note 1)	400 000
Purchases	290 000
Average stock (note 2)	30 000
Net profit	45 000
Debtors at 31 December 1997 (note 3)	80 000
Bank balance	20 000
Creditors at 31 December 1997	50 000
VAT owing at 31 December 1997	25 000
Value of fixed assets	120 000

Notes

1) Turnover is 80% on credit.
2) Stock levels had fallen by £10 000 during the year.
3) Debtors were unchanged from the beginning of the year.

(a) Calculate:
  (i)   mark-up ratio;
  (ii)   rate of stock turnover;
  (iii)   debtors' collection period in days;
  (iv)   expenses ratio;
  (v)   acid-test ratio;
  (vi)   turnover to fixed assets ratio.   **(7 marks)**

  Figures for 1996 for two of the above ratios were:
  Rate of stock turnover: 12 times
  Debtors' collection period: 65 days

(b) Comment on the relative performance of North-East Traders Ltd in 1997.   **(4 marks)**

Part 2

ACE plc has an issued and fully paid share capital of £11 million, comprising
£10 million in 50p ordinary shares and £1 million in 8% preference shares. In addition
ACE plc has issued £1 million 6% debentures.

The ordinary shares have a market value of £1.25.

During the year to 31 December 1997, ACE plc made a net profit before interest and
tax of £2.3 million.

Corporation tax is charged at 25%.

ACE plc paid an interim dividend of 2p per ordinary share and has also declared a
final ordinary dividend of 3p per share.

(a) Calculate the:
  (i)   ordinary dividend percentage;
  (ii)   ordinary dividend yield;
  (iii)   net profit available for distribution to ordinary shareholders;
  (iv)   price–earnings ratio.   **(7 marks)**

(b) Give two possible consequences of being an ordinary shareholder in a highly
    geared company.   **(2 marks)**

Scottish Certificate of Education Higher Grade

Question 12.5

The following are the summarised financial statements of Ball and Gregson Ltd, a
trading company.

Trading and Profit and Loss Accounts for the years ended 31 October

	1994	1995
	£000	£000
Sales	2 100	3 000
Less cost of sales		
Opening stock	350	420
Purchases	1 470	2 190
	1 820	2 610
Closing stock	420	510
	1 400	2 100

Gross profit	700	900
Expenses	353	447
Net profit before tax	347	453
Taxation	87	113
	260	340
Dividends	90	120
Retained profit for the year	£170	£220

Balance Sheets as at 31 October

	1994		1995	
	£000	£000	£000	£000
Fixed assets at net book value		1 700		2 100
Current assets				
Stocks	420		510	
Debtors	400		450	
Bank and cash	100		120	
		920		1 080
Creditors less than one year				
Trade creditors	280		310	
Dividends	60		70	
Accruals	60		130	
Taxation	87		113	
		(487)		(623)
Creditors more than one year				
12% debentures 1995		(400)		
		£1 733		£2 557
£1 ordinary shares, fully paid		1 250		1 500
Share premium		250		604
Retained earnings		233		453
		£1 733		£2 557

Additional information:

(1) 90% of all sales are on credit.

(2) All purchases were made on credit.

(3) Debtors' and creditors' figures at balance sheet dates may be taken as
representative averages for each of the years in question.

REQUIRED

(a) State and calculate **two** ratios relating to the profitability of Ball and Gregson Ltd
for **each** of the years under review.   **(6 marks)**

(b) State and calculate **two** ratios relating to the liquidity of Ball and Gregson Ltd
for **each** of the years under review.   **(6 marks)**

(c) Write a report using the ratios calculated in (a) and (b) to analyse the profitability
and liquidity of Ball and Gregson Ltd over the two-year period. The report should
include an outline of major difficulties encountered in making inter-year comparisons. **(16 marks)**

(d) State **two** ways in which a business could increase its working capital.   **(6 marks)**

(e) What are the disadvantages to a business of having
    (i) excessive working capital   **(6 marks)**
    (ii) limited working capital?   **(6 marks)**

(f) Explain briefly how a business could be profitable yet encounter a liquidity problem.   **(4 marks)**

Associated Examining Board Advanced Level

Question 12.6

Adil Zahir is concerned about the lack of cash in his business and why he has found it difficult to meet orders for customers in the last year.

The following summary information relates to his business for the last two years.

Summarised Profit and Loss Account for the years ended

	31 December 1999	31 December 2000
	£000	£000
Sales	90	120
Cost of goods sold	45	80
Gross profit	45	40
Sundry expenses	30	34
Net profit	15	6

Opening stock as at 1 January 1999 was £15 000.

Balance Sheets as at

	31 December 1999		31 December 2000	
	£000	£000	£000	£000
Net fixed assets		40		30
Current assets				
Stock	5		20	
Debtors	10		20	
Cash at bank	3			
	18		40	
Current liabilities				
Bank overdraft			10	
Creditors	9		30	
	9		40	
		9		
		£49		£30
Financed by				
Opening capital		40		49
Net profit for year		15		6
		55		55
Less drawings		6		25
Closing capital		£49		£30

REQUIRED

(a) A calculation of the following ratios:
  - return on capital employed (based on closing capital)
  - gross profit as a percentage of sales
  - net profit as a percentage of sales
  - current ratio
  - liquid (acid test) ratio
  - stock turnover   **(12 marks)**

(b) An analysis of the changes between the two years, based on the ratios calculated
    and information available in the financial statements. Suggest how Adil Zahir
    could tackle his concerns and improve future liquidity.   **(12 marks)**

OCR Advanced Subsidiary Specimen Paper

13

Computerised Accounting

13.1 Introduction

The application of information technology to business in recent years means that almost all firms nowadays use computers to keep their accounts. At one end of the scale a small business can keep its financial data on spreadsheet programs which will do certain automatic calculations and at the other end are fully computerised accounting packages which perform all the accounting entries and operations connected with each transaction. The principles of double-entry bookkeeping and preparation of final accounts have however not been affected and firms still need to employ personnel who can organise the input and understand the output.

If you are studying computerised accounting, you will need a specialist textbook. If however you are entering for the examinations covered by this book, you do not need to know technical details of how to operate an electronic accounting package. It is sufficient for you to know what the programs do and what the advantages and disadvantages are to firms of using these programs.

13.2 Types of Computerised Accounting Programs

Spreadsheets

A spreadsheet is a computer program with which an operator can do a variety of numerical tasks and which can be used for producing accounts, trial balances, cost grids, profit and loss accounts etc.

The operator works with a grid similar to the one below. It is composed of cells which are filled in with the required data eg monthly sales, the costs of various raw materials etc.

ABACUS LTD FORECAST PROFIT AND LOSS ACCOUNTS				
	2001	2002	2003	2004
	£	£	£	£
Sales	300 000	320 000	450 800	495 000
Cost of Sales	200 000	280 000	350 000	305 000
Gross Profit	100 000	40 000	100 800	190 000
Wages	52 000	56 700	61 800	65 500
Other Overheads	15 000	20 000	25 000	30 000
Net Profit	33 000	(36 700)	14 000	94 500

The spreadsheet does much more than simply set out figures. It can perform a wide range of mathematical functions by entering formulae. For example, in the above spreadsheet, the cost of sales can be subtracted from sales to give gross profit immediately by entering a suitable formula and telling the program which cells it should apply this to.

Another facet of spreadsheets is the 'What If?' function, and this is a great help in decision-making. It allows the operator to ask the program the effect on the figures inserted if one of the variables changes. In the above chart, the businessman might want to know how the profit will be affected if the cost of sales increases by 5%. Keying in the +5% formula instantly updates the cost of sales and all the other figures affected by the change. Again, a manager may be estimating the incomes and costs expected to flow from a new investment and can see the effect on the overall picture of, for example, an increase in the interest rate. This function allows the manager to see the effects of a wide range of possibilities and options without spending valuable time in making mechanical calculations.

13.3 Accounting Packages

These are database programs which are specially designed for bookkeeping and accounts. They work on the double-entry principle but they do not require transactions to be entered twice. A new business could use such a package from the outset but it is not difficult to switch from a manual system. The operator begins by entering all the necessary information eg existing balances from the sales, purchases, nominal and cash ledgers, details of customers and suppliers, defaults for value-added tax, cash discounts etc. After this it is necessary to enter each transaction only once – the computer will complete the double entry in the appropriate accounts and at the same time transfer this to the trial balance, profit and loss account and balance sheet, which are kept on a running basis. Every transaction which is entered goes into a check-list called an **Audit Trail** and this enables the bookkeeper to see exactly what has been recorded and to trace errors more easily.

In addition to the above, the package will raise invoices and print these onto company stationery, produce reports on various aspects of the firm's finances eg cash flow, maintain accurate stock records, keep debtor records and produce **Aged Debtors Analyses** (which show the age of each outstanding debt), do payrolls, manage investments by tracking the current market prices and returns on the firm's investments and perform a wide range of other functions.

13.4 Advantages of Computers in Accounting

There are many advantages to a firm of using computers for accounting tasks. Firstly, the time taken to complete double-entry bookkeeping is much less than in a manual system. For example, when a sale is made on credit, the invoice is raised via the computer program which will then debit the customer's account and credit the sales account, enter both in the trial balance and as an income in the profit and loss account and also enter the transaction in the Audit Trail. This is a much quicker process than if a bookkeeping office had to go through the manual procedures of keeping day books and ledgers and a lot more information can be handled in the same time. Large companies who deal with the accounts of thousands of customers and suppliers would find it impossible to cope with the volume of work without a computerised accounting program. At the same time the work done is more accurate as computers do not make errors when correct information is fed into them.

These increases in speed and accuracy mean a great saving in labour hours as the same work can be done by a smaller accounting staff or, put another way, the same staff can handle a much greater workload. The result is a great saving in bookkeeping and accounting costs to businesses.

Modern computerised accounting packages are user-friendly and it does not take a long period of training for someone to learn how to operate one.

13.5 Disadvantages of Computers in Accounting

Perhaps the worst problem associated with computerised systems happens when they break down, especially in the case of a large company with all its records on disk. We have only to think of the anxiety (largely unfounded, as it turned out) suffered in the run-up to the year 2000 by people who feared that their systems were not 'Y2K compatible'. Although computers do not make many errors, they can lose data and this is why users are always advised to back-up their systems.

Although modern accounting packages are user-friendly, many people operating them do not actually understand the principles of what they are doing – they let the computer complete the operations without having much knowledge of bookkeeping or accounting. Where this is the case, it is desirable for staff to attend training courses in at least basic bookkeeping.

Firms save money on staffing costs but they let themselves in for another set of expenses. The capital and installation costs of a computerised system are high and staff have to be trained to use the system. In addition the rapid advances in technology which are happening continuously mean that a system is out-of-date almost as soon as it has been installed. From time to time firms have to bear the costs of upgrading their systems to faster ones with a larger capacity.

Lastly, computers may hold records safely and produce a lot of valuable information but they are still no substitute for a skilled and experienced accountant who can analyse the figures, read between the lines and understand the deeper implications of the firm's data and who can make decisions based on them.

13.6 The Effects of Computers on the Workforce

People's jobs are made easier when information can be quickly and easily stored and retrieved on a computer and at the same time boring and repetitious manual tasks can be handled by the computer. On the other hand, computer tasks tend to be repetitive and sitting at a computer screen all day is tiring and can produce problems of eye strain, backache, repetitive stress syndrome etc. There can also be psychological problems associated with the anxiety of having access to an almost infinite amount of information and of not being able to claim ignorance of matters about which a wealth of data is now available on the Internet.

When computers are introduced into an office, members of staff who are not 'computer-literate' must be trained, either at a training centre like a local college or on the job. Some people enjoy the challenge and variety of learning something different but others do not take easily to change, feel threatened by the new technology and the fear of the unknown, and are not confident that they will be able to handle it well.

The introduction of computerised systems can certainly mean job losses among those who were previously doing manual operations but at the same time new jobs become available in computer operating and programming. For instance, the commercial banks

in the UK have laid off thousands of employees from their branches but the increase in telephone banking has created new positions in the banks' telephone centres.

13.7 Examination Questions

It is unlikely that a long essay question would be set on this topic but setting part-questions on the various aspects of computerised accounting is becoming popular with examiners. Such a part-question could follow a standard bookkeeping or final accounts question.

Questions

Question 13.1

Barney runs a small plant-hire business. He employs one office assistant who types his correspondence on a personal computer and keeps all his financial records in a system of written ledgers.

(a) Explain to Barney the advantages of buying a computerised accounting software package for his computer.
(b) Advise him what steps he will have to take before the computerised system can be running smoothly.

Author's Question

Question 13.2

(a) Explain in general terms what can be achieved with computerised accounting software.
(b) What are the advantages and disadvantages to a large firm of doing its accounting on the computer?

Author's Question

Part II
Cost Accounting

14

Manufacturing Accounts

14.1 Introduction

Accounting for manufacturing businesses is more complicated than for trading organisations because, in addition to the buying and selling functions of the warehouse and offices, the manufacturing function of the factory also has to be accounted for. This is done in the **manufacturing account**, which is a historic cost statement of all the costs incurred in production. Its purpose is to determine production cost.

Manufacturing accounts are a good starting point to our study of cost accounting because it is the main link between financial accounting and costing. The financial accountant is interested in the manufacturing account because it forms part of the year-end income statement, the cost accountant because it reveals the amounts of the various costs the factory has incurred over the past financial year.

14.2 Basic Layout

There are many costs involved in manufacture and the account lists these by type in a particular order. A distinction is made between **direct costs** and **indirect costs**. Direct costs are those costs which can be attributed to individual units of production whereas indirect costs are overheads which cannot be traced to particular units. For example, the amount of wood used in the manufacture of a table is a direct cost. So is the labour cost of a machine operator since the amount of his wages embodied in each table can be ascertained by multiplying the amount of time spent by his wage rate. In contrast, the labour of the factory supervisor or cleaner is indirect since their work covers all machines and all units of tables generally, making it difficult to allocate their cost to individual units.

Direct costs may be either direct materials, direct labour or direct expenses (such as salesmen's commission or royalty payable on units sold). The sum of direct costs gives us what is called **prime cost**. Adding indirect costs to this gives production cost. To arrive at total cost we need to add selling and distribution costs and administration expenses.

Statement of Costs

	£000	£000
Direct material		4
Direct labour		5
Direct expenses		1
Prime cost		10
Indirect factory overheads		5
Production cost		15

Selling and distribution cost	3
Administration expenses	2
	5
Total cost	20

The total production cost is then transferred to the trading account, adjusted for stocks of finished goods, and deducted from sales to find gross profit in the usual way. Finally, the profit and loss account and balance sheet are drawn up.

These three elements of the income statement can conveniently be regarded as:

Account	Place	Activity	Costs
Manufacturing account	Factory	Production	Production costs
Trading account	Warehouse	Buying and selling	Selling and distribution costs
Profit and loss account	Office	Administration	Administration expenses

The following points should be noted with regard to drawing up manufacturing accounts.

Whereas a trading firm has stocks of only finished goods, a manufacturing concern has three types of stock – raw materials, work-in-progress (representing partly-completed goods) and finished goods. In all three cases, the value of opening stock is added and that of closing stock is deducted.

(a) The stocks of raw materials are included in prime cost as they affect the amount of raw materials used. Opening stock is added to purchases of raw materials and closing stock is deducted to arrive at the cost of raw materials used.

(b) The total cost of production which emerges from adding prime cost to factory overheads is the cost of producing everything, including goods which have not yet been finished and are in a partly-completed state. Since these goods are not ready to be sold yet, they cannot be transferred to cost of sales in the trading account and so we add the opening stock and deduct the closing stock of work in progress to arrive at the total factory cost of finished goods.

(c) The stocks of finished goods are included in the trading account in the usual way, i.e. we add the opening stock to and deduct the closing stock from the cost of production of finished goods plus any purchases of finished goods which the firm may have made.

The year-end stock of finished goods is valued at total manufacturing cost, i.e. it includes a share of factory overheads. In Chapter 20 we shall see that there is some controversy about whether this should be done on an absorption or a marginal costing basis.

The factory and office share some common expenses, such as rent and rates, light and heat. These are apportioned on some logical basis such as area or wattage. Apportionment of overheads is considered in more detail in Chapter 17 on overhead absorption costing. Questions usually disclose the total of the expense in the trial balance and instructions on the split are given in the additional notes. If the expense to be apportioned has an amount owing or prepaid, the accrual or prepayment in the total to be apportioned must be taken into account in the calculation.

Some manufacturers also buy finished goods and sell them alongside their own. In this case, we add the amount of finished goods purchased to the factory cost transferred from the manufacturing account to the trading account and include it in the cost of sales.

Let us now look at an example of the income statement of a manufacturer.

Manufacturing, Trading, and Profit and Loss Account

	£000	£000
Raw materials:		
Opening stock	33	
Purchases	320	
Carriage inwards	6	
Less closing stock	(20)	
Cost of raw materials consumed		339
Manufacturing wages	310	
Royalties	30	
		340
Prime cost		679
Factory overhead expenses		
Indirect labour	55	
Power	70	
Factory rent and rates	25	
Factory light and heat	18	
Depreciation on plant and machinery	60	
		228
Factory cost of production		907
Add opening stock of work in progress		30
Less closing stock of work in progress		(20)
Factory cost of finished goods		£917
Sales		1 500
Less cost of goods sold		
Opening stock of finished goods	12	
Factory cost of finished goods	917	
Less closing stock of finished goods	(9)	
Cost of sales		(920)
Gross profit		580
Discounts received		3
		583
Selling and distribution costs		
Carriage outwards	2	
Depreciation on delivery vans	13	
Advertising	22	
Salesmen's salaries	150	
		(187)
Administration expenses		
Office rent and rates	23	
Office light and heat	5	
General expenses	7	
Administrative salaries	45	
		(80)
Financial costs		
Bank charges	1	
Interest payable	3	
		(4)
Net profit		£312

14.3 Factory Profit

Some firms charge out goods from factory to warehouse at an amount in excess of production cost. A percentage or **profit loading** is added to the factory cost and is a notional profit on the goods produced. This is done to give some credit to the efforts of the factory workforce and managers, at the same time charging the warehouse a more realistic amount for the goods it receives – after all, if it had to buy from outside it would have to pay more than just manufacturing cost. In this way the gross profit can be divided into two – that attributable to manufacturing the goods and that attributable to selling them.

To put this into effect we take the following steps.

(i)   Add the profit loading to the production cost of finished goods to arrive at the transfer price to the warehouse (trading account). The narration for the profit loading should be 'gross profit on manufacture'.

(ii)   Now transfer the increased production cost (i.e. original cost plus profit loading) to the trading account and use it, together with the stocks of finished goods, to find the cost of sales in the normal way. In effect this increases the cost of sales and shows only the gross profit which is attributable to the warehouse – this is less than it would have been if we had not made the adjustment.

(iii)   Now bring the profit loading back from the manufacturing account and add it on to warehouse gross profit to give the total gross profit for the firm as a whole. We therefore have the correct gross profit split into two and we continue the profit and loss account to find the net profit.

There is one more complication of the profit-loading adjustment. Since a business cannot recognise profit until a sale is made and goods delivered to the customer (the realisation concept) we have a problem with the year-end closing stock of finished goods, since they include an element for factory profit. The profit has not yet been realised, so it is necessary to reduce the value of the stock by the amount of factory profit credited to it. This reduced value then appears in the balance sheet. The double entry in the first year of trading is

Debit the profit and loss account, i.e. deduct the amount from net profit

Credit the provision for unrealised profit account and deduct the amount from stock in the balance sheet.

In subsequent years, adjustments will have to be made to the provision according to whether the closing stock is bigger or smaller than the opening stock each year. If closing stock is more than opening stock, we need to increase the provision for unrealised profit by the amount of the difference which represents the unrealised profit. We find this figure in the following way.

Deduct the closing stock from the opening stock. Now multiply this figure by the percentage of the profit loading (i.e. the percentage by which the factory cost is increased on transfer from the factory to the warehouse) and divide the result by this percentage + 100.

For example, if the opening stock is £15 000 and the closing stock £16 600 the difference is £1 600. If the profit loading is 25%, the calculation is:

$$\frac{1\,600 \times 25}{125} = £320$$

This figure represents the amount of the increase in stock (i.e. the profit loading) and it is by this amount that we adjust the provision for unrealised profit. If the closing stock is greater than the opening stock, we increase the provision and if it is smaller, we decrease the provision.

So, if the closing stock is greater than the opening stock:

Debit the profit and loss account with the calculated amount.

Credit the provision for unrealised profit account with the calculated amount (i.e. deduct this amount from the net profit) and deduct the new larger provision from stock in the balance sheet.

If however the closing stock is less than opening stock, we have to decrease the provision. The opposite entries are made.

Debit the provision for unrealised profit account with the calculated amount.

Credit the profit and loss account with the calculated amount (i.e. add the amount to the net profit) and deduct the new smaller provision from stock in the balance sheet.

This adjustment is shown at the end of the profit and loss account as 'provision for unrealised profit'.

The method of treatment of this provision is very similar to that of the provision for doubtful debts, where a new provision may be set up or where an existing provision may be increased or decreased and where each year the new provision is deducted from debtors in the balance sheet.

The purpose of adding a profit loading to factory cost is that it enables a firm to compare the gross profit margin or mark-up on goods it manufactured itself with those which it bought i.e. it attempts to treat the products as if they had been bought from an external supplier. It has no purpose as far as financial reporting is concerned and is simply a cost accounting technique which enables managers to see the market value of the goods they have produced and to make assessments on this basis.

Illustration

The following information relates to the first two years of operations of Hurley Ltd.

Year ended	31 December 2001	31 December 2002
	£	£
Sales	15 000	19 000
Factory cost of finished goods	10 000	12 000
Opening stock of finished goods		1 500
Closing stock of finished goods	1 500	1 100
Selling and distribution costs	800	900
Administration expenses	700	700

It is company policy to charge goods to the warehouse at factory cost + 25%.

Prepare, for both years:

(a) the provision for unrealised profit account
(b) the trading and profit and loss account

Answer
Provision for unrealised profit

		£			£
31.12.2001	Balance c/d	300	31.12.2001	Profit and loss (W_1)	300
31.12.2002	Profit and loss	80	1.1.2002	Balance b/d	300
31.12.2002	Balance c/d (W_2)	220			
		300			300

Workings

W_1

The provision on 31.12.2001 is calculated on the closing stock of £1 500.

$$\frac{1500 \times 25}{125} = £300$$

The provision is *not* £1 500 × 25% as we are working backwards. The £1 500 already includes the provision for profit so we have to find out how much of this is 25% of the original sum.

W_2

The new provision on 31.12.2002 is calculated on the new closing stock i.e. on the £1 100

$$\frac{1100 \times 25}{125} = £220$$

The new provision is therefore less than the old one (this is logical since the new closing stock is less than the opening stock for the year). We thus adjust the profit and loss account with the difference between the old provision and the new one

= £300 – 220 = £80

Since the provision has decreased, we add the £80 to the net profit and deduct the £220 from the stock in the balance sheet.

Hurley Ltd
Manufacturing, Trading and Profit and Loss Account for the years ended

(Beginning at the end of the manufacturing account to show the adjustment)

	31 December 2001		31 December 2002	
	£	£	£	£
Factory cost of finished goods	10 000		12 000	
Gross profit on manufacture (25%)	2 500		3 000	
Factory cost transferred to trading account		£12 500		£15 000
Sales		15 000		19 000
Opening stock			1 500	
Factory cost from manufacturing account	12 500		15 000	
Less closing stock	(1 500)		(1 100)	
Cost of sales		(11 000)		(15 400)
Gross profit		4 000		3 600
Add back profit loading		2 500		3 000
		6 500		6 600
Selling and distribution costs	800		900	
Administrative expenses	700		700	
		(15 00)		(16 00)
Provision for unrealised profit		(300)		80
Net profit		£4 700		£5 080

14.4 The Limitations of a Manufacturing Account

A manufacturing account is actually a cost statement which divides manufacturing costs into their various categories and which gives the totals for each category. It does not however give any idea of how many units were produced for this cost or of the unit cost of the product. Neither does it show how these costs compare with those which were budgeted.

Questions

Question 14.1

The following balances have been extracted from the books of the Staghill Manufacturing Company Ltd at 30 April 1999.

	£
Stocks at 1 May 1998: raw materials	26 740
work in progress	23 170
finished goods	37 440
Factory wages: direct	372 560
indirect	74 280
Royalties	6 500
Heating and lighting	26 650
General factory expenses	47 080
Insurances	15 010
General office expenses	36 740
Purchases of raw materials	278 630
Sales	1 163 750
Plant and machinery at cost	210 000
Provision for depreciation of plant and machinery	126 000
Provision for unrealised profit	6 240

Additional information

1) At 30 April 1999 stocks were as follows:

	£
Raw materials	24 390
Work in progress	24 640
Finished goods	36 720

2) Heating and lighting expenses and insurances are to be apportioned $\frac{2}{3}$ to the factory and $\frac{1}{3}$ to the company's offices.

3) At 30 April 1999 an electricity bill of £800 remained unpaid and insurance policies paid for the year ended 30 April 2000 amounted to £760.

4) The company provides for depreciation on plant and machinery at the rate of 10% per annum on cost.

5) The company always transfers finished goods from the factory to the warehouse at factory cost plus 20%.

REQUIRED

(a) Prepare the manufacturing, trading and profit and loss account for the Staghill
Manufacturing Company Ltd for the year ended 30 April 1999.   **(32 marks)**

(b) Identify and discuss **two** limitations of preparing a manufacturing account.   **(6 marks)**

(c) Why do some businesses transfer finished goods to the trading account at more
than cost price?   **(6 marks)**

(d) Explain the purpose of providing for unrealised profit in the books of a
manufacturing business.   **(6 marks)**

Associated Examining Board Advanced Level

Question 14.2

Sparky Ltd manufactures light bulbs for domestic and industrial use. During the year
ended 31 March 1998, the company added a new product, long-life batteries, to its
manufacturing range. The trial balance of the business at 31 March 1998 included the
following balances:

Trial Balance as at March 1998

	Debit £	Credit £
Sales: Light bulbs		1 821 880
Batteries		523 180
Raw materials purchased	522 600	
Production wages	296 756	
Factory administration costs	412 800	
Factory rent and rates	3 200	
Provision for depreciation on plant and machinery 1 April 1997		12 740
General factory expenses	38 380	
Stocks at 1 April 1997:		
Raw materials	116 540	
Work in progress	34 940	
Finished goods	250 600	

Notes:

1) Closing stocks at 31 March 1998 were:
   Raw materials: £100 204
   Work in progress: Light bulbs £36 300   Batteries £22 080
   Finished goods: Light bulbs £379 780   Batteries £30 010

2) The prime cost of manufacturing is divided 70% light bulbs and 30% batteries
   while factory administration and rent and rates are split in the ratio 3 : 2. £24 198
   of the general factory expenses related to light bulb manufacturing and the
   remainder to batteries.

3) Depreciation is charged at 20% per annum on a straight line basis. Plant and
   machinery used for light bulb manufacturing cost £36 000 and that for battery
   manufacturing £14 000.

4) Finished goods are transferred to the sales department at a notional gross profit
   margin of 10% on factory cost.

REQUIRED

(a) Prepare manufacturing and trading accounts for the year ended 31 March 1998, showing clearly the profit arising from both the manufacture and sale of light-bulbs and the manufacture and sale of batteries.
(Answers must include adjustments for unrealised profit.) **(39 marks)**

(b) Explain why a company might wish to calculate separate profit figures for its manufacturing and trading activities. **(10 marks)**

(c) The management of Sparky Ltd is considering expansion by starting to manufacture torches. What might be the financial implications of such a decision? **(8 marks)**

Welsh Joint Education Committee Advanced Level

Question 14.3

Valley Ltd, a manufacturer, produced the following financial information for the year ended 31 December 1998.

Trial Balance

	Debit £000	Credit £000
Ordinary share capital (£1 each)		240
Share premium		20
Retained profits at 1 January 1998		2
Freehold buildings at cost on 1 January 1998	134	
Plant and machinery at cost on 1 January 1998	100	
Provision for depreciation of plant and machinery on 1 January 1998		36
Office machinery at cost on 1 January 1998	36	
Provision for depreciation of office machinery on 1 January 1998		3
Sales		300
Purchases of raw materials	50	
Direct labour	50	
Direct power	12	
Factory overheads – variable	18	
– fixed	22	
Marketing expenses	20	
Administrative overheads	34	
Stocks: 1 January 1998 – Raw materials	28	
– Work in progress	72	
– Finished goods	25	
	£601	£601

Additional information

* Freehold buildings were revalued at £200 000 during the year 1998 and this figure is to be brought into the accounts.

* Depreciation is to be provided on fixed assets as follows:
  – Freehold buildings: 2% per annum on revalued figure
  – Plant and machinery: 25% per annum on written down figure
  – Office machinery: 10% per annum on cost.

- Depreciation of freehold buildings is to be apportioned between factory and administrative overheads in the ratio of 3:1.

- Direct labour to be accrued at 31 December 1998 amounted to £2 000 and marketing expenses prepaid at 31 December 1998 amounted to £1 000.

- Stock valuations at 31 December 1998:

	£
Raw materials	32 000
Work in progress	80 000
Finished goods at cost	40 000

- The finished goods at 31 December 1998 had a net realisable value of £38 000.

- The market value of goods manufactured during the year ended 31 December 1998 was £220 000.

- A dividend of 10p per share is proposed.

REQUIREMENT

(a) Prepare:

   (i) the Manufacturing, Trading and Profit and Loss Accounts for the year ended 31 December 1998 showing clearly
- prime cost
- cost of production
- manufacturing profit
- gross profit
- net profit.   **(18 marks)**

   (ii) the Appropriation Account for the year ended 31 December 1998.   **(4 marks)**

(b) Discuss the arguments for and against the revaluation of the freehold buildings.   **(8 marks)**

Northern Ireland Council for the Curriculum Examinations and Assessment Advanced Level

Question 14.4

The trial balance of YMB plc at 30th June, 1995 was as follows:

	Debit £000	Credit £000
Ordinary shares of £0.25 each, fully paid		50 000
6% preference shares of £1.00 each, fully paid		2 000
Share premium		8 000
Retained profit at 30 June 1994		36 120
Freehold land and buildings at cost	15 000	
Plant and equipment at cost	80 000	
Motor vehicles at cost	10 000	
Depreciation provisions at 30 June 1994:		
Freehold land and buildings		7 200
Plant and equipment		12 500
Motor vehicles		2 000
Stocks at 30 June 1994:		
Materials	13 000	
Work in progress	84	
Finished products	9 376	
Packaging materials	18	
Trade debtors	23 000	
Provision for bad debts		1 000
Cash at bank	2 000	
Trade creditors		6 000
Sales		200 000
Purchases of materials	62 000	
Manufacturing wages	29 500	
Variable manufacturing overhead expenses	20 000	
Fixed manufacturing overhead expenses	34 895	
Variable distribution costs	2 702	
Fixed distribution costs	2 970	
Variable administration expenses	4 000	
Fixed administration expenses	14 155	
Preference dividend	120	
Interim ordinary dividend	2 000	
	£324 820	£324 820

You are given the following information:

1) There were no additions to fixed assets during the year.

2) Freehold land and buildings are to be depreciated at the rate of 2% per annum by the straight line method, assuming no residual value.

3) Plant and equipment are to be depreciated at the rate of 10% per annum on cost.

4) Motor vehicles are to be depreciated at the rate of 25% per annum by the diminishing (reducing) balance method.

5) The annual depreciation charges are to be allocated as follows:

	Land and buildings	Plant and machinery	Motor vehicles
Fixed manufacturing overhead expenses	75%	80%	
Fixed distribution costs	10%	5%	80%
Fixed administration expenses	15%	15%	20%

6) The bad debts provision is to be increased by an amount equal to 1% of sales. The item is to be regarded as variable distribution cost.

7) Stocks at 30 June 1995, valued at full manufacturing cost where appropriate, were:

	£000
Materials	15 000
Work in progress	80
Finished products	10 900
Packaging materials (variable distribution costs)	20

8) Prepayments and accruals at 30 June 1995 were:

	Prepayments £000	Accruals £000
Manufacturing wages		500
Fixed administration expenses	900	1 100
Variable distribution costs	100	400

9) Provision is to be made for corporation tax at the rate of 50% of the net profit (advance corporation tax is to be ignored) and a final ordinary dividend of £0.02 per share.

YOU ARE REQUIRED TO PREPARE
for YMB plc's internal purposes, the following historic cost financial statements:

(a) a manufacturing, trading and profit and loss account, in vertical and columnar form, for the year ended 30th June, 1995;   **(22 marks)**
(b) a balance sheet, in vertical and columnar form, as at that date.   **(18 marks)**

Chartered Institute of Management Accountants

Question 14.5

The following is the trial balance of Shutter Ltd, a manufacturing company, at 31 December 1997:

	£000	£000
Ordinary shares of £1 each		2 000
Profit and loss account at 1 January 1997		1 100
Debtors and creditors	220	150
Stock of raw materials at 1 January 1997	120	
Stock of finished goods at 1 January 1997	160	
Land and buildings at cost	2 500	
Manufacturing equipment at cost	240	
Sales		3 570
Raw material purchases	1 800	
Heat, light and power	98	
Manufacturing wages	219	

Non-manufacturing wages	101	
Manufacturing expenses	96	
Non-manufacturing expenses	75	
Rates	84	
Bad debts	6	
Provision for bad debts at 1 January 1997		12
Accumulated depreciation on		96
manufacturing equipment at 1 January 1997		
Bank balance	9	
New finance		2 000
Purchase of Bolt & Co	3 000	
Interim dividend paid 30 June 1997	200	
	£8 928	£8 928

You are given the following information:

1. Stocks at 31 December 1997, valued at cost, were:

	£000
Raw materials	135
Finished goods	179

2. Manufacturing equipment is depreciated over a life of ten years using the straight line method and assuming a zero residual value. Assets are only depreciated if they have been held for at least one month during the year. It is the company's policy not to depreciate land and buildings.

3. Heat, light and power and rates are apportioned 80% manufacturing and 20% non-manufacturing. At 31 December 1997, the following adjustments needed to be made:

	£000
Heat, light and power accrual	12
Rates prepayment	14

4. The provision for bad debts at 31 December 1997 is to be increased to £14 000.

5. The balance described as 'new finance' arose on 31 December 1997 when the company issued a debenture for £1 500 000, paying 10% annual interest and 500 000 £1 ordinary shares. This was to help finance the purchase on 31 December 1997 of the business of Bolt & Co at a total cost of £3 000 000. The physical assets acquired were:

	£000
Land and buildings	1 700
Plant and equipment	800
Stock of finished goods	190

The finished goods acquired were not included in the year end stock-take reported in note 1 above.

The policy of the directors of Shutter Ltd is to show as low a gearing position as possible at the year end, consistent with acceptable accounting practice.

6. The directors estimate that the profit for the year will result in a corporation tax charge of £250 000.

7. The directors recommend paying a final dividend of 15 pence per share in issue at
    1 December 1998.

REQUIRED

Prepare the manufacturing, trading and profit and loss account of Shutter Ltd for the
year to 31 December 1997 and the balance sheet at that date.   **(20 marks)**

Institute of Financial Services

15

Cost Classification and Labour Costing

15.1 Introduction

Cost accounting differs from financial accounting in that it prepares information for internal purposes which form the basis of managerial decisions. Costs are one of the most important aspects of a firm's performance and they must be analysed in detail.

Costs can be classified in several different ways according to the purpose required, i.e. whether it is to prepare year-end final accounts, for decision-making, planning, performance evaluation or control.

Direct and Indirect Costs

In the previous chapter, Manufacturing Accounts, we met two ways in which the accountant classifies costs in order to prepare the year-end income statement. One was by function – according to the purpose they serve, e.g. production cost, distribution cost, administration cost. The other was classification into **direct** and **indirect** costs, direct costs being those costs which can be attributed to individual units of production and indirect costs being those which cannot be traced to individual units. This classification was needed in order to distinguish between the prime cost of production and overheads.

Fixed and Variable Costs

A classification vital for decision-making and planning is in terms of cost behaviour in relation to changes in the level of activity. Activity may be measured as the level of output, number of hours worked, number of miles travelled, or number of clients seen, according to the nature of the business. **Fixed costs** do not change with the level of activity. This is because they accrue on a time basis rather than with activity. Examples include rent and rates, interest on loans and executive salaries. **Variable costs** vary directly with the level of activity, examples being direct materials, direct labour and direct expenses (e.g. royalty payable per unit). The graph below illustrates the contrasting nature of fixed and variable costs.

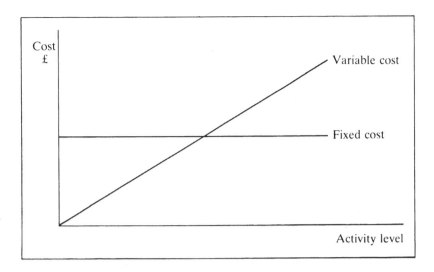

In addition, some costs are of a **semi-variable** nature. As the name implies, these include both a fixed and variable component. For example the cost of electricity and telephone incur a standing charge which is fixed, but also a charge related to usage, which is variable. Thus the total bill rises with increased usage. The graph below illustrates this.

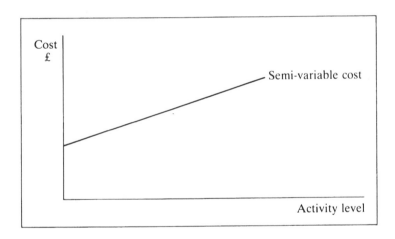

Fixed costs are fixed only over a limited range of output and once this limit is reached, they increase as a 'lump' because the expenditure is indivisible. For example, let us take a supervisor capable of supervising work up to 400 man hours a week. His weekly pay is £200. An activity level of 300 man hours necessitates employment of one supervisor. An increase to 350 hours does not change the cost – it is fixed over this range of activity. If the number of man hours worked rises to 450 however, cost does change by a lump to £400 as a second supervisor is needed. In this case the cost has increased more than proportionately to the increase in activity level as is shown in the graph below. Now the cost of the second supervisor will be fixed until this person reaches full capacity and a third is needed.

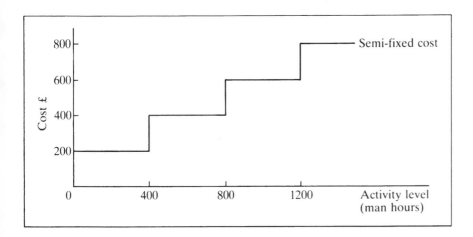

The cost line looks rather like a series of steps – for this reason fixed costs are also known as step costs.

Many examination questions on the costing of processes or projects require you to deal with fixed and variable costs. Variable costs are almost always given per unit and you find the total by multiplying the unit cost by the number of units produced. (Just to make a change, a question could give you the total variable cost for a certain number of units and you would then be expected to adjust this for some new number of units.) Fixed costs, on the other hand, are often quoted in questions as a total since they are not related to the number of units produced but you must be careful. Some questions will give you the fixed cost per unit at some given level of production and expect you to adjust this to a new number of units. In this case you have to multiply the fixed cost per unit by the new number of units and not assume that the original figure you worked with has not changed. It is essential to read the question carefully in order to understand the information you have been given.

The distinction between fixed and variable (or marginal) costs is crucial when making management accounting decisions concerning the number of units to produce, whether to accept an order, whether to make a component or purchase it ready-made etc. When considering whether or not to produce extra units, the cost accountant can either cost the additional production in full by including both fixed and variable costs or take into account only the variable costs. The latter approach is justified by the fact that the fixed costs have already been paid and only the extra (marginal) costs incurred by going ahead with the additional production are relevant. As long as the variable costs can be covered by the price charged for the units, the firm will increase its total profit. We shall consider this in more detail in Chapter 20 on absorption and marginal costing.

In addition to decision-making, the above classification (by cost behaviour with changes in activity level) is important to the process of budgetary control and variance analysis, as we shall see in Chapters 22 and 23. It is also an essential part of break-even analysis, considered in Chapter 24.

Another classification useful for decision-making is whether a cost is relevant or irrelevant to a future decision. For example, in choosing between two alternatives past costs (or **sunk costs**) are irrelevant since their level cannot be affected by a future decision. So too are future common costs. The only relevant costs are the future differential costs, i.e. those costs which are avoidable and which differ between the alternatives under consideration. Relevant costing and decision-making is looked at in Chapter 21.

Large organisations are often de-centralised into divisions with managers being responsible for the performance of their own division. Their performance is frequently monitored by top management using the techniques of standard costing, budgeting and variances. In evaluating performance top management must be careful to classify costs into whether they are **controllable** or **non-controllable** by the person they are seeking to evaluate. Thus while the direct labour cost would be classified as a controllable cost, the head office overhead apportioned to the division would not. If a manager is blamed for an adverse variance on a cost which he cannot control, he is not likely to support and co-operate with the evaluation system. More on this in Chapter 23.

15.2 Cost Units, Cost Centres and Profit Centres

A **cost unit** is simply a unit to which costs are related and to which they are charged. The specific unit will vary from industry to industry. In steel-making the cost unit would be cost per ton of steel, in motor manufacturing cost per car, in dairy farming cost per gallon of milk, in bottle-making cost per thousand bottles and in transport cost per mile travelled.

A **cost centre** is a section of a business to which costs can be charged. It may be a location, a person or an item of equipment, eg a particular factory department or a particular stage in the production process. Each business will choose cost centres which are relevant to its particular circumstances eg a manufacturing firm will allocate costs to each process in the manufacturing cycle, a department store to each department and a civil engineering firm to each contract. The costs charged to the cost centre are attributed to cost units. In other words, a cost centre is a method by which cost units are gathered together. It is possible for a cost unit and a cost centre to be the same thing, but in most medium-sized to large businesses there are many individual cost units in each cost centre.

A business will take the costs contained in its manufacturing, trading and profit and loss account and re-analyse them in order to allocate them to its cost centres. In this way it can find a total cost for each department, process, job or contract.

A **profit centre** is similar to a cost centre but it identifies profits and not just costs. It is a part of the business for which costs and revenues are calculated. A typical profit centre would consist of a number of cost centres.

15.3 Determination of Unit Cost

One of the chief functions of the cost accountant is to determine unit cost. The financial accountant needs this information to value stocks and determine gross profit and the management accountant needs it for performance evaluation, control, decision-making and planning. The total cost of a unit can be split into:

	£
Direct materials	150 000
Direct labour	200 000
Direct expenses	50 000
Prime cost	400 000
Production overhead	60 000
Production cost	460 000
Administration, selling and distribution overhead	40 000
Total cost	£500 000

There are several different methods of costing the amount of direct materials used in a unit – these are looked at in the next chapter. Determination of the unit overhead cost is no simple matter and is considered in the next chapter. In the remainder of this chapter we look at direct labour and direct expenses.

15.4 Labour Remuneration Schemes

There are several alternative methods of remunerating labour, each with a different associated cost. They may be classified into the following types of payment

- salaries;
- time-rate, i.e. on the basis of time worked;
- piecework, i.e. on the basis of output.

Salaries

Salaried employees receive an annual salary paid monthly. It is usually expected that they will perform the job they have contracted to do however long it takes them and so they do not normally claim overtime for long hours worked. However, many firms pay their managers bonuses and these are often performance-related.

Time-Rate

Workers on time-rate are paid according to the number of hours they have done at an agreed rate per hour. Overtime is usually paid at a higher rate for extra hours worked and bonuses may also be paid for high productivity or for good quality of work.

Example

George works a 38-hour week at a basic hourly rate of £5.50 per hour. Hours worked in excess of 38 hours are paid at the overtime rate of £7.50 per hour. Last week George worked 48 hours. His pay will be as follows:

	£
38 hours @ £5.50	209
10 hours @ £7.50	75
Total gross pay for the week	284

Time-rate is a simple system to operate and workers understand it and feel that it compensates them fairly for the time they have sold to their employer. It is suitable for jobs where it is difficult to calculate exactly what each worker has produced, especially in the case of indirect labour where output cannot be measured in units. However, since workers know they will be paid the same whether they work hard or not, there is no incentive to increase output or to discover and implement more efficient working practices and constant supervision is necessary to ensure that people are performing their duties. At the same time resentment may be caused in more efficient workers who see that they are paid no more than idle workers.

To counter the above problems, extra payments can be made:

(a) a high day-rate scheme may be adopted which tries to combine time-rate with an output-based bonus. An output figure is established which is above the normal performance but is still possible to achieve and above-normal time rates are paid to workers who reach this. However if external factors such as material shortages or machine breakdowns etc occur, it becomes impossible to achieve the higher level of output to earn the higher rate and workers can then feel frustrated.

(b) a timekeeping bonus may be paid to workers who are always on time for work and who have a low absentee record.

(c) a continuous working bonus may be paid to workers when the factory has achieved continuous production without stoppages.

Piecework

This is an output-based method of payment whereby the worker is paid an agreed rate per unit produced or per operation carried out. The same rate may be paid for all levels of output (**straight piecework**) or it may increase progressively at higher levels of output (**differential piecework**). Under such a scheme a worker is not paid for units which are rejected by quality control.

Example

Jackie is a production line worker who is paid a straight piecework rate of £1.70 per unit. Last week she produced 125 units 20 of which were rejected by quality inspection. She will be paid for the 105 good units at £1.70 each, i.e. £178.50.

Jackie's factory manager has decided to switch to a differential piecework system by which she will be paid £1.50 per unit for the first 50 units, £1.95 for the next 50 units and £2.20 for all units above that. Her 105 good units will now be paid as follows.

	£
50 units @ 1.50	75.00
50 units @ £1.95	97.50
5 units @ £2.20	11.00
Total pay for week	183.50

There is now a strong incentive for Jackie to exceed the 100 units a week level. Problems arise when external factors make it impossible to achieve higher levels of production (as mentioned above) and piecework is usually accompanied by a safeguard known as a guaranteed day rate. If earnings from piecework fall below what is considered to be a normal day time-rate, the employer guarantees to pay this day rate. Again workers may be unhappy with the various rates paid and with the levels of output necessary to earn those rates, and for this reason trade unions are often involved in the meetings which set the rates.

Bonus Schemes

Bonus schemes involve paying a flat rate per hour plus a bonus for achieving a given output level. There are different ways of doing this.

One scheme pays the worker a bonus by rewarding at the normal rate the time saved by him if he works more quickly than the standard time which has been set for the job; this standard is set by timing a number of workers and establishing an average for the job.

Another scheme increases the hourly rate paid in proportion to the amount of time saved by the worker in producing the average unit in comparison to the standard or average.

Example

Harry is paid £7 per hour for a basic 38-hour week with a bonus of one-third of the hours saved on each job compared with the standard time for each job. Last week he completed four jobs as follows:

Job	Standard hours	Actual hours
1	12	9
2	15	14
3	14	10
4	6	5
Total	47	38

Harry has saved 9 hours over the four jobs and he will be paid in addition for one-third of these hours at the normal rate per hour. His wage for the week will be:

	£
38 hours @ £7	266
Bonus hours (9 ÷ 3) @ £7	21
Total pay for the week	287

Both piecework and bonus schemes are types of performance-related pay. The advantages of such a system are an incentive to increase production and minimise time-wasting, which can result in a fall in the labour cost per unit. More efficient workers are attracted to the job and morale is improved. However, there can be disputes over the performance levels and rates agreed and the incentive to produce more necessitates the employment of quality control inspectors to ensure that quality is not sacrificed for quantity. Also some schemes can be complicated and thus more time-consuming and expensive to administer.

15.5 Recording Labour Costs

Where a time-rate system is used, there must be a method of recording the number of hours worked by each employee. Traditionally this was done by means of a **time clock** into which the employee inserted a card when starting and finishing work. Nowadays such machines have largely been replaced by electronic systems where the employee inserts a swipe card or plastic key and the information is sent to a computer, which calculates the hours worked.

Alternatively individual workers may have **time sheets** which are prepared on a weekly or daily basis which show the number of hours worked. They can also be used to support claims for overtime payment or time off, where a flexi-time system is in operation. Another variable shown on the sheet is idle time. This is time when the employee did no work because of some breakdown beyond his control and for which he is paid but the time cannot be charged to a job sheet as it was non-productive.

Where work is organised around specific jobs, a system of **job sheets** can be used. Each job has a particular code and work done is coded to it and recorded on the job sheet, which will show the total number of hours spent on the job irrespective of the department in which those hours were spent.

Where employees are paid on a piecework basis it is necessary to record the quantity of units produced, together with the number rejected as faulty or inferior. Idle time should also be noted and paid according to an agreed system, e.g. on the basis of average output during productive hours.

15.6 Labour Costing

This is concerned with the determination of the unit labour cost. A direct wage cost can be determined by time and motion studies estimating the standard time needed for an operation. Standard time multiplied by wage rate for each operation gives the direct wage cost embodied in each unit. No attempt is made to calculate the unit indirect wage cost since this is by definition not traceable to individual units. Instead the cost is charged to the product as part of the unit overhead, the determination of which is looked at in Chapter 17. The classification of a labour cost as being direct or indirect is sometimes not clear, as with idle-time due to a machine breakdown and overtime premiums. These are usually treated as overheads, but not in all circumstances. This complication is returned to in the section on job costing in Chapter 18.

Examination questions often ask for a calculation of the effect on a firm's costs of changing from one payment system to another, usually from time rate to a bonus system. The obvious benefit of the latter is increased productivity, but with this being rewarded with a bonus, the labour cost per unit may not fall by much and in some cases it actually rises for a while. The real benefit of increased output to a firm is a decrease in the unit overhead cost. Since most overheads do not increase with output, an increase in output reduces the overhead cost per unit. Put another way, there is better utilisation of fixed overheads. Operating a bonus scheme is thus beneficial to both employees and employer – the employees have the chance to increase their earnings and the employer benefits from a reduction in unit cost.

15.7 Direct Expenses

Direct expenses are those costs other than material and labour which can be traced to particular cost units. If for example a firm is producing a good under licence, for a royalty payment of £1 for every unit sold, this £1 is a direct expense as it can be attributed to each unit sold. Another common direct expense is salesmen's commission since this is usually related to the number of units sold.

Questions

Question 15.1

(a) Explain the following terms associated with the payments made to workers. In each case indicate the possible advantages **to the employer** of adopting the system.

    (i)   Time rates

    (ii) Piece work

    (iii) Bonus schemes

(b) Clock cards and daily time sheets are used in some wage systems. For each of these documents, **state** its purpose and the information it contains.

(15 marks)

Scottish Qualifications Authority Higher Specimen Paper

Question 15.2

You are the Cost Clerk of Jay Ltd and have been recently sent on a seminar called 'Fixed and Variable Costs – the mystery dispelled'. Three topics were examined and discussed:

- Costs and their behavioural patterns.

- Are fixed costs incorrectly named as, when output increases, fixed costs per unit decrease?

- In pricing decisions, only variable costs are relevant as fixed costs are incurred in any event.

REQUIREMENT

Write a report to the Cost Accountant which explains the above three topics.   **(15 marks)**

Northern Ireland Council for the Curriculum Examinations and Assessment Advanced Level

Question 15.3

A small company manufacturing electrical components for the domestic market pays all of its staff on an hourly basis. The managing director is reviewing this policy for the following groups of staff:

- production line workers;
- research staff;
- administration staff;
- maintenance workers.

Draft a report to the managing director explaining the alternatives to hourly rates for **each** of these groups of workers, paying particular attention to the advantages and disadvantages in each case.

                                                                           (20 marks)

London Examinations Advanced Level

Question 15.4

BSE Veterinary Services is a specialist laboratory carrying out tests on cattle to ascertain whether the cattle have any infection. At present, the laboratory carries out 12 000 tests each period but, because of current difficulties with the beef herd, demand is expected to increase to 18 000 tests a period, which would require an additional shift to be worked.

The current cost of carrying out a full test is:

	£ per test
Materials	115
Technicians' wages	30
Variable overhead	12
Fixed overhead	50

Working the additional shift would

(i)   require a shift premium of 50% to be paid to the technicians on the additional shift,

(ii)   enable a quantity discount of 20% to be obtained for all materials if an order was placed to cover 18 000 tests,

(iii)   increase fixed costs by £700 000 per period.

The current fee per test is £300.

REQUIREMENTS

(a) Prepare a profit statement for the current 12 000 capacity.   **(4 marks)**

(b) Prepare a profit statement if the additional shift was worked and 18 000 tests were carried out.   **(7 marks)**

(c) Comment on **three** other factors which should be considered before any decision is taken.   **(4 marks)**

Chartered Institute of Management Accountants

16

Material Costing and Stock Valuation

16.1 Introduction

All businesses use materials to a greater or lesser extent and they are one of the most important inputs to a manufacturing firm. Materials come under various headings:

- raw materials used in manufacture;
- components and sub-assemblies bought ready-made;
- work in progress i.e. partly finished goods which have not finished going through the manufacturing process;
- consumables e.g. cleaning materials;
- maintenance materials eg oil, spare parts etc;
- office materials e.g. stationery, computer supplies etc.

At any time a firm holds a stock of all these materials and, as we have already seen, takes an inventory at the end of each financial year to give a value to the closing stock, which then becomes next year's opening stock.

Valuing stock might at first seem to be a simple exercise but this is not the case because there are several alternative methods of valuation, each producing a different figure. The value placed on stock is of crucial importance because:

1) it affects the charge-out rate of materials issued from stores and hence the unit production cost.
2) it affects the figure for cost of goods sold which in turn affects gross profit.
3) it affects the value of net assets in the balance sheet.
4) the closing stock of one year is carried forward as the opening stock of the next year. Any error in valuation therefore affects not only that year's profit figure but also the subsequent year's.

16.2 Valuation of Stock

SSAP 9 gives guidance on the accounting treatment of stocks and long-term contracts. It is stocks which concern us here. According to this accounting standard, the determination of profit for an accounting period involves the allocation of costs to reporting periods. As part of this process, the cost of unsold or unconsumed stocks is – to the extent that it is believed to be recoverable – carried forward until the period in which the stock is sold or consumed. It is for this reason that we include opening stocks but not closing stocks in the cost of sales in the trading account.

Stocks remaining unsold should be valued at their cost and not their selling price. The specific recommendation of SSAP 9 is for firms to value stock at the '**lower of cost and net realisable value**'.

'**Cost**' is defined as that expenditure which has been incurred in bringing the product to its present location and condition. For middlemen this is just the cost of purchase plus transport costs but for manufacturers it means materials plus conversion costs i.e. money spent on direct labour and overheads to turn the materials into a finished product.

'**Net realisable value**' is the expected selling price less costs of completion, selling and distribution. Since net realisable value is normally greater than cost, stocks are normally valued at cost. However goods can become damaged or out-of-date and the firm may have to reduce the price by a large percentage to sell them off. If the firm estimates that the selling price which can reasonably be expected from the goods in their present state is less than what they cost to buy, then any stocks of these goods should be valued at their expected selling price, since this is below cost. Any additional costs incurred in selling the goods should be deducted from the expected selling price to arrive at net realisable value.

This rule complies with the concept of prudence which requires a firm not to anticipate profits but to provide for losses and to underestimate rather than overestimate future profits. Since closing stock adds on to profit in the trading account, the higher its value the greater will be the gross profit. So it must always be valued at a lower value rather than at a higher.

Example

Elaine has a shop which sells computer software and games. A few months ago she purchased a particular children's game for £25 per unit and has been selling it for £40 each. Now a new version of the game has come out on the market; since nobody wants to buy the old one, Elaine is being forced to sell her stock for £20 each. To every customer who buys the old version of the game, Elaine is giving away free a poster worth £0.50p. At the end of July, Elaine still has 10 of the old games left but she is hoping to sell them by the end of August. At what price should she value the 10 games which remain at the end of July?

The answer is that Elaine should value the games at £19.50 each. The realisable value is £20 (lower than the cost) and is reduced to net realisable value by the £0.50p poster.

In the case of most goods, net realisable value is greater than cost and so most stocks are valued at cost. But what do we mean by cost? There are three subjective areas:

1) For manufactured goods, should cost be taken as direct materials, labour, and direct expenses or should an element of overhead be charged as well? Using only variable costs is a marginal approach whereas an absorption approach includes overheads as well. This question is considered in Chapter 20.
2) If it is decided to use absorption costing and include the overheads, on what basis should fixed overheads be charged to individual stock units? The problem of allocation and apportionment of overheads is looked at in Chapter 17.
3) In a period of changing prices, should materials be issued from stores to production at the latest prices, earlier prices or an average price for the year? Further, should stock records be kept on a periodic or perpetual inventory basis? These questions are considered in this chapter.

16.3 FIFO, LIFO AND AVCO

There are three main methods of determining the cost of unsold and unused stocks:

- FIFO (First In First Out)
- LIFO (Last In First Out)
- AVCO (Average Cost)

Each of these methods produces a different result, as we shall see by working through the following example.

Example

Winston is a dealer in automatic rice cookers. On 1 January he had 15 cookers in stock at cost £30 each. His activities in January are as follows.

Purchases	Jan 04	30 units @ £32	
	Jan 10	22 units @ £34	
	Jan 20	20 units @ £36	
Sales	Jan 06		35 units @ £40
	Jan 25		40 units @ £45

At 31 January Winston had 12 cookers remaining.

Using FIFO

As its name suggests this method assumes that the first goods to come in are the first to go out, in other words that the oldest goods on hand were the first to be issued. Consequently closing stock is valued at the most recent purchase prices.

We can check the number of goods on hand by adding the number of units of the opening stock to those purchased and deducting the number sold.

i.e. 15 + (30 + 22 + 20) − (35 + 40) = 12 units

The question is how to value these 12 units.

Under FIFO they are valued at £36 each, this being the price of the last batch of purchases on 20 January.

Stock valuation: 12 @ £36 = £432.

(If the closing stock had been 21 units, then 20 of these would have been valued at £36 and 1 at £34, i.e. from the period immediately before.)

Using LIFO

As the name again suggests this method assumes that the last goods to come in are the first to go out. In other words it is assumed that the goods most recently received are issued first. Consequently, closing stock is valued at purchase prices pertaining in the earlier part of the period. LIFO calculations are more complicated than FIFO, because it is necessary to work out from which batch of purchases each individual batch of sales is made. Only in this way can closing stock be valued.

Date	Purchases	Sales	Balance	£	£
Jan 01			15 units @ £30		450
Jan 04	30 units @ £32		15 units @ £30	450	
			30 units @ £32	960	1 410
Jan 06		30 units @ £32			
		5 units @ £30	10 units @ £30		300
Jan 10	22 units @ £34		10 units @ £30	300	
			22 units @ £34	748	1 048
Jan 20	20 units @ £36		10 units @ £30	300	
			22 units @ £34	748	
			20 units @ £36	720	1 768
Jan 25		20 units @ £36	10 units @ £30	300	
		20 units @ £34	2 units @ £34	68	368

The final figure of £368 is the closing stock.

Each date in the above table shows the total position on each date.

On 1 January Winston had an opening stock of 15 units which had cost £30 each, i.e. £450.

On 4 January he purchased 30 units at £32 each (£960) and so, together with the opening stock, had a total stock valued at £1 410.

On 6 January he sold 35 units. We assume under LIFO that these came from the most recent batches, i.e. that as many as possible (30) came from the batch which cost £32 and the rest (5) came from the opening stock. The 10 units left over at this point are thus valued at the oldest price of £30. (The fact that Winston sold the goods for £40 each does not concern us here since we value stock at cost.)

On 10 January he purchased 22 units at £34 each (£748), and when we add in the other 10 units on hand he has a stock worth £1 048.

On 20 January he purchased 20 units at £36 each – this transaction has increased the stock to £1 768 (no sales have been made in the meantime).

On 25 January he sold 40 units for £45 each. Again we can ignore the £45 for stock valuation purposes as we need to use the cost price. We have to see from which batches these 40 units came, starting with the most recent; 20 came from the batch which cost £36 each and the other 20 from the batch before that, which cost £34 each. Winston thus has a stock of 12 units, 10 of which are valued at £30 and 2 at £34.

Using AVCO

The unit valuation under this method is the weighted average cost. This is found by dividing the total purchase price by the number of units. This figure is then used to value closing stock. This method aims to resolve the difference in valuation between the FIFO and LIFO methods.

	Date	Units	£
Opening stock	Jan 01	15 units @ £30	450
Purchases	Jan 04	30 units @ £32	960
	Jan 10	22 units @ £34	748
	Jan 20	20 units @ £36	720
		87 units in total cost	2 878

The unit cost is thus £2 878 ÷ 87 = £33.08 (to the nearest penny).

The value of the closing stock is thus 12 units @ £33.08 = £397 (to the nearest £).

16.4 A Comparison of the Methods

Since the different methods produce different stock values, gross profits also differ. The following table compares Winston's trading account under the three methods.

Winston
Trading Account for January

	FIFO	LIFO	AVCO
	£	£	£
Sales	3 200	3 200	3 200
Opening stock (15 × £30)	450	450	450
Purchases*	2 428	2 428	2 428
	2 878	2 878	2 878
Less closing stock	(432)	(368)	(397)
Cost of sales	2 446	2 510	2 481
Gross profit	754	690	719

* Purchases = (30 × £32) + (22 × £34) + (20 × 36) = 2 428

FIFO gives the biggest gross profit since closing stock adds on to profit and, in a period of rising prices, the closing stock is valued from the latest and most expensive goods bought. LIFO, at the other end of the scale, gives the lowest gross profit under the same conditions. AVCO gives a result somewhere between the two.

Note that:

1) sales and purchases are the same under all three methods.
2) in a period of rising prices, FIFO places the highest value on closing stock and consequently produces the highest gross profit. LIFO shows the lowest profit.
3) since this year's closing stock becomes next year's opening stock, the situation will balance off as a higher opening stock will, other things being equal, reduce next year's gross profit.

Of the three methods, FIFO corresponds most closely to the physical flow of goods in businesses trading in perishable products but also in many businesses dealing in goods of a non-perishable nature. It is in fact the most popular method of stock valuation in the UK. The tax authorities do not accept LIFO as a basis for valuation – partly because it leads to lower reported profit. AVCO is suitable for businesses which have no definite policy on the issue of goods.

16.5 Periodic v. Perpetual Inventory

Apart from deciding on the basis of stock valuation, businesses also have to decide whether to keep a constant running check on stock levels, known as perpetual inventory, or to value stock only at the end of a period, which is periodic inventory. The decision depends largely on the size and type of business. A department store with thousands of different stock items, including many of small value, would probably not want to incur the cost of perpetual records and would settle instead for periodic inventory. In contrast, a manufacturing concern which needs to keep detailed costing records of the types and quantities of materials and components in stock at all times might use perpetual inventory. In this all purchases of materials would be recorded in a **Stores Ledger Account**, as would all issues to jobs. In this way the stock level of each item in store is known at all times. See Question 16.2.

Notice that in the LIFO calculations above, we used a perpetual inventory system. Calculating stock value under LIFO would be easier under a periodic system as we would simply calculate the number of units in the closing stock and value them at the earliest prices, going into subsequent batches if numbers make it necessary. However, using the perpetual system is more accurate and it is also the one usually asked for in examinations. It assumes that under LIFO we must always assume that the goods sold were valued at the latest prices at the time of sale and that some of these will not be available at the end of the period to value the closing stock.

The AVCO method described earlier assumes periodic inventory. Where perpetual inventory is used it is necessary to re-calculate weighted average cost after each batch of purchases. This figure is then the unit valuation at which subsequent stock is issued.

Date	Purchases	Sales	Average unit cost £	Units in stock	Value £
Jan 01			30.00	15	450
Jan 04	30 units @ £32		31.33	45	1 410
Jan 06		35 units @ £31.33		10	313
Jan 10	22 units @ £34		33.16	32	1 061
Jan 20	20 units @ £36		34.25	52	1 781
Jan 25		40 units @ £34.25		12	411

Winston began the period with 15 units valued at £30 each = £450.

On 4 January, he purchased 30 units at £32 each, giving a total of £960.
The total value of the 45 units is £450 + 960 = £1 410.
The average value per units is thus £1 410 ÷ 45 units = £31.33.

On 6 January, he sold 35 units. We cost these at the current average cost i.e. £31.33. Now there are 10 units remaining and these are also costed at £31.33 i.e. a total of £313.

On 10 January he purchased 22 units at £34 so the average will now change as follows:
(10 × 31.33) + (22 × 34) = £1 061
This gives an average of £1 061 ÷ 32 units = £33.16.

On 20 January he purchased 20 units at £36. The average is now:
£1 061 + (20 × 36) ÷ 52 units = £34.25.

On 25 January he sold 40 units. The average cost of £34.25 is used to cost both the sales and the closing stock of 12 units
i.e. £12 × 34.25 = £411.

16.6 Standard Cost

Some manufacturing concerns use standard cost, a pre-determined budgeted unit cost, as the basis for valuing stock. Standard costing is considered in Chapter 23.

16.7 Stock Control and Monitoring

In the current information revolution brought on by the application of computers to business, an increasing number of firms, including even department stores and supermarkets, are introducing perpetual inventory. Each stock item is printed with a bar code. When it is sold or issued, a scanner, usually a pen, identifies the code at the check-out point, cash desk or stores department so that an instant record is made of the fact that the item is no longer in stock. The computer can also be programmed to reorder stock when the reorder level has been reached. A computerised system of stock control has the following advantages:

(a) A constant track is kept of stocks of goods received and issued and the accountant can know the number of units in stock and their value at cost at any time. This helps not only in the drawing up of the Stock Account but also enables a check to be kept on fraud, missing items etc.
(b) Once the system has been set up and the stock clerk has learned to use it, such a system saves a lot of time as the computer program will update automatically after each entry.
(c) Since the computer knows when to reorder stock, the firm will not run the risk of running out of items and thus losing customers.

Whether the system used is computerised or manual, the following jobs have to be done in a stores department:

(a) Goods have to be received, either from outside suppliers or from the firm's own factory.
(b) Goods must be issued efficiently and on time.
(c) The storage of all product lines must be organised in logical sequences so that all items can be identified and found when needed and so that available storage space is used ergonomically.
(d) Stock checks must be organised, either continuously or periodically, so that accurate stock figures can be provided whenever necessary. Warehouse managers can encounter certain difficulties when undertaking a physical stock check eg stocks may be so large that the total figure has to be based on a sample, which may or may not be representative. It is not always possible to see whether items have been damaged until they are removed from their packaging and staff must check to ensure that perishable goods have not passed their 'sell-by' date etc.
(e) Stocks must be protected from damage and deterioration and secured against theft and fire. This means that they must be kept in a suitable environment as regards temperature, humidity etc, that their packaging is secure and that they are placed in suitable containers, shelves etc. It is worth a firm investing in good storage facilities to avoid stocks becoming spoiled or damaged. Staff may need to be trained in handling goods, especially those which are fragile or sensitive.

16.8 Ordering Stock

A firm must ensure that it holds just the right amount of stock. If it is too large, it ties up large amounts of working capital, takes up valuable space and needs a large staff to deal with it and there is also the risk that some will become damaged or go out of fashion, with large quantities becoming unsaleable. On the other hand there must be enough to satisfy customers' demands without making them wait so long that they go to another supplier. A modern system of stockholding is 'Just In Time', a Japanese method by which firms hold just enough stocks of goods and raw materials to satisfy one or two days of demand and where supplies are being received constantly. This frees up working capital and space but it means that the firm relies on deliveries always being on time and free of hold-ups.

The Economic Order Quantity

This is a method by which a firm can calculate at what quantity of stock it needs to reorder. The objective is to achieve the right balance between the cost of holding a lot of stock and the cost of not having enough. It makes certain assumptions:

(a) that both the cost of stockholding and the cost of ordering are known and constant;
(b) that the firm is aware of the rate of demand and the price per unit;
(c) that the whole batch of new goods is delivered at one time.

16.9 Examination Questions

Examination questions on this topic usually give information on purchases and sales over a period of time and ask for a calculation of the value of closing stock under two or more methods. Workings need to be shown for LIFO and AVCO. Trading accounts are sometimes asked for.

Questions

Question 16.1

Nazim Rajan is a retailer of garden supplies. You are supplied with the following information for the month of July 2000.

Purchases and Sales of Hanging Baskets

	Purchases			Sales	
Date	Quantity	Price per unit		Date	Quantity
		£			
July 2	10	1.90		July 5	20
4	60	2.00		11	30
16	100	2.20		18	80
22	80	2.10		20	40
28	120	2.30		29	50
				30	80

All sales were made at £5 per hanging basket.

Nazim had an opening stock of 5 hanging baskets costing £1.75 each on 1 July 2000.

REQUIRED

(a) Calculate the closing stock value of hanging baskets at 31 July 2000 under the following methods of stock valuation (perpetual basis):
  (i) FIFO;
  (ii) LIFO.   **(12 marks)**

(b) Trading Accounts for the month ended 31 July 2000 using the following methods of stock valuation (perpetual basis):
  (i) FIFO;
  (ii) LIFO.   **(9 marks)**

(c) Discuss the advantages and disadvantages of using the FIFO and LIFO methods of stock valuation.   **(8 marks)**

(d) State and explain **three** advantages that Nazim Rajan would gain from using a computerised system of stock control.   **(10 marks)**

OCR Advanced Subsidiary Specimen Paper

Question 16.2

An importer deals only in one commodity and has recorded the following transactions for the first six months of the year.

Purchases	Quantity purchased	Gross invoice value	Quantity discount
Date	Units	£	%
1 February	100	30 000	Nil
1 March	200	60 000	2.5
1 May	300	90 000	5

Sales	Quantity Sold	Total Sales Value
Date	Units	£
February	75	30 000
May	350	175 000

There was an opening balance at January 1st of 50 units, valued at £12 500.

REQUIRED

(a) Prepare the stores ledger for the six months using the perpetual inventory system and the FIFO method of pricing issues.   **(10 marks)**

(b) Prepare a trading account to show the gross profit for the period, using the FIFO method of valuation.   **(2 marks)**

(c) Prepare a trading account to show the gross profit for the period, using the LIFO method of valuation.   **(4 marks)**

Association of Accounting Technicians, Final

Question 16.3

Costcutters plc manufactures textiles. The company accountant asks your advice about the following product lines:

Lime Green Tartan: Manufacturing cost £9 000. This stock has been on a shelf since 1990. The accountant believes that the only way of selling it would be to shred it and bundle it (at a cost of £500) and sell it as industrial cleaning wipes for an anticipated sale price of £2 000.

Power Strangers: Originally printed to meet a high demand for garments linked to a popular television series, there is no further demand for the textile in this country. Stocks cost £16 000 and the only possible source of revenue would be to export the material at a cost of £2 750 for use as dusters in Australia. Administration costs to handle the sale are estimated at £2 650 and the sale price is estimated at £4 000.

REQUIRED

(a) Explain what is meant by the term 'stock is valued at the lower of cost and net realisable value' which is found in Statement of Standard Accounting Practice (SSAP) 9: Stocks and long-term contracts.   **(4 marks)**

(b) Explain, with reasons, how each of the above product lines should be accounted for in the annual accounts of the company for the year ended 31 May 1998.   **(8 marks)**

(c) If the average stock of finished textiles was £250 000 and the total cost of goods produced in the year was £25 million, calculate and comment upon the company's rate of stock turnover.   **(3 marks)**

London Examinations Advanced Level

Question 16.4

Sarah Black owns and manages a small retail business. She is concerned that the profit for the year ended 31 March 1999 is below expectations. At present stock is valued using the last in first out method. However Sarah believes that by changing the method her profit will be increased.

The following information on stock is available for the year ended 31 March 1999:

	Purchases (units)	Sales (units)
April – June 1998	256	230
July – September 1998	246	222
October – December 1998	364	342
January – March 1999	244	226

On 1 April 1998 there were 160 units in stock.

Up to 30 June 1998 each unit cost £20; however subsequently the supplier increased his prices by 10% each quarter.

Sarah Black sold her stock in packs of two.

The selling price was £76 per pack.

REQUIRED

(a) Calculate the values of closing stock at 31 March using:

    (i) the last in first out (LIFO) method;
    (ii) the first in first out (FIFO) method.

You should show **all** your working.

State your **final** answers to the nearest pound.   **(11 marks)**

(b) Prepare a statement showing the gross profit for the year ended 31 March 1999 using:

    (i) the last in first out (LIFO) method;
    (ii) the first in first out (FIFO) method.

State your **final** answers to the nearest pound.   **(11 marks)**

(c) Write a memorandum to Sarah Black:

    (i) advising whether she should change her stock valuation method;
    (ii) explaining the limitations of changing the stock valuation method.   **(10 marks)**

Associated Examining Board Advanced Level

Question 16.5

Hasp Ltd is a company which has a number of separate departments, each of which deals with a single product and has its own manager. At the end of the last financial year, 31 March 1998, it was decided to ask each manager to count and value the stock in their department and send the results to the Financial Director, together with an explanation of how the valuation had been carried out. The Financial Director is satisfied that the physical quantities have been counted correctly, but considers that the valuation has not been carried out in all cases in accordance with normal accounting rules. The departmental managers' valuations and notes have been passed to you and are as follows:

Product X – Manager's Valuation £200 000

This is bought in batches and deteriorates with age with the result that its selling price falls. There were three batches left in stock at the year end:

	Cost	Net Realisable Value
	£000	£000
Batch 15	50	25
Batch 16	60	55
Batch 17	90	200
Total	200	280

Product Y – Manager's Valuation £150 000

This is manufactured by Hasp Ltd and, during the year to 31 March 1998, a total of 10 000 units was produced. 1 000 of these remained in stock at the year end. The unit cost of stock is arrived at as follows:

	£
Raw material per unit	100
Variable expenses per unit	50
Cost per unit	150

The department incurred fixed manufacturing overhead costs during the year of £300 000.

Product Z – Manager's Valuation £200 000

This is a very popular line and we can sell it at £200 per unit as many as we can obtain. At the year end there were 1 000 units in stock which had cost £125 each.

Product ABC – Manager's Valuation £100 000

We paid £18 per unit for the 5 000 units we held in stock at the year end. We sell each unit for £40. We were informed by our supplier on 31 March 1998 that the price per unit has gone up from £18 to £20.

Product DEF – Manager's Valuation £360 000

The manager explains that he has read about accountants being cautious and so, although this stock can be sold for £700 000, for valuation purposes 10% has been deducted from what Hasp Ltd paid for it.

REQUIRED

For each product:

(a) Explain the mistake made by the manager when carrying out the valuation.   **(6 marks)**

(b) Calculate the correct valuation for accounting purposes.   **(9 marks)**

(c) State the effect on profit of your revaluation.   **(5 marks)**

Institute of Financial Services

17

Overhead Absorption Costing

17.1 Introduction

The overheads of a business are the indirect costs of running it – indirect materials, indirect labour and indirect expenses. These are costs which cannot be charged directly to products and so must be charged indirectly to them, using the methods described in this chapter.

Overheads may be classified into four main groups:

1) **Production overheads**, also known as factory overheads or works overheads. Examples are factory rent and rates, factory light and heat, power, depreciation of plant and buildings, and supervisors' salaries.
2) **Administration overheads**, such as office rent and rates, office light and heat, clerical and executive salaries, stationery, postage and telephone.
3) **Selling overheads**, such as the cost of advertising, sales promotion, sales staff salaries and research and development. Where research and development is a major item of expenditure, it is classified as an overhead group on its own.
4) **Distribution overheads**, including warehouse costs, packaging, transport, and depreciation of delivery vans.

Overheads may be:

- fixed, e.g. rent and rates and depreciation
- variable, e.g. power and salesmen's commissions
- semi-fixed, e.g. supervisors' salaries, or
- semi-variable, e.g. telephone and electricity.

17.2 Cost Centres

If costs are to be effectively controlled it must be possible for management to trace them to that part of the organisation incurring the cost. This is the cost centre. A cost centre is an area of responsibility, such as a department, to which costs can be related for control purposes. If the persons in the centre have control over the costs, they can be made responsible for them. In this way the organisation can be broken down into several different cost centres, with each centre manager being responsible for his own cost level. Cost centres can be of two types:

1) **production centres**, which are directly involved in production, e.g. the machining department.
2) **service centres**, which exist to facilitate production, e.g. maintenance and canteen.

17.3 Determination of Unit Cost

We know from Chapter 15 that one of the chief functions of the cost accountant is to determine unit production cost. This consists of direct labour, direct materials, direct expenses and overheads. The question of deciding the issue price of materials was looked at in the previous chapter and labour and direct expenses were considered in the chapter previous to that. It is now time to look at the fourth item of unit cost, overheads. Since overheads cannot be charged directly to cost units, they must be shared between them on some equitable basis. This is done by first allocating and apportioning the overheads to cost centres, then absorbing them into cost units. It is possible to identify four separate stages in the calculation of overhead cost per unit:

1) The various factory overhead costs are allocated or apportioned to the production and service cost centres.
2) The costs of the service centres are re-apportioned to the production centres.
3) Appropriate departmental overhead absorption rates are calculated.
4) The overhead costs are absorbed into cost units by applying the absorption rates to jobs passing through each centre.

Let us look in detail at each of the stages. We shall illustrate each in the answer to the following question, which is taken from an Advanced Level paper of the Associated Examining Board.

Example

Caxton plc produces crockery, specialising in mugs for everyday use.

There are three stages to the production of a mug: moulding, firing in the kiln and glazing.

The company also has two service departments – stores and distribution.

The budgeted overheads for the year ended 30 November 1998 were:

	£
Rent	81 000
Rates, lighting, heating	27 000
Fixed asset depreciation	13 200
Fixed asset insurance	6 600
Distribution costs	21 300
Storage costs	3 300
Administration costs	60 000
Fixed asset maintenance	9 900

The following information is available for the five departments:

	Cost of fixed assets £	Floor area m²	Machine hours	Direct labour hours
Moulding	26 000	21 000	120 000	24 000
Firing	72 000	8 000	60 000	6 000
Glazing	9 000	3 000		30 000
Stores	11 000	5 000		
Distribution	14 000	3 000		

The total overheads of the stores department are allocated to the production departments on the basis of machine hours; whereas the total overheads of the distribution department are allocated on the basis of labour hours.

Job number 1245 is the production of 600 mugs.

The job passes through each production department:

	Machine hours	Direct labour hours
Moulding	240	240
Firing	480	36
Glazing	360	84

The direct costs amount to 85p for each mug.

A sum amounting to 30% of the production cost is added to every job to enable a selling price to be quoted.

Job number 1245 is due a 20% trade discount off the selling price.

REQUIRED

(a)

    (i) Prepare a statement to show the total production overheads for each department, showing clearly the bases of apportionment.   **(16 marks)**

    (ii) Prepare a statement to show the total overheads for each **production** department after the service departments are apportioned.   **(5 marks)**

(b) Prepare a computation of the overhead absorption rates for each production department. State your answer to the nearest penny.   **(6 marks)**

(c) Calculate the selling price for job number 1245.   **(11 marks)**

    i)   Write a report to the Board of Caxton plc briefly explaining: **(Report format: 2 marks)**
        (i) the limitations of the bases of apportionment used in (a);
        (ii) the bases of absorption used in (b).   **(10 marks)**

Stage 1: Allocation and Apportionment

Those costs which are wholly identifiable with one cost centre are allocated to that centre. For example, the salary of a machine supervisor can be allocated to the machining department and the wages of a cook to the canteen. There are some overheads however which cannot be charged to just one centre because the benefit of the expenditure is felt by several centres, e.g. rent and rates. The total has to be shared or apportioned over the cost centres on some equitable basis. With rent and rates, since the charge is a function of area, relative areas covered by the cost centres is a fair basis of apportionment. Other occupancy costs such as light and heat should also be shared by floor space. With depreciation of fixed assets and insurance, book value might be the best basis. The cost of power and electricity should be related to usage. In some cases there is more than one possible fair basis of apportionment. Examiners do not always state which basis to apply and you may have to apply your common sense and judgement in each case.

Stage 2: Re-apportionment

Since the beneficiaries of a service department are not actual products but production departments, their costs must be charged to those departments. Here again there is more than one method. The chosen one should be that which best reflects the relative benefits derived by the other departments. For example, the total cost of operating a canteen could be charged on the basis of number of employees in each department and the cost of stores on the basis of value of materials or number of stores requisitions issued (note the scope for more than one basis). In some questions the relative benefits of a service department to other departments is given in percentages and these should then form the basis of your re-apportionment.

In some cases the benefit of a service department is felt by other service departments in addition to production departments. For example personnel benefits other service departments such as stores and maintenance as well as production departments. A difficulty arises here since the costs of a service department written off to other departments may be re-activated by being charged its share of costs of another service department from which it benefits. This charge must now be re-apportioned back to the user departments. In so doing another service department whose costs have been written off can be reactivated and so on. This process can continue for a long time before it is complete. There are three methods of re-apportionment in such cases – the repeated distribution method, specified order of closing, and algebraic solution using simultaneous equations. If cross-charges are in the syllabus of your course, it is sufficient at this level to know just one method. Repeated distribution would be the sensible choice since it is the simplest of the three.

Here is the answer to part (a) of the Caxton question to illustrate how to apportion and re-apportion overheads.

Caxton plc
Production Overhead Statement

Cost	Basis	Moulding £	Firing £	Glazing £	Stores £	Distribution £
Rent	Floor area	42 525	16 200	6 075	10 125	6 075
Rates, lighting, heating	Floor area	14 175	5 400	2 025	3 375	2 025
Fixed asset depreciation	Cost of assets	2 600	7 200	900	1 100	1 400
Fixed asset insurance	Cost of assets	1 300	3 600	450	550	700
Distribution costs						21 300
Storage costs					3 300	
Administration costs	Floor area	31 500	12 000	4 500	7 500	4 500
Fixed asset maintenance	Cost of assets	1 950	5 400	675	825	1 050
					26 775	37 050
Stores	Machine hours	5 950	11 900	8 925	(26 775)	
Distribution	Labour hours	24 700	3 705	8 645		(37 050)
Total overheads		124 700	65 405	32 195		

Set out all the costs in the first column and write beside each the basis on which you have been told to apportion each or which seems to you to be the most appropriate. Rent, rates, lighting and heating are apportioned according to floor area and depreciation, insurance and maintenance of fixed assets according to cost of the fixed assets. Distribution costs will go only to the distribution department and storage costs only to the stores. Administration costs will be apportioned according to floor area

(they must be apportioned to all five departments but we have a total breakdown of all five only under cost of fixed assets and floor area).

Now we calculate the ratios of the various bases and apportion the costs as follows:

Rent: £81 000 to be apportioned between the 5 departments in the ratio of their floor areas: 21 : 8 : 3 : 5 : 3 (see table for figures).

Rates, lighting and heating: £27 000 to be apportioned in the same way.

Administration costs: £60 000 to be apportioned in the same way.

Depreciation: £13 200 to be apportioned between the 5 departments in the ratio of their fixed asset costs: 26 : 72 : 9 : 11 : 14.

Insurance: £6 600 to be apportioned in the same way.

Fixed asset maintenance: £9 900 to be apportioned in the same way.

Distribution costs go only to the distribution department and storage costs only to the stores.

Now we total the costs of the stores and of the distribution departments and reapportion them to the three production departments in accordance with machine hours and labour hours respectively.

The machine hour ratio is 240 : 480 : 360 and the labour hour ratio is 240 : 36 : 84.

Now we find the total overheads for the three production departments by adding the columns. We can check the arithmetic by adding these three totals and to see that they are the same as the total of all the costs given in the question. In this case, total costs are £222 300 and the figures tally.

Stages 3 and 4: Absorption and Application to Jobs

Now that the accountant knows the total amount of overhead charged to each production cost centre, it only remains to establish rates for their recovery through the jobs which pass through them. In this there is again more than one method – in fact there are six. Let us look at them, illustrating their calculation by using the following information on a hypothetical company with just one production cost centre.

Income Statement

	£000	£000
Sales		700
Direct material	200	
Direct labour	100	
Prime cost	300	
Production overhead	200	
Total cost of production		(500)
Gross profit		£200

Direct labour hours worked: 50 000
Machine hours worked: 40 000
Number of units produced: 25 000

(i) Rate per direct labour hour

Cost centre overheads / Cost centre direct labour hours

$$\frac{£200\,000}{50\,000} = £4 \text{ per direct labour hour}$$

For every hour of direct labour spent on a unit in the department it will be charged £4 as its share of overhead. This method is suitable where the departmental overhead incurred is related mainly to time and work is labour-intensive, e.g. the packing department.

Taking a product which has had £4 of direct material and £4 of direct labour spent on it and which has had 2½ hours in the factory, total unit cost would be:

	£
Direct material	4
Direct labour	4
Prime cost	8
Overhead, 2½ hours @ £4	10
Unit production cost	18

(ii) Percentage of direct labour cost

Cost centre overheads / Cost centre direct labour cost   ×   100

$$\frac{200\,000}{100\,000} \times 100 = 200\%$$

Thus for every £1 of direct wage that a unit has spent on it, it is charged £2 of overhead. The implicit assumption in this method is that overheads are a function of direct wages rather than time. Jobs requiring skilled labour at high wage rates will therefore be charged a higher rate of overhead than jobs requiring unskilled labour at low wage rates. Is this fair? It would be if the overheads incurred were a function of direct wages. In reality however, most overheads are a function of time e.g. rent and rates, supervisor's salary. For this reason this method is not as sound as the first from a cost accounting point of view. It is however simpler to use since records do not have to be kept of the time spent by workers on each job, and would be the preferred method where wage rates within a department are uniform, e.g. in an assembly department where all assemblers are paid a standard wage rate.

Note that since the different methods of overhead recovery are likely to produce different rates of absorption they will also produce different figures for unit cost. By this method for example:

	£
Direct material	4
Direct labour	4
Prime cost	8
Overhead, £4 × 200%	8
Unit production cost	16

The unit cost is £16 compared with £18 using the first method. If price is based on cost, the different methods will then also produce different selling prices.

(iii) Percentage of direct material cost

Overheads / Direct material cost $\times$ 100

$$\frac{200\,000}{200\,000} \times 100 = 100\%$$

For every £1 of direct material spent on a unit, it is charged £1 of overhead. For our product, overhead recovered is £4 × 100% =£4.

Although simple to apply, this method cannot really be recommended as it has no logical basis. A job requiring expensive material will be charged more overhead than a job requiring cheap material even though the overhead incurred on the two may be the same. The method fails to account for the different times spent on different jobs. A slow job taking twice as long as another but using the same value of material would be charged the same overhead. This is not likely to produce meaningful rates of absorption and as a consequence the unit costs computed may fail to reflect the true cost of each unit.

(iv) Percentage of prime cost

Overheads / Prime cost $\times$ 100

$$\frac{200\,000}{300\,000} \times 100 = 66.6\%$$

For each of £1 of prime cost spent on a unit, it is charged £0.666 of overhead. For our product, overhead recovered is £8 × 66.6% = £5.33.

As prime cost consists of direct material and direct labour the disadvantages which apply to the percentage of direct material cost and percentage of direct labour cost also apply to this method. It is not one which can be recommended.

(v) Rate per machine hour

Overheads / Machine hours

$$\frac{200\,000}{40\,000} = £5 \text{ per machine hour}$$

For our product, overhead recovered is 4 hours @ £5 =£12.50.

Where work is of a capital-intensive nature this is a good method to use. In the machining department for example, most of the overheads – depreciation, insurance, repairs, power – are related to time and use of the machines, so it seems fair to relate the recovery of the overheads also to time and use of the machines.

(vi) Rate per unit of output

Overheads / Units produced $\times$ 100

$$\frac{200\,000}{25\,000} = £8 \text{ per unit}$$

For our product, overhead recovered is £8.

This method is extremely simple and cheap to operate but is suitable only where the cost centre performs just one standard task for all units passing through it, and each unit takes up the same amount of man and machine time, e.g. car bodies passing through the painting section of a factory. It is suitable for most of the cost centres of mass-production industries producing identical units in an identical way such as chemicals, steel manufacture, motor manufacture, and dairy farming.

Be Careful

Sometimes you have to cost jobs passing through more than one cost centre. Make sure you apply the correct absorption rate to the product in each centre.

Example

The cost accountant of a factory with two production departments has calculated the following overhead absorption rates:

	Machining	Assembly
	£	£
Rate per direct labour hour	8	3
Rate per machine hour	4	5
Rate per unit of output	7	6

The chosen rates are per machine hour for the machining department and per labour hour for assembly. How much overhead should be charged to a product spending 4 hours in machining followed by 1½ hours in assembly?

Answer

Overhead charged:

	£
Machining 4 hours @ £4	16.00
Assembly 1½ hours @ £3	4.50
Total	20.50

In some questions you are given more information than is necessary to perform the task set, as above. In these cases select only that cost data which is relevant.

Now let us see the answer to parts (b) and (c) of the question on Caxton plc, part (a) of which we worked above.

(b) We are asked to compute the overhead absorption rates for each production department. We are not told which basis to use but it must be on either machine hours or direct labour hours. We need to compare the number of machine hours with the number of labour hours for each department to see whether it is capital-intensive or labour intensive. Both the moulding and firing departments are capital-intensive (120 000 hours as opposed to 24 000 hours and 60 000 hours as opposed to 6 000 hours respectively). We are not given machine hours for the glazing department so we use labour hours.

Moulding: £124 700 ÷ 120 000 machine hours = £1.04

Firing: £65 405 ÷ 60 000 machine hours = £1.09

Glazing: £32 195 ÷ 30 000 labour hours = £1.07

(c) We are asked to calculate the selling price for job number 1245, which is for 600 mugs.

Costing Table for Job 1245

	£
Direct costs	0.85
Overheads:	
Moulding (240 × £1.04 ÷ 600)	0.42
Firing (480 × £1.09 ÷ 600)	0.87
Glazing (360 × £1.07 ÷ 600)	0.64
Production cost	2.78
Add 30% mark-up	0.83
	3.61
Less 20% trade discount	(0.72)
Price after discount	2.89

Machine hours were used for all three departments (the glazing on this job uses more machine hours than labour hours).

17.4 The Blanket Absorption Rate

Since most factories are divided into several departments with products passing from one department to another, separate absorption rates are calculated for each department. A simplification of this would be to calculate just one rate for the factory as a whole.

Example

Total overheads of a factory	£750 000
Direct labour hours worked	250 000
Using the rate per direct labour hour	
Blanket overhead rate =	$\dfrac{£750\,000}{25\,000} = £3$

All units would be charged overhead £3 per direct labour hour regardless of the amount of time they spent in different departments.

Be careful of the distinction between the blanket overhead, rate and the rate per unit of output – they are not the same. The latter calculates a separate rate based on units produced independently for each cost centre. A factory with three production cost centres would have three separate absorption rates. With the blanket rate there is no attempt to divide the factory into separate cost centres. In effect the whole of the factory is one large cost centre.

While blanket rates simplify the accounting for overheads they can only be used in certain conditions. If, as is the case in most industries, different departments incur different amounts of overhead and products spend unequal times in the different departments, a single absorption rate for the whole factory would not be appropriate. Jobs spending the bulk of their time in departments with large overheads should be charged proportionately more than those spending most of their time in departments with low overheads. In such a case calculating and applying separate departmental overhead rates, although more expensive to operate, would produce more meaningful

results of unit cost. A blanket rate can be satisfactorily used only when all products spend roughly the same amount of time in each department.

17.5 The Need to Forecast

So far we have been relating actual overhead expenditure to actual activity in determining the absorption rate. In practice there are two difficulties in doing this:

1) It is necessary to wait until the end of a financial year before the totals of the variables are known. Thus for a company with its financial year running from 1 January to 31 December, goods produced in January and February cannot be fully costed until after December. This is impractical. The problem can be overcome by calculating the variables at more frequent intervals, say monthly, but if this is done a second problem is created.

2) Changes in activity level between months will change the absorption rate. Take a company which uses a rate per unit of output:

	January	June
Overhead incurred	£50 000	£45 000
Production	10 000 units	5 000 units
Absorption rate	£5	£9

This company experiences a slow-down in activity in summer, yet overheads being mostly fixed stay much the same. As a result the decrease in production increases the absorption rate. Units produced in January are charged £5 of overhead while identical units produced in June are charged £9. This leads to frequent changes in unit cost, selling price and/or gross profit. In these circumstances it is better to calculate the *average* absorption rate for the whole year by basing total annual overhead to annual activity levels. If we do this, however, we are back to our first problem of having to wait until the end of the accounting year before rates can be established. The dilemma is overcome by predetermining the rate by basing an annual estimated overhead expenditure to estimated levels of activity. This information is generated from preparation of the annual budget, a subject we consider in Chapter 22.

17.6 Under- and Over-absorption

It is most unlikely that actual levels of expenditure and activity will turn out to be exactly as budgeted. If they are not, there will be a discrepancy between the amount of overhead incurred and the amount absorbed into products (which is based on the budgeted rate).

Example

For a Machining Department cost centre:

Budgeted overheads	£200 000
Budgeted machine hours	40 000
Absorption rate per machine hour	£5

	Case A	Case B
Actual overhead incurred	£200 000	£180 000
Actual machine hours worked	30 000	40 000
Overhead absorbed	£150 000	£200 000

In Case A the budgeted number of machine hours has not been reached. As a result only £150 000 of the £200 000 overhead incurred has been charged to jobs – there is an under-absorption of £50 000. In Case B the activity forecast has been achieved but this time the overhead incurred is below plan. £200 000 has been charged to jobs even though only £180 000 has been incurred – there is an over-absorption of £20 000.

Under-absorption will occur if:

(1)   actual activity is below budget, or
(2)   actual overhead is above budget.

Over-absorption will occur if:

(1)   actual activity is above budget, or
(2)   actual overhead is below budget.

Further consideration of overhead variances is given in Chapter 23 on Standard Costing and Variance Analysis.

The better the forecasting the smaller will be the amount of under- or over-absorption. Such incorrect amounts of overhead are not uncommon in practice. They can be avoided only if absorption rates are based on actual expenditure and activity levels but we have seen the two problems this can cause. Most firms choose to forecast the rate in their annual budget and accept the inevitable under/over-absorption. The question is – how should they be dealt with? The perfectionist might like to share the under/over recovery among all jobs worked over the year, but in practice this may prove to be too complicated and expensive an exercise. Another possible solution is to carry forward the discrepancy to the next accounting period, charging it to jobs produced then. This cannot however be justified on theoretical grounds – its effect would be to distort the unit cost of future products simply because of a forecasting error in the past. Instead most firms prefer to write off the amount of the under/over absorption to that year's profit and loss account. This is in fact the official recommendation of SSAP 9, Stocks and Work-in-progress. The ledger accounts would look as follows.

In Case A:

Factory Overheads Account

Incurred – Bank	200 000	Absorbed – Work in progress	150 000
		Under-absorption – P & L	50 000
	200 000		200 000

The under-absorption would be a charge to the profit and loss account.

In Case B:

Factory Overheads Account

Incurred – Bank	180 000	Absorbed – Work in progress	200 000
Over-absorption – P & L	20 000		
	200 000		200 000

The over-absorption would be a miscellaneous income in the profit and loss account. See Question 17.3.

17.7 Non-manufacturing Overheads

A manufacturing concern will have not only a factory but also a warehouse and offices. These also attract overhead expenses. A warehouse incurs distribution costs such as storage space, containers, and delivery vans. An office incurs administration expenses such as clerical and accountancy charges, managerial salaries, and office occupancy costs. It will also incur selling costs such as advertising and publicity, and possibly also research and development.

In this chapter we have looked so far at possible ways of absorbing production overheads to cost units. At the end of the day it is not sufficient for a business to recover just prime cost and production overheads. The administration, selling and distribution overheads have to be recovered as well. The question is – on what basis? Should their recovery be charged directly to products? Since there is no clear link between the manufacture of a product and an indirect non-manufacturing expense most firms do not attempt to charge them to individual cost units. Instead a selected mark-up is added to production cost to cover them.

Example

Let us take a factory manufacturing dining tables:

Per table	£
Direct material	80
Direct labour	40
Prime cost	120
Factory overhead	80
Production cost	200
Mark-up, 25%	50
Total cost	250
Profit	50
Selling price	300

In the year-end financial statements the factory overhead is shown in the trading account as part of the cost of goods sold while the non-manufacturing overhead is shown in the profit and loss account under expenses. Closing stocks therefore incorporate a share of the production overhead but not administration, selling and distribution overhead. (Whether part of the production overhead should be carried forward in closing stock to be charged in the following year is debated in Chapter 20, Absorption and Marginal Costing.)

Some firms boldly attempt to charge non-manufacturing overheads directly to cost units by using bases such as the number of staff in each cost centre for administrative expenses and sales value of each centre for selling costs. Such apportionments are very arbitrary however and often do not reflect the relationship between the chosen basis and incurring of the cost. For example, a popular high-value product may incur a low unit selling cost, because the quality of the product sells itself, while a not-so-popular low-value product may incur a higher unit selling cost. For this reason most firms to do not attempt to charge non-manufacturing overheads directly to products.

Questions

Question 17.1

Driscoll Masters plc uses a system of absorption costing. The product passes through a machining department and an assembly department before it is completed.

The machining department is capital intensive; the assembly department is labour intensive.

The company cost accountant has estimated the following overhead costs for the financial year ended 31 January 1998.

	£
Electricity: power	62 000
heating and lighting	14 000
Supervisory wages	54 000
Rent and rates	21 000
Insurance: machinery	16 740
premises	7 000
Depreciation of machinery	41 850

The following information should be used to determine the appropriate basis of apportionment for the year.

	Production Departments		Service Departments	
	Machining	Assembly	Maintenance	Canteen
Cost of machinery	£810 000	£27 000		
Machine hours	30 000	6 000		
Power (kilowatt hours)	75 000	25 000		
Direct labour hours	35 000	105 000		
Number of employees	20	60	5	5
Floor area (square metres)	11 000	8 000	200	800

The proportion of work done by the service departments is estimated to be:

	Machining	Assembly	Maintenance	Canteen
	%	%	%	%
Maintenance	65	25		10
Canteen	25	75		

It is company policy to apportion the maintenance department's costs between the other three departments to eliminate those costs before apportioning the canteen costs between the production departments.

REQUIRED

(a) Prepare a statement to show the total production overheads for **each** production department. (Work to the nearest £, showing the basis of apportionment selected.) **(21 marks)**

(b) Calculate (to the nearest penny) an overhead absorption rate for **each** production department. **(9 marks)**

(c) Explain how over-absorption or under-absorption of overheads arise and how they would be dealt with by a company accountant. **(12 marks)**

(d) Explain **two** limitations associated with using budgeted overhead absorption rates. **(8 marks)**

Associated Examining Board Advanced Level

Question 17.2

John Barber is considering opening a health club. On investigation, he has discovered an existing building close to the town centre which could be converted for the purpose. The cost of purchase would be £400 000 and equipment a further £100 000.

John Barber intends to offer three main facilities:

- a sauna
- 4 squash courts
- gymnasium.

The building will contain a refreshment bar and has space for administration. He has made an initial assessment of the proposal as follows:

(i)   The club will open for 12 hours per day, 360 days per year.

(ii)   The maximum capacity of each of the facilities at any one time will be:

        sauna   10 customers
        squash courts   16 customers (4 on each of the 4 courts)
        gymnasium   8 customers

(iii)   Staffing and general running costs, other than depreciation, are estimated to be:

Activity	Total staff	Annual salary per employee £	Annual running costs £
Sauna	4	12 500	12 300
Squash courts	2	12 500	18 400
Gymnasium	4	12 500	31 300
Refreshment bar	4	8 000	3 400
Administration	3	15 000	11 600

(iv)   The area occupied by the activities is:

Activity	Area (sq metres)
Sauna	300
Squash courts	800
Gymnasium	400
Refreshment bar	300
Administration	200
	2 000

(v)   It is considered that the building should be depreciated over 50 years and the equipment over 5 years. There will be no residual values.

Three pricing strategies are being considered by John Barber.

Either A

A charge of £4 per hour per person for the use of any of the facilities.

Or B

A charge of £2 per hour per person for the use of any of the facilities, plus an annual fixed membership charge of £150.

Or C

An annual fixed membership charge subscription of £300 for unlimited usage.

Market research has revealed the following customer preferences:

Pricing strategy	A	B	C
Customer projections:			
Annual membership	1 500	1 200	1 000
Daily customers			
Sauna	90	80	60
Squash	50	50	40
Gymnasium	90	70	50

Note: on average, each daily customer will stay for 1 hour.

REQUIRED

(a) Apportion and allocate the costs between the five activities using the basis that is most appropriate from the information given. Calculate the total cost of providing the sauna, squash courts and gymnasium. Re-allocate the costs of the two service departments (refreshment bar and administration) on the basis of maximum customer capacity. **(6 marks)**

(b) Evaluate the three pricing strategies suggested by John Barber by calculating which strategy will maximise his income and profit. **(9 marks)**

(c) John Barber has calculated that the *occupancy rate* for the squash courts is significantly lower than for other activities.

   (i) Explain the term *occupancy rate*. **(3 marks)**

   (ii) Advise of two financial methods by which John Barber might improve the occupancy rate of the squash courts. **(3 marks)**

(d) Advise John Barber of four non-financial methods by which he might improve demand for the services of the club as a whole. **(4 marks)**

London Examinations Advanced Level

Question 17.3

A company is preparing overhead budgets and determining the apportionment of these overheads to products.

Cost centre expenses and related information have been budgeted as follows:

	Total	Machine shop A	Machine shop B	Assembly	Canteen	Maint- enance
Indirect wages (£)	78 560	8 586	9 190	15 674	29 650	15 460
Consumable materials (including maintenance) (£)	16 900	6 400	8 700	1 200	600	
Rent and rates (£)	16 700					
Buildings insurance (£)	2 400					
Power (£)	8 600					
Heat and light (£)	3 400					
Depreciation of machinery (£)	40 200					
Area (sq ft)	45 000	10 000	12 000	15 000	6 000	2 000
Value of machinery (£)	402 000	201 000	179 000	22 000		
Power usage – technical estimates (%)	100	55	40	3		2
Direct labour (hours)	35 000	8 000	6 200	20 800		
Machine usage (hours)	25 200	7 200	18 000			

REQUIRED

(a) Determine budgeted overhead absorption rates for each of the production departments, using bases of apportionment and absorption which you consider most appropriate from the information provided.   **(13 marks)**

(b) On the assumption that actual activity was:

	Machine shop A	Machine shop B	Assembly
Direct labour hours	8 200	6 500	21 900
Machine usage hours	7 300	18 700	

and total production overhead expenditure was £176 533, prepare the production overhead control account for the year (you are to assume that the company has a separate cost accounting system).   **(6 marks)**

(c) Explain the meaning of the word 'control' in the title of the account prepared in answer to (b).   **(3 marks)**

Chartered Association of Certified Accountants

Question 17.4

G Locks Ltd manufactures three different products. Each product is completely made within a different production department, and all three production departments are serviced by two service departments.

The costs allocated to each department are as follows:

Product	Production departments			Service departments	
	Raps	Taps	Baps	Stores	Repairs
	£	£	£	£	£
Indirect labour	153 000	190 000	240 100	42 000	68 000
Other indirect overhead costs	105 000	80 000	125 000	78 000	92 000

The costs of the service departments are allocated to the production departments as follows:

Stores: in proportion to units produced.
Repairs: in proportion to machine hours.

Overhead absorption rates are calculated on a direct labour hour rate for the production of Raps and Taps, and on a machine hour rate for the production of Baps.

The following information is available:

	Raps	Taps	Baps
Direct labour hours	40 000	60 000	15 000
Machine hours	25 000	30 000	45 000
Units produced	63 000	45 000	72 000

REQUIRED

(a) Calculate overhead absorption rates for each of the three production departments.   **(18 marks)**

(b) Outline the factors which should be taken into account in the selection of the labour hour rate and machine hour rate for the absorption of overheads by the company.   **(2 marks)**

(c) In addition to the two methods used for the absorption of overheads, state two other methods the company could use to absorb overheads.   **(2 marks)**

(d) Outline how an unsatisfactory method of overhead absorption can affect the profits of a business.   **(3 marks)**

OCR Advanced Level

18

Job, Batch and Contract Costing

18.1 Introduction

The costs of labour, materials and overheads which we have studied in the last three chapters now have to be applied to actual production situations. The nature of the costing system used in any particular case will depend on the nature of the production process and on the type of good or service being costed.

There are four broad types of costing:
- job costing
- batch costing
- contract costing
- process costing.

Job costing is suitable where the jobs being worked on are unique i.e. not standard. Often they are being made to a specific order such as a custom-built car or a one-off special export order. Since each job is different from the next, it requires different amounts of labour, material, and overhead spent on it and a separate record of its cost needs to be kept.

Batch costing is suitable where a number of identical articles are produced to order as a group or batch. Each unit is not seen individually as it forms part of an identifiable whole. For example, a large retailer might order 5 000 jackets from a clothing manufacturer, to be made according to its own specifications. Costing a batch is similar to costing a job, since the batch is seen as the job.

The techniques of **contract costing** is employed where an individual job is a long-term contract spanning several accounting periods.

In industries where identical units are produced in an identical fashion, usually by mass-production methods, **process costing** is more suitable. Since one unit of output is identical to the next and has incurred the same cost, it is not necessary to keep a record of the cost of each individual unit. Instead it is sufficient to calculate average cost by dividing the total cost of production by the number of units produced. Process costing is used in continuous flow, mass-production industries such as chemicals, oil-refining, flour-milling and motor manufacture. We shall study process costing in the next chapter.

18.2 Job Costing

The purpose of job costing is the keeping of separate cost records for each individual job. This is done on a job order cost sheet which records the material and labour used in a job with their charge-out rates. Allocated overheads are also entered on this sheet (job costing is usually done on an absorption basis whereby all overheads are allocated to the job). The job is, in effect, a cost centre to which the various costs are charged. Job costing is an expensive system to operate and should only be used in circumstances where it is really needed. Here is a typical procedure.

The firm prepares an estimate of what it will cost to do the job to the customer's specifications and a selling price is quoted to the customer. If the customer agrees with the estimate and places an order, a Works Order is raised which is given a specific job number to identify it. Information regarding the job is now sent to all the departments involved – the stores, purchasing, personnel, production etc. – so that the necessary materials, labour and equipment can be made available. A Job Card is then prepared and this gives written instructions for the operations which must be carried out and contains full details of all the costs which will be incurred, including the overheads.

The job is entered into the Production Schedule so that the starting and finishing date can be set and will ensure that the agreed delivery date will be achieved.

Until the job is despatched to the customer, it is entered in the work in progress account at factory cost. It is transferred to the finished goods account on despatch. Selling and administrative overheads and any delivery costs will be added to the works cost to find the total cost and the profit or loss on the job can then be calculated as a percentage or a straight amount.

The total cost of the job is debited to the cost of sales and the total of selling and administrative costs charged to the job is credited to the overhead absorption account. It is here that we can ascertain whether the job has been over-absorbed or under-absorbed.

This final stage is important so that the management accountants can know whether the firm has made the profit it expected to make on the job. The price charged to the customer was based on estimates of the costs which the firm expected to incur plus its profit margin and it needs to see whether there was any variance from the actual outcome.

Example

The following information relates to Job Q2:

Direct materials: In Department A, 20 kilos of material K_2 were issued from stores at £5 per kilo. In addition 12 kilos of L_1 were issued in Department B at £4. Of this a quarter was returned to stores.

Direct labour:

Department	Hours worked	Hourly rate
		£
A	10	11
B	8	9

Direct expense: A special piece of equipment was hired for 2 days for the job. The daily hire charge was £37.

Production overheads: These are charged to jobs at the rate of £6 per direct labour hour.

Non-manufacturing overheads: The company adds 20% to production cost to cover its selling, distribution and administration overhead.

Calculate the cost of Job Q2.

Answer

Job Order Cost Sheet for Job Q2

Direct Materials

Department	Material	Quantity (kilos)	Issue price (£ per kilo)	£	£
A	K_2	20	5	100	
B	L_1	9	4	36	
					136

Direct Labour

Department	Hours worked	Hourly rate £	£		
A	10	11	110		
B	8	9	72		
					182

Direct expense		
Hire of equipment (£37 × 2 days)		74
Prime cost		392
Production overhead		
18 direct labour hours @ £6 per hour		108
Production cost		500
Non-manufacturing overhead (500 × 20%)		100
Total cost of Job Q2		600

18.3 Examination Questions on Job Costing

Examination questions on job costing usually require the answer to be in the above format. Sometimes you may have to do some preliminary workings on the amount of material and direct labour hours chargeable to a job, the issue price of materials and/or the overhead absorption rates.

In some questions you have to apply your judgement on whether a cost incurred on a particular job should in fact be charged to that job. For example, if defects in work carried out on a job necessitate the spending of additional time and material on it, should the cost of this be charged to the customer of that job? Some amount of faulty work can be expected to occur in all factories due to machine or human error. The usual costing practice is to treat the resulting cost as an overhead, to be recovered by charging it to all jobs. Normal losses of material are usually also treated as a production overhead. Abnormal losses however are not expected in the normal course of production and should not be charged to any job but instead written off to the profit and loss account as an expense for the period. Another situation that sometimes arises is overtime being worked on a job to complete it on schedule because of a machine breakdown, non-availability of material, or a strike in the factory. The premium should be treated as a production overhead. Charging premiums for overtime can only be justified if the job has to be finished before the agreed date because of a request from the customer for early completion.

18.4 Usefulness of Job Costing

Keeping a separate record of the cost of individual jobs can be useful in a number of ways:

1) It enables the firm to price the jobs it has undertaken. A common pricing policy is cost plus a percentage mark-up.
2) It contributes to the determination of profit. Where the price for a job has been quoted before it is carried out, a record of how much the job costs to complete must be kept if we are to know the profit earned on the job.
3) It is essential for the valuation of work-in-progress. Those jobs which are still in the process of completion on the last day of the financial year can be easily valued if individual cost records are kept.
4) It is useful as a cost control device as similar jobs can be expected to incur similar costs. By keeping a record of the cost of each job, those jobs which are costing more than they should can easily be identified, and corrective action can be taken.

18.5 Batch Costing

A batch is a group of small individual jobs which constitute a whole. Costing a batch is similar to costing a job, since the batch is seen as the job, and it also has elements of process costing since, if the number of units is large and the units are similar, the firm is approaching mass-production.

Batch costing however has some differences from both job and process costing. In job costing, direct costs are charged directly to the job and overheads are first charged to each cost centre and then reapportioned to the jobs passing through the cost centres, using overhead absorption rates. In batch costing, all costs, whether direct or indirect, are accumulated by cost centres and then averaged over the identical number of units contained within the batch to give a cost per unit, as the batch passes through each cost centre.

Equally it is different from process costing since the batch is of a limited size and comprises an identifiable unit of work whereas a process produces large numbers of the same product indefinitely.

Take, for example, a manufacturer of dining tables which produces cheap, standard, and quality versions of the same table. The production process may be standardised into several operations with the quality table passing through more operations than the cheap table, as shown in the table below:

Operation	Average cost £	Cheap	Standard	Quality
Preparation	30	√	√	√
Assembly 1	50	√	√	√
Assembly 2	40	√	√	√
Varnishing	20	√	√	√
Decoration by hand	40			√
Additional varnishing	30		√	√
Inspection	20	√	√	√
Second inspection	15			√
Packing	20	√	√	√

By calculating the total cost of each operation it is possible to identify the average unit cost of it by dividing the total cost by the number of units in the batch. Hypothetical figures for these are shown above. The cost of a unit is simply the total of the average cost of each operation through which it passes. The final cost is of course an average cost of each unit of that type.

In our example:

Operation	Cheap	Standard	Quality
	£	£	£
Preparation	30	30	30
Assembly 1	50	50	50
Assembly 2	40	40	40
Varnishing	20	20	20
Decoration by hand			40
Additional varnishing		30	30
Inspection	20	20	20
Second inspection			15
Packing	20	20	20
	180	210	265

Batch costing contains elements of both job and process costing. It resembles process costing in that the cost computed is an average per unit, job costing in that separate cost calculations have to be made for each order. Batch costing is used in a lot of multi-product industries where process costing cannot be used and where job costing is prohibitively expensive.

18.6 Contract Costing

Where a job is a long-term contract covering several accounting periods, as is the case in civil engineering and shipbuilding, costing of the job becomes a little more complicated and the techniques of contract costing have to be employed. A double-entry contract account is maintained for each job. All direct costs incurred on the contract and overheads allocated to it are debited to the account, while income from the contract is credited to it. The contract account is, in effect, an individual profit and loss account, from which it is possible to determine the profit on each contract.

The client usually makes several payments during the lifetime of the contract, the amount payable in each instalment being determined by a professional valuation of the partly-completed job by a firm of architects or surveyors. The client is often allowed to withhold some of the payment even after the contract has been completed, for a period of time. This is known as the retention money and its purpose is to allow time for the purchaser to assess whether the job has been completed to their satisfaction. If it has not, the contractor has to make good any defects in the original work before being entitled to the retention money.

In contract work a large percentage of the total cost is made up of costs which would normally be classified as indirect but which, because of the self-contained nature of the work, are here considered to be direct. Examples of such costs are site installations, transportation, the salaries of architects and planners, site clerks etc; these are directly attributable to the contract and will not be used for any other job. Administration costs are considered to be indirect but they are usually a very small proportion of the total cost and are absorbed on an overall basis.

18.7 Recognition of Profit

While the realisation concept states that profit should be regarded as earned when goods are passed to the customer, such an approach is unsuitable for jobs covering several accounting periods. Adherence to it would result in the income statement taking credit only for jobs completed during the year rather than the value of all work carried on during the year. Years in which a large number of jobs are completed would show a disproportionately higher profit compared with years in which the same amount of work is done but fewer contracts completed. To overcome this problem SSAP 9 (stocks and long-term contracts) allows credit to be taken for ascertainable turnover and profit while contracts are still in progress, provided that there is reasonable certainty that the contract will be completed for the sum agreed. This means that the contractor does not take all of a year's apparent profit (being the value of an architect's certificate less cost of certified work) to that year's profit and loss account. A fraction is usually held back as the apparent profit not yet recognised as earned, as a contingency for additional expenditure becoming necessary on the contract, for example for faulty work. It is transferred to the profit and loss account after sufficient time has elapsed during which it becomes clear that no further costs will be necessary on the contract. Meanwhile the amount is shown in the balance sheet under reserves.

Since the outcome of a long-term contract in its early stages is not known with reasonable certainty, no profit should be taken. SSAP 9 also recommends that if a loss on a contract is incurred in any one year the whole of the loss should be charged to that year's profit and loss account, i.e. as soon as it arises, in line with the concept of prudence.

18.8 Contents of a Contract Account

We open a separate account for each contract and debit it with all the costs. Materials may either be purchased and received directly from suppliers or sent to the contract site from stores. At the end of a contract year closing stocks of material are carried down as a debit to the next contract period, to be charged then (in line with the accruals concept).

Direct labour costs are also debited to the account. Employees should fill out time sheets for each contract as they may be working on several at the same time. Any outstanding wages at the year-end should also be debited and carried down as a credit balance of the next period.

Direct expenses are charged directly from invoices received. Work done by sub-contractors is regarded as a direct expense. Overheads are also debited to the account based on a predetermined overhead rate.

Fixed assets used on a contract are treated according to how they have been acquired. If they have been hired or leased, the cost is a direct expense. If it is owned by the firm but is being used on site on a short-term basis, it is charged at an hourly rate. If it is owned and is being used on a long-term basis, then the contract is charged with the difference between its value when it arrives on site and when it leaves, i.e. with the depreciation which it has undergone during the time of the contract. At the end of a period the reduced value of the assets is carried down as a credit balance.

The contract account is then credited with the contract price.

Let us now look at an actual example of a contract account.

Example

Steel Contractors Ltd started work on a two-year factory construction project on 1 April 2005. Details of the contract for the first year are as follows:

	£000
Materials purchased and delivered to site	50
Materials issued from store	40
Materials returned to store	5
Site wages	100
Site direct expenses	35
Architect's fees	15
Paid to Cement Ltd for work sub-contracted	75
Allocated overheads	120
Plant sent to site	250

On 31 March 2006 materials on site cost £10 000 and there was £10 000 outstanding for wages. The value of the plant was estimated at £190 000.

The company received an architect's certificate for £600 000 in respect of work carried out to date. This amount was received at the end of the year less 10 per cent retention money. As a provision for the possibility of further expenditure becoming necessary on the work carried out so far the company takes credit for only two-thirds of the profit on work certified. Work costing £30 000 was not certified as being worthy of payment yet.

(a) Prepare the contract account for the year to 31 March 2006.
(b) What is the value of the work-in-progress at the year-end?
(c) Show an extract of the year-end balance sheet relating to items on this contract.

Answer

(a)

Contract Account

	£000		£000
Materials delivered to site	50	Materials returned to store	5
Materials from store	40	Materials on site 31.3.2006	10
Site wages	100	Value of plant	190
Site direct expenses	35	Cost of work not certified	30
Architect's fees	15	Cost of work certified c/f	460
Paid to sub-contractor	75		
Allocated overheads	120		
Plant sent to site	250		
Wages accrued c/f	10		
	695		695
Cost of work certified b/f	460	Architect's certificate	600
Profit and loss – profit taken (W_1)	84		
Profit not taken (balance)	56		
	600		600
1 April 2006		1 April 2006	
Materials b/f	10	Wages accrued b/f	10
Plant b/f	190	Profit not taken b/f	56
Cost of work not certified b/f	30		

You will note that the contract account is divided into three sections. The purpose of the first section is to establish the total cost incurred on the contract over the year. This is found as a balancing figure on the account. The year-end balances are carried forward to the third section, which then represents part of the future costs still to be incurred on the contract. The calculation of the amount of profit to be credited to this year's profit and loss account is carried out in the second section. The apparent profit is reduced by:

1) the contingency for additional expenditure becoming necessary on the building in the future (one-third) and
2) the amount of the retainer (one-tenth).

$$\mathbf{W_1} \; \text{Profit taken} = \text{Apparent profit} \times \frac{2}{3} \times \frac{\text{Cash received}}{\text{Value of work certified}}$$

$$= \pounds(600 - 460) \times \frac{2}{3} \times \frac{9}{10} = \pounds 84$$

In next year's account the profit taken will be reduced by £84 000, as this is the profit already taken this year.

(b)

Valuation of year-end work in progress

	£000
Cost of work certified to date	460
Cost of work not certified	30
Add profit taken to date	84
	574
Less progress payments received (600 × 9/10)	(540)
Work in progress	34

(c)

Steel Contractors Ltd
Balance Sheet extract as at 31 March 2006

	£000
Fixed assets	
Plant at site	250
Less depreciation	(60)
Current assets	
Materials	10
Work in progress	34
Debtor (retention money)	60
Owners' capital	
Profit and loss account (profit taken)	84
Reserves (profit not taken)	56
Current liabilities	
Wages accrued	10

Questions

Question 18.1

T. Eddy Printing Ltd carries out jobbing contracts to customers' specific requirements. Cost data is currently being collected for the month for which job 5/207 has been started and completed. The cost data for the month are as follows:

Direct labour	Hours worked	Time allowed
Printing department		
Job 5/204	170	160
Job 5/206	220	230
Job 5/207	120	144
Job 5/208	130	130
Colour department		
Job 5/203	115	120
Job 5/206	70	76
Job 5/207	40	50
Job 5/208	200	210
Binding department		
Job 5/201	48	46
job 5/202	55	55
Job 5/203	30	28
Job 5/207	20	22

In the Printing and Colour departments the basic hourly rate is £6 per hour, and in the Binding department the basic hourly rate is £4 per hour. All employees are paid a bonus equal to half of the time saved for each job (the bonus paid is included as part of the direct labour costs to the customer).

Direct materials

All materials used on job 5/207 were bought specifically for the job. Invoice details were:

Paper

30 boxes at £26 per box, less 10% trade discount

Ink

12 litres at £50 per litre, less 15% trade discount

Binders

200 at £1.50 each, less 10% trade discount

Production overheads

Printing and colour departments – overheads are absorbed as a percentage of actual direct labour costs incurred; the current rate is 200%.

Binding department – overheads are absorbed by the direct labour rate method (actual time taken). The current rate is £5.40 per direct labour hour.

Administration overheads

A rate of 20% of total production costs of each job is used.

REQUIRED

(a) A detailed statement to show the total cost of job 5/207.   **(13 marks)**

(b) The selling price to the customer is based on a 10% net profit margin. Calculate
     the selling price to the customer.   **(3 marks)**

(c) Briefly explain the difference between marginal costing and absorption costing.   **(4 marks)**

(d) Job costing is an example of specific order costing. Briefly explain the following
     systems, illustrating the type of industries in which they would be used.

     (i)   Contract costing
     (ii)   Process costing   **(6 marks)**

OCR Advanced Level

Question 18.2

Jetprint Limited specialises in printing advertising leaflets and is in the process of
preparing its price list. The most popular requirement is for a folded leaflet made from
a single sheet of A4 paper. From past records and budgeted figures, the following data
have been estimated for a typical batch of 10 000 leaflets:

Artwork	£65
Machine setting	4 hours at £22 per hour
Paper	£12.50 per 1 000 sheets
Ink and consumables	£40
Printers' wages	4 hours at £8 per hour
Note: Printers' wages vary with volume	

General fixed overheads are £15 000 per period during which a total of 600 labour
hours are expected to be worked.

The firm wishes to achieve 30% profit on sales.

REQUIREMENTS

(a) Calculate the selling prices (to the nearest pound) per thousand leaflets for
     quantities of 10 000 and 20 000 leaflets.   **(7 marks)**

(b) Calculate the profit for a period, assuming that during the period the firm sold
     64 batches of 10 000 and 36 batches of 20 000, and that all costs and selling prices
     were as expected.   **(4 marks)**

(c) Comment critically on the results achieved for the period.   **(4 marks)**

Chartered Institute of Management Accountants

Question 18.3

On 31 March 1997, Shorter plc completed a long-term contract and surplus material valued at £6 300 and plant valued at £8 000 were transferred to a new site for the start of a long-term contract on 1 April 1997.

At the financial year ended 31 March 1998 the following details are available.

	£
Materials purchased	726 000
Materials returned to suppliers	3 400
Materials on site not yet used	21 600
Direct wages	290 000
Administration expenses charged	103 500
Allocated overheads	65 000
New plant delivered to site	44 000
Plant hire	3 100
Paid to sub-contractors	68 000
Architects' fees	10 300
Cost of work not yet certified	110 000
Value of work certified by architect	1 500 000

(i)   Direct wages accrued at 31 March 1998 were £10 200. The sub-contractors were owed £8 600 at that date.

(ii) The plant transferred to the contract on 1 April 1997 is due to be scrapped on 31 March 1999 when it will not have any residual value. The new plant has an estimated life of four years from the date of purchase and an estimated residual value of £4 000. A full year's depreciation is charged in the year of purchase. Shorter plc uses the straight line method of depreciation on plant.

(iii) Shorter plc has an agreement with its customer that the customer will pay for all work certified by the architect, less a 20% retention. The customer has paid in accordance with the agreement.

(iv) The attributable profit formula used by the company is:

$$\text{apparent (notional) profit} \times \frac{2}{3} \times \frac{\text{cash received}}{\text{work certified}}$$

REQUIRED

(a) The Contract Account for the year ended 31 March 1998 together with a calculation of the work in progress at that date.   **(25 marks)**

(b) Explain why the customer has negotiated the 20% retention [see note (iii)].   **(4 marks)**

University of Oxford Delegacy of Local Examinations Advanced Level

19

Process Costing

19.1 Introduction

As was mentioned at the start of the last chapter, process costing is suitable for industries where production occurs in a series of continuous operations or processes. In this situation it is impossible to identify the cost associated with each unit and instead an average cost is computed as the total cost divided by the number of units. This system needs less work than the maintenance of a job costing system. In the latter, costs have to be identified directly with jobs and this necessitates the keeping of timesheets by workers, records of jobs to which materials are issued, and the number of direct labour or machine hours spent on each job if overhead absorption is on that basis. The above tasks are not necessary in process costing since costs do not have to be analysed to individual units of output. Process costing is therefore a cheaper system to operate. The information it generates however is less precise, and, in certain situations, computation of average cost can produce misleading results.

The production process is divided into a number of separate processes or operations. Raw materials start in process 1, are transferred to process 2, and so on. The output of one process becomes the input of the next. An account is maintained for each process, to which the direct costs incurred and overheads allocated are debited. The sum is transferred to the next process thereby closing the account. The account of the second process starts with the costs brought forward from the first process. Costs incurred are again debited and the total transferred to the third process – and so on. As production proceeds therefore, there is an accumulation of costs from previous processes.

A record is kept of the number of units processed or volume in terms of weight. The total process cost divided by total units or weight gives the average cost.

Illustration

A good is manufactured in three distinct processes – 1, 2 and 3. 100 units are produced in the month of June, in which the following costs are incurred:

	Process 1	Process 2	Process 3
Direct material	£1 000	£1 500	£1 750
Direct labour	£2 000	£3 500	£3 250
Direct labour hours	100	200	150

Overheads of £4 500 are apportioned on the basis of direct labour hours. Prepare the process accounts.

Answer

Process 1

	Unit cost	Total		Unit cost	Total
	£	£		£	£
Material	10	1 000			
Labour	20	2 000			
Overhead	10	1000	To Process 2 c/f	40	4 000
	40	4 000		40	4 000

Process 2

	Unit cost	Total		Unit cost	Total
From Process 1 b/f	40	4 000			
Material	15	1 500			
Labour	35	3 500			
Overhead	20	2 000	To Process 3 c/f	110	11 000
	110	11 000		110	11 000

Process 3

	Unit cost	Total		Unit cost	Total
From Process 2 b/f	110.00	11 000			
Material	17.50	1 750			
Labour	32.50	3 250			
Overhead	15.00	1 500	To finished goods c/f	175	17 500
	175.00	17 500		175	17 500

The total cost of production of the 100 units is £17 500, giving an average cost of £175. These figures are transferred to the finished goods account, where they remain as an asset. When sold they are expensed to the trading account.

19.2 Normal and Abnormal Losses

Certain losses occur in production as inputs move from one process to another. These are categorised into

- normal losses, which are expected and take place under normal conditions eg losses due to chemical change
- abnormal losses, which are not expected to occur under normal efficient working conditions
- losses which can be sold at a nominal price as scrap
- losses which have no market value and are known as waste.

Normal losses are unavoidable in the normal course of production. Examples include loss through evaporation, chemical change, and remnants such as the leather lost in making a shoe or the diamond lost in cutting a ring. Since a normal loss is unavoidable it is treated as part of the cost of production as follows:

Debit the normal loss account
Credit the process account, regardless of the actual loss that takes place.

Deviations of actual loss from normal are accounted for in an abnormal loss or gain account. When the scrap is sold the normal loss account is credited, the debit going to the cash, bank or debtor account. If no money is received for the waste, do not credit the process account with any money but credit the amount of weight in the appropriate column. These entries are illustrated in an example later.

Abnormal losses result from errors in production such as carelessness, accidents, and the use of inferior quality material. As these are not expected to occur in the normal course of operations, the costs incurred as a result are not charged to the product but instead are written out to an abnormal loss account with the following entries:

Debit the abnormal loss account
Credit the process account

The value attached to the loss is the full cost of good production. In questions it is often necessary to work out the normal cost of one unit using the following formula:

$$\frac{\text{Total normal process cost - Normal scrap value}}{\text{Normal units processed}}$$

The value of the abnormal loss is given as units of abnormal loss multiplied by the normal cost of one unit. If any of the abnormal loss is sold (for example as scrap) the double-entry is:

Debit the cash, bank or debtor account
Credit the abnormal loss account

The balance on the abnormal loss account is written off to the costing profit and loss account. Abnormal losses are not included in the unit cost calculation. The process account shows the cost of production based on normal efficient working conditions. Any losses of an abnormal nature are not allowed to enter into cost calculations and stock valuation.

Where the loss from a process is less than expected, an **abnormal gain** results. The normal cost of the gain (units of gain multiplied by the normal cost of one unit) is transferred to an abnormal gain account by the following entries:

Debit the process account
Credit the abnormal gain account

The gain is credited to the costing profit and loss account. In an abnormal gain the opportunity is lost of earning the scrap value on the expected loss which did not materialise. The account should therefore be reduced by this amount. The double-entry is:

Debit the abnormal gain account
Credit the normal loss account

with the scrap value of abnormal gain units. This in fact closes the normal loss account (see illustration below).

Scrap is a loss which can be sold at a nominal price, and this must be deducted from the normal process cost when calculating the normal cost of one unit.

Waste is a loss which has no market value eg materials which are thrown away or which disappear into the atmosphere. When waste occurs part-way through a process, some of the loss is charged to the work-in-progress, but if it occurs at the end of the process, only completed units are charged with it.

Some waste is dangerous, e.g. nuclear and chemical waste. Such by-products not only have no marketable value but they actually cause the firm to incur further costs in disposing of them safely.

Illustration

A good is manufactured in two processes. 100 units are introduced into Process 2 at a cost of £440. £300 is spent in process 2. A normal loss is expected at 10 per cent of units introduced and these are sold for scrap at £2 each. Show the ledger accounts recording the above if the actual number of units produced in process 2 is:

(a) 80 units
(b) 95 units.

Answer

(a)

Process 1

	Units	Per unit	Total		Units	Per unit	Total
		£	£			£	£
Costs	100	4.40	440	To Process 2 c/f	100	4.40	440

Process 2

	Units	Per unit	Total		Units	Per unit	Total
		£	£			£	£
From Process 1 b/f	100	4.40	440	Normal loss	10	2	20
Costs			300	Abnormal loss*	10	8	80
				To finished stock c/f	80	8	640
	100		740		100		740

$$* \text{Normal loss} = \frac{£440 + £300 - £20}{(100 \times 0.90)\,\text{units}}$$

$$= \frac{£720}{90} = £8 \text{ per unit}$$

$$\text{Abnormal loss} = (80 - 90)\,\text{units} \times £8$$
$$= £80$$

Normal Loss

	Units	Per unit £	Total £		Units	Per unit £	Total £
In Process 2	10	2	20	Bank	10	2	20

Abnormal Loss

	Units	Per unit £	Total £		Units	Per unit £	Total £
In Process 2	10	8	80	Bank	10	2	20
				Costing P & L			60
	10		80		10		80

Finished Stock

	£		£
From Process 2 b/f	640		

Costing P & L

	£		£
Abnormal loss	60		

Bank

	£		£
Normal loss	20	Process 1 – costs	440
Abnormal loss	20	Process 2 – costs	300

(b)

Process 1

	Units	Per unit £	Total £		Units	Per unit £	Total £
Costs	100	4.40	440	To Process 2 c/f	100	4.40	440

Process 2

	Units	Per unit £	Total £		Units	Per unit £	Total £
From Process 1 b/f	100	4.40	440	Normal loss	10	2	20
Costs			300	To finished stock c/f	95	8	760
Abnormal gain	5	8	40				
	105		780		105		780

Normal Loss

	Units	Per unit £	Total £		Units	Per unit £	Total £
In Process 2	10	2	20	Bank	5	2	10
				Abnormal gain	5	2	10
	10		20		10		20

Abnormal Gain

	Units	Per unit £	Total £		Units	Per unit £	Total £
Normal loss	5	2	10	In Process 2	5	8	40
Costing P & L			30				
	5		40		5		40

Finished Stock

	£		£
From Process 2 b/f	760		

	£		£
		Abnormal gain	30

Bank

	£		£
		Process 1 – costs	440
		Process 2 – costs	300

So far the complications of work-in-progress have been ignored. Let us now bring them into our discussion. The accounting treatment of opening work-in-progress is different from that of closing work-in-progress.

19.3 Closing Work-in-progress

In practice when costs are calculated, perhaps at the end of a month, there are likely to be some units started but not yet complete. The implication of this is that unit cost cannot be calculated as total process cost divided by number of units. It is necessary to convert the incomplete units into their equivalent in terms of complete units. Thus 100 units which are 70 per cent complete are equivalent to 70 complete units. 70 is then the figure which is used in the unit cost computation.

Sometimes the various elements of cost may not all have been incurred up to the same percentage. For example material cost may be wholly incurred at the start of the process. Any work-in-progress at the end of the month therefore represents 100 per cent of the material cost. This may not be so for labour and overhead, which are usually incurred throughout the process. In these cases separate equivalent production units need to be calculated for each item of cost.

Example

Information relating to Process 1 for a period.

Units introduced	1 000
Units completed	800
Closing work in progress	200
Costs incurred:	
Material	£3 000
Labour	£2 300
Overhead	£1 800

The work-in-progress is 100% complete in respect of materials, 60% of labour and 50% of overheads.

What is the cost of the closing work-in-progress and the completed production transferred to process 2?

Answer

	Item of cost		
	Material	*Labour*	*Overhead*
Cost incurred	£3 000	£2 300	£1 800
Completed units	800	800	800
Equivalent units in WIP	200	120	100
Total equivalent units	1 000	920	900
Unit cost	£3 000 ÷ 1 000 = £3	£2 300 ÷ 920 = £2.50	£1 800 ÷ 900 = £2
WIP valuation	200 × £3 = £600	120 × £2.50 = £300	100 × £2 = £200

Total unit cost: £3 + £2.50 + £2 = £7.50

Total WIP valuation: £600 + £300 + £200 = £1 100

The value of completed production is 800 units × £7.50 = £6 000.

The process account would look as follows:

Process 1 Account

	Unit cost	Per unit	Total		Unit cost	Per unit	Total
		£	£			£	£
Material	1 000	3	3 000				
Labour			2 300	To process 2 c/f	800	7.50	6 000
Overhead			1 800	Closing WIP c/f	200		1 100
	1 000		7 100		1 000		7 100

The closing work-in-progress of this period is, of course, the opening work-in-progress of the next period.

19.4 Opening Work-in-progress

When opening work-in-progress exists, a decision has to be made on whether to allow the costs embodied in them to influence the current period's computation of unit cost by using the weighted average cost method. If we decide otherwise we would use the first in, first out method. The difference between the two is best illustrated with an example.

Illustration

The following information applies to Process 2:

Costs embodied in opening work-in-progress, 400 units, ¾ complete:

Material	£800
Conversion costs	£900

Materials are added at the start of a process and conversion costs accrue evenly throughout.

In Process 2:

Units started	3 200
Material cost	£6 400
Conversion costs	£15 600
Closing work in progress	600, ½ complete

What is the value of the closing work-in-progress and completed units?

Answer

We first have to find the number of units completed during the period.

	Units
Opening work in progress	400
Introduced in process	3 200
	3 600
Less closing work in progress	(600)
Completed in process	3 000

Using the Weighted Average Cost Method

		Material	Conversion costs
Opening WIP		800	900
Process 2 costs		6 400	15 600
Total cost		£7 200	£16 500
Completed units		3 000	3 000
Closing WIP equivalent units		600	300
Total equivalent units		3 600	3 300
Unit cost		7 200 ÷ 3 600 = £2	16 500 ÷ 3 300 = £5
Valuation of WIP:			
Material	600 units × £2 =		£1 200
Conversion costs	300 units × £5 =		£1 500
			£2 700

Valuation of completed units:

3 000 units × £7 = £21 000

Note that:

Material + Conversion costs = Completed units + WIP

£7 200	+ £16 500	= £21 000	+ £2 700
	£23 700	= £23 700	

In the above statement costs embodied in the opening work-in-progress have been merged with the costs incurred in the current process to give a figure for average unit cost. No attempt is made to separate the previous process costs (as reflected in the opening WIP £1 700) from the current process costs.

The process account looks as follows:

Process 2 Account

	£		£
Opening WIP b/f	1 700	To finished goods c/f	21 000
Material	6 400	Closing WIP c/f	2 700
Conversion costs	15 600		
	23 700		23 700

Using the First In, First Out Method

This method assumes that the work-in-progress units being first in are also first out, i.e. they are completed before any of the current process units. The whole of the closing work-in-progress is therefore valued at the unit cost of the current process only. The costs embodied in the opening work-in-progress do not enter into the calculation.

The statement of unit cost looks as follows:

	Material	Conversion costs
Process 2 costs	£6 400	£15 600
Units completed in process	3 000	3 000
Less opening WIP equivalent units	(400)	(300)
	2 600	2 700
Add closing WIP equivalent units	600	300
Total equivalent units in process 2	3 200	3 000
	£6 400	£15 600

Material per unit: £6 400 ÷ 3 200 units = £2

Conversion costs per unit: £15 600 ÷ 3 000 = £5.20

Valuation of WIP

		£
Material	600 units × £2	1 200
Conversion costs	300 units × £5.20	1 560
		2 760

Valuation of completed units

		£
Opening WIP		1 700
Material	2 600 units × £2	5 200
Conversion costs	2 700 units × £5.20	14 040
		20 940

Note again that:

Material + Conversion costs   = Completed units + WIP

£7 200   +   £16 500   = £20 940   + £2 760

                    £23 700   = £23 700

The process account looks as follows:

Process 2 Account

	£		£
Opening WIP b/f	1 700	To finished goods c/f	20 940
Material	6 400	Closing WIP c/f	2 760
Conversion costs	15 600		
	23 700		23 700

The decision on which method to use is determined by the nature of production in the process i.e whether the opening work-in-progress is the first to be completed or not. In processes where the opening work-in-progress is in liquid or gaseous form the average cost method is to be preferred since it is not possible to separate them from additional inputs introduced during the process.

Notice the following observations as regards WIP:

1) Costs from a previous process are always complete since incomplete units cannot pass on to the next stage.
2) If it is the practice to add cost elements at the start of the process, these particular costs are not added again later in the process.
3) If it is the practice to add cost elements at the end of the process, these are not included in WIP since, by definition, incomplete units have not yet reached the stage where the final process is carried out.

Questions

Question 19.1

A manufacturing company makes a product by two processes and the data below relate to the second process for the month of April.

A work in progress balance of 1 200 units brought forward from March was valued, in cost, as follows:

	£
Direct materials, complete	10 800
Direct wages, 60% complete	6 840
Production overhead, 60% complete	7 200

During April, 4 000 units were transferred from the first process to the second process at a cost of £7.50 each, this input being treated as direct material within the second process.

Other costs incurred by the second process were:

	£
Additional direct materials	4 830
Direct wages	32 965
Production overhead	35 538

3 200 completed units were transferred to the finished goods store. A loss of 520 units, being normal, occurred during the process. The average method of pricing is used.

Work in progress at the end of April consisted of 500 completed units awaiting transfer to the finished goods store and a balance of unfinished units which were complete as regards direct material and 50% complete as regards direct wages and production overhead.

REQUIRED

(a) Prepare for the month of April the account for the second process.   **(14 marks)**

(b) Present a statement for management setting out the:
    (i) cost per unit of the finished product, by element of cost and total;
    (ii) cost of production transferred to finished goods;
    (iii) cost of production of completed units awaiting transfer to finished goods;
    (iv) cost of uncompleted units in closing work in progress, by element of cost
       and in total.   **(6 marks)**

Chartered Institute of Management Accountants

Question 19.2

Product X is produced through a process. Waste through the process is set at 15% of input. The waste can be sold at a price of 40p per kg.

During period three, there were 16 000 kg of raw material used at a cost of £1.60 per kg. Conversion costs relating to labour and overheads were costed at £4 800 and £4 560 respectively.

The output of Product X was 14 000 kg.

There were no opening or closing stocks in the process.

REQUIREMENT

(a) Prepare the process cost account for period three.   **(8 marks)**

(b) Compare and contrast process costing with job costing and give one example
    of an industry in which each would be appropriate.   **(7 marks)**

Northern Ireland Council for the Curriculum Examinations and Assessment Advanced Level

Question 19.3

Frameit plc produces photograph frames using two processes: heating followed by moulding. The moulding process mixes 2 kg of X (after melting) with 1 kg of Y. Assume that there are no opening stocks of either X or Y.

Details of both processes for April were as follows.

Heating

1 250 kg of material X at £9.72 per kg.
2 500 hours of direct labour at £6.50 per hour.
Overheads are charged to the process on the basis of £4 per direct labour hour.
Normal loss: 4% of input weight.
Good output: 1 210 kg of which 1 000 kg were transferred to the moulding process and the balance held in stock.
Wastage from this process has no sales value.

Moulding

500 kg of material Y at £26.90 per kg.
750 hours of direct labour at £4 per hour.
Overheads are charged to the process on the basis of £8 per direct labour hour.
Normal loss: 5% of input weight.
Good output: 1 375 kg.
All wastage from this process was sold as scrap for £4 per kg.

Prepare the following accounts for April, showing both unit quantities and values.

(a) Heating Process Account	**(9 marks)**
(b) Moulding Process Account	**(7½ marks)**
(c) Abnormal Gain Account	**(1½ marks)**
(d) Abnormal Loss Account.	**(2 marks)**

Scottish Qualifications Authority Higher Specimen Paper

20

Absorption and Marginal Costing

20.1 Introduction

In Chapter 17 we studied overhead absorption, in which we included all manufacturing costs, both variable and fixed, in the calculation of the unit cost of a product. We saw the difficulties of trying to attach indirect overheads to products and the alternative means accountants use to resolve them.

Absorption costing or **full costing** is a system which charges total overheads to cost units and then allocates and apportions them to cost centres. Once the overhead absorption rate has been calculated, each cost unit is charged with its share of the fixed overhead and the valuation of the closing stock includes this share.

Marginal costing (also known as **variable** or **direct costing**) is a system which has been used increasingly in recent years in decision-making. Under this system only the variable manufacturing costs are allocated to the product and are included in the stock valuation. The fixed manufacturing overhead is treated as an overall expense for the period but is not included in the stock valuation, neither is it taken into account when making decisions which are based on the unit cost. Marginal costing includes in the unit cost only those costs which change when the level of activity changes – the variable costs. An increase in the volume of output causes changes only in variable costs in the short-run, as long as the capacity provided by the fixed costs can accommodate such an increase in volume. To understand marginal costing, we need to meet the concept of **contribution**.

20.2 Contribution

Contribution is the difference between sales and the marginal cost:

Sales – Variable Cost = Contribution

The income received by a firm from the sale of one unit of its product has to cover the following items:

(a) the variable cost of production, i.e. direct labour, direct raw materials and any other direct costs
(b) the fixed costs of production, i.e. rent, maintenance, depreciation, administration etc.
(c) the firm's profit.

When extra units are produced, it is only the variable costs which increase as the fixed costs have already been met. The amount left over from the selling price after the direct, variable costs have been met is the 'contribution' to the fixed costs and to the firm's profit (this would not be the case at full capacity as an increase in output at this point would necessitate an increase in fixed costs).

Where spare capacity exists, marginal cost will be equal to total variable cost since an increase in production of one unit will cause an increase in the variable costs only, fixed costs remaining constant. Although all the overheads will be deducted from

revenue in the profit and loss account at the end of the year, it is possible to ignore them when deciding whether or not to accept an extra job or batch. The firm can add to its profits by accepting a job as long as the price paid by the customer covers the variable costs, since the fixed costs have already been paid for and no extra fixed cost will be incurred as a result of taking the job.

Example

A firm has an existing capacity to produce 25 000 units of its product a year. In the year just finished, the firm produced and sold 20 000 units (ignore opening and closing stocks). We are given the following figures:

Sales	£5 per unit
Direct materials	£1.50 per unit
Direct labour	£1.00 per unit
Factory overheads	£20 000
Office overheads	£5 000

At this level of output the firm's profit per unit on an absorption basis is as follows:

	Per unit	
	£	£
Sales		5.00
Direct materials	1.50	
Direct labour	1.00	
Factory overheads (£20 000 ÷ 20 000 units)	1.00	
Office overheads (£5 000 ÷ 20 000 units)	0.25	
Cost of sales		(3.75)
Profit per unit		1.25

The profit and loss account will be as follows:

	£	£
Sales		100 000
Direct materials	30 000	
Direct labour	20 000	
Factory overheads	20 000	
Office overheads	5 000	
Cost of sales		(75 000)
Profit		25 000

A new customer now appears who offers to purchase a batch of 4 000 units if he is allowed a 30% trade discount. This would bring down the selling price from £5 to £3.50. On an absorption basis, the firm will refuse the offer since £3.50 does not even cover its production cost, but the situation changes if it takes a marginal approach.

The contribution in this example is selling price minus direct materials and labour:

$£5 – (£1.50 + £1.00) = £2.50$

The discounted selling price more than covers the variable costs and makes a contribution to the fixed costs and profit, even if does not fully cover the amount of overhead absorbed by each unit.

This will be the profit and loss account after the customer's offer has been accepted:

	£	£
Sales (20 000 units @ £5)		100 000
Sales (4 000 units @ £3.50)		14 000
Direct materials (24 000 units @ £1.50)	36 000	
Direct labour (24 000 units @ £1)	24 000	
Factory overheads	20 000	
Office overheads	5 000	
Cost of sales		(85 000)
Profit		£29 000

The firm's overall profit has increased as a result of accepting the offer since no new fixed costs were involved and since the price paid by the customer exceeded the contribution. The offer would have been refused in the following cases:

(a) If the price offered by the customer had been less than the variable cost of £2.50. Overall profit would fall since the selling price does not even cover the variable costs of production.
(b) If the variable cost increased so that it exceeded the contribution. This could happen if the firm had to pay premium overtime rates to workers in order to finish the job in time.
(c) If the order can be met only by increasing the fixed costs, e.g. by buying new machinery, hiring new premises etc. For the purposes of this job, the fixed cost would become variable and would have to be deducted from the contribution, although it would then become fixed for subsequent jobs.

Example of Marginal Costing

The figures below relate to the activities of a manufacturer for a year:

	£
Direct material	4 000
Direct wages	3 000
Factory overheads	1 000
Sales	10 000
Variable selling costs	500
Fixed selling costs	600
Fixed administrative expenses	900

Costs embodied in stocks:

	Opening £	Closing £
Direct material	600	1 100
Direct wages	400	900
Factory overheads	100	150

A profit and loss account prepared on a marginal costing basis would look like this:

	£	£
Sales		10 000
Less variable cost of goods sold:		
Opening stock (600 + 400)	1 000	
Variable production cost (4 000 + 3 000)	7 000	
	8 000	
Less closing stock (1 100 + 900)	(2 000)	
	6 000	

Variable selling costs	500	
Total variable cost		(6 500)
Contribution		3 500
Less fixed costs:		
Factory overheads	1 000	
Fixed selling costs	600	
Administrative expenses	900	
		(2 500)
Profit		£1 000

Note that:

1) Stock is valued at variable cost only. Under absorption costing, the value of opening stock is £1 100 and of closing stock £2 150.
2) Sales minus variable cost gives the contribution available to cover fixed costs.
3) Profit is contribution less fixed costs.

A positive contribution does not necessarily mean a profit. If fixed costs are greater than contribution, the firm will suffer a loss.

20.3 A Comparison between Absorption and Marginal Costing using a Worked Example

Let us now look at an example of comparative income statements under the two systems.

The following information relates to the Gnome Manufacturing Company Limited:

Per unit	£
Selling price	10
Direct material cost	2
Direct labour cost	1
Variable production overhead	1
Variable selling cost	0.5
Per month	
Fixed production overhead	2 500
Fixed selling costs	600
Fixed administrative expenses	900

There was an opening stock of 50 gnomes at the start of Month 1. Fixed overheads embodied in this were £125. The budget forecast was that production would be equal to sales at 1 000 gnomes per month.

Actual results for the first three months are as follows:

Month	1	2	3
Production in units	1 000	1 100	900
Sales in units	1 000	900	1 100

The method of overhead absorption used by the company is the blanket rate per unit of planned output.

Prepare comparative incomes statements for the three-month period under

(a) marginal costing
(b) absorption costing.

The Gnome Manufacturing Company Limited
Marginal Cost Income Statement for Months 1 – 3

	Month 1 £	Month 1 £	Month 2 £	Month 2 £	Month 3 £	Month 3 £
Sales		10 000		9 000		11 000
Less variable cost of sales:						
Opening stock (W_1)	200		200		1 000	
Direct materials	2 000		2 200		1 800	
Direct labour	1 000		1 100		900	
Variable production overheads	1 000		1 100		900	
	4 200		4 600		4 600	
Less closing stock (W_2) (W_3)	(200)		(1 000)		(200)	
	4 000		3 600		4 400	
Variable selling costs	500		450		550	
		(4 500)		(4 050)		(4 950)
Contribution		5 500		4 950		6 050
Less fixed costs:						
Production overheads	2 500		2 500		2 500	
Selling costs	600		600		600	
Administrative expenses	900		900		900	
		4 000		4 000		4 000
Net profit		£1 500		£950		£2 050

Workings

Stocks are valued throughout at variable cost only i.e. at £4 per unit.

W_1 50 gnomes at £4 each =   £200
W_2 250 gnomes at £4 each = £1 000
W_3 50 gnomes at £4 each =   £200

Note that variable selling costs are not included in the stock valuation – this includes only variable production costs.

And now under absorption costing.

The Gnome Manufacturing Company Limited
Absorption Cost Income Statement for Months 1 – 3

	Month 1 £	Month 1 £	Month 2 £	Month 2 £	Month 3 £	Month 3 £
Sales		10 000		9 000		11 000
Less cost of sales:						
Opening stock (W_4)	325		325		1 625	
Direct materials	2 000		2 200		1 800	
Direct labour	1 000		1 100		900	
Production overheads absorbed (W_5)	3 500		3 850		3 150	
	6 825		7 475		7 475	
Less closing stock (W_6)	(325)		(1 625)		(325)	
	6 500		5 850		7 150	
Under (over) absorption adjustment (W_5)			(250)		250	
		(6 500)		(5 600)		(7 400)
Gross profit		3 500		3 400		3 600

Less non-manufacturing expenses:			
Variable selling costs	500	450	550
Fixed selling costs	600	600	600
Administrative expenses	900	900	900
	(2 000)	(1 950)	(2 050)
Net profit	1 500	1 450	1 550

Workings

W₄ Stocks are now valued at full manufacturing cost, i.e.

50 @ £4 variable cost + £125 fixed cost = £325

W₅ The chosen overhead absorption method is the blanket rate per unit of output

$$\text{Rate} = \frac{\text{Total planned production overhead}}{\text{Planned output}}$$

$$= \frac{£2\,500 \text{ fixed} + £1\,000 \text{ variable}}{1\,000 \text{ gnomes}} = £3.50$$

	Month 1	Month 2	Month 3
Incurred	2 500 + 1 000 = 3 500	2 500 + 1 100 = 3 600	2 500 + 900 = 3 400
Absorbed	1 000 × 3.50 = 3 500	1 100 × 3.50 = 3 850	900 × 3.50 = 3 150
Under (over) absorption	0	(250)	250

W₆ Valuation of closing stock

There are two methods of finding the unit full cost.

Method 1

$$\text{Unit cost} = \frac{\text{Total production cost charged *}}{\text{Units produced}}$$

$$\text{Month 2:} \quad \frac{2\,200 + 1100 + 3\,850}{1100} = £6.50$$

$$\text{Month 3:} \quad \frac{1800 + 900 + 3150}{900} = £6.50$$

* Note that this is not production cost incurred; any under (over) absorption is included in the stock valuation.

Method 2

Unit costs:

	£
Direct material	2.00
Direct labour	1.00
Production overhead	3.50
Total unit cost	6.50

Value of closing stock = 250 gnomes @ £6.50

= £1 625

Follow the illustration through a second time if you did not understand it all in your first reading.

We can now use the illustration to make some observations on the two systems. Firstly note that when:

Production = Sales   Month 1 Absorption cost profit = Marginal cost profit
Production > Sales   Month 2 Absorption cost profit > Marginal cost profit
Production < Sales   Month 3 Absorption cost profit < Marginal cost profit

Since the only difference between the three months is in the treatment of production overheads and valuation of stock, the difference in profit can be reconciled through stock.

Consider Month 2 when there is a build-up of stock. Absorption cost profit is higher than marginal cost profit by £500. This is because with the latter all the production overheads have been charged against profit whilst in the former it has been included in the large year-end valuation and carried forward to the next month. The charge for production overhead has effectively been reduced. This leads to the higher profit figure. A statement can be prepared to clarify the reconciliation.

	Closing stock		Opening stock		Increase in stock	Profit
	£		£		£	£
Absorption costing	1 625	–	325	=	1 300	1 450
Marginal costing	1 000	–	200	=	800	950
Difference					500	= 500

In month 3, when there is a run-down in stock, the opposite happens. Under absorption costing the amount of fixed overhead brought forward from last month is greater than the amount of overhead carried forward to next month. The month then becomes over-burdened with more than one month's share of overhead. Profit is therefore lower than under marginal costing, where the charge is just one month's overhead, and no more.

A reconciliation again:

	Closing stock		Opening stock		Increase in stock	Profit
	£		£		£	£
Absorption costing	325	–	1 625	=	(1 300)	1 550
Marginal costing	200	–	1 000	=	(800)	2 050
Difference					500	= 500

When sales match production and there is no change in stock levels, as in month 1, the two methods produce the same amount of profit. This is because under absorption costing, the amount of overhead deferred to next month in closing stock is exactly equal to the amount of last month's overhead charged to this month in opening stock. In effect the charge is the amount of overhead incurred during the month. As marginal costing also charges this amount we can expect profits under the two systems to be equal.

	Closing stock		Opening stock		Increase in stock	Profit
	£		£		£	£
Absorption costing	325	–	325	=	0	1 500
Marginal costing	200	–	200	=	0	1 500
Difference					0	= 0

The larger the fluctuation in stock levels the greater will be the discrepancy in profits between the two systems. Although fluctuations are common in the short term, in the long term sales and production are usually equal to each other, i.e. there is no continuous build-up or depletion of stock. Taking one period with the next then, total profits under the two systems should be equal. In our example, production is 3 000 units over the three months, and sales are also 3 000 units. The quarterly total profits should then be the same. We can see below that this is so.

Month	Absorption costing profit	Marginal costing profit
	£	£
1	1 500	1 500
2	1 450	950
3	1 550	2 050
Total profit	4 500	4 500

20.4 Features of Absorption and Marginal Costing

Decision-making

One distinction between the fixed and variable components of costs is that fixed costs are unavoidable in the short term whereas variable costs are avoidable. Managers are able to influence the levels of variable cost but not fixed cost since they are sunk costs which have already been incurred. In short-term decision-making it is best to ignore these irrelevant costs and look only at the variable costs associated with different alternatives. Using absorption costing as a basis on which to take decisions may ensure that the firm is taking less risk but it may also lose out on contracts which would have increased the firm's overall profit. A marginal costing system highlighting contribution is therefore likely to be of more use for decision-making than one including irrelevant fixed costs and indeed, marginal costing is an important tool of management accountants. Decision-making and relevant costs are considered in the next chapter.

More Meaningful Results

Under absorption costing it is possible for a business suffering from a slow-down in sales and build-up of stock to show a healthy profit for the year. This is because a large amount of the year's fixed overhead is not charged, being carried forward in the large stock figure. If sales pick up in the following year, profits may actually fall because the year is over-burdened with a large amount of overhead from the previous year in addition to that year's overhead. Under marginal costing such anomalies can never occur. Profits and sales always move in the same direction. If the selling price and cost structure remain unchanged, an increase in sales always leads to an increase in profit, and vice versa. This is because marginal costing profit is influenced by sales volume only whereas under absorption costing profit is a function of both sales and production volume.

Absorption costing flatters the results of an accounting period in which there is a build-up of stocks. Marginal costing does not do this. As a result its profit figure in a period of poor sales is more realistic and alerts management to the problem. Under absorption costing the problem may be hidden in an inflated profit figure, giving management a false sense of achievement. For this reason, comparison of profit from one year to another is more meaningful under marginal costing.

Performance Evaluation

Large businesses are often decentralised into autonomous divisions, for example by function, product or sales area. The manager of each individual division is responsible for its performance. This is frequently monitored by top management for control purposes. The two most widely used measures of performance are divisional sales and divisional profit. Under absorption costing, as mentioned above, it is possible for an increase in sales to decrease profit. A manager is not likely to have much faith in a costing system which rewards his good performance by showing a fall in profit! Worse still, he may be tempted to manipulate profit, by varying the level of stocks. For example, he may inflate it by deliberately building up stocks just before the year-end. No such temptation exists under marginal costing. The results, taking one year with the next, are also fairer and more meaningful.

No Need to Forecast

Under absorption costing, overhead recovery rates are based on forecasts. If actual activity does not turn out to be exactly as forecast, an incorrect amount of overhead is charged to the income statement. Although an adjustment is made for under-absorption or over-absorption later in the statement, closing stock is valued before this and has the incorrect amount of overhead charged to it. The balance sheet figure for stock is therefore also 'wrong'. No such problems arise with marginal costing.

Financial Reporting

In external reporting consistency is an important requirement from year to year for the same business and also between businesses. A choice has to be made and adhered to. The official recommendation in the UK is to use absorption costing (SSAP 9 Stocks and Long-Term Contracts). Financial accountants are more concerned with absorption costing.

20.5 Asset or Expense?

In recent years the debate has centred on whether the production overhead embodied in stock is an asset or expense. If it is considered an asset, the amount should be included in stock and shown in the balance sheet, as in absorption costing. If it is considered an expense, it should be written off to the income statement and excluded from the balance sheet, as in marginal costing. The definition of asset then becomes central to the debate. The problem is that accountants are not in agreement over the definition. The disagreement centres around whether assets are best described as cost-obviators or revenue-producers. An item of expenditure is cost-obviating if it averts the need to incur some future cost. Spending money on fixed production overheads in one year does not reduce the amount that needs to be spent on those overheads in future years – they are therefore not cost-obviating. As such they should be wholly written off to the income statement. This definition of asset supports marginal costing. An item of expenditure is revenue-producing if by its spending the firm's future revenues are boosted. Firms do not spend money on fixed factory overheads just for the sake of it. They do so because it is necessary for the production of goods – goods which will ultimately bring in revenue. Any goods which remain unsold at the end of a year should therefore be charged their share of overhead as this expense will contribute to future revenue. This definition supports absorption costing.

20.6 Examination Questions

Questions usually ask for comparative income statements under the two systems. A reconciliation of the different profit figures, with an explanation, is sometimes also asked for. Essay questions on the theoretical disagreements between the two systems are more a feature of professional examinations than those at this level. You should however be prepared to write about the disagreement over the interpretation of the matching concept, as outlined at the start of the chapter. The dispute about the best definition of asset is not so important at this stage, although knowledge of it will help you to appreciate the difference between the two systems more fully.

Questions

Question 20.1

Kolorglass plc produces stained glass panels at a standard selling price of £72 per unit. You are provided with the following information for years 1998 and 1999.

Annual fixed costs of production were £90 000.

Variable costs per unit:

Direct materials	£22
Direct labour	£4
Variable overheads	£14

Production data

	Units produced
1998	8 000
1999	7 000

Stock data

at 1 January 1998	450 units
at 1 January 1999	300 units
at 31 December 1999	600 units

The production budget shows a normal level of activity of 7 500 units per annum.

Calculate for **1998** and **1999**:

(a) total sales value (assume no wastage);   **(3 marks)**

(b) total variable costs charged to production;   **(2 marks)**

(c) (i) the fixed overhead absorption rate based on the normal level of activity;
     (ii) total fixed overheads charged to production;
     (iii) the value of the over- or under-absorption of fixed overheads;   **(4 marks)**

(d) opening and closing stock values
     (i) for use in marginal cost accounts;
     (ii) for use in absorption cost accounts;   **(5 marks)**

(e) the profit or loss earned
   (i) using marginal costing
   (ii) using absorption costing.   **(6 marks)**

Scottish Qualifications Authority Higher Specimen Paper

Question 20.2

Monteplana Ltd produced the following financial statement for the year ended
31 December 1993:

	£	£
Sales (100 000 units)		300 000
Less		
Direct materials	100 000	
Direct labour	40 000	
Variable factory overhead	10 000	
Fixed factory overhead	100 000	
		(250 000)
Manufacturing profit		50 000
Less		
Selling and distribution expenses	30 000	
Administrative expenses	30 000	
		(60 000)
Net loss		£(10 000)

There were no opening or closing stocks of either finished goods or work in progress.
The factory plant had a production capacity of 200 000 units per annum.

As a result of the net loss arising in 1993, the sales director maintained that the loss
had arisen through not operating the plant at full capacity and that an extensive
advertising campaign would increase sales significantly. Thus the board of directors
agreed that £40 000 would be spent on an advertising campaign in 1994, and that the
plant would be worked to full capacity producing 200 000 units.

The following results were achieved in the financial year ended 31 December 1994.

1) 130 000 units were sold at the 1993 price.
2) All factory variable expenses increased directly in proportion to output.
3) There was no increase in selling and administrative expenses except that due to
   increased advertising.

All the directors agreed that in order to pursue a policy of consistency, stocks of
finished goods should continue to be valued at the full manufacturing unit cost.

The accountant stated that he would prefer to see stock valuation including
manufacturing variable costs only.

REQUIRED

(a) An income statement for the year ended 31 December 1994 on the agreed basis
    of valuing stocks.   **(5 marks)**

(b) An alternative income statement for the year ended 31 December 1994 using the
    accountant's suggestion as the basis of valuing stock.   **(5 marks)**

(c) (i) Use accepted accountancy principles to explain the 'correctness' of the argument
       regarding the stock valuation of the directors.
   (ii) Write a memorandum which the accountant could submit to the directors in an
        effort to persuade them to change to his policy for stock valuation. The
        memorandum should explain the shortcomings of the present policy and the
        advantages which would accrue from the change.   **(10 marks)**

Associated Examining Board Advanced Level

Question 20.3

Duo Limited makes and sells two products, Alpha and Beta. The following
information is available:

	Period 1	Period 2
Production (units)		
Alpha	2 500	1 900
Beta	1 750	1 250
Sales (units)		
Alpha	2 300	1 700
Beta	1 600	1 250

Financial data:

	Alpha	Beta
	£	£
Unit selling price	90	75
Unit variable costs		
Direct materials	15	12
Direct labour (£6/hr)	18	12
Variable production overheads	12	8

Fixed costs for the company in total were £110 000 in period 1 and £82 000 in
period 2. Fixed costs are recovered on direct labour hours.

REQUIREMENTS

(a) Prepare profit and loss accounts for period 1 and for period 2 based on
    marginal cost principles.   **(5 marks)**

(b) Prepare profit and loss accounts for period 1 and for period 2 based on
    absorption cost principles.   **(6 marks)**

(c) Comment on the position shown by your statements.   **(4 marks)**

Chartered Institute of Management Accountants

Part III
Management Accounting

21

Decision-making and Relevant Costs

21.1 Introduction

Financial accounting and the system of absorption costing include historic costs, i.e. costs which have been paid in the past. When it comes to making decisions about the future, historic costs which have already been incurred are irrelevant and the accountant is more interested in avoidable future costs. Such information is not available from the financial accounts. However, not all future costs are relevant to a particular decision. Decision-making is a process of choosing among competing alternatives, each with its own set of costs and revenues. Those costs which are the same under each alternative are irrelevant because they are not affected by the decision taken. A relevant cost is therefore a future differential cost.

For a cost to be relevant to a decision it must be:

1) a future cost, and
2) a differential cost, i.e. its level must be different for each of the alternatives under consideration.

The above applies equally to benefits.

It is the responsibility of the management accountant to identify and separate the differential from the common costs and revenues under each alternative, and present them to management in the form of a differential cost statement. Such statements are widely used in practice and often asked for in examination questions. They can be used for both short-run (tactical) decisions and long-run (investment) decisions. The main distinction is that in the short run the firm is limited to a fixed amount of capacity and has certain fixed costs – those associated with land, capital, and certain types of labour. These fixed costs are not relevant costs because they are unavoidable in the time period under consideration. The relevant costs are the differential variable costs. In the long run all costs are variable, so that the fixed costs irrelevant in the short run become relevant in the long run. This chapter is concerned mainly with short-run decisions. Long-run capital investment decisions are considered in Chapter 25.

Short-run decisions are many and varied but some of the more important ones, which we shall look at in this chapter include:

- dropping a segment
- accepting or rejecting an order
- decision-making in the face of a limiting factor
- making a product internally or buying it from outside
- buying or leasing fixed assets
- selling a by-product or further processing it.

21.2 Dropping a Segment

A segment is an identifiable unit of a business such as a particular product, branch, or sales area. Let us take a firm producing three products – two profitable and one unprofitable – and examine the relevant considerations in the decision on whether to drop the unprofitable product.

Example

General Components Ltd manufactures three components A, B and C, used in the helicopter industry. The estimate of costs and revenues for each for the coming financial year are as follows:

	A	B	C	Total
	£000	£000	£000	£000
Sales	200	150	100	450
Cost of goods sold	(100)	(75)	(60)	(235)
Gross profit	100	75	40	215
Less expenses:				
Factory overhead	40	30	20	90
Selling and distribution costs	15	12	15	50
Head office and administration expenses	20	15	10	37
Total expenses	(75)	(57)	(45)	(177)
Net profit (loss)	£25	£18	£(5)	£38

The factory overhead and 50 per cent of the head office administration expenses are fixed and have been apportioned to the products on the basis of sales value. Should the company cease producing component C? At first sight it appears so. Let us now consider the proposal more carefully.

The first point to note is that the factory overhead and fixed element of the administration expense will continue to be incurred and their levels will be unchanged whether or not C is dropped. They are irrelevant in the context of the decision but the selling and distribution costs and cost of goods sold are avoidable and therefore relevant. Whether or not the company gets any sales revenue from C will also be affected by the decision and it is therefore relevant.

Differential cost statement if C is dropped

	£000	£000
Sales		100
Less differential costs:		
Cost of goods sold	60	
Selling and distribution costs	15	
Variable administration expenses	5	
		(80)
Differential profit		20

The above statement tells us that C should not be dropped since it is contributing £20 000 to the factory overhead and head office administration expenses. If C were dropped (on the basis of the income statement incorporating irrelevant costs) the £20 000 would no longer be covered by C and would have to be absorbed by components A and B thus decreasing their profitability. Total profits of the company would thus fall from £38 000 to £18 000.

21.3 Accepting or Rejecting an Order

Another common type of decision in business is whether or not to accept a special order at a price below the normal selling price. A firm could take the approach that it must make an overall profit on every order accepted, i.e. it would want to cover all variable costs plus a contribution to the overheads. This absorption approach can however cause the firm to reject an order which could have added to its overall profit if it had taken a marginal costing approach.

Example

Fred manufactures wooden clogs. The costs of each unit are as follows:

	£
Direct material	3
Direct labour	1
Fixed overhead	2
	6

Fred receives a large order from abroad to supply 1 000 clogs at £5. On the basis of the above statement he should not accept. The fixed costs however are irrelevant and should be ignored as Fred is committed to incurring them whatever happens.

Differential cost statement if order is accepted

	£	£
Sales		5 000
Less relevant costs:		
Direct material	3 000	
Direct labour	1 000	
		(4 000)
Differential profit		£1 000

Fred should accept the order as he is £1 000 better off in terms of profit. In addition he has secured a new customer who could well increase orders in the future and who could bring new customers. This is especially important in an export market where the domestic firm may not have many contacts.

There is a qualification however. Although fixed costs are usually irrelevant in short-term decision-making, they need not always be so. If in the above example Fred has to purchase machinery for £800 and incur £600 for insurance and supervision costs to satisfy the export order, these fixed costs now become relevant since they are both future and differential. The differential cost statement is now:

	£	£
Sales		5 000
Less relevant costs:		
Direct material	3 000	
Direct labour	1 000	
Additional machinery	800	
Insurance and supervision	600	
		(5 400)
Differential loss		£(400)

The order is no longer worthwhile.

21.4 Decision-making in the Face of a Limiting Factor

Sometimes a firm cannot satisfy its full market demand because of bottlenecks in production. Output may be limited by some scarce factor – this could be a shortage of a particular type of material or component, skilled labour, machinery, or a shortage of cash. It could also be a lack of something which means that production will not go ahead, e.g. the lack of a market for the product or the lack of storage space for extra items. In such a situation management should choose that output which makes the most profitable use of the scarce factor. The limiting factor is sometimes referred to as the 'key factor'.

Example

Expansion Ltd, which makes three products A, B and C has recently been enjoying a period of increasing demand and profitability such that all its machines are now working at full capacity. A further increase in demand is expected in the next year but management will now have to make a decision on which of the three products to cut back on. The following information is available:

	A	B	C
Market demand (units)	1 000	600	600
Contribution per unit	£16	£9	£10
Machine hours per unit	4	3	2
Total machine hours required	4 000	1 800	1 200

If there were no limiting factors, the company should produce up to market demand for each product since they all provide positive contributions. Suppose however that plant capacity is limited to 6 100 machine hours. 7 000 hours (being 4 000 for A, 1 800 for B plus 1 200 for C) are required to produce up to demand for each product. In this situation, management has to set priorities for the three products. Under normal circumstances the criteria to use would be contribution per unit. By this the priority would be A £16, C £10, B £9. However, when one factor is scarce this solution is wrong. In order to make the best possible use of the scarce factor the products should be ranked not in terms of total contribution but contribution per unit of the scarce factor.

Per unit	A	B	C
Contribution	£16	£9	£10
Machine hours required	4	3	2
Contribution per machine hour	£4	£3	£5
Ranking	2	3	1

At £5 contribution per machine hour product C uses the scarce factor most efficiently. C should therefore be given top priority and produced up to market demand. Product A is next best and should also be produced to its demand limit. The balance of machine hours available should be allotted to B. The optimum product-mix can be shown as follows:

Product	Units produced	Machine hours used	Cumulative machine hours used
C	600	1 200	1 200
A	1 000	4 000	5 200
B	300	900	6 100

The quantity of B produced is found by working back from machine hours usable. Since 900 hours are left after allocation to C and A, the quantity is found by

$$\frac{900}{3} = 300 \text{ units}$$

Optimum mix means that it is not possible to increase total contribution by re-arranging the output mix in any way.

Exercise

To check your understanding of the above, work out the optimum product-mix if, as a result of a breakdown in some of Expansion Ltd's machines, capacity is further reduced to only 4 000 machine hours.

Answer

Product	Units produced	Machine hours used	Cumulative machine hours used
C	600	1 200	1 200
A	700	2 800	4 000
B	0	0	4 000

In situations where there are two limiting factors the optimum solution cannot be found by this method. Instead the accountant has to use linear programming techniques which involves constructing a set of simultaneous linear equations reflecting the scarce factors, then solving them. Where three or more constraints exist at the same time advanced mathematical techniques involving matrix algebra have to be used, along with computers to solve them. You are not expected to know these, but will meet them in Management Accounting papers at professional level.

21.5 Make-or-Buy Decisions

A firm could be faced with the choice of purchasing a component or product from an outside supplier or manufacturing the component or product itself. 'Buying in', as it is called, is less risky in that less investment in fixed assets has to be made but the purchase price may be more than the cost of in-house production would be. When making such a decision, a firm must also take into account the longer-term market potential of the product. Making a major investment and borrowing money to do so will be worthwhile only if significant sales are expected for a number of years. The information given to you in a question would probably not be sufficient for you to give an informed opinion on this but you should mention it as a factor which should be taken into account.

Example

The following question is taken from the Chartered Institute of Bankers.

The directors of Fog Ltd are considering the addition of a new product, called Enwrap, to their company's range. They anticipate that annual sales of Enwrap would be 100 000 units, each of which would sell for £7.

There are a number of ways in which Enwrap can be obtained in a condition ready for sale.

1) **Buy Enwrap ready made**

   One of Fog's existing suppliers has offered to provide Enwrap at a price of £6.50 per unit. No additional premises would be required.   *50,000*

2) **Manufacture Enwrap**

   This involves two processes; the entire output of Process A is input to Process B. The costs related to the two processes are:

	Process A	Process B
	£	£
Raw materials per unit	2	Input from Process A
Other variable costs per unit	1	2
Annual fixed costs excluding rent and depreciation	15 000	25 000
Cost of buying plant	100 000	50 000

   The only premises suitable for the manufacture of Enwrap are large enough to house both premises and have to be rented for £20 000 a year.

   The company uses the straight line method of depreciation, assuming a life of 5 years and a zero residual value.

3) **Buy Enwrap part-manufactured ready for input to Process B**

   The product can be purchased in the form that it emerges from Process A at a cost of £3.80 per unit. The manufacturing costs for Process B given above would then be incurred.

   The same premises would be rented as for complete manufacture.

REQUIRED

(a) Calculate the annual profit or loss which would result from the sale of 100 000 units of Enwrap assuming:
   (i) the company buys the product ready-made;
   (ii) the company manufactures the complete product; and
   (iii) the company buys part-manufactured goods and puts them through Process B.   **(14 marks)**

(b) Discuss the factors which management should take into account when deciding which method to adopt.   **(6 marks)**

Solution

(a)

Fog Ltd
Profit and Loss Account using Method 1

	£000
Sales (100 000 units × £7)	700
Purchases (100 000 units × £6.50)	(650)
Profit	£50

Profit and Loss Account using Method 2

	£000	£000	£000
Sales (100 000 units × £7)			700
Process A			
Raw materials (100 000 units × £2)	200		
Variable costs (100 000 units × £1)	100		
Fixed costs	15		
Rent	20		
Depreciation (£100 000 ÷ 5)	20		
Input into Process B		355	
Process B			
Variable costs (100 000 units × £2)	200		
Fixed costs	25		
Depreciation (£50 000 ÷ 5)	10		
		235	
			(590)
Profit			£110

Profit and Loss Account using Method 3

	£000	£000
Sales (100 000 units × £7)		700
Process B		
Purchases (100 000 units × £3.80)	380	
Variable costs (100 000 units × £2)	200	
Fixed costs	25	
Rent	20	
Depreciation (£50 000 ÷ 5)	10	
		(635)
Profit		£65

(b) Some of the factors which would have to be taken into account are:

- the reliability of the sales forecasts; if there is any doubt over the level of future sales, the product should be bought in as this is less risky
- the reliability of cost estimates
- the reliability of the suppliers to supply the required amounts on time
- how easy it will be to finance the project
- the cost of finance, i.e. the interest rate on money borrowed to finance the equipment
- the working capital situation, taking into account the rent payable and other costs
- how the excess premises can be used if method 3 is chosen.

21.6 Buying or Leasing Fixed Assets

Buying fixed assets means that a firm has to find the finance, either by borrowing or by issuing new shares. In the first case it will have to pay interest on the loan whatever happens to its profit; in the second it will have more shareholders who have a claim to dividends. Leasing does not involve the firm in a capital outlay and it pays the lease charge only for the period during which it hires the assets. However, the leasing charge will always have to be paid whereas a good quality fixed asset, if owned, could last for some years and could be cheaper. The following example illustrates the distinction we made earlier between irrelevant costs and future differential costs.

Example

A company is reviewing its policy of purchasing its fleet of vehicles and considering leasing as an alternative. The annual costs per vehicle associated with each alternative are:

	Purchase	Lease
	£	£
Initial outlay	10 000	
Monthly rental		250 per month
Petrol and running costs	500	500
Tax and insurance	600	600

All four costs are future avoidable costs. However, out of these only the first two are relevant costs. Since the petrol, running costs, tax, and insurance are the same whichever alternative is chosen, they are irrelevant to the decision as to whether to buy or lease the vehicles.

21.7 Selling or Processing a By-product

Some productive processes result in a by-product which is not part of the main product but which has some value and is not to be scrapped as waste. Examples might be sawdust in a factory producing wooden furniture or olive skins in an olive oil processing plant. The decision facing the firm is whether to process this by-product further or whether to sell it to another firm as it is. The procedure followed is similar to that used in the examples given above, i.e. the firm must conduct a comparative analysis. Firstly it must find out how much it could sell the by-product for and multiply this by the expected volume and secondly it must estimate the costs of processing the by-product and then deduct these from the expected selling price; this will be more than the unprocessed material.

Such a decision would also be affected by wider factors eg whether spare space is available in which to process the by-product, what investment might have to be made in equipment, what labour would have to be employed, whether processing the by-product might have environmental effects eg whether the process gives off unpleasant smoke or smells.

21.8 The Long Term

You should be clear in all the above cases that, while it is sufficient for an alternative to be accepted in the short run if it covers all variable costs and provides a contribution, firms cannot accept such a situation for all products all of the time. In the long run all costs have to be covered, both fixed and variable, if a firm is to survive.

21.9 Non-financial Factors

Decisions are not made on financial grounds alone and can be affected by factors which cannot be expressed in money terms. These factors are considered in Chapter 26 on Social Accounting.

Questions

Question 21.1

Bell Manufacturing Ltd started business on 1 April 1997. It produces three products and the following information relates to the business for the first year's trading to 31 March 1998.

	Product X	Product Y	Product Z
	£	£	£
Direct materials	60 000	80 000	100 000
Direct labour	20 000	22 000	25 000
Variable overheads	12 000	16 000	20 000
Fixed costs	20 000	20 000	20 000
Sales	90 000	130 000	200 000

The total production was sold for the year and Bell Manufacturing had no closing stock on 31 March 1998.

The total fixed costs of £60 000 must be paid regardless of production. If the production of any product(s) ceases, then the fixed costs must be shared equally by the remaining product(s).

REQUIRED

(a) Prepare separate Profit and Loss accounts for the three products for the year ended 31 March 1998. In addition, calculate the total profit for the company for the year. (You are advised to prepare the profit and loss accounts in columnar form.)   **(6 marks)**

(b) Explain three applications of marginal costing which would help the directors of Bell Manufacturing in decision making.   **(6 marks)**

(c) Identify the product(s) on which Bell Manufacturing should concentrate to increase its profits. Give reasons for your suggestions.   **(11 marks)**

University of Oxford Delegacy of Local Examinations Advanced Level

Question 21.2

Eagle Ltd sells two products called X and Y. The trading results for 1997 were:

	£000	£000
Product X		
Sales	650	
Cost of goods sold (all variable)	520	
		130
Product Y		
Sales	480	
Cost of goods sold (all variable)	420	
		60
		190
General administration expenses		108
Net profit		82

Eagle Ltd manufactures product X and buys in product Y, ready for sale, from an outside supplier. The directors consider that additional profit could be obtained from product Y if it was manufactured internally, but there is no spare capacity in the company's existing premises. The directors have produced two alternative proposals to overcome this:

Proposal 1

- Create spare capacity in the company's existing premises by reducing the production and sale of product X to 80% of its 1997 level. This would enable production and sale of 80% of the 1997 level of product Y; the existing suppliers have indicated that they would not be interested in supplying only 20% of the previous level of sales, and so these sales would be lost.
- To produce product Y at 80% of the 1997 level would require the hire of machinery under a ten-year agreement at an annual cost of £24 000 plus further production costs of £240 000.
- The gross profit percentage of product X and the general administration expenses would remain unchanged.

Proposal 2

- Take out a ten-year lease on additional premises at an annual cost of £48 000.
- This proposal involves hiring machinery under a ten-year agreement at an annual cost of £29 000, plus variable costs of £360 000, at the 1997 level of output.
- The sales and costs of product X would remain unchanged, but general administration expenses would rise to a new fixed level of £126 000.
- This would enable production of product up to 50% above its 1997 level, but the directors expect sales to remain at their 1997 level.

Under both proposals, the selling price per unit remains unchanged.

REQUIRED

(a) Prepare the trading and profit and loss accounts of Eagle Ltd in the same format as that given above, showing the outcome of adopting proposal 1. **(6 marks)**

(b) Prepare the trading and profit and loss accounts of Eagle Ltd, in the same format as that given above, showing the outcome of adopting proposal 2, assuming the same level of output of both X and Y as in 1997. **(6 marks)**

(c) Calculate the additional profit generated for each increase of £1 000 in the sales
of product Y above their 1997 level, if proposal 2 is adopted.   **(2 marks)**

(d) Discuss briefly the merits of the three alternatives facing the directors, namely,
continue as at present or adopt proposal 1 or proposal 2.   **(6 marks)**

Institute of Financial Services Banking Certificate

Question 21.3

Twister Ltd operates a retail shop which consists of three departments and an
administration section; each department sells a separate, distinct product. The
directors have prepared the following forecast for the year to 30 June 1998:

Department	A	B	C	Administration	Total
	£000	£000	£000	£000	£000
Sales	1 000	1 500	2 500		5 000
Cost of goods sold (variable cost)	600	750	1 300		2 650
Gross profit	400	750	1 200		2 350
Direct departmental costs	190	300	400		890
	210	450	800		1 460
Administration costs (all fixed)				960	960
Share of administration costs	320	320	320	(960)	
Net profit (loss)	(110)	130	480		500

The directors are considering what to do about the result expected from Department
A. They have ascertained that the direct departmental costs are fixed in nature so long
as the department remains open; if it is closed, then these costs will no longer be
incurred.

The following courses of action are under consideration:

1) Close Department A and leave it empty.

2) Reduce the selling price of all the goods sold by Department A by 10 per cent; the
volume of its sales should increase by 20 per cent as a result.

3) Use the space currently occupied by Department A to sell Department B goods.
The direct departmental costs would be unchanged, additional sales of £1 200 000
would result, no price reductions would be needed and the sale of existing
Department A products would cease.

REQUIRED

(a) Calculate the revised total forecast profit of Twister Ltd which would result from
each of the alternative courses of action.   **(11 marks)**

(b) Calculate the forecast gross profit percentage and net profit percentage of Department A
based on the above forecast and alternative courses of action numbers 2 and 3.   **(3 marks)**

(c) Prepare a report for the directors of Twister Ltd, explaining the different outcomes,
in terms of both profits and ratios, of the alternative courses of action.   **(6 marks)**

Note: Work to one decimal place.

Institute of Financial Services Banking Certificate

22

Budgeting and Budgetary Control

22.1 Introduction

We do not live our life from day to day without any consideration about the future. We plan – from major things such as our career to small things such as what we are going to do tomorrow and over the week-end. The first is a long-term plan, the second a short-term plan. The same is true of business. However, here the plan is expressed in financial terms and is more formal and deliberate in a process known as budgeting. A budget is a detailed plan of action for a future period, expressed in numbers.

22.2 Long-term and Short-term Budgets

The long-term budget is a financial translation of proposed future capital investments, development of new products and abandonment of existing ones, breaking into new markets, and so on. It looks several years ahead, e.g. a 5-year plan. Each year is broken down into more detail in an operating plan. This is the short-term budget which may in turn be divided into quarterly or monthly budgets. The long- and short-term budgets should not be thought of as being separate from each other. They are interrelated. When the annual budget is prepared, a lot of the decisions affecting activity such as the fixed asset base and the products and markets the business is selling in will already have been made in the long-term plan. In turn, the events of a particular budget year may cause the long-term plan to be amended.

Apart from investment in fixed assets (which we look at in Chapter 25) long-range planning, sometimes called strategic or corporate planning, is not in the syllabus of most bodies at this level. Examination questions tend to concentrate on short-term budgeting and it is this we shall be looking at in this chapter.

22.3 Functions of Budgets

1) **Planning** Forward planning forces managers to consider in a formal way alternative future courses of action, to evaluate them properly and to decide on the best alternative. It also encourages managers to anticipate problems before they arise, thus giving themselves time to consider alternative ways of overcoming them when they do happen. Such an exercise tends to produce better results than decisions made in haste.

2) **Co-ordination** Left to their own devices, department managers may make decisions about the future which are incompatible or even in conflict with other departments. For example, the sales department may be planning to extend the credit period in order to stimulate sales to a point beyond the bank overdraft arrangements. Budgeting helps to avoid such conflicts by encouraging managers to consider how their plans affect other departments and how the plans of other departments affect them.

3) **Control and performance evaluation** While budget preparation aids planning, the way in which budgets are used helps in control and performance evaluation. The system of calculating deviations or variances from the budget after the event fosters cost-consciousness amongst workers and managers and highlights areas of over-achievement and, more importantly, under-achievement. The use of budgets for control and performance is considered in detail in Chapter 23 on standard costing and variance analysis. The behavioural aspects of budgetary control are considered at the end of this chapter.

4) **Participation** By actively involving managers at all stages of the hierarchy, the process of budgeting brings the different levels closer together. The junior members feel that they have a say in the running of the organisation and this leads to enhanced job satisfaction and consequently to increased productivity. It has been said that the actual process of budgeting is as beneficial as the budget itself.

22.4 Who is Involved?

The people who prepare and are responsible for their budgets are the departmental line managers. They may or may not involve their subordinates, depending on their style of management and relationship with their juniors. In converting the budget into money terms they may enlist the help of an accountant. The person whose function it is to co-ordinate the many individual budgets of the line managers is the appointed Budget Officer, who is normally an accountant. In large public companies budgeting for the whole organisation can be a very complex process indeed, co-ordination of which is far beyond the limits of any one person. Here a Budget Committee may be set up which would comprise several high-level executives in charge of the major functional divisions of the business.

22.5 Preparation of the Budget

A number of stages can be identified in the preparation of a budget.

Stage 1

The key aims for the coming year are identified, as are any major external changes likely to affect the business. These are communicated to those preparing the budgets so that they know what overriding factors to keep in mind when preparing their budgets. These will be largely gauged from the long-term corporate plan.

Stage 2

The key factor or limiting factor is determined. Every business has some factor which eventually limits its growth and in most cases it is sales demand. The key factor is significant in two ways in budgeting. Firstly, it is the point at which the process starts and the rest of the budget is built around it. It would be pointless to budget for an activity level of 100 000 units if sales demand is expected to be 20 000 units.

Secondly, it is the most important single sub-budget. An error in the key factor budget would throw out all the subsidiary budgets. (We met the concept of the key factor in Chapter 21.) When used in the context of budgeting it is sometimes called the principal budget factor. If the principal budget factor happens to be production level attainable, the production budget is constructed first and the other budgets are built around it.

Stage 3

Assuming sales is the limiting factor, the sales budget is prepared. Unfortunately this is usually the most difficult budget to prepare because of the many external influences governing it over which the firm has no control. Before the budget is attempted a sales forecast is usually made, by product type and geographical area. There are two broad methods of doing this:

- Asking the sales managers of each product and area to estimate next year's likely sales. The responses are simply added together to give the total for the firm.
- Using mathematical and statistical techniques of interpolating the future from the past, taking into account expected changes in market conditions.

Large companies may use both methods. One advantage of the first method is that it actively involves lower-level managers in the budgeting process.

Stage 4

The subsidiary budgets are prepared. These include the production budget, direct materials budget, direct labour budget, production overhead budget, selling and distribution budget, administration budget, capital expenditure budget and cash budget.

Stage 5

The subsidiary budgets are reviewed and coordinated by the budget officer or budget committee. Their function is to check that there are no inconsistencies or conflicts between the many subsidiary budgets. For example, if the capital expenditure budget includes large amounts for the replacement of assets in a month when the liquidity position is poor, the budget has to be sent back to the person who prepared it with a note of the problem and amendment required. In this way the budgets get sent back and forth until the co-ordinator is satisfied that the many individual budgets are in harmony with each other.

Stage 6

The individual subsidiary budgets are consolidated into a single master budget, which is presented in the form of a budgeted income statement and balance sheet.

Stage 7

The work is now presented to the board of directors for approval. If they are not satisfied with any aspect of it, perhaps because of over-optimism or over-pessimism or because they suspect slack or padding (explained later), they will return it to the budget committee for amendment. The committee will have to return the subsidiary budgets to those who drew them us and Stages 3, 4, 5 and 6 are repeated. The revised budgets are again presented to the board and, if approved, the budgets are finalised.

Although the budgeting is 'finalised' on director approval, in one sense the process of budgeting never ends. A budget is prepared under certain basic assumptions about the future. Any change in these assumptions should lead to the budget being revised. Some organisations operate a continuous or rolling budget where, as one quarter unfolds, the budgets of subsequent quarters are updated in line with any change in market conditions.

22.6 Main Types of Budget

A firm's overall budget is made up of a sub-budget for each section of its activities. A normal sequence of drawing up these budgets would be as follows.

1) **The sales budget** shows the number of sales the firm expects to make in the coming months.
2) **The production budget** is based on the sales budget and on the necessity of keeping stocks.
3) **The purchases budget** is based on the materials and components necessary to achieve the production budget.
4) **The expenses budget** is based on the various costs necessary to produce the budgeted output.
5) **The debtors and creditors budget** is based on expected sales and purchases, the normal credit period and the expected level of bad debts.
6) **The cash budget** includes all receipts and payments of cash based on all of the above budgets.
7) **A budgeted set of final accounts** is drawn up based on all the budgeted figures.

We shall look at each of these budgets in turn.

22.7 Sales Budgets

A sales budget is drawn up based on present sales levels and on market research concerning future trends in demand. Other factors which might affect demand for the product are taken into account:

- expected changes in consumers' incomes
- expected changes in taxes or government regulations affecting the industry
- expected actions by competitor firms
- expected changes in tastes and fashions
- seasonal factors.

Example
Bucket and Spade Ltd manufacture plastic sandplay items for children. Market research indicates that sales for the first five months of 2002 will be:

April	May	June	July	August
80 000	120 000	160 000	120 000	80 000

The following information also applies.

(a) A 10% under-estimate of demand is to be allowed for.
(b) It is hoped that an advertising campaign beginning in March will add a further 20% to each month's sales, based on the original figures.

(c) A fall in unemployment is expected to lead to an increase in beach holidays and this will result in a 2% increase in demand (based on the original figures) for all products from June.

(d) The strength of the £ sterling against other currencies has resulted in an increase in the demand for foreign holidays. This is expected to boost unit sales by 4 000 in May; 8 000 in June; 10 000 in July; and 5 000 in August.

We are asked to prepare a sales budget for the period 1 April to 31 August 2002.

Bucket and Spade Ltd
Sales Budget for April – August 2002

	April	May	June	July	August
Market research figures	80 000	120 000	160 000	120 000	80 000
+ 10% Under-estimate	8 000	12 000	16 000	12 000	8 000
+ Advertising campaign	16 000	24 000	32 000	24 000	16 000
+ Fall in unemployment			3 200	2 400	1 600
Total budgeted sales in units	104 000	156 000	211 200	158 400	105 600

22.8 Production Budgets

Once the firm knows how much it expects to sell, it can organise its production, taking into account how much it wants to add to stock levels. Arranging production necessarily means that it must draw up a purchasing budget to forecast how many units it will need to buy of the various raw materials, parts and components it uses.

Example

Continuing with Bucket and Spade Ltd, whose sales budget we prepared above, we are now asked to prepare the production budget for January to May based on the figures in the sales budget and on the following information.

(a) Each month's output is sold three months after production.

(b) There are no opening stocks in January 2002.

(c) Production in March will fall by 25% because of staff holidays; the shortfall will be made up in equal amounts in April and May.

(d) An extra 20 000 units must be produced in May to allow the firm to build up a stock.

Bucket and Spade Ltd
Production Budget for January – May 2002

	January	February	March	April	May
Output in units	104 000	156 000	211 200	158 400	105 600
March shortfall			(52 800)	26 400	26 400
Stock					20 000
Total monthly output	104 000	156 000	158 400	184 800	152 000

Production takes place three months before sales, eg since the firm expects to sell 104 000 units in April, it must produce them in January etc. We deduct 25% from the March figure and add it on again in two halves in April and May.

22.9 Purchase and Expense Budgets

These are similar to the sales and production budgets in that they set out the expected units to be purchased and the costs which will be incurred to enable the firm to produce the number of finished goods which the production and sales departments have budgeted for. Some purchases will be made in a month previous to that of production and others will be made in the same month. Examination questions always provide you with the necessary information.

22.10 Debtor and Creditor Budgets

These budgets set out the expected value of total debtors and total creditors at the end of each month. The final monthly figure depends on the amount of sales and purchases made on credit and on the amounts received from debtors and paid to creditors.

22.11 Cash Budgets

As we saw in Chapter 12 on ratio analysis and the interpretation of accounts, a large profit does not in itself make for a healthy business. Liquidity is just as important. The cash budget is an attempt by management to ensure that the company does not run into liquidity problems in the future. It involves estimating receipts and payments implied by the other budgets to find the balance in hand or overdrawn at the end of each month or quarter. Apart from the master budget, the cash budget is the last to be prepared since it depends critically on the plans in the other budgets.

We draw up a cash budget in tabular form, with each month of the year having its own column. There are three main sections:

1) The receipts section, which shows all the cash entering the business each month for whatever reason. We must be careful to include the cash actually being received and not the cash which should have been received. Where the firm has sold goods on credit, the receipts for each month will not be the same as sales and it is necessary to read a question carefully to determine exactly when cash is received from sales. For example if one month's credit is given, February's sales will be received in March. Other cash inflows could be for commission or rent or they could be the proceeds of a bank loan or the sale of a fixed asset.

2) The expenditure section, where we show all the cash going out of the business each month for whatever reason. Again we must distinguish between what is paid and what month the liability was incurred. If we purchase goods on two month's credit, we will pay for May's purchases in July. Sometimes a deposit is payable in the month of purchase and the remainder as instructed in the question. Other payments are for all the normal business expenses and for purchases of fixed assets. Bad debts and depreciation of fixed assets are not included in a cash budget since they do not involve an outflow of cash.

3) The final section shows the balance at the end of each month. We begin the first month with any cash balance left over from the previous month, add on to this the total receipts and deduct total payments. The closing balance for the month then becomes the opening balance for the next month. When the opening balance plus

total receipts exceeds total payments, there is a positive closing balance; when the opposite happens there is a negative balance and the bank account is in overdraft.

Here is a typical question on a cash budget. Always read the question very carefully and draw up the format before you begin, filling it in as you go through the instructions.

Example

The following question is taken from OCR Advanced Level.

Leonardo Da Vita runs a marketing agency. He is considering expansion of the business and the following information is relevant to the situation at 1 June 1999 and to the next six months, June to November 1999. His financial year ends 30 November 1999.

(a) Bank balance at 1 June 1999: £12 000.

(b) Total fees income for April 1999 was £12 000 and for May 1999 was £20 000.

(c) Total creditors for expenses for April 1999 were £9 000 and for May 1999 were £12 000.

(d) Salaries accrued at 1 June 1999: £6 000.

(e) Commissions accrued due to employees at 1 June 1999: £4 000.

(f) Budgeted fees income per month:
     June to August inclusive: £45 000
     September to November inclusive: £48 000

(g) Budgeted salaries per month:
     June to August inclusive: £7 000
     September to November inclusive: £8 000

(h) Budgeted expenses per month:
     June to August inclusive: £12 000
     September to November inclusive: £15 000

(i) (i) Debtors' accounts are settled:
         50% one month after fees are earned
         50% two months after fees are earned

     (ii) Salaries are paid one month after being earned.

     (iii) Creditors for expenses are paid:

         $\frac{2}{3}$ one month after being incurred

         $\frac{1}{3}$ two months after being incurred

     (iv) Commission of 20% of fees generated is paid to employees one month after being earned.

(j) Leonardo has decided to use finance leasing to obtain additional equipment (to be acquired 1 July 1999) to assist with the expansion of the business. This will involve a monthly finance lease payment of £400 from July 1999. Leonardo will depreciate this new equipment by £1 500 to cover the period until 30 November 1999. He presently charges depreciation of £9 400 annually in his end-of-year accounts, using the straight-line method. No asset disposals are planned.

REQUIRED

(a) A Cash Budget for the six months June to November 1999 showing the closing
bank balance for each month.   **(23 marks)**

(b) A Budgeted Profit and Loss Account for the half-year ended 30 November 1999.   **(7 marks)**

Solution

Leonardo Da Vita
Cash Budget for the six months June to November 1999

	June	*July*	*Aug*	*Sept*	*Oct*	*Nov*
	£	£	£	£	£	£
Receipts						
Fees income (50%)	6 000	10 000	22 500	22 500	22 500	24 000
(50%)	10 000	22 500	22 500	22 500	24 000	24 000
Total Receipts	16 000	32 500	45 000	45 000	46 500	48 000
Expenditure						
Expenses (2/3)	8 000	8 000	8 000	8 000	10 000	10 000
(1/3)	3 000	4 000	4 000	4 000	4 000	5 000
Salaries	6 000	7 000	7 000	7 000	8 000	8 000
Commissions	4 000	9 000	9 000	9 000	9 600	9 600
Lease payment		400	400	400	400	400
Total Expenditure	21 000	28 400	28 400	28 400	32 000	33 000
Budget						
Opening balance	12 000	7 000	11 100	27 700	44 300	58 800
Receipts	16 000	32 500	45 000	45 000	46 500	48 000
Expenditure	(21 000)	(28 400)	(28 400)	(28 400)	(32 000)	(33 000)
Closing balance	7 000	11 100	27 700	44 300	58 800	73 800

We can check back by adding total receipts to the opening balance and deducting total
expenditures.

A computer spreadsheet program helps the budgeting process considerably. It does
the additions and subtractions for us and allows us to perform the 'What If' function,
where we can analyse the effect of a change in one figure on the rest of the budget.

(b)

Budgeted Profit and Loss Account for the half-year ended 30 November 1999

	£	£
Income from fees		279 000
Less		
Expenses	81 000	
Salaries	45 000	
Commission	55 800	
Lease payments	2 000	
Depreciation on existing equipment	4 700	
Depreciation on new equipment	1 500	
		(190 000)
Profit		£89 000

It is important in a question like this to distinguish between the effect on cash and the effect on profit. The cash budget contains the amounts of cash actually entering and leaving the business, no matter which month or financial year they belong to under the matching concept. The profit and loss account, on the other hand, contains the amounts which belong to the period in question, no matter whether these amounts have actually been paid or received.

In the above question a positive bank balance was forecast for every month but this is not always the case. If a cash deficit is foreseen, arrangements can be made for the required level of bank overdraft during those months in which the company is expected to be 'in the red'. Bank managers are far more willing to entertain requests for a loan or overdraft from a business which has taken the trouble to plan future cash flows in advance than requests from a business which has suddenly found itself short of liquid resources. Another benefit of the cash budget is that months of large surpluses are revealed. Plans can then be made in advance for their investment in the short-term money market; idle cash balances represent an opportunity cost in terms of lost interest.

The cash budget has become increasingly important to firms since the large number of bankruptcies due to insolvency in recent years. There are too many cases of potentially profitable firms going out of business because of cash flow problems. A cash budget is normally required by a bank before considering a request for a business loan. This has reflected itself in the increasing frequency with which they now appear in examination questions.

22.12 Fixed and Flexible Budgeting

One of the functions of budgeting stated at the start of this chapter was performance evaluation and control. Actual performance of each responsibility centre is compared with its budget to evaluate performance. Let us take a firm which budgeted for a monthly production level of 1 000 units, for which the materials purchasing manager was allocated a spending of £10 000. Actual activity during the month was better than expected because of an unexpected increase in sales. 1 100 units were produced at a material cost of £10 800. Under a fixed budget the comparison would be:

Budgeted spending	Actual spending	Variance
£10 000	£10 800	£(800) adverse

Such a system would hardly gain the support and co-operation of the materials purchasing manager. Surely he should be evaluated not on the activity level budgeted but the actual level achieved. Under this flexible budgeting system all costs are translated from budgeted activity level to actual activity level. These figures are then used to evaluate performance. Under this system the comparison for our materials purchasing manager is:

Flexed budget spending	Actual spending	Variance
£10 000	£10 800	£200 favourable

Credit will now be given to him for spending less than budget for the higher level of activity.

Under a flexible budget, costs react differently to changes in activity depending on whether they are of a fixed, variable, or semi-variable nature. Fixed costs stay the same at all activity levels while variable costs increase directly with output. With semi-variable costs only the variable element changes. Try the following exercise.

Exercise

A firm produces the following figures:

Maximum production level	10 000 units
Direct materials cost	£5 per unit
Direct labour cost	£4 per unit
Fixed overhead	£20 000
Power – standing charge	£1 000
variable element	£0.25 per unit

Prepare a flexible budget for production levels 7 000, 9 000 and 10 000 units.

Answer

Production level (units)	7 000	9 000	10 000
% of maximum capacity	70%	90%	100%
	£	£	£
Direct materials	35 000	45 000	50 000
Direct labour	28 000	36 000	40 000
Fixed overhead	20 000	20 000	20 000
Power*	2 750	3 250	3 500
	85 750	104 250	113 500
*Standing charge	1 000	1 000	1 000
Variable element	1 750	2 250	2 500
Power total	2 750	3 250	3 500

It is fairly easy to flex a budget for fixed costs and variable costs. The difficulty arises with semi-variable costs. In examination questions you are not likely to be given the amount of the fixed element of a semi-variable cost but have to deduce it by calculating the change in total cost from one activity level to another and from this working out the variable element per unit. The balance must represent the fixed element and this will be the same at all activity levels. See Question 22.1.

22.13 Forecast Final Accounts

Forecast final accounts are also known as a **master budget** and consist of a forecast profit and loss account and balance sheet. These are a forecast of what the profit or loss will be for the forecast period and of the state of the assets and liabilities. They are drawn up in exactly the same way as ordinary final accounts, except that they do not have to conform with the requirements of published company accounts, since they are not published and are for use by internal management only.

22.14 Behavioural Aspects of Budgeting

A common charge levied against accountants is that, in preparing their budgets and in designing control and evaluation systems, they do not give sufficient attention to human behaviour. Accountants have long suffered an image of being boring, heartless and devoid of human feelings. This is certainly not the case, but the image is unfortunately sometimes justified. Especially in the past, accountants have tended to concentrate on achieving professional and technical excellence in their work at the expense of proper consideration of how their proposals are likely to affect the people they are intended to help and control. At the start of this chapter we looked at four claimed advantages of budgeting. In 1953 Argyris challenged this traditional view in a now famous study in which he found that, far from being a help, budgets had a dysfunctional effect on performance and were widely regarded with suspicion and hostility by employees. ('Dysfunctional' means that results are actually worse than if no budget had been set.) Since Argyris' path-breaking article, the behavioural aspects of budgeting and accounting control systems has been a fertile area for research. The studies have centred on three controversial points:

1) **Tightness of budget**: Should a budget be set at a level which is easy or hard to achieve?
2) **The way in which the budget is used**: To what extent should the budget be used as a performance evaluator?
3) **Participation**: To what extent should those responsible for achieving a budget participate in setting it?

Let us look at each of these points in turn.

1 Tightness of Budget

The question here is whether it matters if the budget is set tight or loose. Hofstede (1968) has found that a budget will lead to improved performance only if it is set at a particular degree of tightness. A loose budget will encourage inefficiency; a very tight budget will cause the budgetee to perceive it as impossible and unattainable and may have a negative dysfunctional effect. The only budget that will be a motivator to efficiency is one that is set a little tighter than the budgetee's expectations. These findings are largely similar to an earlier study on the subject by Stedry (1960). He pointed out that one implication of these findings is that a 'good' budget should produce plenty of adverse variances. If management sets a budget which is not expected to be achieved, how can it then be used for planning purposes? Stedry thinks that it cannot and suggests that firms should produce two budgets each year – a tight one for motivation and control and a more realistic one for planning. Good advice perhaps, but there are practical problems in adopting this, not least of which is the resulting increase in cost and complexity of the budgeting process, which in most companies is already a complex and expensive exercise.

2 How the Budget is Used

Hopwood (1976) found that different companies attach different weight to the budget. He identified two broad styles of performance evaluation – budget-constrained and profit-conscious. In the first, budget achievement is the only consideration in evaluating a manager; in the second a broader more long-term view is taken and adverse variances are tolerated only as long as they are felt to be temporary or for the long-term good of the company. In his research Hopwood found that budgetees regarded with suspicion managers who adopt the budget-constrained style. They

resented the whole process of budgeting and felt that it was there to 'shoot them down if they failed to perform'. He also found that a narrow budget-constrained style gave rise to decisions which, while worth making to a budgetee about to be evaluated, were not in the long-term interests of the organisation as a whole. For example, fear of an adverse variance sometimes led to urgent maintenance work being postponed to a future budget year. However, this critical delay increased the amount of spending needed in the future period. The art of good management is to encourage a state of goal congruence, in which the aims of each individual correspond to the aims of the organisation as a whole. If management focuses exclusively on the budget, it may lead to budgetees becoming obsessed with meeting the budget as an end in itself at the expense of goal congruence. Churchill, Cooper and Sainsbury (1964) found that undue emphasis on budget achievement led managers to regard it as a strait-jacket. As a result they conformed to plans laid down for them even when subsequent changes in the environment made those plans sub-optimal. Such behaviour is clearly not desirable and is the cost of an evaluation system that is narrow and inflexible.

Likert and Seashore (1968) have pointed out the cost in human terms to budgetees evaluated in a narrow manner. They found that they suffered from increased tension and anxiety about achieving targets, and that this led to higher levels of absenteeism and staff turnover. Hopwood found that the more flexible profit-conscious style avoided such problems. The general consensus now is that evaluation of managerial performance is a complex task for which using one single measure is inadequate. For example, the manager of a production department is expected not only to meet his budget with regard to costs, but also to maintain a good working relationship between himself and employees, between the employees themselves, to meet production deadlines on time, and to maintain the quality of the product. It is impossible, even dangerous, to attempt to evaluate all of these criteria by using a single index of performance. A comprehensive performance evaluation should encompass achievement with regard to non-financial objectives as well as the budget.

3 Participation

The question here is to what degree budgetees should participate in the setting of the budget. It is felt that an authoritarian style of management, where the budget has been imposed from the top without any participation or consultation, is a bad thing. If budgetees and workers are unable to relate to the budget, they might reject it without even attempting to conform. The benefit of some participation is that it makes budgetees feel involved in the whole process and removes some of the distrust which exists between management and workers. In 1960 however Vroom claimed that the relationship between participation and performance was not so simple. Participation was not beneficial in all cases and depended on several factors including the personalities of the budgetee and assessor, the type of organisation and the organisation structure. For example, a de-centralised organisation was more conducive to participation than a highly centralized one. Following Vroom's findings several pieces of research have been done specifically on this point but the results do not point to a common conclusion.

While participation seems in most cases to lead to an improvement in workers' attitudes and a better climate of industrial relations, there is a danger in allowing budgetees too much freedom in setting their own budget. This is the problem of slack or padding. It is natural for a manager who is allowed to set his own budget to overstate costs and understate revenues so that the budget is not difficult to achieve; he builds into the budget a certain amount of slack which is in effect an insurance that

the budget will be reached. In a study of sales budgets in 1968, Lowe and Shaw found clear evidence of such padding and also found that the problem was likely to be greatest where the remuneration system was directly tied to sales performance and achievement of the budget. Other studies have confirmed this finding. Management can reduce the amount of slack by remunerating and evaluating employees by criteria other than just budget achievement, i.e. by adopting a profit-conscious style.

Another possible solution is to adopt a technique known as Zero-Base Budgeting, recommended by Phyrr in 1970. Under normal budgeting the starting point for next year's budget is this year's, adjusted for expected changes in the level of activity and inflation. The procedure accepts previous years' expenditures as being necessary without question. Any padding built into the budget in previous years is therefore likely to be repeated in future years. It also encourages managers of efficient cost centres to waste surplus funds towards the end of the budget year in the fear that, if they do not spend the whole of their allowance, it will be reduced in future years. In order to overcome these problems, Phyrr advocated an alternative system of budget-setting in which previous years' figures were to be ignored and each year's budgets were to start from a base of zero. In presenting their budgets for approval, managers would have to justify the whole of their expenditure and not just the increment. The mere fact that an item of expenditure was incurred last year would not in itself be accepted as a reason for approving its spending next year. Such an approach, Phyrr believed, would reduce the amount of slack in two ways:

(i)   managers would not propose as large an expenditure bill in the knowledge that it would be subject to tight scrutiny
(ii) any padding that is proposed is likely to be detected and rejected. In the traditional system, padding is approved without scrutiny.

Unfortunately, most companies have not adopted zero-base budgeting because

(i)   its proper implementation would burden it with additional expenditures; reevaluating each item of expenditure from scratch every year is no mean task

(ii) its implementation has in some instances been resisted by managers for fear that they will lose the luxury of their safety padding.

No doubt the work on the three areas discussed above will continue and new evidence will throw further light on them. It seems that, after a slow start, accountants are finally waking up to their responsibility to take people into account when designing their control systems.

References

Argyris, C., 'Human problems with budgets', *Harvard Business Review*, January-February 1953.

Churchill, N.C., Cooper, W.E. and Sainsbury, T., 'Laboratory and field studies of the behavioural effects of audits', in *Management Controls*, Bonini, E.C., Jaedicke, R.K. and Wagner (Eds) McGraw-Hill, 1964.

Hofstede, G.H., *The Game of Budget Control*, Tavistock, 1968.

Hopwood, A.G., *Accountancy and Human Behaviour*, Prentice-Hall, 1976.

Lowe, E.A., and Shaw, R.W., 'An analysis of managerial biasing: Evidence from a company's budgeting process', *Journal of Management Studies*, October 1968.

Likert, R. and Seashore S.E., 'Making cost control work', in Solomons, D. (Ed) *Studies in Cost Analysis*, Sweet and Maxwell, 1968.

Phyrr, P.A., 'Zero-base budgeting', *Harvard Business Review*, November-December 1970.

Stedry, A.C., *Budget Control and Cost Behaviour*, Prentice-Hall, 1960.

Vroom, V.H., Some Personality Determinants of the Effects of Participation, Prentice-Hall, 1960.

Questions

Question 22.1

The Marketing Director of W Limited is dissatisfied with the variances reported to him on the basis of actual costs being compared with a fixed budget for the costs attributed to the marketing function. He seeks your help and asks you to prepare for him a flexible budget for the calendar year 1997, based on the following information which is stated for an estimated sales level of £10 million unless stated otherwise.

Fixed costs	£000
Salaries – sales representatives	200
– sales office	60
Salary-related costs	32
Rent	100
Depreciation of furniture	5
Depreciation of cars	67
Insurance	20
Advertising	250
Variable costs	
Sales representatives' commission	64
Salary-related costs – 12½ % of commission	8
Sales representatives' ordinary expenses	25
Bad debts	100
Stationery and postage	50
Agency fees	80

Semi-variable costs

Telephone rentals £2 000, metered calls £14 000. Sales representatives' car expenses excluding depreciation: fixed £7 000, variable £48 000.

Sales promotions: the budget figures are to be based on the costs given below which relate to the years 1992 to 1995 and the estimates for 1996.

Year		Costs		Sales
		£000		£ million
1992		384		4.2
1993		402		5.1
1994		368		3.4
1995		450		7.5
1996	Estimate	478	Estimate	8.9

Ignore inflation.

REQUIRED

(a) Prepare a flexible budget for sales levels of £9m, £10m and £11.5m.   **(12 marks)**

(b) Calculate the total marketing cost allowance, assuming sales of £10.75m.   **(3 marks)**

Chartered Institute of Management Accountants

Question 22.2

Hilda Cannon owns a business which supplies materials to clothing manufacturers. The following was Hilda's balance sheet as at 31 May 1999.

	£	£	£
Fixed assets			
Fixtures and fittings at cost		26 000	
Less depreciation		10 400	
			15 600
Current assets			
Stock	4 700		
Debtors	10 400		
Bank balance	700		
		15 800	
Less current liabilities			
Trade creditors		(6 560)	
Net current assets			9 240
			£24 840
Capital			£24 840

20% of Hilda Cannon's sales are for cash. Credit customers are allowed, and take, one month's credit. She receives, and takes, one month's credit on all purchases.

Sales and purchases are as follows.

	Actual		*Forecast*	
	May 1999	June 1999	July 1999	August 1999
	£	£	£	£
Total sales	13 000	12 500	15 000	16 500
Total purchases	6 560	6 300	7 570	8 300

Additional information

1) Rent is paid half yearly in advance on 1 June and 1 December each year. The annual rent payable is £12 000.

2) Other expenses amounting to £1 800 per month are payable in the month in which they are incurred.

3) Hilda Cannon will purchase a new van on 1 July 1999. It will cost £14 700. The garage has agreed to accept £7 700 on 17 July 1999 and the outstanding balance on 17 September 1999. Hilda Cannon will provide for depreciation on the van at the rate of 20% per annum on cost. She provides for depreciation on fixtures and fittings at the rate of 10% per annum on cost. Depreciation is provided for on a monthly basis.

4) Hilda Cannon will withdraw £1 200 per month for her private living expenses.

5) Hilda Cannon has estimated that her stock as at 31 August 1999 should be valued at the cost price of £5 010.

REQUIRED

(a) Prepare a cash budget for Hilda Cannon on a month-by-month basis for the three months ending 31 August 1999. **(15 marks)**

(b) Prepare a forecast trading and profit and loss account for Hilda Cannon for the three months ending 31 August 1999. **(8 marks)**

(c) Prepare a forecast balance sheet extract as at 31 August 1999 showing Hilda Cannon's current assets and current liabilities. **(5 marks)**

(d) Explain the importance of the management of working capital. **(5 marks)**

(e) Explain to Hilda Cannon **three** possible reasons for the difference between the forecast profit earned by her business during the three months ending 31 August 1999 and the forecast bank balance at the end of that period. (Illustrate your answer with examples from the question.) **(11 marks)**

(f) Explain **two** ways in which the preparation of a cash budget may be useful to Hilda Cannon. **(6 marks)**

Associated Examining Board Advanced Level

Question 22.3

The accountant of Riley Ltd is about to introduce a budgetary control system as from 1 July 1998. The factory manager, however, is concerned about the stock and production levels required to meet demand.

Information about the proposed system is as follows.

1) The production year is divided into 13 periods of 4 weeks each. Each week consists of 5 working days.

2) Stocks are to be maintained at a minimum level of 20% of budgeted sales for the next period.

3) There are two production machines each of which has a maximum capacity to produce 88 units per day.

4) Estimated sales are:

Periods	1	2	3	4	5	6
Units	3 100	3 300	3 600	3 800	3 300	3 200

5) Stock at the beginning of Period 1 is expected to be 620 units.

6) Each unit costs £8 to manufacture and is sold for £14. These figures are consistent throughout the year.

The factory manager believes that production will not meet anticipated demand and the above minimum stock requirements. He feels that there are **two** options open to him.

Option 1

Increase production to the maximum in periods when demand is small to stockpile finished units. Units should be stored for the shortest time possible to keep storage costs to a minimum.

Option 2

Buy finished units from another manufacturer to meet any shortfall in output in any particular period. These will cost £13 each.

REQUIRED

(a) (i) Prepare a production budget in units for the Periods 1 to 5, which satisfies the criteria for minimum stock requirements **but** assumes that there are no limitations on output.   **(10 marks)**

    (ii) Calculate the shortfall in output for the periods where demand plus minimum stock requirements exceeds the production capacity.   **(5 marks)**

(b) Prepare a production budget in units for the Periods 1 to 5 if Option 1 is adopted, applying the criteria for maximum output where necessary.   **(9 marks)**

(c) Prepare the budgeted trading accounts for Options 1 and 2 covering the Periods 1 to 5 inclusive.
(**Note**: separate trading accounts for each period are **not** required.)   **(11 marks)**

(d) Write a short report to the factory manager: **(Report format: 2 marks)**
    (i) recommending which of the two options should be adopted, giving both financial and non-financial reasons for your choice.   **(8 marks)**

    (ii) stating **one** alternative course of action which could be considered, including any financial implications of this action.   **(5 marks)**

Associated Examining Board Advanced Level

Question 22.4

Lamb Ltd operates a system of budgetary control and it is now drawing up budgets for the first quarter of its next financial year beginning on 1 July 1998.

It has been decided that production levels should be kept even during the three-month period commencing July 1998, and that a closing stock of 10 000 units is required in September 1998. Market research details show that sales for July are expected to be 20 000 units and to increase by 6% in August, and by a further 6% in September (on August levels). there will be an opening stock of 8 344 units on 1 July 1998. Production in June was 41 600 units.

The variable cost of production per unit is £25 throughout the period, of which materials account for 50%. These materials are always bought the month before they are used in production. Until recently, suppliers gave two months' credit before requiring payment. However, a new arrangement is being phased in. From August, any purchases will be paid for in the next month. May was the last month for buying materials carrying two months credit. Of the purchases made in June, 50% will have to be paid in July and the remainder in August. Of the purchases in July, 80% will have to be paid for in August and the remainder in September.

Lamb Ltd sells 80% of its goods on credit terms. Credit customers pay in the month after receiving their goods. The selling price per unit of the product is £30. June sales were 20 000 units.

REQUIRED

(a) Outline the stages the Lamb Ltd would need to go through in order to draw up its overall budget, and the advantages it would gain from using a system of budgetary control. **(12 marks)**

(b) Draw up monthly budgets for July, August and September 1998 for Lamb Ltd for:
    (i) stocks of finished goods in units; **(5 marks)**
    (ii) creditors in £s; **(5 marks)**
    (iii) debtors in £s. **(5 marks)**

University of Oxford Delegacy of Local Examinations Advanced Level

Question 22.5

Ballygawley Batteries is proposing to introduce a system of budgetary control.

REQUIREMENT

Draft a memorandum to the Board of Directors which:

(a) outlines the objectives of a system of budgetary control; **(9 marks)**

(b) highlights the behavioural problems which may be associated with the introduction of such a system; **(12 marks)**

(c) suggests ways of overcoming the behavioural problems identified in part (b) above. **(9 marks)**

Northern Ireland Council for the Curriculum Examinations and Assessment Advanced Level

Question 22.6

'The annual operating budget of a business is the most important document to be prepared in the accounting cycle.'

REQUIRED

(a) Explain the stages in the preparation and implementation of the annual budget of a manufacturing business. **(15 marks)**

(b) To what extent do you agree with the above statement? **(5 marks)**

London Examinations Advanced Level

23

Standard Costing and Variance Analysis

23.1 Introduction

Standard costing is the setting of pre-determined levels of costs and revenues which then represent a target for achievement. Variances are the difference between actual results and standards. Conceptually, standard costing is similar to budgeting and the only difference is one of degree. While budgets relate to the activities of the firm as a whole, standard costs relate to individual cost units. For example, if the budgeted manufacturing cost is £6 000 for an output of 1 000 units, the standard cost is £6 per unit. This can be analysed into standard material cost, standard labour cost, and so on.

Like budgeting, standard costing is a managerial aid to planning and control. By setting cost standards and comparing actual costs with standards, managers and workers are made cost-conscious since they know that they will be evaluated on their performance. In this way standard costing promotes efficiency.

23.2 Types of Standard

In the previous chapter we saw that management has to make a decision on whether to set a tight, loose, or medium budget. So it is with standards. Again there are three types.

Basic Standards

These are standards which are left unchanged for many years. Since they are not updated they are not suitable as the basis for budgeting from year to year. Their main function is to highlight trends over time. For example, the effect of the introduction of new technology on productivity can be gauged by observing the change in labour efficiency variances over time.

Ideal Standards

Ideal standards represent maximum performance and are consistent with a very tight budget. As we saw in the last chapter, such standards are likely to be regarded as unattainable by employees and the resulting mass of adverse variances might discourage them and serve as a disincentive to effort. As a result they are not often used.

Currently Attainable Standards

These represent costs that should be incurred under normal efficient operating conditions and they are consistent with a medium to tight budget. While not easy to achieve, they are by no means impossible. This is because, unlike ideal standards, allowances are made for normal wastage of materials, machine breakdowns, and some labour inefficiency. They are tight enough to motivate and be taken seriously by employees, yet not too tight that they cannot be used for the setting of budgets. Unlike the other two types, currently attainable standards can therefore be used for both planning and control. Because of this, most budgets are prepared under this type of standard.

23.3 Setting Standard Costs

Setting standard costs is a complicated task involving a large number of people including engineers, technicians, management, and workers. Four separate standards have to be established to arrive at standard unit cost:

- standard material cost
- standard labour cost
- standard variable overhead cost
- standard fixed overhead cost.

The four added together give us the overall standard unit cost.

In multi-product firms, the above has to be done for each type of product. Although setting standard cost is a complicated exercise, it is imperative to get it right because incorrect standards will throw up variances that have little meaning and cannot be used as the basis for performance evaluation and control.

Standard Material Cost

This is determined by the type and quantities of materials used and the price of each. The first should be set by engineers, technicians, and other members of the production department and should take into account normal wastage. The standard price should be obtained from the purchasing department, who should quote not current but expected prices during the period in which the standards are to apply. Thus there is some element of guesswork in their estimate.

Standard Labour Cost

This is determined from the grades of direct labour required to manufacture a product from start to finish, the time needed for each operation and the wage rate of each grade. To establish the first two, time and motion studies could be conducted for each product. These should allow for an element of labour inefficiency through idle time, poor concentration and fatigue. The wage rate of each grade should be forecast by supervisors and management.

Standard Overhead Cost

Overhead standards are established by using the information generated in predetermining overhead absorption rates, as described in Chapter 17.

$$\text{Standard variable overhead cost} = \frac{\text{Budgeted variable overhead}}{\text{Budgeted output}}$$

If the absorption method is the rate per unit of output, the standard variable overhead cost is in fact equal to the overhead absorption rate. If the method is the rate per labour hour or machine hour, the absorption rate has to be multiplied by the standard labour or machine hours to arrive at total standard variable overhead cost. The above applies similarly to standard fixed overhead cost.

Since separate overhead absorption rates are calculated for each cost centre, the total standard overhead cost has to be found by multiplying the appropriate absorption rate by time spent in each cost centre, then adding these together.

23.4 Variance Analysis

Let us now look at variance analysis, which involves the following:

1) measuring deviations of actual performance from standards, and
2) analysing the possible causes of the variances so that corrective action may be taken.

There is almost no end of possible variances that may be computed. They all have one thing in common however – they represent the difference between what was and what should have been. We shall be looking at some of the more important variances in this chapter, demonstrating their calculation with an example and mentioning possible causes. Adverse or unfavourable variances are bracketed, with the letter 'A' next to them. Favourable variances have the letter 'F' next to them.

23.5 Material Variances

The total material variance measures by how much the actual cost of materials used differs from the standard cost. The cost of materials used is determined by:

*   the price of the material per unit
*   the amount of material used per unit or batch of production.

The formula for finding this is:

Total material variance = (standard units × standard price) – (actual units × actual price)

Consider the following information:

Standards
Material price   £4 per kg
Usage   5 kg per unit

During a given period, 100 units of the finished article were produced. The material purchase price was £3.80 and the total used was 525 kg.

Since the cost of material used is determined by both price and usage it is possible to break down the total variances into two material sub-variances:

1) the price variance
2) the usage variance.

1. The Materials Price Variance
= (standard price – actual price) × actual quantity of materials purchased

£(4.00 – 3.80) × 525 kg = £105 F

Since the purchase price was £0.20 per kg less than expected, we have a favourable variance.

Possible Causes of a Favourable Price Variance

(a) An unexpected fall in market price
(b) Efficiency on the part of the purchasing department taking advantage of special offers and large volume discounts
(c) The purchase of inferior quality material

The opposites of these factors could cause an adverse materials price variance.

2. The Materials Usage Variance
= (standard quantity for actual production – actual quantity used) × standard price.

Standard usage = 100 units × 5 kg = 500 kg
Variance = (500 – 525) kg × £4 = £(100) A

Since 25 kg more material was used than expected, the variance is adverse.

Be careful

1) The under- or over-usage is multiplied by the **standard** and not the actual price. If we used the actual price, the computation of the usage variance would be affected by the efficiency or inefficiency of the purchasing department. Since we are trying to separate the price variance from the usage variance, we cannot do this. We have already performed a calculation for the price variance and bringing it into our calculation again would be double-counting it.

2) If budgeted output was not 100 units we should not compare budgeted total usage with actual usage. The budget should first be flexed to the actual level of activity. This flexed amount (representing standard usage) should then be compared to the actual to determine variance.

Illustration

Budgeted output	110 units
Budgeted usage, 110 × 5 kg	550 kg
Actual output	100 units
Actual usage	525 kg

Under a fixed budget the variance is:

$(550 - 525)$ kg × £4 = £100 F

This is wrong. The standard amount of material that should have been used is

$$550 \text{ kg} \times \frac{100}{110} = 500 \text{ kg}$$

This flexed amount should be the basis for the comparison. Now the variance is

$(500 - 525)$ kg × £4 = £(100) A

Possible Causes of an Adverse Materials Usage Variance

(a) Inferior materials leading to excessive waste
(b) Abnormal losses in production
(c) Poor stock control and pilferage

The opposites of these situations could lead to a favourable usage variance.

A favourable price variance often leads to an unfavourable usage variance. The cheaper supplies obtained may have been from a disreputable supplier selling poor quality material or 'seconds'. This lead to excessive wastage.

Standard material price and usage variances should be calculated for each type of material used. The total of the sub-variances (taking into account that a favourable variance is a plus and an adverse variance is a minus) give us the overall variance and this is a good way of checking your answer to a question. This applies to the sub-variances to all types of cost, i.e. materials, labour, variable overheads and fixed overheads.

23.6 Labour Variances

The total labour variance measures by how much the actual total cost of labour differs from the standard cost. The cost of labour is determined by:

- the price of labour per unit
- the amount of labour used per unit.

The formula for finding this is:

Total labour variance = (standard labour hours produced × standard rate)
– (actual hours × actual rate)

Consider the following information:

Standards	
Wage rate	£6 per hour
Time per unit	2 hours

The 100 units produced used 190 direct labour hours at a wage rate of £6.25.

Since the total wage bill is determined by two factors – the quantity of labour used and the wage rate – as with materials, the variance can also be sub-divided into:

1) the labour rate variance
2) the efficiency variance.

1. The Labour Rate Variance = (standard rate – actual rate) × actual number of hours

£(6.00 – 6.25) × 190 hours = £(47.50) A

Since the rate turned out to be higher than expected, the variance is adverse.

Possible Causes of an Adverse Labour Rate Variance

(a) Trade unions successfully negotiating a larger wage increase than management had anticipated.
(b) A scarcity of a particular type of skilled labour which necessitated an increase in rates to attract personnel.
(c) Use of a higher grade of labour than normal for some operations.

The opposite situations could lead to a favourable labour rate variance.

2. The Labour Efficiency Variance = (standard time for actual production – actual time) × standard wage rate

Standard time = 100 units × 2 labour hours = 200 labour hours
Variance = (200 – 190) hours × £6 = £60 F

Since 10 less hours than expected were worked, the variance is favourable.

As with the material usage variance, note again that:

1) The under (over) use is multiplied by the **standard** and not the actual wage rate.
2) The budget should be flexed to the actual activity level before comparison between standard and actual is made.

Possible Causes of a Favourable Labour Efficiency Variance

(a) A large increase in pay may have boosted worker morale and employer-employee relationships.
(b) The use of better grades of labour than standard may have speeded up operations of those processes.
(c) Less time than usual was lost by workers being idle because of machine breakdowns and bottlenecks in production (caused by poor scheduling or late delivery of components).
(d) Workers working with better quality material to that budgeted.

The opposite situations could lead to an adverse efficiency variance.

23.7 Variable Overhead Variances

The variable overhead variance measures by how much the actual variable overheads incurred differ from the standard variable overheads. The formula is as follows:

The Variable Overhead Variance =
(standard variable overhead absorbed for the activity level achieved
– actual variable overhead incurred)

Illustration

Budgeted variable overhead	£330
Budgeted output	110 units
Standard variable overhead per unit	£3
Actual production	100 units
Variable overhead incurred	£380

First, we need to flex the budget to the level of activity achieved. Variable overheads should have been

$$£330 \times \frac{100}{110} = £300$$

This represents the standard variable overhead

$= 100$ units $\times$ £3 $=$ £300

Variable overhead variance $=$ £300 $-$ £380
$=$ £(80) A

The allowed expenditure for an output of 100 units was £300. Since actual expenditure was £380 we have an adverse variance of £80.

When variable overheads accrue on the basis of direct labour hours or machine hours it is possible to analyse them into the expenditure and efficiency variances. Suppose that the standard variable overhead was not £3 per unit but 2 hours at £1.50 per direct labour hour. Remember from our labour variance example that direct labour hours budgeted was 200 hours, actually worked 190 hours.

A variable overhead variance is sub-divided into:

1) the expenditure variance and
2) the efficiency variance.

1. **The Variable Overheads Expenditure Variance =**
   (standard variable overhead per direct labour hour – actual variable
   overhead per direct labour hour) × number of direct labour hours worked

Since variable overheads now vary with labour hours it is necessary to flex the budget on this basis.

Actual variable overhead per direct labour hour $\dfrac{£380}{190 \text{ hours}} = $ £2 per hour

The standard is £1.50 of variable overhead per direct labour hour. There is therefore an adverse expenditure variance of
£(0.50) × 190 hours $=$ £(95) A

Another approach to calculating the expenditure variance is to see it as the difference between the budgeted overhead adjusted to the level of operations and the actual overhead incurred. By this approach:

	£
Variable overhead absorbed, 190 hours × £1.50	285
Incurred	380
Variance	£(95) A

Possible Causes of an Adverse Variable Overhead Variance

(a) Indirect materials costing more than expected, or usage being greater than expected
(b) Indirect labour being paid more than expected or efficiency being lower than expected
(c) Charges for utilities such as electricity and power increasing. The total of the variable overhead expenditure variance in itself has little meaning. For example, a nil variance does not necessarily mean that everything went according to plan. A large adverse variance on indirect materials could have been offset by a large favourable variance on indirect labour. For the variance to be useful to management, the cost accountant needs to prepare a report setting out the variance of each cost item.

Situations opposite to the above could result in a favourable variable overhead variance.

2. The Variable Overhead Efficiency Variance
  = (standard input hours – actual input hours) × standard variable overhead rate

Because fewer labour hours than expected were worked we could expect there to be a favourable efficiency variance.

Labour hours variance is 200 – 190 = 10 hours F
Efficiency variance = 10 hours × £1.50 = £15 F

Possible Causes of a Favourable Efficiency Variance

Since this variance arises from the efficiency of labour its causes are the same as those mentioned under labour efficiency variance.

Note that:

	£
Variable overhead expenditure variance	(95) A
Variable overhead efficiency variance	15 F
Variable overhead total variance	£(80) A

23.8 Fixed Overhead Variances

The fixed overhead variance measures by how much the actual fixed overheads incurred differ from the standard fixed overheads. The formula is as follows:

The Fixed Overhead Variance = (standard fixed overhead absorbed by actual production – actual fixed overhead incurred)

Illustration

Budgeted fixed overhead	£1 100
Budgeted output	110 units
Standard fixed overhead per unit	£10
Actual production	100 units
Fixed overhead incurred	£1 250

$$(100 \text{ units @ £10}) - £1\,250$$
$$1\,000 - 1\,250 \quad = £(250)A$$

This is the same as saying that there has been a £250 under-recovery of fixed overhead. Under-recovery is caused either by excessive expenditure or by budgeted production not being achieved. To reflect this, the total fixed overhead variance can be sub-divided into:

1) the fixed overhead expenditure variance
2) the fixed overhead volume variance.

1. The Fixed Overhead Expenditure Variance
= (budgeted – actual fixed overhead)

It is not necessary to flex the budget this time since fixed overheads do not vary with output.

Variance is £1100 – £1 250 = £(150) A

Possible Causes of an Adverse Fixed Overhead Expenditure Variance

(a) A greater than expected increase in factory occupancy costs
(b) An increase in insurance or any other fixed factory cost

The opposite could result in a favourable fixed overhead expenditure variance.

The total of the fixed overhead variance in itself has little meaning, for the same reason as for the total variable overhead variance. Again, the cost accountant should prepare a statement showing the variance on each cost item.

If the budgeted volume of production, 110 units, had been achieved, then the only variance would have been excessive expenditure. However, there is a shortfall in production, implying under-absorption. The extent of this under-absorption reflects the volume variance.

2. The Fixed Overhead Volume Variance
= budgeted cost – standard cost absorbed by production achieved

$$£1100 - (100 \text{ units} \times £10)$$
$$1100 - 1\,000 = £(100)A$$

Where actual output exceeds planned output, the volume variance is favourable.

Possible Causes of an Adverse Fixed Overhead Volume Variance

(a) Over-estimation of sales demand leading to a slow-down in production
(b) Industrial action slowing down production
(c) Production being held up by machine breakdowns, poor scheduling of work, or delays in receiving materials and components

The opposite could result in a favourable volume variance.

Note that:

	£
Fixed overhead expenditure variance	(150) A
Fixed overhead volume variance	(100) A
Fixed overhead total variance	£(250) A

The cause of the volume variance is that production did not match up to expectations. This can be caused by:

(a) inefficiency of work
(b) capacity available and paid for but not utilised.

It is possible further to split the volume variance into two parts to reflect this:

1) the efficiency variance
2) the capacity variance.

1. The Efficiency or Productivity Variance =
    (standard hours – actual hours)
    × standard fixed overhead rate per direct labour hour

Since only 190 hours were worked when the standard was 200 hours, we have a favourable efficiency variance.

$$\text{Standard Fixed Overhead Rate per Direct Labour Hour} = \frac{\text{Standard fixed overhead per unit}}{\text{Standard labour hours per unit}}$$

$$= \frac{£10}{2} = £5$$

Variance $= (200 - 190)$ hours $\times £5$
       $= £50$ F

Possible Causes of a Favourable Efficiency Variance

These are the same as for the labour efficiency variance.

2. The Capacity Variance = (capacity available – capacity used)
                         × standard fixed overhead rate per direct labour hour

On the budget of 110 units at 2 direct labour hours per unit, capacity available for production was 220 direct labour hours. Since actual hours worked were only 190 hours, the firm has failed to make use of 30 hours of available capacity.

Variance $= (220 - 190)$ hours $\times £5$
       $= £(150)$ A

If the 30 hours had been worked, an additional $30 \times £5 = £150$ fixed overhead would have been absorbed by production, resulting in a nil capacity variance.

Possible Causes of an Adverse Capacity Variance

These are the same as for the fixed overhead volume variance.

Note that:

	£
Fixed overhead efficiency variance	50 F
Fixed overhead capacity variance	(150) A
Fixed overhead volume variance	£(100) A

23.9 Sales Variances

The sales variance measures by how much actual sales differ from standard or budgeted sales. It is calculated by using the following formula:

Overall Sales Variance = (actual sales in units × actual selling price)
– (standard sales in units × standard selling price)

Since revenue is a function of both price and quantity it is possible to sub-divide the overall sales variance into two separate sub-variances:

1) the price variance and
2) the volume variance.

Consider the following information:

	Budget	Actual
Selling price	£60	£59
Quantity	120 units	125 units
Total revenue	£7 200	£7 375

1. The Price Variance = (actual price – standard price) x actual sales volume

$£(59 - 60) \times 125$ units $= £(125)$ A

The adverse variance indicates that selling price was lower than planned.

2. The Volume Variance = (actual volume – standard volume) × standard price

$(125 - 120)$ units $\times £60 = £300$ F

Since 5 more units than budgeted were sold the variance is favourable.

Interpretation

As there is an inverse relationship between selling price and quantity sold, the adverse price variance has led to a favourable volume variance.

With income variances, when the actual is greater than the planned, the variance is favourable. For this reason the actual is written before the planned in the formula. With cost variances the reverse is true and the planned is written before the actual.

With the growing popularity of marginal costing for internal management purposes, a new set of sales variances have recently come into use which calculate the impact of the variances not on total revenue but on contribution or profit margin.

23.10 An Alternative Approach to Calculation

In some questions the nature of the information given makes it awkward to adopt the approach we have used so far in variance calculations. Consider the following information:

Standard direct labour cost per unit: 3 hours at £4.50 per hour

Actual total direct labour use: 2 000 hours at a cost of £9 315

What is the wage rate variance?

By the approach we have used so far

The rate variance = (Standard wage rate − Actual wage rate) × Actual hours worked

$$\text{Actual wage rate} = \frac{£9\,315}{2\,000}$$
$$= £4.6575$$

This is when things become awkward as the actual wage rate does not come to a simple figure. In some cases it can run to many more decimal places. An alternative method in these situations is as follows:

	£
Standard cost for actual hours: 2 000 × £4.50	9 000
Actual cost	9 315
Rate variance	£(315) A

We have got to our answer by avoiding any awkward figures. The reasoning behind each route is essentially the same, the only difference being in the nature of the calculation. Performed accurately, our original method will produce the same answer.

Check:

Rate variance = £(4.6575 − 4.50) × 2 000
               = £0.1575 × 2000
               = £(315)A

Which is the better method to use? They are equally good. You can either use our original method for all calculations, use the second method for all calculations or use the first method as a general rule, resorting to the second when the figures become awkward.

23.11 Unrealistic Standards

Another factor which can explain a variance, whether favourable or adverse, is that the original standard may have been set at an unrealistic level. It might be too tight or too loose, or it might not have been updated to take recent changes into account. Whatever the reason, management accountants should always be ready to accept that the targets being set are not feasible and that the standards they are working with need to be changed.

23.12 Standard Costs and Selling Prices

Standard, rather than actual, costs are often used as the basis for setting selling prices. In this way it is ensured that efficiencies in production are rewarded in the form of a larger profit margin and that inefficiencies are not passed on to the consumer in the form of higher prices. Raising prices because of inefficiencies is, in any case, not a good idea since it may erode the competitive position of a business.

23.13 Interpretation of Variances

Examination questions require you not only to compute variances but also to interpret them and comment on possible causes. In this, it is important to look out for inter-relationships, not only between sub-variances of the same type but also between the different classes of variance, i.e. between material, labour, overhead and sales variances. There are many possible combinations but here are two situations to consider.

A firm purchases a raw material at a price which is cheaper than the standard price and so there is a favourable material price variance. However, the material is of an inferior quality, and because it breaks easily, more of it is wasted, resulting in an adverse material usage variance. Workers have to spend more time dealing with the material and so they produce less per hour, resulting in an adverse labour efficiency variance. The workers may become so frustrated that they demand more money per hour and this leads to an adverse labour rate variance. As the material is sub-standard, it causes problems with the machinery itself and more time has to be spent on maintenance, thus causing an adverse overhead variance. The finished product is of inferior quality and consumers buy less of it, resulting in an adverse sales volume variance; alternatively the selling price is dropped to reflect the reduced quality and there is an adverse price variance.

Another situation is as follows. The workers in a factory receive a wage rise over and above the standard labour rate and there is thus an adverse labour rate variance. In addition the workers have been told that they can have further wage increases if they improve their productivity. They feel more motivated and their production per hour rises, resulting in a favourable labour efficiency variance. Because industrial relations are now better, the workers are more careful in how they use the materials and there is less wastage, resulting in a favourable materials usage variance. Because they are working more carefully, their machines break down less often and there is less need for maintenance, resulting in a favourable overhead variance.

23.14 Profit Reconciliation Statements

These are drawn up when the actual profit for the year differs from that which was forecast in the budgets, the purpose being to explain why the two figures are different. It begins with the budgeted profit and finishes with the actual profit, the first figure being turned into the other by adding or subtracting all the individual variances.

In preparing a reconciliation statement, proceed as follows:
1) Begin with the budgeted profit.
2) Adjust this for the sales variances, adding favourable ones and deducting adverse ones. The two sub-sections of the sales variance should be shown separately.

Inclusion of the sales volume variance gives us the standard (expected) profit on actual sales; adding on the selling price variance gets us to the actual profit on actual sales.

3) Next we include the cost variances, breaking each down into its parts. Favourable variances are added and adverse variances deducted. It is a good idea to devote separate columns to the favourable and adverse variances. Total up the lists and deduct one from the other. If the result is an overall favourable cost variance, add this to the adjusted budgeted profit figure and vice versa.

4) The final figure will be the actual profit.

Example

This question is taken from Northern Ireland Council for the Curriculum Examinations and Assessment Advanced Level.

Down Chemicals Limited manufacture large plastic containers which sell at £200 each. The following budget details relate to period 2.

	£	£
Sales (50 × £200)		10 000
Less variable costs		
Material X (1 000 kg × £1 per kg)	1 000	
Material Y (500 kg × £2 per kg)	1 000	
	2 000	
Labour (250 hours × £4 per hour)	1 000	
Total variable costs	3 000	
Fixed costs	4 000	
Total costs		(7 000)
Net profit		£3 000

Actual results for period 2 were as follows:

	£	£
Sales (50 × £200)		10 000
Less variable costs		
Material X (800 kg) 1.50/	1 200	
Material Y (600 kg) 1.40/	1 080	
	2 280	
Labour (240 hours)	1 080	
Total variable costs	3 360	
Fixed costs	4 000	
Total costs		(7 360)
Net profit		£2 640

(a) Prepare a statement reconciling the budgeted profit with the actual profit for period 2, detailing the following variances:

    (i)   material price

    (ii)   material usage

    (iii)   labour rate

    (iv)   labour efficiency   **(24 marks)**

(b) As the management accountant, draft a report to the managing director on
     the statement you have prepared, outlining the possible action which might
     be taken by management.   **(16 marks)**

Solution

(a)

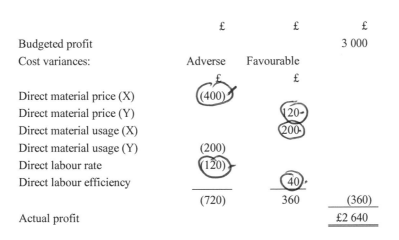

	£	£	£
Budgeted profit			3 000
Cost variances:	Adverse	Favourable	
	£	£	
Direct material price (X)	(400)		
Direct material price (Y)		20	
Direct material usage (X)		200	
Direct material usage (Y)	(200)		
Direct labour rate	(120)		
Direct labour efficiency		40	
	(720)	360	(360)
Actual profit			£2 640

(b) The adverse overall variance is explained by the price of X and the labour wage
     rate being higher than expected. A possible solution might be to find a cheaper
     supplier for the materials. It is hard to decrease a wage rate but labour efficiency
     might be encouraged by higher motivation of workers.

23.15 Examination Technique

As far as the calculations are concerned, it is desirable but not necessary for you to
memorise the formulae. If you understand a variance you will be able to work out the
formula for yourself. If you are really stuck, go back to basics, adopt a common sense
approach, and ask yourself the question: 'What is the difference between what
happened and what should have happened?' This will often lead you to the right
answer. A check on whether sub-divisions of a variance add up to the total variance is
recommended, e.g. whether the variable overhead expenditure variance plus the
efficiency variance equals the total variance. Be careful always to make clear whether
the variance you have calculated is a favourable one (plus) or an adverse one (minus).

23.16 Departmental Performance Reports

It is common for cost accountants to prepare performance reports from variances for
each responsibility centre at regular intervals. Such reports separate those variances
that are significant from those that are not. Management attention can then be focused
on areas where variances are exceptionally large. This system is known as
Management by Exception.

Performance reports should distinguish controllable costs from non-controllable costs.
The departmental manager should be held responsible only for those costs which he
can influence. This is an obvious point but also an important one. A manager will not
co-operate with an evaluation system which assigns responsibility to him over costs
his department incurs but over which he has no control. Thus the manager of a
production department can in most situations be justifiably assigned responsibility
over material usage and labour efficiency variances but not over material price or

wage rate variances. A material price variance is the responsibility of the purchasing department, and wage rates are set by negotiations between unions and management. An example of a possible format for a departmental performance report is shown below (figures have not been included but you can see how it works from the way it is set out).

Performance Report for Month

	Budget	Actual	Variance	Percentage variance
Production: hours				
Production: units				
Controllable costs:				
Direct material				
Direct labour				
Indirect labour				
Other variable overheads				
Non-controllable costs				
Rent and rates				
Light and heat				
Depreciation				
Other fixed overheads				

Analysis of Variances

		Controllable	Non-controllable	Controllable	Non-controllable
Direct material:	Price				
	Usage				
Direct labour:	Rate				
	Efficiency				
Variable overhead:	Expenditure				
	Efficiency				
Fixed overhead:	Expenditure				
	Volume				

As mentioned in the last chapter, it is important that managers have faith in the evaluation system and see it as a device to help rather than judge or blame them. It helps if managers have participated in the setting of the budget. Also, they are more likely not to fear the report if they know they will be evaluated on a profit-conscious rather than budget-constrained style. In addition to the traditional financial measures, the evaluation should encompass non-financial qualitative measures such as relationship with employees, the meeting of production schedules on time, and maintaining product quality.

Having digested the report, managers should investigate significant variances to identify their causes. Corrective action should then be taken. This final act is one of the rewards of an effective system of standard costing. Businesses do not take the trouble and expense of maintaining a standard costing system just for the sake of it; it is not an end in itself. It is a means to an end and the end is cost minimisation and control.

Questions

Question 23.1

Sun plc has budgeted to produce 5 000 units of Beam per month. On this basis the standard cost per Beam is set as follows:

Direct materials	50 kilos at £0.18 per kilo
Direct labour	45 minutes at £1.60 per hour
Fixed overheads	£0.80 per unit

For the month of May the actual production was 4 800 Beams and the actual costs incurred for the month were:

Direct materials: 241 000 kilos at a total cost of £43 300
Direct labour: 3 400 hours at a cost of £5 500
Fixed overhead incurred: £4 140

Mr Ray, the Management Accountant, has asked you to calculate the variances for the month and prepare a report, briefly giving reasons for each variance.

REQUIRED

Calculate the variances and prepare the report asked for by Mr Ray.   **(15 marks)**

Institute of Chartered Accountants, Foundation

Question 23.2

Dash Ltd manufactures liquid cleaning products from chemical raw materials. It uses the following standard costs for the production of a batch of its product Sparkleen.

Material

Ammonia solution	200 litres at £1.10 per litre
Colouring	1 000 litres at £0.10 per litre
Fragrance agent	10 litres at £14.20 per litre

Labour operations

Blending	8 hours at £12.00 per hour
Mixing	12 hours at £8.00 per hour

The actual costs for batch S4120 were:

Material

Ammonia solution	240 litres costing £216.00
Colouring	950 litres costing £85.50
Fragrance agent	11 litres costing £165.00

Labour operations

Blending	11 hours costing £143.00
Mixing	10 hours costing £90.00

REQUIRED

(a) Calculate the following variances from standard for batch S4120.
  (i)   Material price variances
  (ii) Material usage variances
  (iii) Total direct material cost variance
  (iv) Labour rate variances
  (v)   Labour efficiency variances
  (vi) Total direct labour cost variance   **(12 marks)**

(b) Suggest possible reasons why the labour and material variances may have occurred.   **(10 marks)**

(c) Evaluate the usefulness of standard costing to Dash Ltd.   **(2 marks)**

OCR Advanced Level

Question 23.3

A company manufactures a single product. The product is manufactured by processig
through two sections, Cost Centre A and Cost Centre B. The company is introducing
standard costing.

The standards will be based upon the following budgeted information:

	Cost centre A	Cost centre B
Material usage (per product)	3 kilos	1 kilo
Material price (per kilo)	£5	£6
Labour hours (per product)	1.5	1.75
Labour rate (per hour)	£3	£4
Overheads	£40 000	£60 000
Annual production (products)	50 000	50 000

During the month of May the following actual results were achieved:

	Cost centre A	Cost centre B
Products produced	5 000	5 000
Materials used (kilos)	15 500	5 100
Materials consumed	£70 050	£30 090
Total labour hours	7 200	8 800
Total labour cost	£22 680	£33 440
Overheads	£42 000	£59 000

REQUIRED

(a) Explain the term 'Cost Centre'.   **(3 marks)**

(b) Calculate the standard cost of one completed product.   **(4 marks)**

(c) Calculate separate variances for Cost Centre A and Cost Centre B in May
    for each of the following:
    (i)   Material price
    (ii) Material usage
    (iii) Labour efficiency
    (iv) Labour rate   **(8 marks)**

London Examinations Advanced Level

Question 23.4

Hanson Ltd is a small manufacturing company which produces one product. The production budget for May 1998 had shown the following costs per unit.

	£
Materials (£4 per kg)	2
Labour (£6 per hour)	12
	14

Budgeted sales for the month were 2 000 units at £20 each.

In June 1998 the management accountant reviewed the actual performance for the previous month and produced the following information based on sales of 1 800 units at £22 each.

	£
Materials (880 kg)	3 718
Labour (3 900 hours)	23 985

There were no opening or closing stocks of the finished product.

REQUIRED

(a) Calculate:
    (i)   the overall sales variance, together with volume and price variances;   **(6 marks)**
    (ii)   the overall material variance, together with usage and price variances;   **(6 marks)**
    (iii)   the overall labour variance, together with efficiency and rate variances.   **(6 marks)**

(b) Prepare a statement reconciling the budgeted profit to actual profit for May 1998.   **(9 marks)**

(c) Calculate the actual contribution per unit to the nearest penny.   **(5 marks)**

(d) Write a short report to the management accountant:
                                (Report format: 2 marks)
    (i) commenting on the results from the variance analysis;   **(6 marks)**
    (ii) evaluating the company's performance, making recommendations for
       improving sales, materials and labour costs.   **(10 marks)**

Associated Examining Board Advanced Level

24

Break-even Analysis

24.1 Introduction

An important piece of information for a business to know is how many units it must make and sell before it begins to make a profit. Break-even analysis is a management accounting tool which is used to make this calculation.

As a firm's production increases, so do its variable costs, so producing a small quantity incurs only a small amount of variable cost. But fixed overheads like rent and administration have to be paid before any units are produced and are the same regardless of output. (Remember that the cost of producing zero units is the total of the fixed costs.)

As we saw in Chapter 20, the contribution is the selling price of a product minus the variable costs incurred in producing it. The difference between these two figures is the amount contributed by each unit sold to the fixed costs and to the firm's profit.

If the firm produces only a small output, there will be insufficient revenue to cover all fixed costs, i.e. not enough units are contributing, and the firm is making a loss. As output increases, however, contributions build up as more and more units are sold until the point where the firm's total revenue just equals its total costs. This is the break-even point where

Total revenue = Fixed costs + Variable costs

No firm is satisfied simply with breaking even and its objective is to achieve as much profit as possible, but it needs to know at what point it covers its total costs and after what point it will begin to make a profit. After fixed costs have been covered by the break-even number of units, the firm starts to make a profit as the fixed costs are being spread over a larger output and cost per unit falls.

Consider the following situation. Dermatino Ltd is a factory which manufactures leather jackets. Each jacket incurs variable costs of £40 and the firm sells it at £60. The fixed costs of the factory are £20 000 a year. Each jacket is sold for £20 more than its variable production cost but fixed costs also have to be covered. Dermatino wants to know how many jackets they have to sell before they start making a profit.

The following chart shows the costs paid and revenues received by Dermatino at different levels of production. Fixed costs are the same at all levels of production but variable costs and sales revenue vary directly with the number produced and sold. We can see from the chart that the firm is making a loss up to 1 000 units and beyond that is making a profit, so the break-even point is 1 000 units. As long as the firm can produce and sell more than 1 000 jackets, it will make a profit.

No of units (x)	Total fixed costs	Total variable costs (40x)	Total cost i.e. FC + VC	Sales revenue (60x)	Profit	Loss
	£	£	£	£	£	£
0	20 000	0	20 000	0		20 000
250	20 000	10 000	30 000	15 000		15 000
500	20 000	20 000	40 000	30 000		10 000
750	20 000	30 000	50 000	45 000		5 000
1 000	20 000	40 000	60 000	60 000	Break-even point	
1 250	20 000	50 000	70 000	75 000	5 000	
1 500	20 000	60 000	80 000	90 000	10 000	

24.2 The Break-even Point

Rather than drawing up a table and inserting figures at different hypothetical levels of production, we can use a simple formula to find the break-even point.

$$\text{Break - even point} = \frac{\textbf{Total fixed costs}}{\textbf{Selling price per unit - variable cost per unit}}$$

The total fixed costs are divided by the contribution per unit.

Using this formula in our example of the leather jackets:
£20 000 ÷ £(60 – 40) = 1 000 units

From our table above, we can see that Dermatino makes a loss before 1 000 units and starts to earn a profit after this point, assuming that all costs and revenues are constant.

From this we can conclude that:

1) when total contribution is less than fixed costs, losses are suffered
2) when contribution is greater than fixed costs, profits are enjoyed
3) when contribution is exactly equal to fixed costs there is neither profit nor loss and we are in a break-even position.

24.3 The Break-even Chart

It is possible to represent the break-even point on a chart which shows the levels of fixed cost, variable cost, and total revenue at all output levels from zero to capacity. This provides a visual impression of the critical relationship between costs, volume, and profit. For this reason break-even analysis is sometimes referred to as **cost–volume–profit analysis**, or CVP analysis for short.

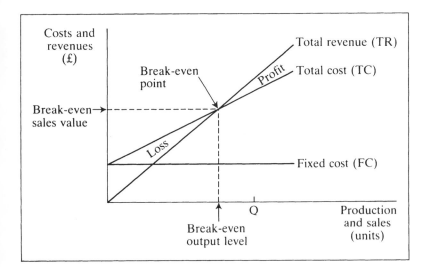

Note from the above chart that:

1) fixed costs are a constant in relation to production level.
2) variable costs are indicated by the area above fixed costs and below total costs. They increase directly with output.
3) total revenue increases directly with sales volume.
4) the slope of the total revenue line is steeper than variable cost because for each unit produced and sold selling price is greater than variable cost (£60 > £40).
5) at an output level of zero, loss is equal to the whole of fixed costs. As the firm starts to produce and sell, fixed costs are gradually recovered and consequently losses get smaller, until the break-even point. Thereafter additional sales earn increasing amounts of profit.
6) at all points before break-even total cost is greater than total revenue.
7) at all points after break-even total revenue is greater than total cost.
8) at the break-even point, where the two lines intersect, total revenue is exactly equal to total cost and profit is zero.

24.4 The Margin of Safety

Entrepreneurs do not set up in business to break even – their main objective is to achieve profit and output levels in excess of break-even point. The **margin of safety** is the amount by which sales exceed the break-even point. On the chart at level of sales of Q units, the margin of safety is indicated by the distance between the break-even output level and Q. The greater the margin of safety the greater are profits and the safer is the firm's position.

The margin of safety can be calculated as a percentage:

$$\frac{\text{Sales beyond break - even point}}{\text{Units required to break even}} \times 100$$

For example, in the example of Dermatino whose break-even point was 1 000 units, if the firm actually sells 1 500 units, its margin of safety is

$$\frac{500}{1\,000} = 50\%$$

The break-even analysis can also be used to calculate the number of units a firm must sell in order to make a target profit. We simply add the target profit to the fixed costs and divide by the contribution as usual.

Suppose that Dermatino Ltd has a target profit of £40 000 per annum. The number of jackets it must sell to achieve this is:

$$\frac{\text{Total fixed costs} + \text{target profit}}{\text{Selling price per unit} - \text{variable cost per unit}}$$

$$= \frac{20\,000 + 40\,000}{60 - 40}$$

$$= 3\,000 \text{ units}$$

24.5 Constructing a Break-even Chart

Questions on this topic usually ask for construction of a break-even chart from information supplied. The following steps should be followed.

Step 1

Calculate total cost at various levels of output. There is no need to do this at all levels since the relationship between output and cost is assumed to be linear. Choose three output levels – zero, capacity and one in between. For example in the case of Dermatino we would write:

No of units (x)	Total fixed costs	Total variable costs (40x)	Total cost i.e. FC + VC	Sales revenue (60x)
	£	£	£	£
0	20 000	0	20 000	0
750	20 000	30 000	50 000	45 000
1 500	20 000	60 000	80 000	90 000

Step 2

Select suitable scales for the axes.

Step 3

Draw axes and plot lines in the following order:

(a) FC – horizontal at the given level.
(b) TC – from your workings. Having marked your three points, join them with a ruler. If it does not come to a straight line check your calculations.
(c) TR – the same instructions apply as for TC.

Step 4

Label the break-even point.

If you are asked to state the amount of profit or loss at a particular output level, do not be tempted to answer this from the chart. Since profit is the difference between two lines you will not be able to state it precisely. It is better to do a little calculation of total revenue minus total cost for an accurate answer.

24.6 Limitations of Break-even Charts

Users of break-even charts should be aware of their limitations to prevent the possibility of false conclusions being drawn from them. These limitations lie in the assumptions which underlie them, most of which are suspect. The assumptions are as follows:

1 The cost functions are linear

In practice this is not so, for either fixed cost or variable cost, in either the short run or the long run, as the economist will tell us. From a given asset base, as output expands in the short run, the rate of increase in variable cost initially falls as the firm benefits from increasing returns to the variable factors. Eventually a point is reached when diminishing returns set in – this increases the rate of increase in variable cost. The short-run cost function is therefore non-linear. In the long run, when time is allowed for changes in the scale of operations, again businesses do not experience constant costs. In the early stages of growth economies of scale are reaped as the firm benefits from increased specialisation of manpower and machines (technical economies) and enjoys certain other benefits such as discounts on bulk-buying (trading economies), and cheaper loans (financial economies). At very high levels of output however diseconomies of an administrative and managerial nature set in as the organisation becomes too large and unwieldy for efficient management. The long-run cost function is therefore also non-linear.

With fixed costs the assumption that they are constant over the whole range of output from zero to maximum capacity is unrealistic. In reality fixed costs are stepped, as shown below.

2 The revenue function is linear

While this may be so for a firm operating in a perfectly competitive market, where imperfections exist (as they do in the majority of markets) economists will at once tell us that firms have to reduce prices in order to sell more. This gives us a curvilinear revenue function, as shown below.

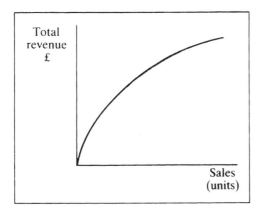

3 Volume is the only factor affecting costs and revenues

In practice costs may also be affected by a number of other factors such as inflation, technological change, and an increase in workers' productivity. Revenue may be affected by the need to change prices in response to a change in market conditions. The break-even chart ignores these and makes the assumption that, other things being equal, all other factors affecting costs and revenues remain constant.

4 A single product is sold

Break-even charts cannot handle multi-product situations. A multi-product firm earning different amounts of contribution on each product will find that there is more than one break-even point, this depending on the sales mix.

5 All output is sold

The break-even chart does not incorporate the possibility of changing stock levels.

24.7 The Usefulness of Break-even Analysis

Given that in the short term the firm's capacity is fixed, and its range of output is limited, break-even charts do have value because in this limited range the extent of the curves in the cost and revenue functions are so slight that they can be approximated as being linear. Management is often concerned with decision-making at the margin. Over this limited range the functions are pretty much linear. For this reason, despite the unrealistic assumption of linearity, break-even analysis does have relevance in the real world. The range over which the assumptions hold true is known as the relevant range. Strictly speaking when drawing the chart the accountant should only include the functions within this range, and not extend them to very low and very high levels of output.

Although the break-even chart as presented in this chapter cannot handle multi-product situations and changing stock levels, more complicated versions can be adapted for use even in these situations.

Break-even charts are an excellent way for the accountant of a firm to present financial information to management, who may be non-accountants. Most non-accountants prefer to look at information in the form of charts and diagrams rather than a table of figures or financial statements.

Perhaps the greatest value of the chart is its highlighting of the underlying relationship between costs, volume and profit. In so doing it provides an excellent framework for exploring the effect on the firm's finances of management following different courses of action. In this way the chart is a useful tool for decision-making. For example the effect of an increase in wages would be to increase the slope of the variable cost curve. This would increase the break-even point and reduce profit, as shown in the chart below.

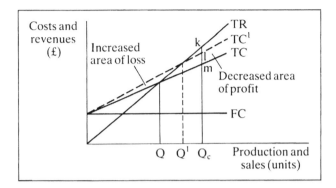

The dotted total cost function TC' represents the new level of costs after the change. The break-even output level is increased from Q to Q'. If the firm is currently producing Q_c, the amount of profit is reduced from km to kl and the margin of safety from $Q_c - Q$ to $Q_c - Q'$.

As a useful exercise you might like to construct break-even charts to represent the following:

(i) an increase in fixed costs

(ii) a decrease in selling price

(iii) a decrease in variable costs.

Questions

Question 24.1

Lonard plc is investigating ways of improving the profitability of one of its products. The following forecast is available for the production and sales of 20 000 units for the next financial year.

	£000
Direct labour	500
Direct material	300
Variable production overheads	150
	950
Fixed overheads	300
	1 250
Sales	1 450

The following options are being considered with a view to increasing profitability. Lonard plc has the capacity to increase production by 5 000 units.

(i)   Invest in new technology which would reduce direct labour costs by £5 per unit, and the variable production overhead by £1.50 per unit. Selling price, direct material and quantity would remain unchanged. Fixed overheads would increase by £50 000.

(ii)   Increase advertising by £100 000 per year, and introduce a sales commission of £4 per unit. The selling price would be increased by £8 per unit, and sales quantity would increase by 3 000 units. All other costs would remain unchanged.

(iii)   Improve the quality of the product by increasing material and labour costs by 25%. Selling price would increase by £15 per unit. Sales quantity, variable production overheads and fixed overheads would remain unchanged.

REQUIRED

(a) Based upon the original forecast calculate:

    (i) contribution per unit;
    (ii) total profit;
    (iii) break-even point in both units and sales value.   **(6 marks)**

(b) Taking each option independently, calculate the total profit for each option.   **(8 marks)**

(c) Calculate the margin of safety in units and sales value for option (iii).   **(4 marks)**

(d) Discuss the limitations of using break-even analysis for decision making.   **(6 marks)**

(e) Comment on the implications for the workforce if Lonard plc undertakes
    option (iii).   **(3 marks)**

OCR Advanced Level

Question 24.2

Businesses, after reaching their break-even points, always accumulate profits in direct proportion to further increases in the level of output.

REQUIRED

(a) Comment upon the validity of the above statement.   **(8 marks)**

The Special Occasions restaurant has a capacity of 25 customers per day and opens for 300 days in the year.

Details of the costs and income of the restaurant are as follows:

1) Each customer will spend an average of £12 on a meal.

2) Raw material costs represent one third of income.

3) There are two full-time members of staff who are each paid £10 000 per annum.

4) The premises were purchased at a cost of £200 000 with fixtures and fittings costing a further £50 000. Depreciation is to be charged at the rate of 2% on the cost of premises and 20% on the cost of fixtures and fittings.

5) Other fixed overheads amount to a total of £16 000 per annum.

REQUIRED

(b) Calculation of:

   (i)   the number of meals which must be sold for the business to break even.

   (ii)   the profit or loss of the business for the year, assuming that full capacity is achieved.

   (iii) the margin of safety. Comment upon the sufficiency level of the margin of safety for this business.   **(8 marks)**

The owners have the opportunity of purchasing the premises next to the Special Occasions Restaurant and expanding its operations to cover both premises. The owners calculate that the number of customers would double and that:

1) Each customer would continue to spend an average of £12 on a meal.

2) Raw material costs would remain at the rate of one third of income.

3) The number of staff would be increased to five, each of whom will be paid £10 000 per annum.

4) The new premises would cost £300 000. In addition, a further £50 000 of fixtures and fittings would be purchased. Deprecation rates would continue to be at the rates of 2% and 20% on cost respectively.

5) Other fixed overheads will rise to £50 000 per annum because of increased interest payments.

REQUIRED

(c)

  (i) A calculation of the number of meals which must be sold for the business to break even if the business is expanded.

 (ii) The calculation of the profit or loss of the expanded business, assuming that full capacity is achieved.

(iii) Comment upon the reasons for the difference in the break-even points before and after the proposed expansion.   **(9 marks)**

London Examinations Advanced Level

Question 24.3

Armagh Ltd manufactures a radio which is marketed through only specially approved dealers who receive a trade discount of 30% on the retail price of £20.

Armagh Ltd's accountant has produced the following summary of the actual operating results for the year to 31 May 1998.

	£	£
Sales		33 600
Costs:		
Direct material	14 400	
Direct labour	4 800	
Total overheads	5 800	
		(25 000)
Net profit		£8 600

Fixed overheads, included in the total overheads figure, amount to £3 400.

There are no stocks or work in progress.

All of the following decisions will be implemented for the year to 31 May 1999:

- The trade discount allowed to approved dealers is to be increased by £1 for each radio.

- An advertising campaign will be launched on 1 June 1998 at a cost of £5 000. This is expected to increase the number of radios sold over the next 12 months by 50%.

- Arrangements have been made with suppliers of some of the components used in the manufacture of the radio for bulk orders to be placed and it is expected that the material cost will, as a result, be reduced by £1 per unit.

- Fixed overheads will remain the same for both years.

REQUIREMENT

(a) Prepare a net profit forecast for the year to 31 May 1999, taking account of all of the above decisions.   **(13 marks)**

(b) Calculate the following figures for 1998 and 1999 (forecast):

    (i)   break-even volume of sales (units)
    (ii) margin of safety (units)   **(8 marks)**

(c) Evaluate the feasibility of the proposals for the year to 31 May 1999.   **(9 marks)**

Northern Ireland Council for the Curriculum Examinations and Assessment Advanced Level

Question 24.4

(a) Ferguson plc manufactures a standard product in two factories situated in Perth and Inverness. The following are the forecasts for the forthcoming year.

	Perth	Inverness
Selling price per unit	£60	£60
Variable costs per unit:		
Direct material	£15	£16
Direct labour	£20	£16
Variable overhead	£10	£8
Fixed costs per annum	£42 000	£67 000

Calculate for each factory

(i)   the break-even point in units and sales value;   **(4 marks)**

(ii)   the profit or loss if sales had been
       (1) 4 000 units
       (2) 2 500 units;   **(4 marks)**

(iii) the value of sales necessary to make a profit after tax of
       £48 000 if profits are taxed at 20%;   **(5 marks)**

(iv)   the margin of safety in units and sales value at the current output
       level of 7 500 units in each factory;   **(3 marks)**

(v)   the Profit / Volume Ratio (PVR).   **(2 marks)**

(b) Calculate the uniform level of output at which each factory will make the
    same profit.   **(2 marks)**

Scottish Certificate of Education Higher Grade

25

Capital Investment Appraisal

25.1 Introduction

In contrast to the short-term business decisions considered so far such as dropping a segment, accepting a special order, and decision-making based on break-even analysis, investment decisions are long term, i.e. the effects are felt over several years. Capital investment is concerned with the type and mix of fixed assets employed by a firm. When a fixed asset is due for replacement a decision has to be taken on which of several competing assets to purchase. When a business is planning for expansion, investment decisions have to be taken regarding plant and machinery and land and buildings. Such decisions are usually taken by top management for three reasons:

1) They usually involve very large sums of money.
2) The quality of the decisions taken affect the profitability of the firm for many years.
3) Having purchased an item of fixed asset or embarked on a long-term project the decision is usually irreversible. To find subsequently that the wrong decision has been taken and to attempt to change it could be very costly.

Given the crucial importance of 'getting-it-right' in selecting between alternatives, management does not choose on the basis of feelings or hunches but uses tried and tested techniques and concrete financial data.

This analysis deals with the quantitative aspect of an investment but there are also qualitative issues to be taken into account. The main qualitative considerations are:

- the firm's objectives
- external costs and benefits
- past experience
- the current state of the economy.

25.2 Cash Flows

The first step in making a quantitative assessment of an investment is to estimate and calculate the expected cash flows over the relevant years. These flows are:

(a) the cash inflows coming from the net revenue receipts from the sale of the product which will result from the investment. These net receipts are the difference between sales revenue and expenses (materials, labour, overheads etc). A loss would result in a negative net receipt.
(b) the cash outflows resulting from the initial cost of the investment.

When measuring these cash flows, we must specify during which year they take place. The initial outflow when the investment is paid for is assumed to take place in Year 0 (i.e. the first day of the period). Year 1 shows the flows for the first year, Year 2 for the second year and so on.

When cash outflows are deducted from cash inflows, we can see the net result of the investment over its lifetime. A net cash inflow is positive and a net cash outflow is negative. The firm could take the view that if the net cash flow is positive the investment is worthwhile. If the firm has to choose between two or more alternative investments, it will choose the one which has the greatest positive cash inflow. As we shall see below, this is a very simplistic way of assessing matters. We shall consider the following methods of capital investment appraisal:

- payback
- accounting rate of return
- net present value
- internal rate of return.

The first two of these are simple and rather crude but the second two use the more sophisticated principles of discounted cash flow. We shall now look at these methods in turn.

25.3 The Payback Method

The simplest method is payback. This ranks projects by the time it takes for the expected net cash inflows to pay back the initial outlay. The quicker the outflow is repaid, the more attractive the investment. 'Net cash inflows' means cash inflows less cash outflows.

Example
Stone plc is considering investing £1 million on one of two competing projects.

Details are as follows:

	Project A	Project B
	£000	£000
Initial outlay	1 000	1 000
Expected net cash inflows:		
Year 1	450	200
Year 2	550	500
Year 3	250	600
Year 4	150	300

The estimated residual value of both projects after four years is zero. The cost of capital is 10%.

Payback periods

   Project A = 2 years
   Project B = 2 years + 300 / 600 of year 3 = 2½ years

Project A: the initial outlay of £1 000 is paid back within two years by the expected inflows of £450 plus £550.

Project B: the initial outlay of £1 000 is paid back within 2½ years, i.e. £200 plus £500 plus £300 of the £600 in year 3.

By this criteria, the company would select Project A. The payback method prefers projects whose returns are concentrated in earlier years.

This is an easy method to follow and it does take into account the timing of cash flows but it does not measure profitability and it looks at the short term only. It does not take account of monies received after the payback period and it ignores the longer-term profitability of projects. In our example the rejected project B in fact returns more than A over the full four-year period – £1.6 million compared with £1.4 million. These drawbacks are overcome by our second method.

25.4 The Accounting Rate of Return (ARR)

The criterion here is profitability rather than speed of return. The procedure is as follows:

(a) Calculate the total profit arising over the lifetime of the project (i.e. deduct the investment outlay from the net cash inflows).
(b) Divide the answer by the number of years of the investment.
(c) Calculate ARR as follows:

$$\frac{\text{average annual profit}}{\text{initial outlay}} \times 100$$

Only revenues and costs flowing from the investment should be included in the calculation.

In the above example of Stone plc, the average annual net cash inflow from project A, in £000s, is

$$\frac{£450 + £550 + 250 + 150}{4 \text{ years}} = £350$$

The figures for project B are:

$$\frac{£200 + 500 + 600 + 300}{4 \text{ years}} = £400$$

To calculate the average annual profit we need to account for depreciation in addition to the cash flows given. By the straight-line method the annual charge is £250. The average annual profit is therefore £100 for project A and £150 for Project B. The average investment, in £000s, is its book value at the mid-point of the project's life, i.e.

$$\frac{1000}{2} = £500$$

This gives us:

For project A : $\text{ARR} = \dfrac{£100}{£500} \times 100 = 20\%$

For project B : $\text{ARR} = \dfrac{£150}{£500} \times 100 = 30\%$

This method measures profitability and takes into account all the cash flows over the life of the project, but it ignores the timing of the cash flows and also the time value of money. This is the opportunity cost of

the money invested and it is very important to take it into consideration if we want to make a reliable and accurate appraisal.

What we have done in our calculations so far is to add together money expected in year 1 to that expected in year 2, and so on. But money in different time periods is worth different amounts, for two reasons:

1) Money received earlier is worth more than money received later since once received, it can be invested to earn a return.
2) Inflation reduces the purchasing power (real value) of money over time.

In other words, a person would rather have £100 now than £100 in a year's time because he could earn interest on it in the meantime and make it up to, say, £105 by next year. In addition, if he wants the £100 to buy a new radio which costs that amount, again he would rather have the money now because inflation may push the price of the radio up to £110 by next year.

The payback and accounting rate of return methods do not account for the time value of money. Both add together cash flows from different years. Since £1 received in year 1 is worth more than £1 received in year 2, it is possible to add them only by first converting one in terms of the other by means of an exchange rate between the two. What is needed is a similar exchange rate such that money received in the future can be converted back to what it is worth today, the time of the initial outlay, so that we can compare like with like.

25.5 Discounted Cash Flow (DCF)

It is possible to do just this by discounting, the purpose of which is to reduce the value of future cash flows to their present-day value by using an appropriate discount factor.

Suppose that the interest rate is 10% per annum and we want to know how much £1 invested today will be worth in one year's time:

£1 + £0.10 = £1.10

And in two years' time?

£1.10 + £0.11 = £1.21

This process, which you have probably met before, is known as compounding.

Discounting is the opposite of compounding. It asks the question 'Given that the rate of interest is 10 per cent, how much is £1 received in one year's time worth today?'

$$\frac{£1}{1.10} = £0.9091$$

And £1 received in two years' time

$$\frac{£1}{1.21} = £0.8264$$

The compounded values are calculated by the formula $A = P(1 + i)$.

The discounted values are calculated by the formula : $P = \dfrac{A}{(1+i)^n}$

where P is the principal (original sum invested), A the sum to which it will amount, i the rate of interest, and n the number of years.

Fortunately you will not have to make these calculations as there are net present value tables which give the discount factor for £1 in various future years at various percentage interest rates. Examination questions provide you with the discount factors and you just have to know how to use them.

Despite the fact that DCF techniques are more complicated than the first two methods, firms still use them because, in practice, the time value of money is an important consideration, especially in times of high interest rates and inflation. We did not meet this problem in short-run decisions because the elements of interest and inflation over short periods of time are usually insignificant. Over a long period they are significant and should therefore be brought into the calculations. There are two specific discounted cash flow methods – net present value and internal rate of return.

25.6 Net Present Value (NPV)

The estimated future cash flows are discounted at the minimum rate of return acceptable to the firm. This total sum, expressed in today's £s, is compared with the initial outlay. If it is greater, the project is worthwhile. The criteria for setting the minimum acceptable rate of return is discussed later in the chapter.

Illustration

Let us evaluate project A on the assumption that the minimum acceptable rate of return is the cost of capital, 10%.

Year	Cash flow	Discount factor	Present value
	£000	at 10%	£
0	(1 000)	1.0000	(1 000 000)
1	450	0.9091	409 095
2	550	0.8264	454 520
3	250	0.7513	187 825
4	150	0.6830	102 450

The calculation tells Stone plc that the project will add to the value of the company by £153 890 at today's money value.

Present value of expected net cash inflows – Initial outlay = NPV of project

$$£1\ 153\ 890 - £1\ 000\ 000 = £153\ 890$$

This would be compared with the NPVs of competing projects, the one with the largest NPV being selected. Where NPV is negative the project should be rejected.

Examination questions usually require you to comment on your findings and to recommend a course of action. As well as quoting the quantitative results of your calculations, you should also bring in any qualitative factors you think may be relevant, taking into account the nature of the product if you have been told what this is. Always choose a project and back it up with your findings.

25.7 The Internal Rate of Return (IRR)

The IRR, or yield, is the true annual percentage return earned on a project. It is given by that interest which, when applied to the future cash flows, reduces the NPV of the project to zero. It has to be found by trial and error.

Illustration

For Project A

Year	Cash flow	Discount factor	Present value	Discount factor	Present value
	£000	at 18%	£	at 19%	£
0	(1 000)	1.0000	(1 000 000)	1.0000	(1 000 000)
1	450	0.8475	381 375	0.8403	378 135
2	550	0.7182	395 010	0.7062	388 410
3	250	0.6086	152 150	0.5934	148 350
4	150	0.5158	77 370	0.4987	74 805
			NPV = 5 905		NPV = (10 300)

The IRR is between 18% and 19%. This return is compared with the minimum acceptable rate. If it is greater, the project is worthwhile. Note how the return using discounted cash flow is lower than that obtained by the simple ARR method (20%) which does not take the time value of money into account.

The IRR represents the maximum a firm is willing to pay for finance. (Economists amongst you will recognise the similarity of this to Keynes' concept of the marginal efficiency of capital, which also represents the maximum rate of interest a firm is prepared to pay for investment funds.)

Where projects are mutually exclusive and all have an IRR greater than the minimum acceptable rate of return, the project with the largest IRR is to be selected.

25.8 The Minimum Acceptable Rate of Return

A common criteria is cost of capital to the firm. In practice, businesses raise finance through several sources each with a different cost attached to it. The cost of capital then has to be calculated as the weighted average cost.

Example

A company has the following capital structure:

Source	Cost	£
Ordinary shares	12%	60 000
Debentures	8%	30 000
Bank loan	10%	10 000

What is its cost of capital?

Answer

Source	£000	Weight	×	Cost	= Weighted cost
Ordinary shares	60	6		12	72
Debentures	30	3		8	24
Bank loan	10	1		10	10
	100	10			106

Divide the weighted cost by the sum of the weights, i.e.
$106 \div 10 = 10.6$
Weighted average cost = 10.6%

The company's cost of capital is 10.6%.

Economists advocate the use of the opportunity cost concept in setting the minimum acceptable rate. By this criterion, the rate should be at least equal to the return the firm could obtain if it invested the funds outside the business eg in shares of corporate stocks or bonds.

Example

The company above could earn a return of 14% if it invested externally. A project offering a return of 12% would be accepted by the cost of capital criteria, but rejected by the opportunity cost criteria. Accepting the project would be a bad decision in the sense that the opportunity would be lost of earning a better return on the capital in an alternative use.

In addition, the minimum acceptable rate of return should be adjusted in line with the degree of risk attached to various projects. Risky projects should be evaluated with a higher rate than safe projects, to compensate for the additional risk.

25.9 Comparison of Methods

Only the DCF methods are theoretically sound. ARR suffers from the failure to take the time value of money into account. Payback also suffers from this, and in addition it fails to take relative profitability of projects into account. It may seem surprising then that payback is the most widely used method in industry. This is partly because of its simplicity and also because, in times of rapid change when forecasting becomes particularly hazardous, projects offering a quick return are favoured. Another possible reason for the popularity of payback is that people are motivated by the short term. Ambitious young managers who want to work their way up the corporate ladder in as short a time as possible display a preference for projects offering quick spectacular returns, rather than those equally profitable in the long run but whose returns are more spread out. In most situations management uses more than one method before reaching a decision. In major investments involving very large sums of money all four methods may be used.

25.10 Limitations

All methods of investment appraisal suffer from the fact that the figures used in the calculations are only estimates. One of the main problems in practice is quantifying future cash flows likely to emanate from different projects. In a dynamic world it is not possible to do this with certainty. Since the timescale in investment decisions is long rather than short, forecasting is made even more difficult. The correctness of decisions taken often relies on the quality of the original forecast. In this respect DCF methods are at a disadvantage to the simple crude methods since in addition to cash flows, estimates have to be made about future interest rates and inflation.

The other main limitation of the techniques presented in this chapter is that they do not incorporate non-financial factors, such as how worthwhile socially projects are and what degree of risk is involved. It should be said however that more advanced methods can take these into account. Investment decisions in the public sector for example often try to attach money values to social costs and benefits emanating from a project, such as construction of a ring-road, in an exercise known as cost-benefit analysis. Risk can also be allowed for in more complicated methods.

Questions

Question 25.1

Darton plc manufactures designer kitchen doors. The machine which cuts and shapes the doors is frequently breaking down. The management is considering two possible courses of action. These are as follows:

Proposal 1

The purchase of a new updated machine at a cost of £420 000 which would be capable of producing 6 500 doors per year.

Proposal 2

Major repairs to be carried out on the existing machine at a cost of £300 000. If this proposal is adopted, it is anticipated that annual repair and maintenance costs would be £12 000 for each of the next four years after which time the machine would be replaced. This machine can produce a maximum of 90 doors per week but it would be necessary to shut the machine down for two weeks each year for maintenance purposes. A part-time maintenance and repair engineer would also need to be employed at a cost of £4 000 per annum.

Additional Information

1) The company is expecting to sell 4 000 doors per year for the next two years and thereafter to sell 4 400 doors per year. The current selling price is £80 per door but the company is expecting to raise the selling price by 20% with effect from the beginning of year 4. Company policy is to produce in any year only the number of doors which can be sold in that year.

2) The material for each door at present costs £40 but this is expected to rise by 10% at the beginning of year 2 and remain constant thereafter.

3) Direct labour costs are expected to be £5.50 per door in year 1 and will rise by 50 pence per door in each of the three subsequent years.

4) The company's cost of capital is 10% per annum.

The discount factor is:

Year	10%
1	0.909
2	0.826
3	0.751
4	0.683

REQUIRED

(a) Prepare statements showing the net cash revenue receipts per year for each proposal if demand is as expected over the next four years. **(20 marks)**

(b) Prepare a table of computations using the net present value for each proposal over the next four years. **(12 marks)**

(c) Write a report to the Directors of Darton plc analysing the two proposals and indicating which proposal should be implemented. **(Report format: 2 marks)**
(8 marks)

(d) Identify and briefly discuss **one** advantage and **one** disadvantage of having machinery which is capable of output greater than anticipated sales. **(8 marks)**

Associated Examining Board Advanced Level

Question 25.2

(a) What is meant by the terms 'discounting' and 'non-discounting' methods of investment appraisal? Illustrate your answer with an example of each method. **(10 marks)**

(b) What difficulties will be encountered when applying methods of investment appraisal, including discounting, to long-term projects? **(10 marks)**

London Examinations Advanced Level

Question 25.3

Lakeside plc is considering purchasing one of two businesses in order to expand its operations. The options are:

Turner Ltd

Estimated cost of the take-over bid: £2.15 million.

Production: 100 000 units per annum.

Sales: 80% of the output will be sold under an existing fixed price contract which has a further four years to run at £15 per unit. The remainder of the production will be sold on the open market at the following selling prices:

Year	1	2	3	4
Selling price per unit	£14	£14	£15	£16

Operating costs (including depreciation): £750 000 over each of years 1 and 2, £800 000 over each of years 3 and 4.

Depreciation: £60 000 per year.

Paxton Ltd

Estimated cost of take-over bid: £3.5 million.

Production: 200 000 units per annum.

Sales: A contract already exists covering the next four years under which the entire product will be taken at a price of £13 per unit for years 1 and 2, £14 per unit in year 3 and £15 per unit in year 4.

Operating costs (including depreciation): £1.2 million in the first year, £1.3 million in the second year, £1.5 million in the third year and £1.7 million in the fourth year.

Depreciation: £90 000 per year.

The cost of capital for Lakeside plc is 12%. All receipts and payments take place at the end of each year.

Extract from present value tables of £1 @ 12%:

Year 1	0.893
Year 2	0.797
Year 3	0.712
Year 4	0.636

REQUIRED

(a) Calculate the net present value of each of the two businesses, and make a recommendation, with reasons, as to which business appears to be the better investment.   **(14 marks)**

(b) Briefly describe **two** other methods of capital investment appraisal. What are the advantages and disadvantages of each method?   **(6 marks)**

OCR Advanced Level Specimen Examination

Question 25.4

The Rovers Football Club are languishing in the middle of the First Division of the Football League. The Club has suffered a loss of £200 000 in their last financial year and, whilst receipts from spectators have declined over the last five years, recently receipts have stabilised at approximately £1 000 000 per season. The Club is considering the purchase of the services of one of two new football players – Jimmy Jam or Johnny Star.

Jimmy Jam is 21 years old and considered to be a future international footballer. He is prepared to sign a five-year contract with Rovers for a salary of £50 000 per annum. His present club would require a transfer fee of £200 000 for the transfer of his existing contract. With Jam in the team, the Rovers Club would expect receipts to increase by 20%.

Johnny Star is 32 years old and a leading international footballer who is prepared to sign for Rovers on a two-year contract before retiring completely from football. He would expect a salary of £200 000 per annum and his present club would require a transfer fee of £100 000 for the transfer of his existing contract. Rovers believe that, as a result of signing Star, receipts would increase by 40%.

The rate of interest applicable to the transaction is 12% and the following is an extract from the present value table for £1:

	12%
Year 1	0.893
Year 2	0.797
Year 3	0.712
Year 4	0.636
Year 5	0.507

It should be assumed that all costs are paid and revenues received at the end of each year.

REQUIRED

A report, incorporating an evaluation of the financial results of engaging each player by the net present value method, providing the Rovers Football Club with information to assist it in deciding which alternative to adopt. Indicate any other factors that may be taken into consideration.

(18 marks)

Associated Examining Board Advanced Level

26

Social Accounting

26.1 Introduction

Throughout this book we have assumed that a firm's main objective is to make as much profit as possible and that a higher profit is always better than a lower one. We have seen how to record and calculate profit, how to adjust it for errors and omissions and how to increase it by keeping costs down and revenues up. We have looked at some of the principles on which businesses make decisions of both a short-term and a long-term nature and, in all cases, the main criterion has been profit maximisation.

However there are situations where profitability as the sole or main determinant of a firm's policy is increasingly being challenged. As we have seen, there are various groups of people who are interested in the progress and activities of a firm besides the owners or shareholders, eg employees, customers, local residents and society as a whole. Firms have a responsibility not only to make a profit for their shareholders but also to take into account in their decisions and actions the needs and rights of other groups. This is know as a firm's **social responsibility**.

26.2 Social Responsibility Accounting

An important development in recent decades has been a re-consideration of the motives of the firm. The traditional and rather narrow view is that the only motive is profit maximisation. It is now realised that there may be more than one motive. A business decision affects not only profits accruing to owners but also has consequences on employees, consumers, and in some cases the environment. In practice, firms try to balance conflicting interests with one another. Decisions taken in this way may not lead to maximum profits. For example, a firm may decide to keep open an unprofitable segment out of a sense of responsibility to the local community and perhaps a desire to avoid the adverse publicity and resentment that goes with a closure. Again a business may install pollution-reducing devices, thereby reducing profits, out of a sense of responsibility to the environment and in reaction to local environment protection pressure groups. This is a complex and growing field of study called social responsibility accounting.

Groups of people who have an interest in the activities of firms are known as their **stakeholders**. We can identify the following:

- **the firm's employees**, who are mainly concerned with fair wages, good working conditions (taking into account health and safety), job security, the existence of good pension benefits etc.

- **the consumers** who buy the firm's product. They want a high-quality good or service at a fair price, quick delivery and in many cases they need guarantees and after-sales service.

- **creditors** who have lent or who are considering lending money to the firm. They are concerned that the firm should make a profit insofar as this affects the firm's ability to repay its debt to them but beyond that they are also interested in its creditworthiness and its payment policy.

- **the local population** who live in the area near or around the firm. They are concerned that the company should not create pollution in the form of bad air, emissions of smoke and gases, dangerous waste, radiation, noise etc. They may be concerned that heavy works traffic passes through residential areas.

- **the population of the country as a whole and of neighbouring countries** are concerned with similar issues to those just stated – pollution does not stop at city or country boundaries. In addition people are also concerned about social and moral issues like the employment of minorities, foreign aid, trading with unacceptable regimes etc. Multinational companies are often criticised for using the resources of developing countries to increase their profits but for taking these profits out of the countries.

Firms are thus increasingly being forced to reconsider their objectives by pressure groups, the press, local organisations and by a general change in public opinion which is beginning to expect social responsibility from large corporations. The power of the mass media is an important factor both in forming public opinion and in transmitting it to those who make industrial decisions.

26.3 Social Issues

In the interests of social responsibility, firms should be willing to adjust some of their activities and incur greater costs. Here are some examples of issues which should cause firms to take the wider view.

(a) **the closure of an unprofitable branch in a deprived area**: in the interests of profit maximisation, a firm may wish to close a branch which is losing money but there will be strong pressure on it to keep the branch open for the sake of the local labour force, especially if unemployment in the area is already high. The cost of closure to the local community could be extremely high and would include the multiplier effect of the drop in incomes, a fall in the standard of living of the area and all the associated social problems of family break-up, crime, social deprivation etc.

(b) **the replacement of labour by advanced technology**: this is similar to the above case in that the social cost is unemployment and its associated problems. Social considerations do not usually prevent companies from investing in the technology necessary to keep their product competitive and their costs low. It is true that many workers made redundant because of machinery eventually find jobs elsewhere but the process of adjustment can be too slow for many. Commercial banks in the UK are closing down their branches and replacing them with computerised telephone centres. Some of those made redundant may find jobs in the new centres but others will not. The banks will make redundancy payments but this may not compensate for the loss of a livelihood.

(c) **the effects of redundancy and early retirement on the labour force:** the chances of finding alternative employment can be very slight in some areas. For a younger person, being made redundant means losing not only income but also valuable experience, and the longer the period of unemployment, the more remote the chance of finding another job. For someone over the age of 50, redundancy can mean retirement as it is even more difficult for an older person to find an employer. But retiring early means living on a smaller pension and redundancy money is not usually so large that a family can live off the interest. The stress and anxiety associated with unemployment can cause both physical and mental illness and perhaps the company who dismissed the employees should make some contribution towards helping the people involved.

(d) **the effects of using non-renewable, rare or scarce materials:** there can be conflict between a firm which wants to use large quantities of a material which is in very short supply and those who want to protect the supply source. An example is the deforestation of large areas in many countries which is taking place in the interests of the profits of timber companies. This deforestation is not only destroying natural habitats and killing ecosystems but it is also blamed for altering global weather patterns.

(e) **the effects on the environment of the use of dangerous materials:** firms which handle materials such as radioactive substances or poisons have a real and obvious responsibility to both their employees and the community as a whole to deal with and dispose of these safely. The measures involved include:

- the provision of a safe working environment
- the purchase of special containers, tanks, carts etc for the storage of hazardous materials
- special arrangements for the transportation of hazardous materials
- the labelling of materials which are flammable, explosive, caustic, radioactive etc
- training of staff in all of the above to minimise accidents caused by human error.

All of these measures are costly and eat into a firm's profits. There is a temptation for a firm to cut its costs to the point where it is not breaking the law but where it is still increasing the risk of accident and this is a clear case of a conflict between the firm's desire for profit and its social responsibility. Failure to take adequate precautions can have serious consequences: death and injury, pollution of air, water and crops, loss of property etc.

(f) **trading which has political or ethical implications:** certain industries are controversial by the very nature of their products and society may wish to place some restrictions on their freedom to sell wherever and however they wish. A good example is the tobacco industry, whose product is now generally accepted as being potentially dangerous to health. Although advertising of the product is restricted, cigarettes and tobacco have not been banned and their manufacturers are able to make profits out of something which causes harm. Other examples here are the arms and alcohol industries.

(g) **excessive economy in health or safety measures**: firms are bound by law to provide a healthy and safe working environment for their employees but they may be tempted to skimp on those areas which cause them the greatest cost.

(h) **keeping to a code of ethics in advertising**: the Advertising Standards Authority in the UK is a self-regulating body which tries to ensure that all advertisements are legal, decent, honest and truthful. It provides a mechanism by which people can complain about the content of advertisements and attempts to give a framework within which firms can publicise their products without offending anyone.

26.4 Social Accounting

A profit-oriented organisation can produce a social accounting statement alongside and as an extension of its normal financial statements. This statement can show:

- the effects of its social policies on the company's financial performance
- the effects on the community of those actions taken in the interests of profit
- the value of the workforce to the organisation (this is known as Human Resource Accounting).

Since certain actions taken by the company become costs which are borne by the community, these costs should be included in the fixed overheads and allocated to the products and processes which are causing the environmental problem. Some costs can certainly be traced to particular cost centres but perhaps a cost such as smoke pollution from a steel works should be spread over all the steel products coming out of the plant. An amount of money could be put aside out of profits in order to limit the pollution or to deal with its consequences. Local residents might wish nothing less than the closure of the steel plant but this would not be a practical solution.

However it is done, an attempt should be made to give a financial value to the social costs created but some firms may confine themselves simply to giving a narrative of the social effects of their activities. There is also a tendency for such reports to have a positive bias and to state the positive actions being taken by the company without admitting to the negative ones. After all the report is being written by the firm and this might point to the advisability of an external environment audit being undertaken by a neutral firm.

26.5 Conclusion

Public opinion is increasingly forcing companies to set themselves environmental and community objectives as well as financial ones, i.e. to recognise that their shareholders are not the only stakeholders in the organisation. While they will always be faced with the constraint of making enough profit to allow them to pay their shareholders enough dividend to encourage them to keep their shares and to buy new ones, they can also be made to behave in a way which takes other groups of people into account and which recognises other objectives besides financial ones. Legislation can require firms to behave in certain socially and ethically acceptable ways but it is also possible for them, on their own initiative, to go further than simply not breaking the law.

Acting responsibly towards the environment has its positive side for a firm as it can use its actions to gain valuable publicity as a firm which cares. A firm which practises effective social accounting will ensure its own long-term survival and profitability.

The topic of social accounting normally comes up in an examination as part of a financial question, often one where a decision has to be made. As well as considering the financial aspects of the courses of action you are given, you would also be expected to take into account the social consequences.

Questions

Question 26.1

Eurasifrac, a multi-national company of diverse interests, was reviewing a number of its activities in order to determine possible courses of action.

1) The company owned a coal mine where increased geological difficulties had resulted in the full cost per ton of coal mined rising from £70 to £90 in the last year. The current market price of coal was £80 per ton, and was likely to remain at that level in the forseeable future. The normal level of output was 10 000 tons per annum. A director has argued that the mine should be closed, so that the company's profits would increase. All of the employees should be made redundant.

2) A factory owned by the company was located in a rural environment close to a small town. The local community had complained that poisonous effluent was being discharged into a river passing through the town. Scientific tests had shown that fish were being killed, and that seepage of poison had occurred into agricultural and residential land adjacent to the river.

Summarised Revenue Statement of the Factory for the last three years

	Year 1	Year 2	Year 3
	£m	£m	£m
Sales	10.0	12.0	15.0
less			
Variable costs	5.0	6.7	9.1
Fixed costs	4.0	4.1	4.1
Profit	1.0	1.2	1.8

The fixed costs include £3m of the parent company costs allocated to the factory annually.

The local community had requested that the pollution be stopped, but the company replied that the factory was not very profitable. In order to eliminate the poisonous effects, a capital outlay on new plant of £4m over three years would be required.

3) Over the past two years the company had stockpiled a very scarce material known as Igoxi, which it used in a high-technology process. The material had cost £6.50 per lb and all of the stockpile of 10 tons had been purchased at this price. The material was not used in normal production, but only on special contract orders.

In the last three months world demand had increased the market price of Igoxi to £10 per lb.

REQUIRED

Prepare a report advising the company as follows:

(a) Whether the company should proceed to close the coal mine.   **(8 marks)**

(b) Whether the company can justify continuing to operate the factory and allow the river to remain polluted.   **(10 marks)**

(c) What should be the basis of valuing the stock of Igoxi:
   (i) for balance sheet purposes
   (ii) for production purposes.   **(7 marks)**

Associated Examining Board Advanced Level

Question 26.2

What social considerations should be taken into account in the following situations?

(a) An international car-manufacturing plant has plans to close down a branch in the UK which is in an area of high unemployment. It intends to resite the plant in China.

(b) A soft drink bottling plant is investing in new automated machinery which will allow it to cut one-third of its current workforce.

(c) A building firm has just acquired a green-field site on which it is seeking planning permission to build 2 000 houses. Woodland will have to be cleared.

(d) A television advertisement promoting a confectionery manufacturer hints that children who eat the firm's sweets enjoy better health than those who do not. Health groups have complained.

(e) A beer company is promoting its product in a country where few people drink alcohol for religious reasons. The promotion is proving so successful that there is an increasing trend of alcoholism among the young people of the country.

(f) A consultancy employs ten people in an old premises which has been converted into offices. Fire precautions are minimal and there is no fire escape from the upper floors of the building. The management say that they cannot afford to make structural changes but that there is virtually no risk of fire since it enforces a no-smoking policy in all rooms.

(g) The food technology industry is trying to promote the use of genetically modified crops but environmentalists argue that these pose a danger to health.

Author's question

Extra Questions

The questions which follows are on miscellaneous topics. Some of them test areas which have been covered in several chapters.

Questions

Question E.1

One of the directors of Sleet Ltd has prepared the following draft balance sheet for the company at 30 June 1996:

Draft Balance Sheet at 30 June 1996

	£000	£000	£000
Fixed assets at cost			500
Less accumulated depreciation			(250)
			250
Stock		69	
Debtors	87		
Less provision for bad debts	(2)		
		85	
Balance at bank		6	
		160	
Trade creditors		(90)	
			70
			£320
financed by			
Ordinary shares of £1 each			195
Profit and loss account			125
			£320

You ascertain the following information:

1. The balance at bank was taken from the cash book, but the director did not prepare a bank reconciliation. On checking, you find at 30 June 1996:

	£000
Cheques issued but not yet cleared	12
Lodgements in the cash book not on the bank statement	6
Bank charges not in the cash book	4
Returned cheque not in cash book	3

   The returned cheque was to settle a debt, but the customer had forgotten to sign it. There is no reason to suppose that the debt is bad.

2. The provision for bad debts is no longer required.

340

3. Some goods were sent to a customer on 27 June 1996 on 'sale or return'. The goods cost Sleet Ltd £5 0000 and had a selling price of £7 000. They were recorded as a credit sale when sent to the customer and no accounting entries have been made to record the fact that all of the goods were returned on 15 July 1996.

4. On checking the stock lists for 30 June 1996 it was found that some goods had been recorded at their cost of £6 000 but their realisable value was £5 000.

5. The depreciation charge for the year had been calculated incorrectly. It is the company's policy to write its assets off over their estimated life of 10 years using the straight line method and assuming a residual value of £100 000. The director had omitted the estimated value from his calculation.

REQUIRED

(a) Prepare the company's bank reconciliation statement at 30 June 1996, showing the balance on the bank statement and the adjusted cash book balance. **(4 marks)**

(b) Prepare the balance sheet of Sleet Ltd at 30 June 1996, revised in the light of the additional information. Show clearly how any revised figures are calculated. **(12 marks)**

(c) Explain, with reference to the **single** accounting concept which you consider most appropriate, your treatment of item 3 above. **(2 marks)**

(d) Explain, with reference to the **single** accounting concept which you consider most appropriate, your treatment of item 4 above. **(2 marks)**

Institute of Financial Services Banking Certificate

Question E.2

Rain, Squall and Deluge traded in partnership for a number of years until 30 June 1995, sharing profit in the ratio 3 : 2 : 1 respectively. After preparing the accounts for the year to 30 June 1995, but before including the effects of Rain's retirement, the following credit balances appeared on the partners' accounts:

	Current Account	*Capital Account*
	£000	£000
Rain	10	300
Squall	15	250
Deluge	20	200

Rain decided to retire from the partnership on 30 June 1995. The assets of the partnership were revalued on that date; it was found that their current value was £120 000 greater than their book value and the partners' capital accounts were adjusted accordingly. Rain was then paid the full amount due to him in cash.

Squall and Deluge decided to continue trading as a partnership, leaving the assets at their revalued amounts and putting all further adjustments through their current accounts.

The Squall and Deluge partnership made a profit of £180 000 during the year to 30 June 1996 and decided that it should be divided between them in a manner which reflected their relative contributions to the firm. They agreed that the balances on their capital accounts could be invested elsewhere, with a similar risk, to earn an annual return of 10%. Squall could earn a salary of £20 000 and Deluge a salary of £31 000 a year if they worked elsewhere. Any remaining profits or losses would be divided equally.

During the year to 30 June 1996, Squall's drawings were £25 000 and Deluge's drawings were £35 000.

REQUIRED

(a) Calculate the amount paid to Rain when he left the partnership. **(3 marks)**

(b) Calculate the balances of Squall's and Deluge's capital accounts at 30 June 1995 after giving effect to the revaluation. **(2 marks)**

(c) Prepare the partnership appropriation account for the year to 30 June 1996 and the partners' current accounts for the same period. **(7 marks)**

(d) Show how the profit of the partnership for the year to 30 June 1996 would be divided if the terms of the Partnership Act 1890 were applied. **(2 marks)**

(e) Squall and Deluge are considering converting the firm to a limited company. State **three** advantages and **three** disadvantages of taking this course of action. **(6 marks)**

Institute of Financial Service Banking Certificate

Question E.3

Patmann plc is a company which sells sportswear from a number of retail outlets. The company currently holds 10% of the ordinary share capital of Quinoxite plc which is one of its major competitors.

The following information is available for each of the companies.

Balance Sheets as at 30 September 1997

	PATMANN PLC		QUINOXITE PLC	
	£000	£000	£000	£000
Authorised share capital				
600 000 ordinary shares of £1 each		600		
720 000 ordinary share of 25p each				180
200 000 8% preference shares of 50p each		100		
Issued Share Capital and reserves				
240 000 ordinary shares of £1 each, fully paid		240		
720 000 ordinary shares of 25p each, fully paid				180
120 000 8% preference shares of 50p each, fully paid		60		
Share premium account		50		40
Profit and loss account		340		120
		£690		£340
Fixed assets		570		380
Investment in Quinoxite plc at cost		80		

Current assets	280		210
Creditors: Amounts falling due within one year	190		250
Net current assets (liabilities)		90	(40)
		740	340
Creditors: Amounts falling due after more than one year			
10% debenture stock		(50)	
		£690	£340

During October the Directors of Patmann plc decided that they would like to increase their company's holding of ordinary shares in Quinoxite plc in order to become the majority shareholder.

In order to raise the necessary finance, the Directors of Patmann plc declared a rights issue of one ordinary share for every three ordinary shares currently held by existing shareholders. The issue price was agreed at £3 per share and all the shares were taken up and paid for by 7 October 1997.

On 10 October 1997, Patmann plc purchased sufficient ordinary shares in Quinoxite plc to achieve a 75% holding in total. The market price of Quinoxite plc's ordinary shares at that date was 50p per share.

REQUIRED

(a) Briefly explain the phrase 'majority shareholder'. **(4 marks)**

(b) Prepare the balance sheet of Patmann plc as at 10 October 1997 after accounting for the rights issue and showing the 75% holding of ordinary shares in Quinoxite plc. **(17 marks)**

(c) (i) Define the term 'gearing' as it would apply to a limited company. **(2 marks)**

(ii) Calculate the gearing ratio for Patmann plc as at 30 September 1997 and as at 10 October 1997, stating the formula used. **(7 marks)**

(iii) Briefly comment on the change in gearing calculated in (c) (ii), indicating how it would affect an ordinary shareholder of Patmann plc. **(6 marks)**

(d) (i) Briefly explain what is meant by a 'wholly-owned subsidiary' company. **(4 marks)**

(ii) Calculate the total price that Patmann plc would have had to have paid if sufficient ordinary shares in Quinoxite plc had been acquired on 10 October 1997 in order to make it a wholly-owned subsidiary. **(5 marks)**

(iii) Calculate the minimum issue price per preference share if the purchase of shares in (d) (iii) above had been financed by the rights issue and by issuing all the remaining available preference shares in Patmann plc. **(5 marks)**

Associated Examining Board Advanced Level

Question E.4

The following trial balance was extracted from the books of Bashmetal Limited, a manufacturing company, at 31 October 1995:

	£	£
Share capital (authorised and issued):		
Ordinary shares of 25p each		60 000
Profit and loss account, 1 November 1994		18 550
Share premium account		5 000
6% debentures		20 000
Debtors and creditors	64 947	20 260
Opening stocks:		
Raw materials	18 260	
Work-in-progress	12 480	
Finished goods	18 060	
Bank	38 400	
Factory buildings	42 000	
Plant and machinery	28 420	
Fixtures and fittings	9 600	
Provision for depreciation:		
Factory buildings		4 200
Plant and machinery		17 052
Fixtures and fittings		3 840
Production wages	71 940	
Raw materials purchased	49 770	
Bad debts written off	460	
Carriage inwards	190	
Carriage outwards	2 840	
Non-productive factory labour	21 450	
Light, heat and power	2 200	
Rent, rates and insurance	3 650	
Directors' salaries	41 205	
Audit fee	1 600	
Sales		300 000
Bank charges	1 400	
Advertising	1 200	
Debenture interest paid	600	
Administration expenses	18 230	
	£448 902	£448 902

You are given the following extra information:

(1)   Closing stocks are valued as follows:
Raw materials: £19 460
Work-in-progress: £14 444
Finished goods: £24 215

(2)   Factory buildings are depreciated at 2% per annum. All other fixed assets are depreciated at 20% of cost.

(3)   There were accruals at 31 October 1995 as follows:
Advertising: £150
Carriage inwards: £90

(4)   £150 of the rent, rates and insurance was paid in advance at 31 October 1995.

(5)   The rent, rates and insurance is to be split in the proportion: $\frac{3}{5}$ factory and $\frac{2}{5}$ administration, and the light, heat and power is apportioned $\frac{1}{2}$ factory, $\frac{1}{4}$ administration and $\frac{1}{4}$ selling expenses.

(6)   A corporation tax provision of £30 000 is to be made, and the directors propose a dividend of 20%.

344

REQUIRED

(a)   Prepare the manufacturing, trading and profit and loss accounts of Bashmetal
       Limited for the year ended 31 October 1995 (including an appropriation account).   **(22 marks)**

(b)   Prepare the balance sheet of the company as at 31 October 1995.   **(8 marks)**

Note: The above accounts and balance sheet need not be in a form suitable for publication.

London Examinations Advanced Level

Question E.5

Plato Ltd started business on 1 January 1991. The company has two
separate divisions; one manufactures a product called 'Aristo' and the
other a product called 'Tottle'. The following information is provided
about the company:

	Aristo	*Tottle*
Plant purchased 1 January 1991:		
Cost	£1 000 000	£250 000
Residual value at end of life	£100 000	£50 000
Life	10 years	10 years
Maximum output	50 000 units	70 000 units
Production and sales (in units) for the years to 31 December:		
1991 (actual)	30 000	20 000
1992 (actual)	40 000	30 000
1993 (forecast)	50 000	40 000
Selling price per unit	£9.00	£9.50
Material cost per unit (variable)	£1.80	£1.60
Labour cost per unit (variable)	£2.20	£0.90
Annual fixed costs (excluding depreciation)	£100 000	£92 000

The company uses straight line depreciation. There were no stocks of any
kind held at the end of any of the years.

Management is satisfied that production and sales of both products will
continue to grow at the annual rate of 10 000 units in future years, but the
department producing Aristo will be a full capacity by the end of 1993.
The further increase in the demand for Aristo during 1994 can be met in
either of two ways:

1.   Buy the finished product from Hume Ltd for £8.00 per unit and resell them. No
      further processing would have to be done by Plato.

2.   Double the capacity of the Aristo department by purchasing an additional set of fixed
      assets. These would be identical in all respects to those purchased on 1 January 1991.

The fixed costs excluding depreciation would not be affected by either course of action.

REQUIRED

(a) Prepare, in columnar form, the separate profit and loss accounts for the two products
    for each of the three years to 31 December 1993.   **(6 marks)**

(b) Calculate the break-even points of Aristo and Tottle in 1991, in terms of the number of units to be sold. **(4 marks)**

(c) Discuss the relative profitability of the two products. **(4 marks)**

(d) Advise management on which method should be selected to meet the anticipated additional demand in 1994. You should include appropriate calculations in your answer. **(6 marks)**

Institute of Financial Services Banking Certificate Specimen Paper

Question E.6

Use the Worksheet for your final answers to part (a). You will find this together with the Solutions.

The following information concerns the movements of stocks of a material, Prolux, held by Stag Products during March.

March 1	Stock in hand	500 units at £20
8	Purchased	500 units at £24.00
9	Issued to Job 2018	600 units
14	Purchased	500 units at £25.60
16	Returned to supplier	100 units purchased on 14 March
17	Issued to Job 2019	300 units
21	Purchased	500 units at £26.20
26	Issued to Job 2018	400 units
30	Issued to Job 2019	300 units

(a) Complete Stock Record Cards for the material Prolux for March to show the effect of each of the following pricing methods:
   (i) LIFO;
   (ii) AVCO. **(14 marks)**

(b) Assuming that Stag Products operates AVCO, calculate the total charge to Job 2019 for the material Prolux. **(1 mark)**

In addition to material Prolux, the following cost data for Job 2019 are available. This Job was started and completed in March.

Other direct material	£1 500
Direct labour (£12 per hour)	220 hours
Variable overheads	200% of direct labour
Fixed factory overheads	?

Fixed factory overheads are absorbed using the basis of Direct Labour Hours and the following budgeted information is available:

Fixed factory overheads	£96 000
Direct labour hours	15 000

(c) Calculate the total cost of Job 2019. **(5 marks)**

Scottish Qualifications Authority Higher Specimen Paper

Solutions

Chapter 1

Question 1.1

Muriel
Ledger

Capital

	£			£
31 May Balance c/d	7 000	1 May Bank		5 000
		1 May Cash		2 000
	7 000			7 000
		1 June Balance b/d		7 000

Bank

	£			£
1 May Capital	5 000	9 May L Jones		200
10 May Loan	1 000	9 May A Smith		150
29 May B Black	725	14 May Desk Ltd		500
		14 May Rent		175
		31 May Salary		450
		31 May Rent		175
		31 May Balance c/d		5 075
	6 725			6 725
1 June Balance b/d	5 075			

Cash

	£			£
1 May Capital	2 000	2 May Purchases		400
7 May Sales	250	17 May Purchases		500
23 May Sales	275	31 May Balance c/d		1 625
	2 525			2 525
1 June Balance b/d	1 625			

Purchases

	£			£
2 May Cash	400	31 May Balance c/d		1 800
2 May L Jones	200			
2 May A Smith	300			
17 May Cash	500			
17 May L Jones	400			
	1 800			1 800
1 June Balance b/d	1 800			

L Jones

	£			£
9 May Bank	200	2 May Purchases		200
31 May Balance c/d	400	17 May Purchases		400
	600			600
		1 June Balance b/d		400

A Smith

	£		£
9 May Bank	150	2 May Purchases	300
31 May Balance c/d	150		
	300		300
		1 June Balance b/d	150

Desk Ltd

	£		£
12 May Fixtures	100	4 May Fixtures	600
14 May Bank	500		
	600		600

Fixtures

	£		£
4 May Desk Ltd	600	12 May Desk Ltd	100
		31 May Balance c/d	500
	600		600
1 June Balance b/d	500		

Sales

	£		£
31 May Balance c/d	2 175	7 May Cash	250
		7 May B Black	350
		7 May K White	450
		23 May Cash	275
		23 May B Black	375
		23 May K White	475
	2 175		2 175
		1 June Balance b/d	2 175

B Black

	£		£
7 May Sales	350	29 May Bank	725
23 May Sales	375		
	725		725

K White

	£		£
7 May Sales	450	31 May Balance c/d	925
23 May Sales	475		
	925		925

Loan (A. Friend)

	£		£
		10 May Bank	1 000

Rent

	£		£
14 May Bank	175	31 May Balance c/d	350
31 May Bank	175		
	350		350
1 June Balance b/d	350		

Salary

	£		£
31 May Bank	450	31 May Balance c/d	450
1 June Blanace b/d	450		

Trial Balance as at 31 May

	Debit	Credit
	£	£
Capital		7 000
Bank	5 075	
Cash	1 625	
Purchases	1 800	
L Jones		400
A Smith		150
Fixtures	500	
Sales		2 175
K White	925	
Loan		1 000
Rent	350	
Salary	450	
	£10 725	£10 725

Question 1.2

Transaction No	(a) Document	(b) Book of original entry	(c) Double-entry
1	Purchase invoice	Purchase day book	Dr monthly total to purchases account, GL Cr individual amounts to suppliers' accounts PL
2	Sales invoice	Sales day book	Dr individual amounts to debtors' accounts SL Cr monthly total to sales account GL
3	Cheque received	Cash book	Dr bank account Cr debtors accounts SL
4	Cheque sent	Cash book	Dr creditors accounts PL Cr bank account
5	Credit note	Returns inward day book	Dr monthly total to returns inwards account GL Cr individual customers SL
6	Paying-in slip	Cash book	Dr bank account Cr cash account
7	Wages slip	Cash book	Dr wages and salaries account GL Cr bank account
8	Stock sheets	Main journal	Dr stock account GL Cr trading account (year-end income statement)

Question 1.3

P Blunt

	£		£
4 Oct Cash	1 225	1 Oct Balance b/d	1 250
4 Oct Discount	25	4 Oct Purchases	6 000
28 Oct Returns	600	4 Oct VAT	1 050
28 Oct VAT	105	15 Oct Purchases	12 000
		15 Oct VAT	2 100

J Hall

	£		£
21 Oct Cash	150	1 Oct Balance b/d	150

J Bolton

	£		£
3 Oct Returns	2 000	11 Oct Purchases	30 000
3 Oct VAT	350	11 Oct VAT	5 250

Z Rhawandala

	£		£
13 Oct Purchases	5 000	13 Oct Purchases	5 000
		13 Oct VAT	875
		13 Oct Office equipment	5 000

Purchases

	£		£
4 Oct P Blunt	6 000	13 Oct Z Rhawandala	5 000
11 Oct J Bolton	30 000		
13 Oct Z Rhawandala	5 000		
15 Oct P Blunt	12 000		

Sales

	£		£
		31 Oct Cash (W_1)	52 000

Returns Outwards

	£		£
		3 Oct J Bolton	2 000
		28 Oct P Blunt	600

VAT

	£		£
4 Oct P Blunt	1 050	3 Oct J Bolton	350
11 Oct J Bolton	5 250	28 Oct P Blunt	105
13 Oct Z Rhawandala	875	31 Oct Cash sales (W_1)	9 100
15 Oct P Blunt	2 100		

Postage

		£		£
6 Oct	Cash	65		
14 Oct	Cash	24		
18 Oct	Cash	27		

Travelling Expenses

		£		£
10 Oct	Cash	20		
12 Oct	Cash	125		
16 Oct	Cash	85		

Office Equipment

		£		£
13 Oct	Z Rhawandala	5 000		

Workings

W_1

The cash sales of £61 100 include VAT so we have to work backwards to find the amount of tax included. Since £61 100 is 100% of the transaction + 17.5% VAT, we can call it 117.5%. Now we find out what 17.5% is by:

£(61 100 × 17.5) ÷ 117.5 = £9 100 (amount of the tax)
£61 100 – £9 100 = £52 000 (value of the sales)

Note the entries required to correct the error of classifying the goods bought from Z Rhawandala as purchases and not office equipment. The entry in his own account must be adjusted to show what was bought and the entry in the purchases account must be taken out and transferred to the office equipment account. If we want to remove an item from an account, we cannot take it away from the side it is on but must enter it on the other side of the account to cancel it out.

The profit for the year will be larger now that the £5 000 is classed as a fixed asset and not as purchase of stock. Purchases are deducted from profit but fixed assets are not.

Section (c) of this question has been included here as it forms part of the same question on the examinatifon paper concerned. The answer to it is contained in the material covered in Chapter 13.

Chapter 2

Question 2.1

(a)

Workitt Ltd

Sales Ledger Control Account

Debits	£	Credits	£
Balances b/d	56 000	Cheques received	676 000
Sales	800 000	Cash received	1 000
Dishonoured cheques	2 000	Discounts allowed	20 000
		Purchase Ledger contra	4 000
		Balances c/d	157 000
	858 000		858 000

Corrected Sales Ledger Control Account

Debits	£	Credits	£
Balances b/d	56 000	Cheques received	676 000
Sales (+ 1 000)	801 000	Cash received	1 000
Dishonoured cheques	2 000	Discounts allowed (+ 700)	20 700
		Purchase Ledger contra	4 000
		Returns	2 000
		Balances c/d	155 300
	859 000		859 000

Reconciliation Statement of Debtors Schedule

	£	£
Opening balance		156 125
+ Sales returns	1 000	
+ Dishonoured cheque	600	
		1 600
– Contra entry	(425)	
– Returns	(2 000)	
		(2 425)
Balance as per control account		155 300

Workings

i) No entries had been made for this item at all so it must be entered both in the control account and in the debtors' schedule.

ii) The control account had received this information but the £425 (£500 – £75 trade discount) is deducted from the debtors' schedule since this cancels out part of the money owed.

iii) The discount in the cash book was £700 short and so therefore was the total amount of discounts transferred to the control account, so we add this to the discounts total. The debtors' schedule is correct since each account would have included the correct amount of discount.

iv) The returns have been completely omitted so they must be added to both the control account and the debtors' schedule.

v) The £600 was included in the total of dishonoured cheques, so the control account figure is correct but it must be added back to the debtors' schedule.

(b)

Two advantages of operating a control account are:

(a) it provides a check on the accuracy of the ledgers and helps to prevent fraud;

(b) it acts as a summary of the ledger.

Question 2.2

(a)

	£		£
1 Feb 1995 Balance b/d	12 087	Receipts (90 019 – 600)	89 419
Sales	117 635	Discounts allowed	3 000
Sales omitted – note 1	3 400	Returns inward	4 200
Purchases ledger – note 5	400	Bad debts	1 550
31 Jan 1996 Balance c/d	185	31 Jan 1996 Balance c/d	35 538
	133 707		133 707
1 Feb 1996 Balance b/d	35 538	1 Feb 1996 Balance b/d	185

(b)

Statement of Reconciliation of sales ledger balances with the sales ledger control account

	£	£
Debit balances extracted from sales ledger		35 588
Add (1) sales omitted		3 400
		38 988
Less (3) Discounts allowed omitted	350	
(4) Bad debts entered on wrong side	3 100	
		(3 450)
Corrected balance		35 538

(c) Credit balances should be shown as part of current liabilities.

Question 2.3

Sales Ledger Control Account

	£		£
30 November 1993		30 November 1993	
Amended balance b/d (N₁)	29 411.18	Balance b/d	171.08
(1) Bad debt recovered	161.20	Purchases ledger (N₂)	1 527.40
Balance c/d (171.08 + 63.27)	234.35	Discounts allowed (N₂)	2 828.56
		(2) Discounts undercast	100.00
		Balance c/d (balancing figure)	25 179.69
	29 806.73		29 806.73
1 December 1993		1 December 1993	
Balance b/d	25 179.69	Balance b/d	234.35

Notes

N₁ The accountant has made a casting error of £1 000.00 on the credit side of his control account. In addition the total of his credit side is also out by £5.00.

N₂ Entry in wrong side of account, now corrected.

Schedule of adjustments to the sales ledger balances

	£	£
Net balance on individual accounts		25 586.83
Add:		
(4) Transposition error	9.00	
(5) Credit balance overstated	10.00	
(8) Debtor omitted	571.02	
		590.02
		26 176.85
Less:		
(3) Discount allowed not posted	341.27	
(6) Credit balance taken as debit balance	126.54	
(£63.27 × 2)		
(7) Purchases ledger contras	763.70	
		(1 231.51)
Corrected net balance		£24 945.34

Chapter 3

Question 3.1

Victor Chan

Trading and Profit and Loss Account for year ending 30 September 2004

	£	£	£
Sales		18 600	
Less returns inwards		(205)	
			18 395
Opening stock		2 368	
Purchases	11 874		
Less returns outwards	(322)		
		11 552	
Carriage inwards		310	
Less closing stock		(2 592)	
Cost of sales			(11 638)
Gross profit			6 757
Less revenue expenses			
Carriage outwards		200	
Salaries and wages		3 862	
Rent		304	
Insurance		78	
Motor expenses		664	
Office expenses		216	
Light and heat		166	
General expenses		314	
			(5 804)
Net profit			£953

Balance Sheet as at 30 September 2004

	£	£	£
Assets			
Fixed Assets			
Premises		5 000	
Motor Vehicles		1 800	
Fixtures and Fittings		350	
			7 150
Current Assets			
Closing Stock	2 592		
Debtors	3 896		
Cash at Bank	482		
		6 970	
Current Liabilities			
Creditors		(1 731)	
Working Capital			5 239
Net Assets			£12 389
Financed by:			
Capital		12 636	
Net Profit		953	
Less drawings		(1 200)	
Capital Employed			£12 389

Question 3.2

Marian Eliott

Trading and Profit and Loss Account for the year ending 31 December 2000

	£	£	£
Sales		261 800	
Less returns inwards		(1 100)	
			260 700
Opening stock		47 720	
Purchases	184 200		
Less returns outwards	(614)		
		183 586	
Carriage inwards		430	
Less closing stock		(39 220)	
Cost of sales			(192 516)
Gross profit			68 184
Less revenue expenses			
Carriage outwards		618	
Motor expenses		3 260	
Rent		5 940	
Telephone		810	
Wages and salaries		26 620	
Insurance		984	
Office expenses		2 754	
Interest on loan		568	
			(41 554)
Net profit			£26 630

Balance Sheet as at 31 December 2000

	£	£	£
Assets			
Fixed Assets			
Motor van		8 200	
Office equipment		12 500	
			20 700
Current Assets			
Closing stock	39 220		
Debtors	24 600		
Cash at bank	6 230		
Cash in hand	590		
		70 640	
Current Liabilities			
Creditors		(18 740)	
Working Capital			51 900
Net Assets			£72 600
Financed by:			
Capital		52 810	
Net profit		26 630	
Less drawings		(16 840)	
Capital Employed			62 600
Long-term Liabilities			
Loan from F Holt			10 000
Capital Employed			£72 600

Question 3.3

(a) See text

(b) If the accruals concept is ignored, profit would be affected by the extent to which there are prepayments and amounts owing at the end of the year. For example, if there is a wages bill outstanding of £1 000 and this is not included in the wages figure, the profit will be £1 000 too large and the current liabilities will be too small. Equally, the omission of a prepayment at the end of the year will result in the profit being too small, as will the current assets. (See Chapter 4 for more detail).

Question 3.4

See text

Chapter 4

Question 4.1

Claire Voyant

Trading and Profit and Loss Account for the year ended 31 December 2000

	£	£
Sales		20 000
Opening stock	2 000	
Purchases	13 000	
Less closing stock	(3 000)	
Cost of sales		(12 000)
Gross profit		8 000
Discounts received		500
Total income		8 500
Discounts allowed	560	
Light and heat	900	
Rent and rates (1 700 – 200)	1 500	
Wages (1 850 + 150)	2 000	
Depreciation	500	
Provision for doubtful debts (100 – 60)	40	
Total expenses		(5 500)
Net profit		£3 000

Balance Sheet as at 31 December 2000

	£	£	£
Fixed Assets			
Fixtures and fittings at cost		14 000	
Less accumulated depreciation			
(3 500 + 500)		(4 000)	
			10 000
Current Assets			
Stock		3 000	
Trade debtors	2 000		
Less provision for doubtful debts	(100)		
		1 900	
Rent and rates prepaid		200	
Bank balance		4 900	
Cash		2 000	
		12 000	
Less Current Liabilities			
Trade creditors	6 850		
Wages accrued	150		
		(7 000)	
Working Capital			5 000
Net Assets			£15 000
Financed by			
Capital 1 January 2000		14 500	
Add net profit		3 000	
Less drawings		(2 500)	
Capital Employed			£15 000

Question 4.2

Mr Yousef

Trading and Profit and Loss Account for the year ended 31 May 1996

	£	£
Sales		138 078
Opening stock	11 927	
Purchases	82 350	
Carriage inwards	2 211	
Less closing stock	(13 551)	
Cost of sales		(82 937)
Gross profit		55 141
Less expenses		
Carriage (5 144 – 2 211)	2 933	
Rent, rates and insurance (6 622 + 210 – 880)	5 952	
Postage and stationery	3 001	
Advertising	1 330	
Salaries and wages	26 420	
Bad debts	877	
Increase in provision for bad debts	40	
Depreciation (58 000 × 15%)	8 700	
		(49 253)
Net profit		£5 888

Balance Sheet as at 31 May 1996

	£	£	£
Fixed Assets			
Equipment at cost		58 000	
Less accumulated depreciation		(27 700)	
			30 300
Current Assets			
Stock		13 551	
Debtors	12 120		
Less provision for doubtful debts	(170)		
		11 950	
Rates prepaid		880	
Cash at bank		1 002	
Cash on hand		177	
		27 560	
Less Current Liabilities			
Creditors	6 471		
Rent accrued	210		
		(6 681)	
Working Capital			20 879
Net Assets			£51 179
Financed by			
Capital		53 091	
Add net profit		5 888	
Less drawings		(7 800)	
Capital Employed			£51 179

Question 4.3

(a)

PLJ

Trial Balance at 30 April 1997

	£000	£000
Capital at 1 May 1996		230
Drawings	14	
Plant at cost	83	
Plant depreciation at 1 May 1996		13
Office equipment at cost	33	
Office equipment depreciation at 1 May 1996		8
Debtors	198	
Creditors		52
Sales		813
Purchases	516	
Returns inwards	47	
Discounts allowed	4	
Provision for doubtful debts at 1 May 1996		23
Administration costs	38	
Salaries	44	
Research costs	26	
Loan to a friend, repayable in 6 months	25	
Bank		50
Bad debts written off	77	
Stock at 1 May 1996	84	
	£1 189	£1 189

To get this to balance, you must put every item on the correct side. A few points need to be explained:

(i)   Include the opening stock figure as a debit. Closing stock does not normally go into a trial balance as the value of the unsold stock at the end of the year is implicit in the figures for opening stock, purchases and sales.

(ii) The loan is **to** a friend, not **from** a friend, meaning that PLJ has lent money to someone. This is an asset and a debit balance.

(iii) The computer brought into the business is added to the office equipment and to the capital, as it is value introduced into the business by the owner.

(iv) We are not told whether the bank balance is a positive balance or an overdraft but the trial balance will balance only if we include it as an overdraft.

(b)

Trading and Profit and Loss Account for the year ended 30 April 1997

	£	£
Sales	813 000	
Less returns inwards	(47 000)	
		766 000
Opening stock	84 000	
Purchases	516 000	
Less closing stock	(74 000)	
Cost of sales		(526 000)
Gross profit		240 000

Less expenses

Depreciation on plant (10% of 83 000)	8 300	
Depreciation on equipment (20% of [33 000 – 8 000])	5 000	
Discounts allowed	4 000	
Administration costs (38 000 – 3 000 prepaid)	35 000	
Salaries (44 000 + 2 000 accrued)	46 000	
Research costs*	26 000	
Bad debts	77 000	
		(201 300)
Net profit		£38 700

* Pure research costs and applied research costs are written off profit in the year in which they are incurred while development costs may be carried forward to future periods. In this case the research is pure and so its cost is treated as a current expense.

(c)

Balance Sheet as at 30 April 1997

	£	£	£
Fixed Assets			
Plant at cost		83 000	
Less accumulated depreciation		(21 300)	
			61 700
Office equipment at cost		33 000	
Less accumulated depreciation		(13 000)	
			20 000
Total Fixed Assets			81 700
Current Assets			
Stock		74 000	
Debtors	198 000		
Less provision for doubtful debts	(23 000)		
		175 000	
Insurance prepaid		3 000	
Loan		25 000	
		277 000	
Less Current Liabilities			
Creditors	52 000		
Salaries accrued	2 000		
Bank overdraft	50 000		
		(104 000)	
Working Capital			173 000
Net Assets			£254 700
Financed by			
Capital		230 000	
Add net profit		38 700	
Less drawings		(14 000)	
Capital Employed			£254 700

Question 4.4

(a)

Alan Watson

Trading and Profit and Loss Account for the year ended 31 March 1998

	£	£
Sales		580 000
Opening stock	94 000	
Purchases	220 000	
Less stock drawings	(1 500)	
Less closing stock	(51 000)	
Cost of sales		(261 500)
Gross profit		318 500
Add revenue receipts		
Discounts received		2 000
Rent received (26 000 + 3 000)		29 000
		349 500
Less expenses		
Wages	30 000	30 000
General expenses (38 000 – 600 – 2000)	35 400	
Depreciation on fixtures	18 000	
Depreciation on motor vans	21 000	
		(104 400)
Net profit		£245 100

Balance Sheet as at 31 March 1998

	£	£	£
Fixed Assets	*At cost*	*Depreciation*	*Net value*
Premises at cost	236 000		236 000
Fixtures	90 000	(54 000)	36 000
Motor vans	84 000	(69 000)	15 000
			287 000
Current Assets			
Stock		51 000	
Debtors		10 000	
Rent owing		3 000	
Electricity prepaid		600	
		64 600	
Less Current Liabilities			
Creditors	6 000		
Bank	56 000		
		(62 000)	
Working capital			2 600
Net assets			£289 600
Financed by			
Capital		80 000	
Add net profit		245 100	
Less drawings (32 000 + 2 000 + 1 500)		(35 500)	
Capital employed			£289 600

(b) Making a provision for bad debts complies with the prudence concept which tells us not to overestimate profit or assets. It also complies with the going concern concept as it assumes that the business will be continuing.

(c) Alan must monitor his debtors to ensure that he receives the majority of the money owing to him in the interests of his cash flow and working capital. He can encourage prompt payment by offering cash discounts, he should keep track of money owed to him, especially those debts which have been outstanding for a long time, and he should check customers' credit ratings before offering them credit in the first place.

(d) An accountant would prepare the year end accounts to comply with the matching and consistency concepts. This person would know how to treat outstanding and prepaid amounts and also how to separate personal from business expenses.

Answers to Case Study – Kilburn Tandoori

This is the answer to both parts of the Case Study which were given in Chapter 1 and in this chapter.

The books of original entry should be written up first. These are the Purchases Day Book, Sales Day Book, Cash Book and Petty Cash Book.

Purchases Day Book (Journal)

Week	Supplier	£
1	T Green	80
	Hakim Meat	300
	Robinson Wines	50
2	Williams Farms	500
	T Green	100
	Hakim Meat	350
	Robinson Wines	110
3	Williams Farms	450
	T Green	110
	Hakim Meat	350
	Robinson Wines	175
4	Williams Farms	550
	T Green	100
	Hakim Meat	350
	Robinson Wines	150
Credit purchases for the month		£3 725

Sales Day Book (Journal)

Week	Customer	£
2	Sun Finance	110
	Chrome Metals	60
3	Sun Finance	155
	Chrome Metals	80
4	Sun Finance	150
	Chrome Metals	100
Credit sales for the month		£655

Cash Book (Debit side)

Week	Item	Discount allowed	Total	Capital	Sales	Debtors
		£	£	£	£	£
1	Capital		50 000	50 000		
	Cash		625		625	
	Cheques		810		810	
2	Cash		830		830	
	Cheques		1 050		1 050	
3	Cash		1 055		1 055	
	Cheques		1 100		1 100	
	Sun Finance	3	107			107
4	Cash		1 210		1210	

	Discount	Total				
Cheques		1 175		1 175		
Sun Finance	5	150				150
Chrome Metals	2	138				138
	10	58 250	50 000	7 855		395
Balance b/d		3 832				

Cash Book (credit side)

Week	Item	Discount received £	Total £	Wages £	Creditors £	Fixed assets £	Petty cash book £	Drawings £	Rates £
1	Premises		40 000			40 000			
	Furniture		4 000			4 000			
	Conversion Costs		6 000			6 000			
	Wages		100	100					
	Wages		180	180					
	Petty Cash		30				30		
2	T. Green	2	78		78				
	Hakim Meat	6	294		294				
	Robinson's	1	49		49				
	Wages		100	100					
	Wages		180	180					
	Petty cash		30				30		
	Drawings		55					55	
	Cash Register		200			200			
3	Williams	10	490		490				
	T. Green	2	98		98				
	Hakim Meat	7	343		343				
	Robinson's	2	108		108				
	Wages		110	110					
	Wages		200	200					
	Petty cash		30				30		
	Drawings		10					10	
4	Williams	9	441		441				
	T. Green	2	108		108				
	Hakim Meat	7	343		343				
	Robinson's	4	171		171				
	Wages		100	100					
	Wages		200	200					
	Petty Cash		30				30		
	Drawings		70					70	
	Rates		270						270
		52	54 418	1 170	2 523	50 200	120	135	270
Bal c/d			3 832						
			58 250						

Note: The entries for discounts allowed and discounts received in the cash book are not part of the double-entry. They are included merely to provide additional information to the cashier.

Petty Cash Book

Dr	Week		Cr Total	Cleaning materials	Flowers	Napkins
£			£	£	£	£
30	1	Cash book				
		Expenditures	27	5	10	12
30	2	Cash book				
		Expenditures	25	7	4	14
30	3	Cash book				
		Expenditures	27	7	5	15
30	4	Cash book				
		Expenditures	29	8	6	15
			108	27	25	56
		Balance c/d	12			
120			120			
12	5	Balance b/d				

Postings to the ledgers are made at the end of the month, from the books of original entry.
First the individual creditor and debtor accounts in the Purchase and Sales Ledgers.

Purchase Ledger
Williams Farms

Week		£	Week		£
3	Bank	490	2	Purchases	500
	Discount	10	3	Purchases	450
4	Bank	441	4	Purchases	550
	Discount	9			
	Balance c/d	550			
		1 500			1 500
			5	Balance b/d	550

T Green & Sons

Week		£	Week		£
2	Bank	78	1	Purchases	80
	Discount	2	2	Purchases	100
3	Bank	98	3	Purchases	110
	Discount	2	4	Purchases	100
4	Bank	108			
	Discount	2			
	Balance c/d	100			
		390			390
			5	Balance b/d	100

Hakim Meat

Week		£	Week		£
2	Bank	294	1	Purchases	300
	Discount	6	2	Purchases	350
3	Bank	343	3	Purchases	350
	Discount	7	4	Purchases	350
4	Bank	343			
	Discount	7			
	Balance c/d	350			
		1 350			1 350
			5	Balance b/d	350

Robinson Wines

Week		£	Week		£
2	Bank	49	1	Purchases	50
	Discount	1	2	Purchases	110
3	Bank	108	3	Purchases	175
	Discount	2	4	Purchases	150
	Bank	171			
	Discount	4			
	Balance c/d	150			
		485			485
			5	Balance b/d	150

Note

The entries for 'discount' represent discounts received. The books of original entry are: the purchases day book for purchases and the cash book for bank and discount.

Sales Ledger

Sun Finance Co

Week		£	Week		£
2	Sales	110	3	Bank	107
3	Sales	155		Discount	3
4	Sales	150	4	Bank	150
				Discount	5
				Balance c/d	150
		415			415
5	Balance b/d	150			

Chrome Metals plc

Week		£	Week		£
2	Sales	60	4	Bank	138
3	Sales	80		Discount	2
4	Sales	100		Balance c/d	100
		240			240
5	Balance b/d	100			

Note

The entries for 'discount' represent discounts allowed. The books of original entry are: the sales day book for sales and the cash book for bank and discount.

General Ledger
Capital

Week		£	Week		£
			1	Bank	50 000

Premises

Week		£	Week		£
1	Bank	40 000			
1	Bank (conversion)	6 000			

Fixtures and Fittings

Week		£	Week		£
1	Bank	4 000			
2	Bank (cash register)	200	28 Feb	Balance c/d	4 200
		4 200			4200
1 Mar	Balance b/d	4 200			

Total Creditors

Week		£	Week		£
	Bank	2 523		Purchases	3 725
	Discounts received	52			
28 Feb	Balance c/d	1 150			
		3 725			3 725
			1 March	Balance b/d	1 150

Total Debtors

Week		£	Week		£
	Sales	655		Bank	395
				Discounts allowed	10
			28 Feb	Balance c/d	250
		655			655
1 March	Balance b/d	250			

Sales

Week		£	Week		£
28 Feb	Trading account	8 510		Cash and bank	7 855
				Sundry debtors	655
		8 510			8 510

Purchases

Week		£	Week		£
	Sundry creditors	3 725	28 Feb	Trading account	3 725

Wages

Week		£	Week		£
	Bank	1 170			
28 Feb	Balance c/d	20	28 Feb	Profit and loss	1 190
		1 190			1 190
			1 March	Balance b/d	20

Rates

Week		£	Week		£
	Bank	270	28 Feb	Profit and loss	90
			28 Feb	Balance c/d	180
		270			270
1 March	Balance b/d	180			

Drawings

Week		£	Week		£
	Bank	135			

General Expenses

Week		£	Week		£
	Petty cash	27	28 Feb	Profit and loss	108
	Petty cash	25			
	Petty cash	56			
		108			108

Discounts allowed

Week		£	Week		£
	Sundry debtors	10	28 Feb	Profit and loss	10

Discounts received

Week		£	Week		£
28 Feb	Profit and loss	52		Sundry creditors	52

Electricity

Week		£	Week		£
28 Feb	Balance c/d	100	28 Feb	Profit and loss	100

Provision for Doubtful Debts

Week		£	Week		£
28 Feb	Balance c/d	10	28 Feb	Profit and loss	10
			1 March	Balance b/d	10

Provision for Depreciation on Fixtures and Fittings

Week		£	Week		£
28 Feb	Balance c/d	35	28 Feb	Profit and loss	35
			1 March	Balance b/d	35

Stock

Week		£	Week		£
28 Feb	Trading account	250	28 Feb	Balance c/d	250
1 March	Balance b/d	250			

The above represent the general ledger accounts as they would appear after:

(i)   performing the double entry of the transactions during the month;

(ii)   effecting the month-end adjustments;

(iii)   closing the income and expense accounts to the trading and profit and loss accounts and

(iv)   bringing down the balances remaining in the books of the asset, liability and capital accounts.

On completion of (i) above and before (ii):

(1) the individual debtor and creditor accounts in the sales and purchase ledgers should be checked with their respective control accounts;

(2) a trial balance should be extracted from the general ledger to check that the total of the debit balances equals the total of the credit balances. This looks as follows:

Trial Balance at 28 February 2000

	Debit £	Credit £
Capital		50 000
Premises	46 000	
Fixtures and fittings	4 200	
Creditors		1 150
Debtors	250	
Sales		8 510
Purchases	3 725	
Wages	1 170	
Rates	270	
Drawings	135	
General expenses	108	
Discounts allowed	10	
Discounts received		52
Bank	3 832	
Cash	12	
	£59 712	£59 712

When the trial balance has been balanced, steps (ii) and (iii) above can be performed. The resulting income statement looks like this.

Kilburn Tandoori
Trading and Profit and Loss Account for the month ended 28 February 2000

	£	£
Sales		8 510
Purchases	3 725	
Less closing stock	(250)	
Cost of sales		(3 475)
Gross profit		5 035
Add discounts received		52
		5 087
Less expenses		
Wages (1 170 + 20)	1 190	
Rates (270 − 180)	90	
General expenses	108	
Discounts allowed	10	
Electricity	100	
Provision for doubtful debts	10	
Depreciation on fixtures*	35	
		(1 543)
Net profit		£3 544

$$* £4\,200 \times 10\% \times \frac{1}{2} = £35$$

The final task is (iv), followed by preparation of the balance sheet. This looks as follows:

Kilburn Tandoori
Balance Sheet as at 28 February 2000

	£	£	£
Fixed Assets			
Freehold premises			46 000
Fixtures and fittings at cost		4 200	
Less depreciation		(35)	
			4 165
			50 165
Current Assets			
Stock		250	
Debtors	250		
Less provision for doubtful debts	(10)		
		240	
Rates prepaid		180	
Bank		3 832	
Cash		12	
		4 514	
Less Current Liabilities			
Creditors	1 150		
Accrued wages	20		
Accrued electricity	100		
		(1 270)	
Working capital			3 244
Net assets			£53 409
Financed by			
Capital, 1 February 2000		50 000	
Add net profit		3 544	
Less drawings		(135)	
Capital employed			£53 409

Chapter 5

Question 5.1

(a)

Statement of Depreciation on Motor Vans at 31 March 1995

Delivery Van	Year	Value at start of year £	Annual depreciation £	Total depreciation £	Value at end of year £
VEH 101	1991/92	18 000	(3 600)		14 400
	1992/93	14 400	(2 880)		11 520
	1993/94	11 520	(2 304)		9 216
	1994/95	9 216	(1 843)		7 373
Total depreciation on VEH 101				(10 627)	
VEH 102	1992/93	18 600	(3 720)		14 880
	1993/94	14 880	(2 976)		11 904
	1994/95	11 904	(2 381)		9 523
Total depreciation on VEH 102				(9 077)	
VEH 103	1994/95	19 500	(3 900)		15 600
Total depreciation on VEH 103				(3 900)	
Total depreciation on all vans				(23 604)	

(b)

The following are the amounts of depreciation using the straight line method and the adjustments necessary to convert the reducing balance amounts to the straight line amounts:

VEH 101: £(18 000 – 500) ÷ 5 = £3 500 depreciation per annum
£3 500 × 4 years = £14 000
The adjustment necessary is £14 000 – 10 627 = + £3 373

VEH 102: £(18 600 – 500) ÷ 5 = £3 620 depreciation per annum
£3 373 × 3 years = £10 860
The adjustment necessary is £10 860 – 9 077 = + £1 783

VEH 103: £(19 500 – 500) ÷ 5 = £3 800 depreciation per annum
The adjustment necessary is £3 800 – 3 900 = – £100

The total amount which will be added to the provision for depreciation account and to the profit and loss account is therefore £3 373 + 1 783 – 100 = + £5 056

(c)

Delivery Van

		£			£
1.4.1995	Balance b/d	56 100	1995/96	Disposal VEH 102	18 600
1995/96	Brownlee Ltd VEH 104	20 800	31.3.96	Balance c/d	58 300
		76 900			76 900
1.4.1996	Balance b/d	58 300			

Provision for Depreciation

		£				£
1995/96	Disposal VEH 102	10 860	1.4.95	Balance b/d		23 604
31.3.96	Balance c/d	29 160	1.4.95	Adjustment P&L		5 056
			31.3.96	VEH 101		3 500
			31.3.96	VEH 103		3 800
			31.3.96	VEH 104		4 060
		40 020				40 020
			1.4.96	Balance b/d		29 160

Disposal (VEH 102)

	£			£
Delivery Van A/c	18 600	Provision for depreciation		10 860
		Cash		6 000
		Profit and loss account		1 740
	18 600			18 600

(d)

The answer to this written part is contained in the chapter.

Question 5.2

(a)

Firstly, here are the fixed asset accounts:

Land

		£			£
1.4.97	Balance b/d	120 000	31.3.98	Balance c/d	120 000
1.4.98	Balance b/d	120 000			

The land was revalued on 31 March 1997 and revaluation will not take place again until 31 March 2000.

Building

		£			£
1.4.97	Balance b/d	80 000	31.3.98	Balance c/d	80 000
1.4.98	Balance b/d	80 000			

Plant

		£			£
1.4.97	Balance b/d	144 000		Disposal (C)	26 000
	Bank (E)	17 000	31.3.98	Balance c/d	174 950
	Bank (F)	39 950			
		200 950			200 950
1.4.98	Balance b/d	174 950			

The capitalised value of Machine F is the total cost minus the maintenance charge, as this is revenue expenditure; the cost of delivery and installation is classed as capital expenditure. The amount included in the plant account is therefore £42 300 – 2 350 (2 000 plus 17.5% VAT) = £39 950.

Office Equipment

		£			£
1.4.97	Balance b/d	21 600		Printer adjustment	400
	Computer upgrade	2 000		Balance c/d	23 200
		23 600			23 600
1.4.98	Balance b/d	23 200			

The computer upgrade is an improvement to the asset therefore it is capitalised. The printer must be taken out to adjust for the previous error.

Small Tools

		£			£
1.4.97	Balance b/d	1 200	31.3.98	Profit and loss	400
			31.3.98	Balance c/d	800
		1 200			1 200
1.4.98	Balance b/d	800			

Now here are the provision for depreciation accounts:

Provision for Depreciation on Buildings

		£			£
31.3.98	Balance c/d	20 000	1.4.97	Balance b/d	18 000
			31.3.98	Profit and loss	2 000
		20 000			20 000
			1.4.98	Balance b/d	20 000

Provision for Depreciation on Plant

	£			£
Disposal (Machine C)	11 700	1.4.97	Balance b/d	76 200
Balance c/d	77 621		Machine A	4 500
			Machine B	3 000
			Machine D	1 350
			Machine E	1 275
			Machine F	2 996
	89 321			89 321
		1.4.98	Balance b/d	77 621

The depreciation for the year is 7.5% of the cost of each machine.

Provision for Depreciation on Office Equipment

		£			£
	Printer adjustment	200	1.4.97	Balance b/d	8 050
31.3.98	Balance c/d	9 440		Computer	1 500
				Scanner	75
				Printer	15
		9 640			9 640
			1.4.98	Balance b/d	9 440

The depreciation on the old printer is removed to compensate for the previous error.

(b)

Disposal of Machine C

	£		£
Machine C	26 000	Provision for depreciation	11 700
		A Jones	13 000
		Profit and loss account	1 300
	26 000		26 000

(c) A fixed asset register can give details of purchases, upgradings, sales and depreciation. It can also hold information regarding the assets, model and serial numbers, date of expiry of guarantees etc. Maintaining a computerised register is easier, quicker and more accurate as the balance on each asset is given after each transaction.

Question 5.3

(a)

Plant

		£			£
1.4.1995	Balance b/d	372 000	1.9.1995	Disposal	44 400
30. 11.1995	Bank	96 000	31.3.1996	Balance c/d	423 600
		468 000			468 000
1.4.1996	Balance b/d	423 600			

(b)

Provision for Depreciation on Plant

		£			£
1.9.1995	Disposal (W_1)	25 200	1.4.1995	Balance b/d	205 400
31.3.1996	Balance c/d	228 880	31.3.1996	P & L (W_2)	48 680
		254 080			254 080
			1.4.1996	Balance b/d	228 880

(c)

Disposal of Plant at 1 September 1995

	£		£
Plant at cost	44 400	Provision for depreciation	25 200
		Bank	13 700
		Profit and loss account	5 500
	44 400		44 400

Workings

W_1 To find accumulated depreciation on plant sold

		Accumulated depreciation
	£	£
Bought 31 October 1991	40 000	
Depreciation 31 March 1992	(8 000)	8 000
	32 000	
Depreciation 31 March 1993*	(6 400)	14 400
	25 600	

New motor December 1993	4 400		
	30 000		
Depreciation 31 March 1994*	(6 000)	20 400	
	24 000		
Depreciation 31 March 1995	(4 800)	25 200	

*Repairs and the overhaul are revenue expenditure and therefore do not affect the capital cost of the plant.

W_2 Depreciation charge for the year ended 31 March 1996:

£[423 600 – (205 400 – 25 200)] × 20% = £48 680

Question 5.4

The information which was given is presented here in bold. The columns completed in regular type contain the answers which the candidates were expected to give.

(i)

(a)

ASSET	COST (£)	ANNUAL DEPRECIATION (£)				TOTAL DEPRECIATION (£)
		1995	1996	1997	1998	
Machine 101	20 000	3 000	3 600	3 600	3 600	13 800
Machine 102	30 000		4 050	5 400	2 250	11 700
Machine 103	7 200			432	1 296	1 728
Vehicle A	12 800	3 200	2 400	1 800		7 400
Vehicle B	24 000			6 000	4 500	10 500
Vehicle C	18 000				4 500	4 500
Total depreciation for year		6 200	10 050	17 232	16 146	

(b)

Disposal of Machine 102

	£		£
Machine at cost	30 000	Depreciation	11 700
		Bank	16 300
		Loss	2 000
	30 000		30 000

(c)

Disposal of Vehicle A

	£		£
Vehicle at cost	12 800	Depreciation	7 400
Profit	800	Bank	6 200
	13 600		13 600

(d)

Balance Sheet Extract as at 31 December 1998

FIXED ASSETS	Cost (£)	Aggregate Depreciation (£)	Net Book Value (£)
Machinery	27 200	(15 528)	11 672
Vehicles	42 000	(15 000)	27 000

(ii) See text.

Question 5.5

(a)

The question asks for a fixed asset schedule but, to make the answer clear to you, the ledger accounts have been prepared separately, followed by a summary schedule of the fixed assets and the depreciation on them. The disposal accounts have also been shown, even though not asked for, to explain how the profit or loss on sale has been calculated.

Freehold Properties

		£			£
1.4.98	Balance b/d	200 000	1998/99	Disposal	80 000
1998/99	Revaluation	150 000	31.3.99	Balance c/d	270 000
		350 000			350 000
1.4.99	Balance b/d	270 000			

Plant and Machinery

		£			£
1.4.98	Balance b/d	250 000			
1998/99	Purchase	120 000	31.3.99	Balance c/d	370 000
		370 000			370 000
1.4.99	Balance b/d	370 000			

Motor Vehicles

		£			£
1.4.98	Balance b/d	40 000	1998/99	Disposal	8 000
1998/99	Purchase	10 000	31.3.99	Balance c/d	42 000
		50 000			50 000
1.4.99	Balance b/d	42 000			

Provision for Depreciation on Freehold Property

		£			£
1998/99	Disposal	14 400	1.4.98	Balance b/d	36 000
31.3.99	Balance c/d	27 000	31.3.99	Profit and loss (W$_1$)	5 400
		41 400			41 400
			1.4.99	Balance b/d	27 000

Provision for Depreciation on Plant and Machinery

		£				£
31.3. 99	Balance c/d	114 469	1.4.98	Balance b/d		69 375
			31.3.99	Profit and loss (old) (W₂)		27 094
			31.3.99	Profit and loss (new) (W₂)		18 000
		114 469				114 469
			1.4.99	Balance b/d		114 469

Provision for Depreciation on Motor Vehicles

		£			£
1998/99	Disposal	4 800	1.4.98	Balance b/d	24 000
31 3.99	Balance c/d	27 600	31.3.99	Profit and loss (W₃)	8 400
		32 400			32 400
			1.4.99	Balance b/d	27 600

Disposal of Freehold Property

	£			£
Asset at cost	80 000	Bank		140 000
Profit	74 400	Depreciation (W₄)		14 400
	154 400			154 400

Disposal of Motor Vehicle

	£		£
Asset at cost	8 000	Bank	2 500
		Depreciation (W₅)	4 800
		Loss	700
	8 000		8 000

Workings

W₁

Depreciation on freehold properties = 2% on the carrying amount
i.e. on the balance of 270 000 = 5 400.

W₂

Depreciation on plant and machinery = 15% on the reducing balance
i.e. on (250 000 + 120 000) − (69 375) = 300 625
15% of 300 625 = 45 094 (27 094 on the old machinery and 18 000 on the new)

W₃

Depreciation on motor vehicles = 20% on cost
i.e. on the balance of 42 000
20% of 42 000 = 8 400

W₄

Depreciation on freehold property sold = 2% for each of 9 years
= 80 000 × 2% × 9 = 14 400

W₅

Depreciation on motor vehicle sold = 20% for each of 3 years on cost
= 8 000 × 20% × 3 = 4 800

This information from the ledger can be reformatted into a fixed asset schedule as follows.

Fixed Asset Schedule at 31 March 1999

	Freehold Properties	Plant and Machinery	Motor Vehicles
	£	£	£
Balances b/d	200 000	250 000	40 000
Add purchase		120 000	10 000
Less disposal	(80 000)		(8 000)
Add revaluation	150 000		
Balance at cost	270 000	370 000	42 000
Less depreciation balance	(36 000)	(69 375)	(24 000)
Less depreciation for 1998/99	(5 400)	(45 094)	(8 400)
Net value of asset	228 600	255 531	9 600

(b)

The profit and loss account entries relating to the fixed assets are:
(i) the depreciation for 1998/99 on each asset and
(ii) the profit or loss on the sale of the assets disposed of.

Profit and Loss account extract for the year ending 31 March 1999

	£	£
Depreciation on:		
Freehold properties	5 400	
Plant and machinery	45 094	
Motor vehicles	8 400	
		58 894
Profit on sale of freehold property	74 400	
Loss on sale of motor vehicle	(700)	
		73 700

(a) Refer to chapter 5.

(b) Refer to chapter 10.

Chapter 6

Question 6.1

(a)
Jackson Printing Company Limited
Journal

		Dr	Cr
		£	£
1)	Retained profits	1 000	
	Motor van disposal		1 000
	Motor van disposal	10 000	
	Motor vans at cost		10 000
	Provision for depreciation on vans	8 000	
	Motor van disposal		8 000
	Retained profits	1 000	
	Motor van disposal		1 000
2)	Land and buildings	10 000	
	Revaluation reserve		10 000
	Retained profits	1 000	
	Provision for depreciation on buildings		1 000
3)	Bad debts	1 000	
	Debtors		1 000

(b) It is first necessary to revise the profit figure.

Statement of adjustment to profit

	Dr	Cr
	£	£
Retained profits b/f		30 200
Less		
Reduction in sales	1 000	
Loss on sale of van	1 000	
Depreciation on buildings	1 000	
Increase in bad debts	1 000	
		(4 000)
Corrected profit		£26 200

Jackson Printing Company Limited
Balance sheet as at 31 March 1994

	£	£	£
	Cost or valuation	Depreciation	Net
Fixed assets			
Freehold land, at valuation	20 000		20 000
Buildings, at valuation	50 000	(1 000)	49 000
Plant and machinery	40 000	(18 000)	22 000
Motor vans	15 000	(3 000)	12 000
	125 000	(22 000)	103 000

Current assets

Stock	10 000	
Debtors	13 000	
Cash	1 200	
	24 200	

Less current liabilities

Creditors	10 000		
Bank overdraft	6 000		
Working capital		(16 000)	8 200
Net assets			£111 200

Financed by:

Called-up share capital	75 000
Revaluation reserve	10 000
Retrained profits	26 200
Capital employed	£111 200

Question 6.2

(a)

RST Ltd
Statement of Corrected Net Profit for the year ended 30 April 1995

		£	£
Net profits as per draft accounts			78 263
Add			
1) (ii)	↓provision for doubtful debts (W$_1$)	208	
5)	↓purchases (W$_4$)	9 800	
6)	↑closing stock	2 171	
7)	↓insurance charge	162	
8)	↓wages	100	
			12 441
			90 704
Less			
1) (i)	bad debts	610	
1) (ii)	provision for discounts on debtors (W$_2$)	1 070	
2)	↑rates	491	
3)	reduction in sales	1 350	
3)	loss on sale of vehicle (W$_3$)	1 470	
5)	depreciation on equipment (W$_4$)	1 960	
7)	↑electricity charge	543	
	Corrected net profit for the year		7 494
			£83 210

Workings

W$_1$ 1) (ii)
Provision for Doubtful Debts

	£
Required (55 210 – 610) × 2%	1 092
Existing provision	(1 300)
Reduction necessary	(208)

W₂ 1) (iii)
Provision for Discounts on Debtors
£(55 210 – 610 – 1 092) × 2% = £1 070

W₃ 3)

Vehicle Disposal

	£			£
Cost	8 100	Depreciation		5 280
		Bank		1 350
		P & L (loss)		1 470
	8 100			8 100

W₄ 5)
Equipment – correcting entries

	£	£
Dr equipment	9 800	
Cr purchases (trading a/c)		9 800
Dr P & L	1 960	
Cr provision for depreciation on equipment		1 960

Note: Error (4) affects the figure for creditors, a balance sheet item. The profit figure is **not** affected.

(b)
The suspense account will contain those items above for which correcting the error involved **one** account only, i.e. (2) rates, (4) creditors, and (8) wages.
Corrections for all the other errors involve two accounts.

Suspense

	£		£
30 April 1995 Balance b/f	301	(2) Rates	491
(4) Creditors	90		
(8) Wages	100		
	491		491

Question 6.3

(a)
A trial balance is used to check the arithmetical accuracy of the double-entry accounting system.
It is limited in that there are certain types of errors which do not cause the trial balance to disagree.

(b)
(3) Error of Principle. (5) Error of Original Entry.

Kathleen Mason
Journal

	Dr	Cr
	£	£
(1) Suspense	192	
Expense creditor		192
(2) Wages	40	
Suspense		40

(3) Shop fittings	320	
Purchases		320
(4) Suspense	160	
Sales		160
(5) Suspense	18	
Expenses		18
(6) Suspense	20	
Discount allowed		10
Discount received		10

Explanations:

1) Only one entry has been made here (the heating account has been debited). Since the invoice is unpaid, the amount must be credited to the expense creditor's account. The double entry for the correction is to debit suspense. This error does not affect the profit since the heating account was correct but we would have to increase the creditors in the balance sheet.

2) Another example of a single entry only. The wages account must now be debited and the double entry for the correction is to credit the suspense account. As the wages account total was too low, we must reduce profit by £40.

3) This is an error of principle which does not affect the trial balance and which therefore does not involve the suspense account. Simply shift the amount from the purchases account to the shop fittings account by debiting the shop fittings and crediting purchases. An item of capital expenditure has been treated as revenue expenditure and has thus been incorrectly deducted from profit; profit must now be increased by £320 as must the total of fixed assets.

4) Another single entry. Complete it by crediting sales and debiting suspense. As sales were too low, the profit is also too low and we must add back £160.

5) An error of original entry in which the wrong amount has been posted. The question does not say what figure was entered in the bank or cash account (i.e. whether this was correct or whether the same mistake was made) but we should take the wording literally and assume that the only account affected is the one specifically mentioned. We thus adjust the expense account for the difference and credit it with £18 (in order to deduct the extra amount); the double entry for the correction is on the debit side of suspense. Too much was deducted from profit so we add £18 back.

6) Here we must first calculate the amount of the discount. £240 was paid after the 4% discount so we must work back to find the original figure owing. £240 is 96% of the full amount and we calculate 100% by £240 × 100 ÷ 96 = £250. The discount was therefore the difference of £10. This was a discount received by Kathleen but she entered it as a discount allowed. When a figure has been entered on the wrong side of the ledger, it is necessary to double the amount for correction purposes. Here we must credit the discount allowed account with £10 to cancel the error and then credit the discount received account with another £10 to enter it correctly; we debit the suspense account with the doubled amount of £20. As discount received was treated as discount allowed, £10 has been deducted from profit so we must add back £20, i.e. £10 to cancel out the deduction and £10 to make it right.

(c)

Suspense

	£		£
Electricity	192	Trial balance	350
Sales	160	Wages	40
Expenses	18		
Discount	20		
	390		390

In the trial balance, total debits come to £35 370 while total credits amount to £35 020 so the first entry in the suspense account is the difference between the two totals, £350, on the side which is lower, i.e. credit. Now we follow what we wrote in the journal and enter up the suspense account accordingly. Since it balances off, we are almost certain that we have done it correctly.

(d)

Statement of Corrected Net Profit for year ended 30 April 1998

	£	£
Net Profit as per P & L account		3 100
+ Purchases	320	
+ Sales	160	
+ Expenses	18	
+ Discount	20	
		518
− Wages		(40)
Corrected net profit		£3 578

We start off with the net profit given to us in the trial balance i.e. £3 100 and then adjust for each relevant item. The above explanations include reference to the profit adjustments and also to how the balance sheet would be corrected even though the question has not asked for this.

Question 6.4

In answering this question it is useful to remember that every correction must be entered in the balance sheet twice in order to make the corrected version balance.

(a)

Our first task is to adjust the net profit. We do not know how much this year's profit was but we can calculate whether it should be increased or decreased and by how much and this figure will be distributed equally between the partners.

Net Profit Adjustment

	£
+ Increase in closing stock	4 000
+ Profit on sale of fixtures and fittings (see below)	500
− Provision for doubtful debts	(1 200)
+ Stock drawing (Black)	1 000
− Loan interest (8% of £21 000)	(1 680)
+ Rates drawing (Brown)	1 500
Adjustment to profit	+4 120

The extra £4 120 profit will be divided equally between the partners.

We now adjust the other balance sheet items:

- Stock: this is increased to £30 000
- Sale of fixtures and fittings: several adjustments have to be made here.
  We deduct the cost price of the fittings sold from the total fittings at cost
  i.e. £30 000 – 10 000 = £20 000
  We now deduct the accumulated depreciation on the asset from the depreciation
  column. This is 10% of cost for 6 years (1990 to 1995 inclusive as depreciation
  is not deducted in the year of sale) i.e. (10% of £10 000) × 6 = £6 000.
  Depreciation in the balance sheet will now be £10 000 – 6 000 = £4 000.
  We add the proceeds of the sale to the bank account
  i.e. £10 000 + 4 500 = £14 500.
  The profit on sale is the difference between the proceeds and the net value of the
  asset when sold, i.e. £4 500 – (10 000 – 6 000) = £500.
- Deduct 5% from the debtors, i.e. £24 000 – (5% of 24 000) = £22 800
- Deduct drawings of £1 000 from R Black's current account
- Add interest owing to the current liabilities (since we are not told that the interest
  has been paid)
- Deduct drawings of £1 500 from B Brown's current account
- Calculate the new current account balances of the partners:
  Black: £5 000 + extra profit £2 060 – drawings £1 000 = £6 060
  Brown: £4 000 + extra profit £2 060 – drawings £1 500 = £4 560

The corrected balance sheet looks like this:

	£	£	£
	Cost	Depreciation	NBV
Fixed Assets			
Premises	50 000		50 000
Plant and machinery	40 000	(25 000)	15 000
Fixtures and fittings	20 000	(4 000)	16 000
	110 000	(29 000)	81 000
Current Assets			
Stock	30 000		
Debtors	22 800		
Banks	14 500		
		67 300	
Current Liabilities			
Creditors		(26 680)	
Net current assets			40 620
Net book value of assets			£121 620
Financed by:			
Capital accounts			
R Black	60 000		
B Brown	30 000		
			90 000
Current accounts			
R Black	6 060		
B Brown	4 560		
			10 620
Long-term Liabilities			
Bank loan			21 000
Capital Employed			£121 620

(b) The policy of not depreciating premises is justified by the fact that land and
buildings often hold or even increase their value over time, depending on the
market. After a sustained increase in the market value of a building, a firm might
decide to revalue its balance sheet value upwards; if the market value falls, the firm
could equally decide to revise it downwards.

Question 6.5

(a)

Journal

	Dr £	Cr £
(1) Suspense account	1 000	
Sales account		1 000
(2) Plant account	240	
Delivery expenses account		240
(3) Discount received account	150	
Creditors (JW) account		150
(4) Stock account	240	
Profit and loss account		240
(5) Suspense account	500	
Purchases account		500
(6) Purchases returns account	230	
Sales returns account	230	
Suspense account		460

(b)

Suspense

	£		£
Sales	1 000	Trial balance	1 040
Purchases	500	Purchases returns	460
	1 500		1 500

(c)

Statement of Adjusted Profit

	£	£
Gross profit as per trading account		35 750
+ Sales	1 000	
+ Reduction in purchases (850 – 350)	500	
		1 500
– Returns		(460)
Corrected gross profit		£36 790
Net profit as per P & L account		18 500
+ Gross profit adjustment (36 790 – 35 750)	1 040	
+ Delivery and installation costs	240	
+ Stock of stationery	240	
		1 520
– Discount received		(150)
Corrected net profit		£19 870

Chapter 7

Question 7.1

An interesting question. The trading account is quite testing. Be careful with the determination of cash sales. Also, watch the dates very closely.

Jean Smith

Trading and Profit and Loss Account for the year ended 31 March 1996

	£	£
Sales (W_1)		50 400
Less cost of goods sold		
Purchases	27 400	
Less closing stock	(1 900)	
		(25 500)
Gross profit		24 900
Less Expenses		
Electricity (760 + 180)	940	
Rent (3 500 × $\frac{12}{15}$)	2 800	
Rates	1 200	
Wages	14 700	
Van licence and insurance (250 × $\frac{6}{12}$)	125	
Van running expenses	890	
Postages, stationery and other sundry expenses	355	
Depreciation on van (W_2)	750	
Loan interest (£10 000 × 5% × $\frac{3}{12}$)	125	
		(21 885)
Net profit		£3 015

Workings

W_1 Determination of sales

	£
Purchases (26 400 + 120 + 880)	27 400
Excluding goldfish	(600)
	26 800
Less closing stock	(1 900)
	24 900
Mark-up at 100%	24 900
Sales value	49 800
Sale of goldfish at cost	600
Total sales	50 400

W_2 Annual depreciation on van $= \dfrac{7\,600 - 100}{5} = £1500$

Since the date of purchase is given it is assumed that depreciation is charged on a monthly basis. 1 Oct 1995 to 31 March 1996 = 6 months.

Depreciation charge $= £1\,500 \times \dfrac{6}{12} = £750$.

Workings for balance sheet

We are not given the amount of cash drawings, so it is necessary to reconstruct the Cash Book and deduce it as a balancing figure.

Cash Book

		Cash £	Bank £		Cash £	Bank £
1 April 1995	Capital		15 500	Creditors (26 400 + 120)		26 520
1 Jan 1996	Loan		10 000	Electricity		760
Takings banked			42 340	Takings banked	42 340	
Cash sales (W_3)		48 100		Rent		3 500
				Rates		1 200
				Wages		14 700
				1 Oct 1995 Van		7 600
				Caravan		8 500
				Motor vehicle expenses	890	250
				Postages, stationery, etc.	355	
				Drawings	3 875	
				31.3.1996 Bals c/d (W_4)	640	4 310
		48 100	67 340		48 100	67 340

		£
W_3	Sales during the year	50 400
	Less debtors outstanding at year end	(2 300)
	Cash received from sales	48 100
W_4	Balance as per bank statement	4 090
	Add lodgement not yet credited	340
		4 430
	Less unpresented cheque	(120)
	Balance as per Cash Book	4 310

Jean Smith
Balance Sheet as at 31 March 1996

	£	£	£
Fixed Assets			
Van at cost			7 600
Less depreciation			(750)
			6 850
Current Assets			
Stocks		1 900	
Debtors		2 300	
Rent prepaid		700	
Van licence and insurance prepaid		125	
Bank (W_4)		4 310	
Cash		640	
		9 975	
Less Current Liabilities			
Trade creditors	880		
Electricity accrued	180		
Loan interest accrued	125		
		(1 185)	
Working Capital			8 790
Net assets			£15 640

Financed by:	
Capital	15 000
Add profit	3 015
	18 015
Less drawings (3 875 + 8 500 caravan)	(12 375)
Capital owned	5 640
Long-term loan	10 000
Capital Employed	£15 640

Question 7.2

Linda Bernt

(a)

Statement of Affairs as at 1 November 1996

	£	£
Equipment	910	
Fixtures & fittings	210	
Ironing fees due	1 710	
Cash	2 150	
Wages owing		750
Telephone unpaid		190
Delivery van	4 100	
Capital		8 140
	9 080	9 080

Computations for financial statements:

Ironing fees: £480 × 6 = 2 880 x 12 = £34 560

Wages: Staff   £5 500 × 2 = £11 000
            Secretary   £50 × 12 = £600
Rent: £250 × 12 = £3 000 (owing £750 i.e. 3 months)

Total fees = 34 560 + fees due 1 710 – fees owing for last year £1 920
            = £34 350

Drawings calculation:
Total fees – Fees banked = £34 350 – 19 650 = £14 700
£14 700 – Wages – Van costs = Drawings
£14 700 – (2 750 + 150 + 640) = £11 160
Drawings = £11 160 + 50 (sales proceeds) = £11 210

Ironing equipment: £910 + 190 – 60 = £1 040

Profit and Loss Account for the year ended 31 October 1997

	£	£
Revenue		
Fees		34 560
Less expenses		
Wages	11 000	
Wages (secretary)	600	
Rent (2 250 + 750)	3 000	
Electricity (1 350 + 450)	1 800	
Telephone (620 + 280 – 190)	710	
Van costs (2 200 + 640)	2 840	
Bookkeeper	2 477	
Advertising (800 + 240)	1 040	
Depreciation on ironing press (10% of 1 040)	104	
Depreciation on fixtures & fittings (10% of 210)	21	
Depreciation on van (10% of 4 100)	410	
Loss on ironing press	10	
Bonus to staff (2½ % of [34 500 – 11 000] × 2)	1 178	
		(25 190)
Net Profit		£9 370

(b)

Balance Sheet as at 31 October 1997

	£	£	£
Fixed Assets			
Ironing equipment		1 040	
Less depreciation		(104)	936
Fixtures & fittings (210 – 21)			189
Van			3 690
			4 815
Current Assets			
Debtors		1 920	
Cash		2 463	
		4 383	
Current Liabilities			
Rent	750		
Electricity	450		
Telephone	280		
Advertising	240		
Bonus	1 178		
		(2 898)	
			1 485
Net assets			£6 300
Capital 1 November 1996			8 140
Add Net Profit			9 370
Less Drawings			(11 210)
Capital employed, 31 November 1997			£6 300

(c)

Memorandum

To: Linda Bernt
From:
Date:
Subject: Treatment of Drawings

You should keep a record of the amounts you take out as drawings because otherwise you might enter the amounts spent as business expenses, with the result that the profit will be too small. Also you need to control how much value you take out of the business; limit your drawings or you will find yourself with negative capital.

Question 7.3

This is a typical type 2 question where no system of recording has been maintained – not even single entry. Income statements cannot be prepared and profit has to be deduced from successive balance sheets.

(a)

Ben
Statement of affairs as at 30 September 1991

	£	£	£
Fixed Assets			
Cars			35 000
Current Assets			
Stocks of spares		470	
Trade debtors		1 860	
Bank		2 190	
		4 520	
Less Current Liabilities			
Deposits in advance	250		
Trade creditors	2 110	(2 360)	
Working capital			2 160
Net assets			£37 160
Financed by:			
Initial capital, 1 Oct 1988			2 500
Profit, 1 Oct 1988 to 30 Sept 1991			47 140
			49 640
Less drawings (£80 x 52) × 3 years			(12 480)
Capital employed, 30 Sept 1991			£37 160

(b)

Statement of affairs as at 30 September 1993

	£	£	£
Fixed Assets			
Cars			55 000
Current assets			
Stocks		2 100	
Debtors		5 630	
		7 730	

Less Current Liabilities

Deposits in advance	350		
Creditors	6 300		
Bank overdraft	1 190		
		(7 840)	110
Net assets			£54 890

Capital, 30 Sept 1991		37 160
Profit, 1 Oct 1991 to 30 Sept 1993		43 730
		80 890
Less drawings (£250 × 52) × 2 years		(26 000)
Capital employed, 30 Sept 1993		£54 890

(c)

Statement of affairs as at 30 September 1993

	£
Capital, 1 Oct 1991	37 160
Add new capital introduced	10 000
	47 160
Add profit (balancing figure)	33 730
	80 890
Less drawings	(26 000)
Capital employed, 30 Sept 1993	£54 890

Yes. Profit would be reduced by £10 000.

Question 7.4

Julie Ross

Trading and Profit and Loss Account for year ended 31 December 1997

	£	£
Sales (W$_1$)		50 800
Opening stock (by deduction)	3 560	
Purchases (W$_2$)	23 400	
Less closing stock (W$_{3)}$	(4 800)	
Cost of sales (sales – gross profit)		(22 160)
Gross profit (60% of 55 400)		28 640
Loss on sale of car (W$_4$)	900	
Loss on sale of machinery (6 500 – 4 300)	2 200	
Rent and rates (4 200 – 500 + 600)	4 300	
Telephone and electricity	2 400	
Motor running expenses	1 200	
Stationery	80	
Increase in provision for doubtful debts (300 – 250)	50	
Interest on loan (W$_5$)	600	
Depreciation on plant and machinery (W$_6$)	4 500	
Depreciation on new car (25% of cost)	2 500	
		(18 730)
Net profit		£9 910

Balance Sheet as at 31 December 1997

	£	£	£
Fixed Assets	*At cost*	*Depreciation*	*Net value*
Motor car	10 000	(2 500)	7 500
Plant and machinery	26 500	(8 500)	18 000
			25 500
Current Assets			
Stock	4 800		
Debtors (6 000 – PBD of 300)	5 700		
Bank	2 400		
		12 900	
Less Current Liabilities			
Creditors	2 400		
Rent and rates owing	600		
		(3 000)	
Working capital			9 900
Net assets			£35 400
Financed by			
Capital (W_7) + 80		21 690	
Net profit		9 910	
Less drawings		(5 200)	
			26 400
Bank loan (W_8)			9 000
Capital employed			£35 400

Workings

In the trading account, we can calculate the sales, purchases, closing stock and gross profit as shown below; the opening stock can then be deduced.

W_1

Sales = Cash banked – proceeds of sale of car + money used to pay supplier's invoice and motor running expenses – opening debtors + closing debtors

= 52 000 – 4 600 +800 + 1 200 – 4 600 + 6 000 = 50 800

W_2

Purchases = Bank payments to suppliers + supplier's invoice paid in cash – opening creditors + closing creditors
= 22 000 + 800 – 1 800 + 2 400
= 23 400

W_3

Closing stock at selling price = £12 000 and gross profit is 60% of sales.
Therefore closing stock at cost price = 40% of 12 000 = 4 800

W_4

Loss on sale of car = book value of car – proceeds of sale
5 500 – 4 600 = 900

W₅

Calculation of loan interest:
Amount of loan = 12 000
Amount repayable = 8 × 1 800 = 14 400
14 400 – 12 000 = 2 400 interest
2 400 ÷ 8 = 300 interest per quarter
Interest for the year = 300 × 2 quarters = 600

W₆

Depreciation on plant and machinery:
Cost of plant in the business on 31 December 1997 = existing plant + new plant – plant sold
18 000 + 15 000 – 6 500 = 26 500
Depreciation on new plant = 20% of 15 000 = 3 000
Depreciation on rest of plant = 20% of net value at the end of the year, deducting the plant sold (this was not depreciated in the year of sale)
= 18 000 – 6 500 – 4 000 depreciation to date = 7 500
20% of 7 500 = 1 500
Total depreciation on plant for 1997 = 3 000 + 1 500 = 4 500

W₇

Opening capital = opening assets – opening liabilities
Debtors + car + plant and machinery + stock – bank – creditors – rent owing – provision for doubtful debts
4 600 + 5 500 + 14 000 + 3 560 – 3 500 – 1 800 – 500 – 250
= 21 610

W₈

Of the 3 600 in loan repayments, 600 (300 × 2 quarters) represents interest. The remainder represents repayment of the principal sum i.e. 3 600 – 600 = 3 000.
12 000 – 3 000 = 9 000 loan still outstanding

Question 7.5

Bhupesh Chaughan

(a)

To find the amount stolen, we first have to calculate the true level of sales, as shown in the trading account below. We then compute the level of sales suggested by the accounting records provided in the question.

Sales from the example = Receipts from debtors – opening debtors + closing debtors + cash banked + cash which funded purchases, wages and drawings

= 6 170 – 1 750 + 1 160 + 41 120 + 1 360 + 15 240 + 14 150
= 77 450

The amount stolen is thus the difference between the true sales of 80 000 and 77 450 i.e. £2 550. We deduct from this the £20 increase in cash between the beginning and end of the year, since this is otherwise unaccounted for and has not been stolen.

i.e. 2 550 – 20 = 2 530

Since the owner was not insured against theft, we must write this off profit.

(b)

We have to find the correct sales figure and so we cannot work from the sales information given, as this will be less than the true figure because of the theft. We can however find the true sales from the trading account as we know that the gross profit margin is 50%.

Trading and Profit & Loss Account for year ending 30.4.95

	£	£
Sales (W₂)		80 000
Opening stock	6 000	
Add purchases (W₁)	41 000	
Less closing stock	(7 000)	
Cost of sales (W₂)		(40 000)
Gross Profit		40 000
Rent and rates (4 170 – 250 + 200)	4 120	
Light and heating	2 140	
Advertising	850	
Insurance (1 200 + 340 – 400)	1 140	
Motor expenses	2 110	
General expenses	3 180	
Wages	15 240	
Depreciation on fixtures & fittings (9 000 – 8 100)	900	
Depreciation on van PFQ (9 000 – 6 750)	2 250	
Loss on sale of van XBA (7 000 – 4 500)	2 500	
Cash stolen	2 530	
		(36 980)
Net Profit		£3 040

Balance Sheet as at 30.4.95

	£	£
Capital (W₃)	24 610	
Net Profit	3 040	
Drawings	(14 150)	
Capital employed		£13 500
Fixed Assets		
Fixtures & fittings	8 100	
Van	6 750	
		14 850
Current Assets		
Stock	7 000	
Debtors	1 160	
Insurance prepaid	400	
Cash	160	
	8 720	
Current Liabilities		
Creditors	700	
Bank overdraft	9 170	
Rent	200	
	(10 070)	
Working capital		(1 350)
Net assets		£13 500

Workings

W_1

Purchases = Cash purchases + extra cash purchases + payments to creditors – opening creditors + closing credit
$$= 35\ 670 + 1\ 360 + 4\ 120 - 850 + 700$$
$$= 41\ 000$$

W_2

Since gross profit is 50% of sales, the other 50% must be cost of sales i.e. gross profit is equal to cost of sales. Sales are therefore £80 000.

W_3

Opening Capital:

	£	£
Fixtures and fittings	9 000	
Van	7 000	
Stock	6 000	
Debtors	1 750	
Creditors		850
Insurance prepaid	340	
Rent accrued due		250
Balance at bank	1 480	
Cash in hand	140	
Capital		24 610
	£25 710	£25 710

Chapter 8

Question 8.1
Bourne Ladies Hockey Club

(a)

Bar Trading Account for the year ended 31 May 1998

	£	£
Bar sales		2 850
Opening bar stock	600	
Bar purchases (W_1)	1 240	
Less closing bar stock	(810)	
	1 030	
Bar staff wages	900	
Cost of sales		(1 930)
Profit, to income and expenditure account		£920

Income and Expenditure Account for the year ended 31 May 1998

	£	£
Income		
Bar profit	920	
Subscriptions (W_2)	5 150	
Fundraising evening profit (630 – 590)	40	
Christmas raffle profit (250 – 150)	100	
		6 210
Less expenditure		
Ground maintenance	2 800	
Club house running costs (W_3)	2 620	
Depreciation on equipment (W_4)	1 620	
Depreciation on hockey sticks (W_5)	420	
		(7 460)
Deficit of income over expenditure		£(1 250)

(b)

Balance Sheet as at 31 May 1998

	£	£	£
Fixed Assets	*Asset at Cost*	*Accumulated Depreciation*	*Net Value of Asset*
Clubhouse	120 000		120 000
Equipment	4 860	(1 620)	3 240
Hockey sticks	1 260	(420)	840
			124 080
Current Assets			
Bar stock	810		
Subscriptions owing	630		
		1 440	
Less Current Liabilities			
Club house running costs owing	280		
Subscriptions prepaid	40		
Creditors	170		

Overdraft	510	
		(1 000)
Working capital		440
Net assets		£124 520

Financed by:

Accumulated fund (W_6)	125 770	
Less deficit for the year	(1 250)	
		£124 520

Workings

W_1

Bar purchases = Amount paid – Opening creditors + Closing creditors
   = £1 200 – 130 + 170 = £1 240

W_2

Subscriptions = Membership subscriptions – Opening subs owing + Closing subs owing
   + Opening subs in advance – Closing subs in advance
   = £4 740 – 240 + 630 + 60 – 40 = £5 150

W_3

Club house running costs = Amount paid – Opening costs owing + Closing costs owing
   = £2 490 – 150 + 280 = £2 620

W_4

Depreciation on equipment is calculated by subtracting the closing equipment figure from the opening one (no new equipment has been purchased except for the hockey sticks and these are accounted for separately)
i.e. £4 860 – 3 240 = £1 620

W_5

The new hockey sticks are to be depreciated at the same rate as the other equipment so we need to find what percentage the depreciation is of the opening equipment figure, i.e. 1 620 ÷ 4 860 × 100 = 33.3% (one-third). We thus depreciate the new hockey sticks by deducting one-third of their cost, i.e $\frac{1}{3}$ of £1260 = £420

W_6

Accumulated fund as at 31 May 1997 = Assets – Liabilities at that date
i.e. £(120 000 + 4 860 + 600 + 410 + 240) – (150 + 60 + 130)
= £126 110 – 340 = £125 770

(c)

Memorandum

To: The Treasurer of the Bourne Ladies Hockey Club

From:

Date:

Subject: Ways of improving the club's cash resources

The main way of obtaining more revenue is to increase the annual subscription, although this should not become prohibitively expensive. If you introduced a life membership scheme, you would receive a large amount of cash in the first year, although your cash receipts will fall in the future if you do not find new members.

You should also think of how to cut costs. Your ground maintenance charge was very high; perhaps you could find a cheaper contractor? You might also run the bar with members working on a voluntary basis to save the wages of the bar staff.

Question 8.2

(a)

Since we are not given the opening value of the accumulated fund, it is necessary to derive it as a balancing figure from the opening balances, i.e. deduct total opening liabilities from total opening assets (not forgetting the opening cash balance).

Happy Wanderers Rambling Club
Statement of Accumulated Fund as at 1 January 1992

	Debit	Credit
	£	£
Equipment and fittings	1 200	
Stock	30	
Subscriptions	40	
Rent and rates prepaid	100	
Cash	300	
Bar creditors		40
Insurance accrued		15
Wages accrued		20
Accumulated fund as at 1 January 1992		1595
	£1 670	£1 670

(b)

Trading Account for the year ended 31 December 1992

	£	£
Takings		1 030
Less cost of food and drinks sold		
Opening stock	30	
Purchases (W_1)	570	
	600	
Less closing stock	(60)	
Cost of sales		(540)
Gross Profit		490
Wages (W_2)		(205)
Net profit, to income and expenditure account		£285

Income and Expenditure Account for the year ended 31 December 1992

	£	£
Income		
Subscriptions (W_3)		500
Outing and excursions		505
Profit on bar		285
		1 290
Less Expenditure		
Rent and rates (400 + 100 + 75)	575	
Insurance (80 − 15 − 20)	45	
Light and heat (110 + 15)	125	
Repairs to equipment	40	
Telephone, postage and stationery (85 + 15)	100	
Magazines and periodicals	76	
Depreciation on equipment (2 100 @ 10%)	210	
Bad debt on subscriptions	10	
		(1 181)
Surplus of income over expenditure		£109

Workings

W₁

Bar purchases = Payments to creditors – opening creditors + closing creditors

=£500 – 40 + 110 = £570

W₂

Wages = wages paid to bar staff – opening accrual + closing accrual

= £200 – 20 + 25 = £205

W₃

Subscriptions = fees for 1992 + owing for 1992 – fees prepaid + bad debt

= £450 + 50 – 10 + 10 = £500

(The bad debt comes from those members who have still not paid for 1991. We were told that four members had not paid for 1991 on 1 January 1992 but we can see from the Cash Book that three members paid during the year.)

Where a question splits the subscriptions paid into the various years, you have only to include those which relate to the year for which the accounts are being prepared. If, however, you are given a total for subscriptions received without being told how much is for which year, you have to adjust for each amount owing and prepaid.

(c)

Happy Wanderers Rambling Club
Balance Sheet as at 31 December 1992

	£	£	£
Fixed Assets			
Equipment and fittings – at cost			2 100
Less accumulated depreciation			(1 010)
Net book value			1 090
Current Assets			
Stock	60		
Subscriptions receivable	50		
Outings fee receivable	15		
Prepayments	20		
Cash and bank	719		
		864	
Current Liabilities			
Bar creditors	110		
Subscriptions prepaid	10		
Accrued expenses	130		
Working capital		(250)	614
Net assets			£1 704
Financed by:			
Accumulated fund (derived)			1 595
Add surplus for the year			109
			£1 704

Question 8.3

(a)

Tennis Club

Income and Expenditure Account for the year ended 31 December 1993

Income	£	£	£
Subscriptions (W_1)			9 150
Entry fees for club championship		210	
Less cost of prizes		(90)	
Profit on championship			120
Bank interest received			85
			9 355
Less Expenditure			
Groundsman's wages		4 000	
Rent (W_2)		2 000	
Rates (W_3)		1 725	
Annual dinner/dance:			
Sale of tickets	420		
Less cost	(500)		
Loss on dinner/dance		80	
Secretarial expenses		400	
Miscellaneous expenses		100	
Depreciation on equipment (W_4)		600	
Bank interest		250	
			(9 155)
Surplus of income over expenditure			£ 200

Workings

W_1

Subscriptions = Subs for 1993 + subs owing at 31.12.93 + subs prepaid during 1992
= £8 220 + 700 + 230 = £9 150

W_2

The rent was paid for the year to 30 September 1993, which means that part of what was paid was for three months of last year and that the amount for the last three months of this year is still owing. However, since the annual rent is the same as before, no calculation is necessary and we simply include the rent for the year, i.e. £2 000.

W_3

Rates for the six months to 31 March 1993 were paid last year, i.e. half of this amount must be included this year on behalf of January – March. During 1993, rates of £1 800 were paid for twelve months. Three-quarters of this figure relate to April – December 1993. So the rates to be included in the Income and Expenditure Account are £375 + (75% of £1 800) = £1 725.

W_4

Fixed assets

Since in part (b) of the question we need to construct balance sheets at the start and end of the year it is necessary to find, for equipment, the:

- accumulated depreciation up to 31 December 1992
- charge for the year
- accumulated depreciation up to 31 December 1993

Since the exact dates of purchase are given it is assumed that depreciation is charged on a monthly basis.

Date of purchase	Years held up to 31 Dec 1992	Cost	Annual depreciation @ 10%	Accumulated depreciation up to 31 Dec 1992	Charge for 1993	Accumulated depreciation up to 31 Dec 1993
		£	£	£	£	£
30 June 1982	10½	5 000	500	5 000		5 000
1 Jan 1987	6	1 000	100	600	100	700
30 Sep 1991	1¼	1 000	100	125	100	225
30 June 1993	0	8 000	800		400	400
		15 000		5 725	600	6325

(b)

Again in this question we have to derive the opening accumulated fund. This time it is shown in balance sheet form to the left of this year's balance sheet.

Tennis Club
Balance Sheet as at

	31 December 1992				31 December 1993		
£	£	£			£	£	£
			Fixed Assets				
	7 000		Equipment -- at cost				15 000
	(5 725)		Less accumulated depreciation				(6 325)
	1 275		Net book value				8 675
			Current Assets				
620			Debtors for subscriptions	700			
375			Rates prepaid	450			
2 000			Bank deposit account				
1 160			Bank current account				
100			Cash	50			
	4 255				1 200		
			Less Current liabilities				
230			Subscriptions prepaid	125			
500			Rent accrued	500			
	(730)		Bank interest accrued	250			
			Bank overdraft	4000			
					(4 875)		
	3 525						(3 675)
	£4 800		*Net assets*				£5 000
			Financed by:				
			Accumulated fund (derived)				4 800
			Add surplus for the year				200
	£4 800						£5 000

Question 8.4

Players Sports and Social Club

Income and Expenditure Account for year ended 31 December 1998

	£	£
Income		
Subscriptions (W_1)		14 980
Expenditure		
Loss on sale of van (W_2)	1 250	
Bad debts (W_3)	820	
Loss on dances (1 778 – 2 060)	282	
Wages	8 450	
Loss on competitions (W_4)	10	
Printing and advertising	2 070	
Repairs to sports equipment	800	
Motor expenses	1 200	
Sundry expenses	1 180	
Depreciation on van (25% of 6 300)	1 575	
Depreciation on computer (1 600 – 1 400)	200	
Depreciation on sports equipment (6 200 – 5 400)	800	
		(18 637)
Deficit		£(3 657)

Balance Sheet as at 31 December 1998

	£	£	£
Fixed Assets	*At cost*	*Depreciation*	*Net value*
Motor vans	6 300	(1 575)	4 725
Computer	2 000	(600)	1 400
Sports equipment (depreciated value)	6 200	(800)	5 400
			11 525
Current Assets			
Subscriptions due	1 620		
Stock of prizes	450		
		2 070	
Less Current Liabilities			
Subscriptions prepaid	720		
Bank	2 722		
		(3 442)	
Working capital			(1 372)
Net assets			£10 153
Financed by			
Accumulated fund (W_5)		13 810	
Less deficit		(3 657)	
Capital employed			£10 153

Workings

W_1

Subscriptions = Subs for 1998 + owing for 1998 – prepaid for 1999

$$= 14\ 080 + 1\ 620 - 720 = 14\ 980$$

W₂

Loss on sale of van:
Van at cost = 4 000
Depreciation on reducing balance method
= 1 000 for year 1 and 750 for year 2 = 1 750
Book value of van at time of sale = 4 000 – 1 750 = 2 250
Proceeds of sale = 1 000
Loss on sale = 2 250 – 1000 = 1 250

W₃

Bad debts:
Subscriptions owing at the beginning of the year were 1 440 but only 620 of these
were received on behalf of 1997
Bad debts = 1 440 – 620 = 820

W₄

Loss on competitions:
Receipts = 2 590
Cost of competitions = opening stock of prizes + purchases of prizes – closing stock
850 + 2 200 – 450 = 2 600
Loss on competitions = 2 590 – (2 600) = (10)

W₅

Opening accumulated fund = opening assets – opening liabilities (there are none in
this question)
Subscriptions due + stock of prizes + computer + sports equipment + van + bank
= 1 440 + 850 + 1 600 + 6 200 + 2 250 + 1 470
= 13 810

Chapter 9

Question 9.1

(a) (i)

Philip, Simon and Ann
Appropriation Account for the year ending 31 December 1996

	£	£
Profit		31 000
Interest on capital		
Philip	800	
Simon	800	
Ann	400	
		(2 000)
Salaries:		
Philip	10 000	
Simon	6 000	
Ann	5 000	
		(21 000)
Remainder		£8 000
Share of profits:		
Philip (50%)		4 000
Simon (25%)		2 000
Ann (25%)		2 000
		£8 000

(ii)

Philip's Current Account

	£		£
Balance b/d	5 000	Interest on capital	800
		Salary	10 000
Balance c/d	9 800	Share of profit	4 000
	14 800		14 800
		Balance b/d	9 800

Simon's Current Account

	£		£
		Balance b/d	2 000
		Interest on capital	800
		Salary	6 000
Balance c/d	10 800	Share of profit	2 000
	10 800		10 800
		1 Jan Balance b/d	10 800

Ann's Current Account

	£		£
		Balance b/d	3 000
		Interest on capital	400
		Salary	5 000
Balance c/d	10 400	Share of profit	2 000
	10 400		10 400
		1 Jan Balance b/d	10 400

(iii)

Revaluation Account

	£		£
Assets decreased in value		*Assets increased in value*	
Motor vehicles	2 000	Stock	1 000
Debtors	3 000	Deficit to capital accounts:	
		Philip (50%)	2 000
		Simon (25%)	1 000
		Ann (25%)	1 000
	5 000		5 000

(iv)

Philip's Capital Account

	£		£
Revaluation	2 000	Balance b/d	8 000
Goodwill (W₁)	8 000	Goodwill	10 000
Balance c/d	8 000		
	18 000		18 000
		Balance b/d	8 000

Simon's Capital Account

	£		£
Revaluation	1 000	Balance b/d	8 000
Goodwill (W₁)	6 000	Goodwill	5 000
Balance c/d	6 000		
	13 000		13 000
		Balance b/d	6 000

Ann's Capital Account

	£		£
Revaluation	1 000	Balance b/d	4 000
Goodwill (W₁)	4 000	Goodwill	5 000
Balance c/d	4 000		
	9 000		9 000
		Balance b/d	4 000

Kate's Capital Account

	£		£
Goodwill (W₁)	2 000	Bank	10 000
Balance c/d	8 000		
	10 000		10 000
		Balance b/d	8 000

Workings

W₁

The first division of goodwill is between the original partners according to the old profit-sharing ratio i.e. 2:1:1.

i.e. Philip: £10 000; Simon: £5 000; and Ann: £5 000

The second division of goodwill is between all the partners, including Kate, in the new profit-sharing ratio i.e. 4:3:2:1.

i.e. Philip: £8 000; Simon: £6 000; Ann: £4 000; and Kate: £2 000.

 (b) See text.

Question 9.2

(a)

Scotby and Wetheral
Partnership Profit and Loss Appropriation Account for the year ended 30 November 1997

	£	£
Net profit		37 500
Interest on loan (**W₁**)		(300)
Profit after interest		37 200
Wetheral's salary	6 000	
Interest on capitals		
Scotby	7 500	
Wetheral	4 500	
		(18 000)
Remainder		£19 200
Share of profits:		
Scotby ($\frac{2}{3}$rds)		12 800
Wetheral ($\frac{1}{3}$rd)		6 400
		£19 200

W₁: (6% of £20 000) ÷ 4 = £300

(b)

Scotby's Current Account

	£		£
Balance b/d	1 700	Interest on capital	7 500
Drawings	15 600	Share of profits	12 800
Capital account	3 000		
	20 300		20 300

Wetheral's Current Account

	£		£
Drawings	18 400	Balance b/d	7 200
Capital account	5 700	Salary	6 000
		Interest on capital	4 500
		Share of profit	6 400
	24 100		24 100

(c)

Scotby's Capital Account

	£		£
Preference shares	50 000	Balance b/d	75 000
Ordinary shares	100 000	Current account	3 000
Bank	2 200	Profit on sale of business (**W₁**)	74 200
	152 200		152 200

Wetheral's Capital Account

	£		£
Preference shares	30 000	Balance b/d	45 000
Ordinary shares	50 000	Current account	5 700
Bank	7 800	Profit on sale of business (**W₁**)	37 100
	87 800		87 800

Calculation of Profit on Sale of Business

	£	£
Capital accounts (75 000 + 45 000)	120 000	
Transfers to capital accounts (3 000 + 5 700)	8 700	
Less cash	(10 000)	
Value of assets taken over		118 700
Purchase consideration		(230 000)
		£111 300

Profit on sale split between partners:

Scotby ($\frac{2}{3}$)		74 200
Wetheral ($\frac{1}{3}$)		37 100
		£111 300

(d) A partner would be paid a salary to compensate for the amount of work done by that person in the business. Interest on capital would be paid so that those partners who invested more in the business would get a larger payment.

(a) Preference shares receive a share of profit before ordinary shares. They carry a fixed rate of dividend whereas the dividend on ordinary shares is variable. (See Chapter 10).

(b) If a share is issued at par, the new investor is asked to pay the nominal value of the share. If it is issued at a premium, the new investor has to pay more than the nominal value. (See Chapter 10).

Question 9.3

(a)

Parks, Langridge and Sheppard
Revaluation Account

31 March 1995	£	31 March 1995	£
Plant and machinery	1 000	Land and buildings	4 000
Increase in doubtful debts provision	300	Decrease in creditors provision	500
Stock	800		
Revaluation surplus to:			
Parks ($\frac{1}{2}$)	1 200		
Langridge ($\frac{1}{3}$)	800		
Sheppard ($\frac{1}{6}$)	400		
	4 500		4 500

(b)

Capital Accounts

	Parks £	Langridge £	Sheppard £		Parks £	Langridge £	Sheppard £
31 March 1995				31 March 1995			
Plant and machinery	1 500			Balance b/d	24 000	12 000	8 000
Motor car	1 000			Revaluation	1 200	800	400
Goodwill out (**W₁**)	6 000	16 000	8 000	Goodwill in	15 000	10 000	5 000
Loan	31 700						
Balances c/d		6 800	5 400				
	40 200	22 800	13 400		40 200	22 800	13 400
				1 April 1995			
				Balance b/d		6 800	5 400

W₁

Goodwill to be written out	30 000
Charged to Parks	(6 000)
Balance to be written out	£24 000
Charged to:	
Langridge ($\frac{2}{3}$)	16 000
Sheppard ($\frac{1}{3}$)	8 000
	£24 000

(c)

Langridge and Sheppard
Balance Sheet as at 31 March 1995

	£	£	£
Fixed Assets			
Freehold land and buildings			20 000
Plant and machinery (5 000 – 1 500)			3 500
Motor cars (2 400 – 1 000)			1 400
			24 900
Current Assets			
Stock		10 400	
Debtors	12 000		
Less provision for doubtful debts	(1 500)		
		10 500	
Bank		9 600	
		30 500	
Less Current Liabilities			
Creditors		(7 500)	
Working Capital			23 000
Net Assets			£47 900
Financed by			
Capital:			
Langridge		6 800	6 800
Sheppard		5 400	5 400
			12 200
Loan from Parks (4 000 + 31 700)			35 700
Capital Employed			£47 900

(d) See text.

Chapter 10

Question 10.1

Notice that this question does not require you to prepare the Balance Sheet; you are given only some of the balances.

R R Hood plc
Profit and Loss Account for the year ended 31 December 1998

	£	£
Turnover (W_1)		967 600
Cost of sales (W_2)		(412 800)
Gross profit		554 800
Distribution costs (W_3)	143 720	
Administration expenses (W_4)	150 245	
		(293 965)
Trading profit		260 835
Other operating income (W_5)		9 900
		270 735
Income from investments		14 700
Interest payable and similar charges		(13 100)
Profit or loss on ordinary activities before taxation		272 335
Tax on profit or loss on ordinary activities		(81 000)
Profit or loss on ordinary activities after taxation		191 335
Transfers to reserves		(70 000)
Dividends paid and proposed		(85 000)
Retained profit for the year		36 335
Profit and loss credit balance b/f		78 300
Profit and loss account transferred to Balance Sheet		£114 635

Workings

W_1

Turnover = Sales − Returns

$= £981\,000 − 13\,400$

$= £967\,600$

W_2

Cost of sales = Opening stock + Net Purchases − Closing stock

$= £69\,800 + (426\,000 − 8\,700) − 74\,300$

$= £412\,800$

W_3

Depreciation on plant and equipment = 25% of (20% of £682 000 − 298 000)

$= 25\%$ of £76 800

$= £19\,200$

Depreciation on motor vehicles $\quad = 15\%$ of £(146 600 − 53 800)

$= £13\,920$

Distribution costs = Costs paid + Costs owing + Depreciation on plant + Depreciation on vehicles

$= £110\,200 + 400 + 19\,200 + 13\,920$

$= £143\,720$

W$_4$

Depreciation on Plant and Equipment = 75% of £76 800

$$= £57 600$$

Increase in provision for bad debts $\quad$ = £3 700 − (400 + 2.5% of (158 200 − 400)

$$= £3 700 − (400 + 3 945)$$

$$= − £645 \text{ (add this to the expenses)}$$

Administrative expenses = Expenses paid + net discounts allowed − prepayment
$\qquad\qquad\qquad$ − legal costs* + increase in provision for bad debts
$\qquad\qquad\qquad$ + depreciation on plant and equipment

(*Legal costs incurred in the purchase of a fixed asset are capitalised.)

$$= £93 200 + (7 200 − 5 500) − 900 − 2 000 + 645 + 57 600$$

$$= £150 245$$

W$_5$

Other operating income = Rent receivable + rent receivable outstanding

$$= £8 700 + 1 200$$

$$= £9 900$$

(b) See text.

Question 10.2

(a)

Salutin plc
Journal

	Debit	Credit
(1) Land and buildings	130 000	
$\quad$ Revaluation reserve		130 000
Being revaluation of land and buildings		
(2) Disposal account	35 000	
$\quad$ Motor vehicles		35 000
$\quad$ Provision for depreciation	28 000	
$\quad$ Disposal account		28 000
$\quad$ Insurance owing	9 000	
$\quad$ Disposal account		9 000
$\quad$ Disposal account	2 000	
$\quad$ Profit and loss account		2 000
Being profit of £2 000 made on disposal of a motor vehicle (**W$_1$**)		
(3)Share premium account	140 000	
$\quad$ Capital redemption reserve	10 000	
$\quad$ Revaluation reserve	130 000	
$\quad$ Share capital		280 000
Being the issue of 1,120,000 bonus shares at 25p each (**W$_2$**)		
(4) Profit and loss account	56 000	
$\quad$ Dividends owing		56 000
Being proposed dividend of 2.5p per share (**W$_3$**)		

Workings

W₁

The book value of the vehicle on sale was £35 000 – 28 000 = £7 000

Since the insurance company has agreed to pay £9 000, the company has made a profit of £2 000.

W₂

The bonus issue is one share for every two held, i.e. 50% of £560 000 = £280 000. Since the company maintains reserves in their most flexible form, we must work from the top. The amounts contained in the share premium account, the capital redemption reserve and the new revaluation reserve exactly cover the amount of the share issue and the profit and loss account remains untouched.

W₃

The dividend is 2.5p per share on 2 240 000 shares (£560 000 × 4 since each share is worth 25p) = £56 000

(b)

Redrafted Balance Sheet as at 31 May 1998

	Valuation	*Cost*	*Aggregate depreciation*	*Net book value*
	£000	£000	£000	£000
Fixed Assets				
Land and buildings	750			750
Machinery		430	272	158
Vehicles		515	272	243
	750	945	544	1 151
Current Assets			177	
Creditors: amounts falling due within one year				
Trade creditors and accrued expenses			(102)	
Net Current Assets				75
				1 226
Creditors: amounts falling due after more than one year				
9% Debentures (2009)				(200)
				£1 026
Capital and Reserves				
Ordinary shares of 25 pence each				840
Profit and loss account				186
				£1 026

(a) and (d) See text.

Question 10.3

The question does not require conformity with the Companies Acts but the answer has nevertheless been prepared with them in mind.

Brampton Ltd
Profit and Loss Account for the year ended 30 April 1996

	Notes	£	£
Turnover	(2)		466 668
Cost of sales (W_1)			(325 878)
Gross profit			140 790
Distribution costs (W_2)		(39 750)	
Administration expenses (W_3)		(59 770)	
			(99 520)
Trading profit	(3)		41 270
Interest payable and similar charges	(4)		(1 800)
Profit on ordinary activities before taxation			39 470
Provision for taxation			(7 000)
Profit on ordinary activities after taxation			32 470
Transfers to reserve	(12)	(16 000)	
Dividends paid and proposed	(5)	(8 640)	
			(24 640)
Retained profit for the year			£7 830

Workings

		£
W_1	Opening stock	15 400
	Purchases	326 978
	Less closing stock	(16 500)
	Cost of sales	325 878
W_2	General expenses (17 040 ÷ 2)	8 520
	Salaries (31 420 ÷ 2)	15 710
	Depreciation on plant	3 200
	Depreciation on motor lorries	12 320
	Distribution cots	39 750
W_3	General expenses	8 520
	Salaries	15 710
	Bad debts	4 800
	Insurance (2 600 – 420)	2 180
	Directors' fees	32 000
		63 210
	Discounts received	(3 280)
	Reduction in provision for doubtful debts (1 060 – 900)	(160)
	Administration expenses	59 770

(In the absence of any information, wages and salaries and general expenses have been apportioned equally between distribution costs and administration expenses.)

Balance Sheet as at 30 April 1996

	Notes	£	£
Fixed Assets			
Tangible assets	(6)		62 080
Current Assets			
Stock	(7)	16 500	
Debtors	(8)	88 480	
Cash at bank		72 170	
		177 150	
Creditors: amounts falling due within one year	(9)	(66 640)	
Net current assets			110 510
Total assets less current liabilities			172 590
Creditors: amounts falling due after more than one year	(10)		(18 000)
Net assets			£154 590
Capital and reserves			
Called-up share capital	(11)		80 000
Share premium	(12)		20 000
Other reserves	(12)		16 000
Profit and loss account	(12)		38 590
Capital employed			£154 590

Notes to the accounts

1) Accounting policies
   (a) Basis of accounting: the accounts are prepared under the historical cost system.
   (b) Depreciation: depreciation on fixed assets is provided on a reducing balance basis at 20 per cent.
   (c) Stock: stock is valued at the lower of cost and net realisable value.

2) Turnover
   Turnover is exclusive of VAT.

3) Trading profit
   Trading profit is stated after charging:
   Depreciation   £15 520
   Directors' fees £32 000

4) Interest payable and similar charges
   Interest payable is on 10% debentures.

5) Dividends
   Preference interim dividend paid £640 + Ordinary final dividend proposed £8 000
   = £8 640

6) Tangible assets

	Plant and machinery	Motor lorries	Total
	£	£	£
Cost at 1 May 1995	76 000	114 000	190 000
at 30 April 1996	76 000	114 000	190 000
Accumulated depreciation:			
at 1 May 1995	60 000	52 400	112 400
Charge for the year	3 200	12 320	15 520
at 30 April 1996	63 200	64 720	127 920
Net book value			
at 1 May 1995	16 000	61 600	77 600
at 30 April 1996	12 800	49 280	62 080

7) Stock
Stock consists of goods for resale.

8) Debtors
Debtors comprise amounts falling due within one year as follows:

	£
Trade debtors	88 060
Prepayments	420
	88 480

9) Creditors: amounts falling due within one year

	£
Trade creditors	50 740
Debenture interest	900
Proposed dividend	8 000
Provision for tax	7 000
	66 640

9) Creditors: amounts falling due after more than one year
This consists of 10% debentures.

10) Called-up share capital

	Authorised	Issued
	£	£
8% redeemable preference shares of £1 each	16 000	
Ordinary shares of £1 each	100 000	80 000
	116 000	80 000

On 1 November 1995, 16 000 8% redeemable preference shares of £1 each were redeemed at par value.

12) Reserves

	Share premium	Capital redemption reserve	Profit and loss account
	£	£	£
At 1 May 1995	20 000		30 760
Transfers from profit and loss account		16 000	7 830
At 30 April 1996	20 000	16 000	38 590

The capital redemption reserve was created on redemption of the preference shares to maintain the company's capital.

Question 10.4

Brighton Ltd

Profit and Loss Account for year ended 31 March 1998

	£	£
Net profit before debenture interest		565 000
Less debenture interest omitted (9% of 20 000)		(1 800)
Net profit after debenture interest		563 200
Profit and loss account 1 April 1997		400 000
		963 200
Less		
Bonus to directors	20 000	
Corporation tax	160 000	
Ordinary dividend	30 000	
Interim preference dividend	4 800	
Final preference dividend	4 800	
Transfer to general reserve	30 000	
		(249 600)
Profit and loss account balance 31 March 1998		713 600

Balance Sheet Extract as at 31 March 1998

	£	£	£
Authorised Share Capital			
8% preference shares of £1 each		200 000	
Ordinary shares of £1 each		800 000	
			1 000 000
Issued Share Capital and Reserves			
8% preference shares of £1 each (fully paid)		120 000	
Ordinary shares of £1 each (fully paid)		600 000	
Share premium account		100 000	
Profit and loss account		713 600	
General reserve		30 000	
Shareholders' funds			1 563 600
Creditors falling due after one year			
9% debentures			20 000
Capital Employed			1 583 600
Current Assets			
Stock	310 000		
Debtors	120 000		
Cash at bank	60 000		
		490 000	

Creditors falling due within one year		
Creditors	80 000	
Directors' bonus	20 000	
Corporation tax	160 000	
Ordinary dividend	30 000	
Final preference dividend	4 800	
	(294 800)	
Working Capital		195 200

Question 10.5

Gupta plc

Journal

		£000	£000
		Dr	*Cr*
(1)	Stock account	54	
	Profit and loss account		54
(2)	Profit and loss account	9	
	Disposal account		9
	Disposal account	48	
	Plant account		48
	Provision for depreciation account	23	
	Disposal account		23
	Profit and loss (loss on sale of plant)	16	
	Disposal account		16
(3)	Fixed assets account	600	
	Revaluation reserve account		600
(4)	Share premium account	250	
	Revaluation reserve	600	
	Profit and loss account	50	
	Ordinary shares account		900
(5)	Bank account	4 950	
	Ordinary shares account		1 980
	Share premium account		2 970
(6)	Profit and loss account (ordinary dividend)	594	
	Ordinary dividend outstanding		594
	Profit and loss account (preference dividend)	16	
	Preference dividend outstanding		16

Explanations

(1) The extra £54 000 increases both the closing stock and the profit.

(2) The only correct entry which has been performed is that of debiting the bank with the proceeds of the sale. The sales account should not have been credited since it was not a sale of stock, so we reduce the profit by debiting the profit and loss account and credit the plant disposal account, which should have been done in the first place. Then we complete the disposal process as shown in the journal (note that the depreciation plus the loss on sale equal the original cost i.e. 23 000 + 9 000 = 48 000).

(3) The increase in the asset value is credited to the revaluation reserve.

(4) Since there are 9 000 000 ordinary shares, there will be 900 000 new bonus shares (1 for every 10 held), increasing share capital by £900 000. This is taken from the existing reserves, using all the share premium account at the time (250 000), all of the new revaluation reserve (600 000) and the remaining 50 000 from the profit and loss account so as to retain as much of the reserves as possible in the more flexible form of the profit and loss account.

(5) The calculation of the rights issue is based on the old ordinary shares plus the new ones, i.e. on 9 000 000 + 900 000 shares = 9 900 000 shares. The rights issue is on the basis of 1 for 5 so 1 980 000 new shares are issued at a price of £2.50 each. £1 of this price is the nominal value and the remaining £1.50 is share premium.

(6) The ordinary dividend is paid on all shares issued at 31 March 1999, i.e. on the original shares, bonus issue and rights issue.
9 000 000 + 900 000 + 1 980 000 = 11 880 000 shares
5 pence on each of 11 880 000 shares = £594 000
The preference dividend is 4% (half a year) on £400 000 = £16 000.
Neither dividend has been paid so both are current liabilities.

(b)

Summarised Balance Sheet as at 31 March 1999

	£000
Fixed assets [(10 000 + 600 – (48 – 23)]	10 575
Net current assets (1 160 + 54 + 4 950 – 594 – 16)	5 554
	£16 129
Capital and reserves:	
11 880 000 ordinary shares of £1 each	11 880
400 000 8% preference shares of £1 each	400
Share premium account	2 970
Profit and loss account	879
	£16 129

(c) The advantage of a rights issue over a bonus issue is that the company actually receives cash whereas the bonus issue is simply a capitalisation of existing reserves.

(d) (i) An advantage of raising funds by issuing ordinary shares is that the company's gearing falls. Funds have been provided by shareholders who will be paid dividends only if there is a profit.
A disadvantage is that the capital base of the company is being widened and existing shareholders may lose control, i.e. their holding becomes divided. It is also a complex and costly process to issue new shares.

(ii) Gupta plc could have issued debentures (loan stock) or borrowed from the bank. This might have been easier if the company has a good credit record and good profits but it will increase the gearing and interest will have to be paid, regardless of performance.

(e) (i) A provision is a reduction in the value of an asset to provide for a possible or probable future loss eg provision for depreciation of fixed assets or of doubtful debtors.

(ii) A capital reserve (eg the share premium account) is an amount of money belonging to the shareholders of a limited company. It is not available for transfer to the profit and loss account to enable an increased payment of dividends to take place.

(iii) A revenue reserve (eg the retained profit reserve) is an amount transferred from the profit and loss account and can be used in future years for dividend purposes.

Chapter 11

Question 11.1

(a)

(i) Purchase of tangible fixed assets means that the company has bought assets such as land, buildings, equipment, fittings etc.

(ii) Purchase of intangible fixed assets means that the company has bought items such as goodwill in another company, patents, copyrights etc.

(iii) Equity dividends are the payments made to shareholders out of profits as a return on their investment.

(b) Three material changes are as follows:

(i) The net cash inflow from normal operating activities has increased by 37.3%. 1998 was a more profitable year than 1997. This is a positive factor for the company.

(ii) Clifton used some of its cash inflows to repay loans and debt. This reduces the amount of gearing in the financing structure and increases the safety of the company's shares – a positive factor.

(iii) The company has reduced both its issue of new shares and acquisitions of new subsidiaries. This is probably a neutral change.

(c) Clifton plc's underlying cash flow in 1998 was better than in 1997. Overall there was a decrease in cash of £54 600 but this was due to a deliberate decision by management to repay a lot of debt. While this has caused 1998 to take a one-time hit, the action will reduce interest payable in future years and boost cash flow then.

Question 11.2

(a)

Tower plc

Cash Flow Statement for year ending 31 May 1998

	£000	£000	£000
Operating activities			
Operating profit (W_1)	49 400		
Add depreciation (W_2)	12 000		
Add loss on sale of fixed assets	6 400		
		67 800	
Less increase in stock	(2 000)		
Less increase in debtors	(23 000)		
Less decrease in creditors	(7 600)		
		(32 600)	
Net cash inflow from operating activities			35 200
Returns on investments and servicing of finance			
Less dividends paid			(4 000)
Taxation			
Tax paid			(8 000)

Investing activities

Sale of fixed assets	3 600	
Purchase of fixed assets	(44 000)	
		(40 400)

Financing

Ordinary share issue	6 000	
Preference share redemption	(4 000)	
Share premium	200	
		2 200
		£(15 000)

Decrease in bank and cash (9 600 + 5 400)	£(15 000)

Workings

W₁

	£000	£000
Increase in retained profit (79 800 – 46 400)		33 400
Add back:		
Tax charge	10 000	
Proposed dividends	6 000	
		16 000
Profit before tax		49 400

W₂

Calculation of depreciation for year:

	£000
Book value of assets on 31 May 1998	86 000
Less book value of assets on 31 May 1997	(64 000)
Less new asset purchased	(44 000)
Add book value of asset sold	10 000
Depreciation for year	(12 000)

The difference in the book value of assets between the two years is accounted for by three factors – the disappearance of the asset sold, the appearance of the asset purchased and the depreciation for the year. If we adjust the difference (86 000 – 64 000) by taking out the new asset and adding back the old one, we are left with the depreciation for the year. Although this is a minus figure in the calculation, it is added back to the operating profit in the usual way.

(b)

A company might invest more in its fixed assets than it pays to its shareholders in dividends because:

- it sees a growth in demand for its products and needs to invest in more equipment to be able to make higher profits in the long-run.
- it cannot borrow easily or cheaply from external sources and chooses to finance growth from internally generated profits.
- its fixed assets have become obsolete and it is forced to invest in new ones to be able to compete on efficiency and product quality.

(c)

The investment in fixed assets has been largely financed by the worsening in the cash position and by retained profits. Assuming that the investment was necessary, the company should have financed it with a long-term loan or by issuing more shares.

The increase in debtors can be controlled by offering cash discounts for prompt payment and by reviewing Tower's procedures for granting credit and chasing slow payers. Alternatively management could sell some of the sales invoices to a debt factoring agency for cash.

Question 11.3

(a)

B B Wolf plc
Cash Flow Statement for year ending 31 December 1998

	£	£	£
Operating activities			
Operating profit (W$_1$)	127 000		
Add depreciation on machinery (W$_2$)	155 400		
Add depreciation on office equipment (W$_3$)	39 000		
Add loss on sale of fixed assets (8 000 – 6 500)	1 500		
		322 900	
Add decrease in stock	11 800		
Add decrease in debtors	6 900		
Add increase in creditors	8 700		
		27 400	
Net cash inflow from operating activities			350 300
Returns on investments and servicing of finance			
Less dividends paid			(80 000)
Taxation			
Tax paid			(41 000)
Investing activities			
Sale of office equipment		6 500	
Purchase of machinery		(195 000)	
Purchase of office equipment		(19 000)	
			(207 500)
			£21 800
Increase in bank and cash (64 100 – 42 300)			£21 800

Workings

W$_1$

	£	£
Decrease in retained profit (146 000 – 182 000)		(36 000)
Add back:		
Tax charge	48 000	
Proposed dividends	65 000	
Transfer to general reserve	50 000	
		163 000
Profit before tax		127 000

W₂

Calculation of depreciation on machinery for year:

	£
Book value of machinery on 31 December 1998	579 600
Less book value of machinery on 31 May 1997	(540 000)
Less new machinery purchased	(195 000)
Depreciation for year	(155 400)

W₃

Calculation of depreciation on office equipment for year:

	£
Book value of office equipment on 31 December 1998	110 000
Less book value of office equipment on 31 May 1997	(138 000)
Less new office equipment purchased	(19 000)
Add book value of asset sold	8 000
Depreciation for year	(39 000)

Note: The increase in the book value of the premises is covered exactly by the Revaluation Reserve and so does not involve any cash.

(b)

Since the bonus issue of shares was covered exactly by the Share Premium, no cash was received by the company and so the item does not appear in the cash flow statement.

(c) See text.

Question 11.4

To do this question we have to reverse the normal cash flow procedure. We start with the opening balance sheet and make adjustments to the items from the information given in the cash flow statement until we reach the closing balance sheet.

(a)

Brenda O'Flynn Ltd
Balance Sheet as at 31 May 1997

	£000	£000	£000
Fixed assets (net book value) (W_1)			10 950
Investments (at cost) (W_2)			1 020
			11 970
Current assets			
Stock (W_3)		641	
Debtors (W_4)		981	
Bank balance (W_5)		907	
		2 529	
Creditors – amounts falling due within one year			
Creditors (W_6)	687		
Proposed ordinary dividend (W_7)	801		
Taxation (W_8)	140		
		(1 628)	
Net current assets			901
			£12 871
Capital and reserves			
Ordinary share capital (£1 shares) (W_9)			10 000
Share premium account (W_{10})			1 108
Retained earnings (W_{11})			1 763
			£12 871

Workings

W_1

Fixed assets: balance as per opening balance sheet + new acquisitions + revaluation of land and buildings – depreciation for the year
$= 7\ 535 + 638 + 3\ 200 - 423 = 10\ 950$

W_2

Investments: balance as per opening balance sheet + new acquisitions
$= 780 + 240 = 1\ 020$

W_3

Stocks: balance as per opening balance sheet + increase in stocks over the year
$= 587 + 54 = 641$

W_4

Debtors: balance as per opening balance sheet + increase in debtors over the year
$= 828 + 153 = 981$

W_5

Bank balance $= 907$ (we are given this in the cash analysis)

W₆

Creditors: balance as per opening balance sheet + decrease in creditors over the year
= 761 – 74 = 687

W₇

Proposed ordinary dividend = 801 (we are given this in the net profit reconciliation)

W₈

Taxation = 140 (we are given this in the net profit reconciliation)

W₉

Ordinary share capital: balance as per opening balance sheet + new rights issue +
bonus shares
= 6 400 + 400 + 3 200 = 10 000

N.B.

(i) only the nominal value of the rights issue is shown under share capital;
(ii) the bonus issue is the full amount of the revaluation reserve,
       i.e. 8 000 000 – 4 800 000 = 3 200 000

W₁₀

Share premium: balance as per opening balance sheet + premium on new issue
(400 000 shares @ 25p each = 100 000)
= 1 008 + 100 = 1 108

W₁₁

Profit and loss account: balance as per opening balance sheet + retained profit
1 268 + 495 = 1 763

(a)

Memorandum
From: (Your name)   To: Jayne Smart

Date:

Subject: Cash Flow Statements

(i)   Depreciation is added to operating profit in calculating profit for cash flow
        purposes because it is not a cash cost and has not resulted in an outflow of
        cash. We must therefore compensate for this by adding it back on to show
        what the profit would have been without it.

(ii)   The increase in stocks is deducted from operating profit because it represents
        a fall in cash, since the stocks must have been paid for out of cash.

(iii)   The increase in debtors is similarly deducted because it represents a situation
        where cash is not coming in.

(iv)   The decrease in creditors is deducted because it represents cash payments by
        us.

(c) A cash flow statement is useful because it reconciles the profit and cash situations.
     It shows, for example, how it is possible for a large profit to be accompanied by a
     low cash position or vice versa. It is also useful to users of accounting information
     because it analyses in detail the effect of the year's transactions on cash.

Chapter 12

Question 12.1

(a)

Becky plc

Gross margin	47.22%
Net margin	34.16%
Return on capital employed	16.16%
Current ratio	1.98:1
Acid-test ratio	0.78:1
Debtors' collection period	101 days
Creditors' payment period	92 days
Earnings per share	13.07 pence
Dividend cover	1.74 times
Dividend yield	6%

Workings

Gross margin:
$$\frac{\text{Gross profit}}{\text{Sales}} \times 100$$
$$= \frac{13\,685}{28\,980} \times 100$$
$$= 47.22\%$$

Net margin:
$$\frac{\text{Net profit}}{\text{Sales}} \times 100$$
$$= \frac{9\,900}{28\,980} \times 100$$
$$= 34.16\%$$

ROCE:
$$\frac{\text{Net profit before taxation}}{\text{Capital employed}} \times 100$$
$$= \frac{61\,270}{28\,980} \times 100$$
$$= 16.16\%$$

Current ratio: Current assets : current liabilities
$$= 22\,970 : 11\,610$$
$$= 1.98 : 1$$

Acid-test ratio: (Current assets – stock) : current liabilities
$$= (22\,970 - 13\,860) : 11\,610$$
$$= 0.78 : 1$$

Debtors' collection period:
$$\frac{\text{Debtors}}{\text{Credit sales}} \times 365$$
$$= \frac{8\,030}{28\,980} \times 365$$
$$= 101 \text{ days}$$

Creditors' payment period:

$$\frac{\text{Creditors}}{\text{Credit purchases}} \times 365$$

$$= \frac{4\,650}{18\,515} \times 365$$

$$= 92 \text{ days}$$

Earnings per share:

$$\frac{\text{Profit after tax}}{\text{Number of ordinary shares issued}}$$

$$= \frac{6\,900}{52\,800}$$

$$= 13.07 \text{ pence}$$

Dividend cover:

$$\frac{\text{Profit after tax}}{\text{Dividend}}$$

$$= \frac{6\,900}{3\,960}$$

$$= 1.74 \text{ times}$$

Dividend yield:

$$\frac{\text{Ordinary dividend price per share}}{\text{Market price per share}} \times 100$$

Ordinary dividend per share = 3 960 ÷ 52 800 = 7.5 pence

$$= \frac{7.5 \text{ pence per share}}{£1.25} \times 100$$

$$= 6\%$$

(a)

Report to Laura Labbatt

From:

Date:

Subject: A Comparison of the Results of Becky plc and Charlotte plc

Findings

Charlotte plc is a more profitable company as evidenced by the return on capital employed which is 21.39% compared with Becky's 16.16%. This means that Charlotte is achieving a better return on the long-term funds invested in it. This could be explained by Charlotte having a better product – its gross margin is higher than Becky's but its costs are being kept lower.

Becky's acid-test ratio is slightly lower than Charlotte's but both are inadequate. Although both companies are achieving a satisfactory current ratio, they are relying too much on stocks and could soon experience a liquidity crisis.

Becky's debtors take 102 days on average to pay their invoices whereas Charlotte's credit control seems to be much tighter at only 32 days. Charlotte's creditors' period is greater than the debtors' period whereas the opposite is true of Becky.

Becky's dividend cover is lower than Charlotte's which means that the divided yield was more and that the shareholders received a higher percentage of the profit in the

form of dividend. While this policy might keep the shareholders happy, it might also mean that less resources are being reinvested into the business.

Conclusions

Charlotte has a better position on both profitability and liquidity and collects its debts more quickly. It pays out less of its profit in dividends but it may be a safer investment for the future.

Recommendations

You should invest in the shares of Charlotte.

Notes

The question asked for comments on four ratios and, although any four could have been chosen, it is better to choose one from each type, i.e. profitability, liquidity, working capital management and investment. In this case there is not much to choose between the two companies and recommending either is acceptable as long as it is backed up with relevant figures and sound reasoning.

The answers to (c) and (d) are covered in the chapter.

Question 12.2

(a)

(i)   gearing ratio $= \dfrac{\text{long term loans}}{\text{shareholders' funds and long - term loans}} \times 100$

London: $= \dfrac{0}{730\,000} \times 100 = 0\%$

Bridge: $= \dfrac{520\,000}{1\,250\,000} = 41.6\%$

London has no gearing as all its long-term capital is in the form of shares. Bridge on the other hand has a relatively high level of debentures to long-term capital.

(ii)   working capital ratio: current assets : current liabilities

London   = 458 000 : 472 000

                    = 0.97 : 1

Bridge   = 958 000 : 336 000

                    = 2.85 : 1

London's working capital ratio is dangerously low as current assets do not even cover current liabilities. Bridge's ratio is higher than it needs to be, 2 : 1 being normally accepted as safe.

(iii)   the acid test ratio: current assets – stock : current liabilities

                    London = 192 000 : 472 000

                    = 0.4 : 1

Bridge   = 684 000 : 336 000

                    = 2.04 : 1

London's acid test ratio is also too low whereas Bridge's is higher than necessary.

(iv)   return on capital employed: $= \dfrac{\text{net profit before interest}}{\text{capital employed}} \times 100$

London $= \dfrac{60\,000}{730\,000} \times 100$

                         $= 8.22\%$

Bridge $= \dfrac{60\,000}{1\,250\,000} \times 100$

                         $= 4.8\%$

Although both companies are making exactly the same amount of profit, London's return is almost twice that of Bridge because it has less long-term capital invested.

(b)   The rate of return earned by an investor is higher in the case of London as the same profit is being earned on a lower amount of long-term capital. However the fact that London has no gearing means that profit has to be allocated between more shares. Although London has no debenture holders to be paid interest out of the profits, the company's liquidity position is bad. Current assets are insufficient to pay the current liabilities and the firm could well find itself becoming insolvent.

(a) If the going-concern concept were not applicable this means that London Ltd is about to go into liquidation. Even if the investor were prepared to risk the liquidity position because of the higher return on capital, he or she would not put money into a firm which is about to be wound up.

Question 12.3

(a)

i) The gross profit margin is the percentage of gross profit on sales and shows how much of the selling price of the product is made up of gross profit. Slipshod's gross profit margin is higher than the average for the industry, which could mean that its prices are not competitive.

ii) The operating profit margin is the percentage of net profit on sales and shows how much of the selling price of the product is made up of net profit, i.e. after expenses have been taken into account. Again, Slipshod's percentage is slightly higher than that of the industry; this might mean that its prices are higher but it could also be the result of the company keeping its costs down.

iii) The return on capital employed is the percentage of profit to long-term capital employed in the business and shows the return being made by the firm on its investment. Despite possibly having higher prices, Slipshod is making a higher return than the industry average.

iv) The acid-test ratio is current assets excluding stock to current liabilities and shows the relation between liquid assets (debtors, bank and cash) to creditors which will have to be paid in the short term (up to 12 months). Slipshod's ratio is less than the industry average but 1:1 is considered to be the norm and the firm probably does not have a cash problem.

v) The gearing percentage shows the relationship between the firm's long-term debt and its total capital employed. The fact that Slipshod is much more highly geared than other firms in the same industry means that its loans and debentures are high when compared with its share capital; this is risky as the firm will have to pay interest on these loans whether it makes a profit or not

(b) The current ratio is current assets : current liabilities and 2:1 is considered to be safe. The fact that Slipshod has 5:1 does not mean that it is in a better position however as the ratio is much higher than is necessary. It means that the firm is tying up more funds in current form than is desirable and is not investing this money in more profitable long-term assets.

Question 12.4

Part 1

(a)

(i) Mark-up ratio $= \dfrac{\text{Gross profit}}{\text{Cost of sales}} \times 100$

We have to find both these figures.

Gross profit = Turnover – Cost of sales

Cost of sales = Opening stock + Purchases – Closing stock

We know that average stock is £30 000 and that stock levels have fallen by £10 000 during the year. Opening stock must therefore have been £35 000 and closing stock £25 000, as these are the only figures with that difference which give us that average.

Cost of sales = £35 000 + 290 000 – 25 000 = £300 000

Gross profit = £400 000 – 300 000 = £100 000

Mark-up ratio = £100 000 / £300 000 x 100 = 33.3%

(ii) Rate of stock turnover $= \dfrac{\text{Cost of sales}}{\text{Average stock}} = \dfrac{300\,000}{30\,000} = 10$ times

(iii) Debtors' collection period in days $= \dfrac{\text{Debtors}}{\text{Cost of sales}} \times 365$

Credit sales are 80% of turnover i.e. 80% of 400 000 = 320 000

$\dfrac{80\,000}{320\,000} \times 365$

= 91.25 days

(iv) Expenses ratio $= \dfrac{\text{Expenses}}{\text{Sales}} \times 100$

Expenses = Gross profit – net profit

£100 000 – 45 000 = £55 000

$\dfrac{55\,000}{400\,000} \times 100$

= 13.75%

(v) Acid-test ratio = Current assets excluding stock : current liabilities

= Debtors + Bank balance : Creditors + VAT owing

= 80 000 + 20 000 : 50 000 + 25 000

= 100 000 : 75 000

= 1.33 : 1

(vi) Turnover to fixed assets = Sales : Fixed assets

= 400 000 : 120 000

= 3.33 : 1

(b)

The rate of stockturn last year was 12 times while it is only 10 times this year. The debtors' collection period last year was 65 days while this year it has sharpened up considerably to only 25 days. While this is good for credit control policy, it may be a reason why the stock is being turned over less quickly. If debtors are being given less time to pay, some sales are probably being lost.

Part 2

(a)

(i) The ordinary dividend percentage is the dividend declared on the ordinary shares by the directors.
A total of 2p + 3p was paid on the ordinary shares i.e. 5p per share
The shares have a nominal value of 50p
So the percentage dividend is $\frac{5}{50} \times 100 = 10\%$

(ii) the ordinary dividend yield is the $\dfrac{\text{ordinary dividend per share}}{\text{market price per share}}$

$$= \frac{5p}{125p}$$

$$= 4\%$$

(iii) the net profit available for distribution to ordinary shareholders is:

	£
Net profit before interest and tax	2 300 000
Less interest on debentures (6% of £1 million)	(60 000)
	2 240 000
Less tax (25% of 2 240 000)	(560 000)
	1 680 000
Less preference dividend (8% of £1 million)	(80 000)
Net profit available for distribution	£1 600 000

(iv) the price earnings ratio $= \dfrac{\text{market price per share}}{\text{earnings per share}}$

earnings per share $= \dfrac{\text{profit after interest, tax and preference divided}}{\text{number of ordinary shares}}$

$$= \frac{1\,600\,000}{10\,000\,000}$$

$= 16p$ per share

The P/E ratio is thus $\dfrac{1.25}{0.16}$

$= 7.8$ times

(b) The consequences of being an ordinary shareholder in a highly geared company are:

i) There will be less profit to share out since a lot of interest will have been paid first to the debt holders.

ii) On the other hand there will be less shareholders to share the profit with.

Returns fluctuate more year to year than for shareholders in a similarly profitable low geared company.

Question 12.5

(a)

Profitability ratios: Net profit margin and return on capital employed

Net profit margin = Net profit before tax / Sales x 100

$$1994: \frac{347}{2\,100} \times 100$$
$$= 16.5\%$$

$$1995: \frac{453}{3\,000} \times 100$$
$$= 15.1\%$$

Return on capital employed (using shareholders' funds since the debentures will be repaid in 1995)

$$1994: \frac{347}{1\,733} \times 100$$
$$= 20\%$$

$$1995: \frac{453}{2\,557} \times 100$$
$$= 17.7\%$$

(b)

Liquidity ratios: Current ratio and acid test ratio

Current ratio = Current assets : current liabilities

1994: 920 : 487 = 1.89 : 1

1995: 1 080 : 623 = 1.73 : 1

Acid test ratio = Current assets minus stock : current liabilities

1994: 500 : 487 = 1.02 : 1

1995: 570 : 623 = 0.91 : 1

(c)

The firm's profitability has fallen between 1994 and 1995. This was due to both a fall in gross profit and to an increase in expenses of 26%. The return on investment continues to be good when compared with the rate of interest paid on a bank account, however. New share capital has been issued and new fixed assets purchased. Perhaps the fruits of this investment will be realised in the longer term, i.e. over the next few years.

Liquidity has also deteriorated and the ratios for 1995 are near to the margin of safety. This could be partly due to the repayment of the debentures. The company needs to boost its liquid assets and not rely on its stocks.

It is difficult to make inter-year comparisons using financial ratios as it is necessary to see trends in the light of changes in the external environment. However inter-firm comparisons could be made and the industry average could be looked at.

(d)

A business could increase its working capital by issuing new shares for cash or borrowing long-term funds and not spending all of the money on fixed assets. It could also sell off fixed assets which are no longer necessary.

(e)

 (i) Excessive working capital means that a business is holding too many resources in liquid form and is not able to invest this money in more profitable assets eg to purchase more advanced equipment etc.

(ii) Limited working capital means that a business is not able to meet all of its short-term obligations to suppliers and creditors on time. Prolonged or serious shortage of working capital often causes insolvency.

(f)

A firm could be making profits 'on paper' and yet not be receiving money from its debtors and so be experiencing a liquidity problem. Expenditure on fixed assets could have increased but unwisely have been financed with short-term liabilities like a bank overdraft. A firm which increases its sales rapidly by offering very favourable prices and credit terms may be overtrading and risks bankruptcy.

Question 12.6

(a)

$$\text{Return on capital employed} = \frac{\text{net profit}}{\text{closing capital}*} \times 100$$

$$1999 : \frac{15}{49} \times 100 = 30.61\%$$

$$2000 : \frac{6}{30} \times 100 = 20\%$$

* We could use average capital, i.e. (opening + closing capital) ÷ 2

$$\text{Gross profit as a percentage of sales} = \frac{\text{gross profit}}{\text{sales}} \times 100$$

$$1999 : \frac{45}{90} \times 100 = 50\%$$

$$2000 : \frac{40}{120} \times 100 = 33.3\%$$

$$\text{Net profit as a percentage of sales} = \frac{\text{net profit}}{\text{sales}} \times 100$$

$$1999 : \frac{15}{90} \times 100 = 16.67\%$$

$$2000 : \frac{6}{120} \times 100 = 5\%$$

Current ratio = current assets : current liabilities
1999: 18 : 9 = 2:1
2000: 40 : 40 = 1:1

Liquid ratio = current assets excluding stock : current liabilities
1999: 13 : 9 = 1.44:1
2000: 20 : 40 = 0.5:1

Stock turnover $= \dfrac{\text{cost of goods sold}}{\text{average stock}}$

$1999 : \dfrac{45}{(15 + 5) \div 2} = 4.5$ times

$2000 : \dfrac{80}{(5 + 20) \div 2} = 6.4$ times

(b)

Adil's profitability has fallen significantly. Although his sales figure has increased by 33% from 90 to 120, his gross profit margin has fallen from 50% to 33%. This has been caused by the sharp increase in cost of sales from 50% to 66%. Perhaps the business has been cutting prices over the past year; this boosts sales but also reduces the gross margin. Adil has been able to control his sundry expenses, these rising by only 13.3%.

Liquidity has deteriorated. The current ratio has fallen from 2:1 (good) to 1:1 (which is not) and the liquid ratio from 1.44:1 (which is good) to 0.5:1 (extremely unsatisfactory). The bank balance is now in overdraft. The stock turnover has increased from 4.5 times to 6.4 times, which reflects the increased activity during the year.

The following additional changes have taken place over the year:

Net fixed assets have fallen in value i.e. existing fixed assets have depreciated but no new fixed assets have been purchased.
Stock decreased from 15 to 5 in 1999 and then increased by four times to 20 in 2000.
Debtors have doubled.
Creditors have risen by more than three times.
Adil has put £9 000 more capital into the business.
His drawings have increased by more than four times.

Conclusions:
Adil is trying to grow too fast. Demand for his product is high and he can hardly cope. However the price cuts have hurt his profitability and large amounts of money tied up in stocks and debtors have hurt his liquidity.

Suggestions:
1. Adil should consider raising selling prices. This would reduce sales but would be a welcome relief in view of the fact that the business is being stretched to cope with current demand. It would also boost the gross margin and profitability.

2. Adil should reduce the period of credit allowed to his creditors. He could also offer a small cash discount on accounts settled promptly, eg within ten days of a sale. Selling some of his debtors to a factoring agency is another option – he would have to sell at a discount to invoice terms but this would boost liquidity.

3. Adil has to exercise restraint on drawings in years when profit is low. Failure to do this erodes the capital base of his business.

Chapter 13

See text.

Chapter 14

Question 14.1

(a)

Staghill Manufacturing Company Ltd
Manufacturing, Trading and Profit and Loss Account for the year ended 30 April 1999

	£	£	£
Raw materials			
Opening stock	26 740		
Purchases	278 630		
Less closing stock	(24 390)		
Cost of raw materials consumed	280 980		
Direct factory wages	372 560		
Royalties	6 500		
Prime cost		660 040	
Factory overhead expenses			
Indirect labour	74 280		
Heating and lighting (2/3 of [26 650 + 800])	18 300		
General factory expenses	47 080		
Insurances (2/3 of [15 010 − 760])	9 500		
Depreciation on plant and machinery (10% of 210 000)	21 000		
		170 160	
Factory cost of production		830 200	
Add opening stock of work in progress		23 170	
Less closing stock of work in progress		(24 640)	
Factory cost of finished goods		828 730	
Gross profit on manufacture		165 746	
Factory cost transferred to trading account			£994 476
Sales			1 163 750
Opening stock of finished goods		37 440	
Factory cost of finished goods		994 476	
Less closing stock of finished goods		(36 720)	
Cost of sales			(995 196)
Gross profit			168 554
Add gross profit on manufacture			165 746
Add decrease in provision for unrealised profit (W_1)			120
			334 420
Heating and lighting (1/3 of [26 650 + 800])		9 150	
Insurances (1/3 of [15 010 − 760])		4 750	
General office expenses		36 740	
			(50 640)
Net profit			£283 780

Workings

W₁

The new provision for unrealised profit $= \dfrac{£36\,720 \times 120}{120\,(\text{a 20\% profit loading})} = £6120$

The existing provision is £6 240 so the new one is £120 less.
The provision for unrealised profit must be reduced by £120 (closing stock was less than opening stock).

(b), (c) and (d) See text.

Question 14.2

In this question we have to show separate columns for two different products. However we are told that the prime cost of manufacturing is split 70:30 and so, to save time, we can calculate the prime cost as a total and then split it. Notice that there are no opening stocks of batteries under any of the three categories.

Sparky Ltd

(a)

Manufacturing and Trading Account for the year ended 31 March 1998

	£	0	£
Raw materials:			
Opening stock	116 540		
Purchases	522 600		
Less closing stock	(100 204)		
Cost of raw materials consumed		538 936	
Production wages		296 756	
Prime cost			£835 692

	Light Bulbs		Batteries	
	£000	£000	£000	£000
Prime cost (70% : 30%)		584 984		250 708
Factory administration costs (3:2)	247 680		165 120	
Factory rent and rates (3 2)	1 920		1 280	
General factory expenses (24 198 and [38 380 – 24 198])	24 198		14 182	
Depreciation on plant and machinery	7 200		2 800	
		280 998		183 382
		865 982		434 090
Add opening work in progress		34 940		
Less closing work in progress		(36 300)		(22 080)
Factory cost of production		864 622		412 010
Gross profit on manufacture (10%)		86 462		41 201
Factory cost transferred to trading account		£951 084		£453 211
Sales		1 821 880		523 180
Opening stock of finished goods	250 600			
Factory cost from manufacturing account	951 084		453 211	
Less closing stock of finished goods	(379 780)		(30 020)	
Cost of sales		(821 904)		(423 191)
Gross profit		999 976		99 989
Add back profit loading		86 622		41 201
Less in provision for unrealised profit (W₁)		(11 744)		(2 729)
Net profit		£1 074 854		£138 461

Workings

W$_1$

We are not given a provision for unrealised profit from last year but we can assume that one had been created for the light bulbs.
This will now be increased since the closing stock is greater than the opening stock.

£379 780 – 250 600 = £129 180

$$= \frac{£129\,180 \times 10}{110\,(a\,10\%\,profit\,loading)}$$

= £11 744

The batteries are a new product and so a new provision must be created.

$$= \frac{£30\,020 \times 10}{110} = £2\,729$$

(a) See text

(b) If Sparky expands by manufacturing a new product, it will have to invest in new equipment, train workers into new techniques and find new suppliers. It will need to finance the exercise, either from existing reserves, by issuing new shares or by borrowing from a financial institution. It will have to cost out the new product very carefully in order to know what price to charge and it should also do market research to discover how much consumers will be willing to pay for the new product.

Question 14.3

Valley Ltd

(a) (i) and (ii)

Manufacturing, Trading and Profit and Loss Account for the year ended 31 December 1998

	£000	£000
Raw materials:		
Opening stock	28	
Purchases	50	
Less closing stock	(32)	
Cost of raw materials consumed	46	
Direct labour (50 000 + 2 000)	52	
Direct power	12	
Prime cost		110
Factory overhead expenses		
Variable factory overheads	18	
Fixed expenses	22	
Depreciation on freehold buildings (**W$_1$**)	3	
Depreciation on plant and machinery (**W$_2$**)	16	
		59
Factory cost of production		169
Add opening stock of work in progress		72
Less closing stock of work in progress		(80)
Factory cost of finished goods		161
Gross profit on manufacture (220 – 161)		59
Factory cost transferred to trading account		£220

Sales		300
Less cost of goods sold		
Opening stock of finished goods	25	
Factory cost of finished goods	220	
Less closing stock of finished goods (NRV)	(38)	
		(207)
Gross profit		93
Marketing expenses (20 – 1)	19	
Administrative overheads	34	
Depreciation on freehold buildings (W_1)	1	
Depreciation on office machinery (W_3)	4	
Provision for unrealised profit (W_4)	8	
		(66)
Net profit		27
Retained profit		2
Profit available for distribution		29
Less appropriations		
Final ordinary dividend proposed (10p × 240 000)		(24)
Retained profit		£5

(b) Revaluing the premises is justified if the market price of the land and buildings has increased enough and over a long enough period of time to make its new increased value stable. However the firm takes the risk that the property market might fall again, as it will then have an overvalued asset on its balance sheeet.

Workings

W_1

2% on revalued figure of £200 000 = £4 000
This is to be apportioned between factory and office in the ratio of 3 : 1 i.e. £3 000 and £1 000.

W_2

25% of £(100 – 36)
= £16 000

W_3

10% on cost
i.e. 10% of £36 000 = £3 600 (rounded up to £4 000)

W_4

Provision for unrealised profit:
The factory cost of £161 000 has been increased to a market value of £220 000.
This is an increase of 27% (rounded up).
The provision is calculated on the closing stock of finished goods (there is no existing provision)

i.e. £38 000 $\times \dfrac{27}{127}$ = £8 000

This is added to cost and deducted from net profit.

Question 14.4

YMB Ltd

(a)

Manufacturing, Trading and Profit and Loss Account for the year ended 30 June 1995

	£000	£000
Raw materials:		
Opening stock	13 000	
Purchases	62 000	
Less closing stock	(15 000)	
Cost of raw materials consumed		60 000
Manufacturing wages		30 000
Prime cost		90 000
Factory overhead expenses		
Variable expenses	20 000	
Fixed expenses	34 895	
Depreciation on land and buildings (W_1)	225	
Depreciation on plant and equipment (W_2)	6 400	
		61 520
Factory cost of production		151 520
Add opening stock of work in progress		84
Less closing stock of work in progress		(80)
Factory cost of finished goods		£151 524
Sales		200 000
Less cost of goods sold		
Opening stock of finished goods	9 376	
Factory cost of finished goods	151 524	
Less closing stock of finished goods	(10 900)	
		(150 000)
Gross profit		50 000
Distribution costs		
Variable (W_1)	3 000	
Fixed	2 970	
Depreciation on land (W_1)	30	
Depreciation on plant (W_1)	400	
Depreciation on motor vehicles (W_1)	1 600	
Provision for doubtful debts	2 000	
		(10 000)
Administration expenses		
Variable	4 000	
Fixed (14 155 – 900 + 1 100)	14 355	
Depreciation on land (W_1)	45	
Depreciation on plant (W_1)	1 200	
Depreciation on motor vehicles (W_1)	400	
		(20 000)
Net profit		20 000
Less provision for corporation tax		(10 000)
Profit after tax		10 000
Retained profit 30.6.1994		36 120
Profit available for distribution		46 120

Less Appropriations		
Preference dividend paid	120	
Interim ordinary dividend paid	2 000	
Final ordinary dividend proposed	4 000	
		(6 120)
Retained profit 30.6.1995		£40 000

Workings

W₁ Depreciation

	Land	Plant	Vehicles
	£000	£000	£000
Manufacturing expenses	225	6 400	
Distribution costs	30	400	1 600
Administration expenses	45	1 200	400
	300	8 000	2 000

W₂ Variable distribution costs

	£
Variable distribution costs paid	2 702
Less prepayment	(100)
Add accrual	400
Add opening stock of packaging materials	18
Less closing stock of packaging materials	(20)
Amount transferred to profit and loss account	3000

(b)

Balance Sheet as at 30 June 1995

	£000	£000	£000
	Cost	*Depreciation*	*Net*
Fixed assets			
Freehold and buildings	15 000	7 500	7 500
Plant and equipment	80 000	20 500	59 500
Motor vehicles	10 000	4 000	6 000
	105 000	32 000	73 000
Current assets			
Stocks – materials		15 000	
work in progress		80	
finished products		10 900	
packaging materials		20	
Trade debtors	23 000		
Less provision for doubtful debts	(3 000)		
		20 000	
Prepayments		1 000	
Cash at bank		2 000	
		49 000	
Current liabilities			
Trade creditors	6 000		
Accrued expenses	2 000		
Ordinary dividend proposed	4 000		
Provision for tax	10 000		
		(22 000)	
Working capital			27 000
Net assets			£100 000

Financed by:		
Ordinary shares of £0.25 each, fully paid		50 000
6% preference shares of £1 each, fully paid		2 000
		52 000
Reserves		
Share premium	8 000	
Retained profit	40 000	
		48 000
		£100 000

Question 14.5

Shutter Ltd

Manufacturing, Trading and Profit and Loss Account for the year ended 31 December 1997

	£000	£000
Raw materials		
Opening stock	120	
Purchases	1 800	
Less closing stock	(135)	
Cost of raw materials consumed		1 785
Wages		219
Prime cost		2 004
Factory overheads		
Depreciation of manufacturing equipment (10%)	24	
Heat, light and power (80% of 110 000)	88	
Manufacturing expenses	96	
Rates (80% of 70 000)	56	
		264
Cost of production		£2 268

	£000	£000
Sales		3 570
Opening stock of finished goods	160	
Cost of production	2 268	
Less closing stock of finished goods	(179)	
Cost of sales		(2 249)
Gross profit		1 321
Heat, light and power (20% of 110 000)	22	
Non-manufacturing wages	101	
Non-manufacturing expenses	75	
Rates (20% of 70 000)	14	
Bad debts	6	
Increase in provision for bad debts (14 – 12)	2	
		(220)
Net profit		1 101
Corporation tax		(250)
Net profit after tax		851
Interim dividend	200	
Proposed dividend (15p x 250 000 000 shares)	375	
		(575)
Retained profit		276
Profit and loss account 1 January 1997		1 100
Profit and loss account 31 December 1997		£1 376

Balance Sheet as at 31 December 1997

		£000
Fixed Assets		
Land and buildings		4 200
Equipment at cost	1 040	
Less accumulated depreciation (96 + 24)	(120)	
		920
Goodwill **(W₁)**		310
		5 430
Current Assets		
Stock (135 + 179 + 190)	504	
Debtors (220 – 14)	206	
Prepayments	14	
Cash	9	
	733	
Current Liabilities		
Creditors	150	
Accrual	12	
Corporation tax	250	
Proposed dividend	375	
	(787)	
Working capital		(54)
		5 376
Debentures		(1 500)
		£3 876
Ordinary shares (2 000 + 500)		2 500
Profit and loss account		1 376
		£3 876

W₁

Goodwill is the difference between the amount paid for Bolt & Co and the value of the assets acquired
i.e. 3 000 000 – (1 700 000 + 800 000 + 190 000) = 310 000

Chapter 15

Questions 15.1 and 15.2

See text.

Question 15.3

(a) Production line workers could be paid on a piecework system according to the number of units they make.
(b) Research staff could be paid a salary with a bonus for results.
(c) Administrative staff could be paid a salary with a performance bonus.
(d) Maintenance workers could be paid a basic time-rate but with a productivity bonus on top.

Each answer should be justified and the advantages and disadvantages of each set out.

Question 15.4
BSE Veterinary Services
(a)

Profit Statement on 12 000 units

	£
Sales (12 000 units × £300)	3 600 000
Less costs:	
Materials (12 000 units x £115)	(1 380 000)
Technicians' wages (12 000 units × £30)	(360 000)
Variable overhead (12 000 units × £12)	(144 000)
Fixed overhead (12 000 units × £50)	(600 000)
Profit	£1 116 000

(b)

Profit Statement on 18 000 units

	£
Sales (18 000 units × £300)	5 400 000
Less costs:	
Materials (18 000 units × £92) (W_1)	(1 656 000)
Technicians' wages (W_2)	(630 000)
Variable overhead (18 000 units × £12)	(216 000)
Fixed overhead (600 000 + 700 000)	(1 300 000)
Profit	£1 598 000

Workings

W_1
There is a discount of 20% on all materials at this level of production
i.e. £115 − (20% of 115) = £92

W_2
The technicians' wages on the first shift have not changed but there is a 50% premium on the additional shift i.e. £30 + (50% of 30) = £45 per unit
Total wages = £(30 x 12 000) + (45 × 6 000) = £630 000

(c)

Three other factors to consider:

- Are the staff willing to work the extra shifts or can other qualified staff be found?
- Can the supplier of the materials make enough extra material available?
- Has the firm got enough liquidity to enable it to pay the extra costs before receiving the extra revenue from the customers?

Chapter 16

Question 16.1

(a)

Closing stock in units = opening stock + purchases − sales

$$= 5 + (10 + 60 + 100 + 80 + 120) − (20 + 30 + 80 + 40 + 50 + 80)$$
$$= 75 \text{ units}$$

(i) FIFO: Since the last batch of purchases contained 120 units, all the 75 units of closing stock can be valued at £2.30

  i.e. $75 \times £2.30 = £172.50$

(ii) LIFO: The closing stock of 75 units must be valued on a perpetual basis.

Date	Purchases	Sales	Balance	£	£
July 1			5 units @ £1.75		8.75
July 2	10 units @ £1.90		5 units @ £1.75	8.75	
			10 units @ £1.90	19.00	27.75
July 4	60 units @ £2.00		5 units @ £1.75	8.75	
			10 units @ £1.90	19.00	
			60 units @ £2.00	120.00	147.75
July 5		20 units @ £2.00	5 units @ £1.75	8.75	
			10 units @ £1.90	19.00	
			40 units @ £2.00	80.00	107.75
July 11		30 units @ £2.00	5 units @ £1.75	8.75	
			10 units @ £1.90	19.00	
			10 units @ £2.00	20.00	47.75
July 16	100 units @ £2.20		5 units @ £1.75	8.75	
			10 units @ £1.90	19.00	
			10 units @ £2.00	20.00	
			100 units @ £2.20	220.00	265.75
July 18		80 units @ £2.20	5 units @ £1.75	8.75	
			10 units @ £1.90	19.00	
			10 units @ £2.00	20.00	
			20 units @ £2.20	44.00	91.75
July 20		40 units @ £2.20	5 units @ £1.75	8.75	8.75
July 22	80 units @ £2.10		5 units @ £1.75	8.75	
			80 units @ £2.10	168.00	176.75
July 28	120 units @ £2.30		5 units @ £1.75	8.75	
			80 units @ £2.10	168.00	
			120 units @ £2.30	276.00	452.75
July 29		50 units @ £2.30	5 units @ £1.75	8.75	
			80 units @ £2.10	168.00	
			70 units @ £2.30	161.00	337.75

July 30	70 units @ £2.30	5 units @ £1.75		8.75
	10 units @ £2.10	70 units @ £2.10	147.00	155.75

The 75 units remaining are thus costed at £155.75.

Notice that, if we had used the periodic system, we would have valued the closing stock from the earliest batches available as follows:

$[(5 \times £1.75) + (10 \times £1.90) + (60 \times £2.00)] = £147.75$

(b)

(i)

Trading Account for the month ending 31 July 2000 under FIFO

	£	£
Sales (300 × £5)		1 500.00
Opening stock	8.75	
Purchases *	803.00	
Less closing stock	(172.50)	
Cost of sales		(639.25)
Gross profit		£860.75

* Purchases:

$[(10 \times £1.90) + (60 \times £2.00) + (100 \times £2.20) + (80 \times £2.10) + (120 \times £2.30)] = £803$

(ii)

Trading Account for the month ending 31 July 2000 under LIFO

	£	£
Sales		1 500.00
Opening stock	8.75	
Purchases	803.00	
Less closing stock	(155.75)	
Cost of sales		(656.00)
Gross profit		£844.00

(c) See text.

(d) See Chapter 13.

Question 16.2

(a)

Stores Ledger Account

		Receipts			Issues			Balance	
Date	Quantity	Unit cost £	Total cost £	Quantity	Unit cost £	Total cost £	Quantity	Unit cost £	Total cost £
1 Jan							50	250	12 500
1 Feb	100	300	30 000						
Feb				50	250	12 500			
				25	300	7 500	75	300	22 500

1 Mar	200	292.50*	58 500						
1 May	300	285*	85 500						
May				75	300	22 500			
				200	292.50	58 500			
				75	285	21 375	225	285	64 125
			174 000			122 375			

*Determination of unit cost of receipts:

£ (60 000 × 0.975) ÷ 200 units = £292.50
£ (90 000 × 0.95) ÷ 300 units = £285

(b)

Trading Account for the six months 1 January – 30 June

	£	£
Sales		205 000
Opening stock	12 500	
Purchases	174 000	
Less closing stock	(64 125)	
Cost of sales		(122 375)
Gross profit		£82 625

(c) It is first necessary to work out the closing stock valuation under LIFO.

Date	Purchases	Sales	Balance	£	Total £
01 Jan			50 @ £250		12 500
01 Feb	100 @ £300		50 @ £250	12 500	
			100 @ £300	30 000	42 500
Feb		75 @ £300	50 @ £250	12 500	
			25 @ £300	7 500	20 000
01 March	200 @ £292.50		50 @ £250	12 500	
			25 @ £300	7 500	
			200 @ £292.50	58 500	78 500
01 May	300 @ £285		50 @ £250	12 500	
			25 @ £300	7 500	
			200 @ £292.50	58 500	
			300 @ £285	85 500	164 000
May		300 @ £285	50 @ £250	12 500	
		50 @ £292.50	25 @ £300	7 500	
			150 @ £292.50	43 875	63 875

Trading Account for the six months 1 January – 30 June under LIFO

	£	£
Sales		205 000
Opening stock	12 500	
Purchases	174 000	
Less closing stock	(63 875)	
Cost of sales		(122 625)
Gross profit		82 375

Question 16.3

(a) See text.

(b)

Lime Green Tartan: The material will be costed at net realisable value since this is less than manufacturing cost i.e. expected selling price – costs incurred
i.e. £2 000 – £500 = £1 500.

Power Strangers: To sell the material in Australia, the firm will make a loss, i.e. the marginal cost will exceed the marginal revenue:
£4 000 – (£2 750 + £2 650) = £(1 400)
It is more likely that the firm will decide to scrap the material rather than incur more expenses just for the sake of selling it and it will probably be given a zero value.

(c)

Rate of stock turnover = Cost of goods sold / average stock

$$= \frac{25\,000\,000}{250\,000} = 100 \text{ times}$$

This means that the company is selling its average stock every three days approximately. To be able to comment we would need to know the rate of stock turnover for previous periods and for similar firms.

Question 16.4

(a) General calculations:

The number of units of closing stock is opening stock + purchases – sales
= 160 + (256 + 246 + 364 + 244) – (230 + 222 + 342 + 226)
= 250 units

The price per unit is as follows:

Opening stock	160 units @ £20 per unit = £3 200
April – June 1998	256 units @ £20 per unit = £5 120
July – September 1998	246 units @ £22 per unit = £5 412
October – December 1998	364 units @ £24.20 per unit = £8 808.80
January – March 1999	244 units @ £26.62 per unit = £6 495.28

The price for each quarter is 10% higher than the quarter before.

Total purchases = £5 120 + 5 412 + 8 808.80 + 6 495.28 = £25 836.08

Sales = (230 + 222 + 342 + 226) units
= 1 020 units

$$= \frac{1\,020}{2\,\text{packs}} = 510\,\text{packs}$$
$$= 510 \times £76 \text{ per pack}$$
$$= £38\,760$$

(i) under LIFO:

Date	Purchases	Sales	Balance	£	£
April – June			160 units @ 20	3 200	3 200
	256 units @ 20		256 units @ 20	5 120	8 320
		230 units @ 20	160 units @ 20	3 200	
			26 units @ 20	520	3 720
July – Sept	246 units @ 22		160 units @ 20	3 200	
			26 units @ 20	520	
			246 units @ 22	5 412	9 132
		222 units @ 22	160 units @ 20	3 200	
			26 units @ 20	520	
			24 units @ 22	528	4 248
Oct – Dec	364 units @ 24.20		160 units @ 20	3 200	
			26 units @ 20	520	
			24 units @ 22	528	
			364 units @ 24.20	8 808.80	13 056.80
		342 units @ 24.20	160 units @ 20	3 200	
			26 units @ 20	520	
			24 units @ 22	528	
			22 units @ 24.20	532.40	4 780.40
Jan – March	244 units @ 26.62		160 units @ 20	3 200	
			26 units @ 20	520	
			24 units @ 22	528	
			22 units @ 24.20	532.40	
			244 units @ 26.62	6 495.28	11 275.68
		226 @ 26.62	160 units @ 20	3 200	
			26 units @ 20	520	
			24 units @ 22	528	
			22 units @ 24.20	532.40	
			18 units @ 26.62	479.16	5 259.56

The closing stock is valued at £5 260 (rounded).

(ii) under FIFO:

250 units are valued at the latest prices as follows:
£(244 × 26.62) + (6 × 24.20)
= £6 495.28 + 145.20
= £6 640.48. This rounds to £6 640.

Solutions

(b)

(i)

Trading Account for the year ending 31 March 1999 under LIFO

	£	£
Sales		38 760
Opening stock	3 200.00	
Purchases	25 836.08	
Less closing stock	(5 259.56)	
Cost of sales		23 776.52
Gross profit		£14 983.48

Gross profit = £14 983

(ii)

Trading Account for the year ending 31 March 1999 under FIFO

	£	£
Sales		38 760
Opening stock	3 200.00	
Purchases	25 836.08	
Less closing stock	(6 640 48)	
Cost of sales		22 395.60
Gross profit		£16 364.40

Gross profit = £16 364

(c)

To: Sarah Black

From: Her Accountant

Date:

Subject: Stock Valuation Method

Although using the FIFO method gives a larger profit, the concept of consistency says that a firm should not change methods of valuation unless absolutely necessary. Using FIFO makes this year's profit larger but, other things being equal, it will make next year's profit smaller since this year's closing stock will become next year's opening stock.

Question 16.5

Product X

The manager has not valued each batch individually but has simply compared the totals and chosen the lower of the two. The correct valuation is as follows:

	Cost	Net Realisable Value	Lower of Cost and Net Realisable Value
	£000	£000	£000
Batch 15	50	25	25
Batch 16	60	55	55
Batch 17	90	200	90
Total	200	280	170

The profit is reduced by £30 000 as the value of the closing stock has fallen by £30 000.

Product Y

The manager has not included in the costing the appropriate manufacturing overheads. The correct valuation is:

= 1 000 x (100 + 50 + [300 000 ÷ 10 000])
= 1 000 x (150 + 30)
= 180 000

The profit is increased by £30 000 as the value of the closing stock has increased by this amount.

Product Z

The manager has valued the stock at net realisable value and not at cost. The lower figure of the two should be used, no matter how sure the business is of selling the stock for the expected selling price.

The correct valuation is 1 000 units x 125 = £125 000.

The profit will be reduced by £75 000.

Product ABC

The manager has valued the stock at replacement cost and not at original cost.

The correct valuation is 5 000 units × £18 = £90 000.

The profit will be reduced by £10 000.

Product DEF

The manager has valued the stock at below cost but this is neither necessary nor desirable.

The correct valuation is $360\,000 \times \dfrac{10}{9} = £400\,000$.

The profit will be increased by £40 000.

Chapter 17

Question 17.1

(a)

Driscoll Masters plc
Production Overhead Statement

Cost	Basis	Machining	Assembly	Maint- enance	Canteen
		£	£	£	£
Power	Kilowatt hours	46 500	15 500		
Heating and lighting	Area	7 700	5 600	140	560
Supervisory wages	Number of employees	12 000	36 000	3 000	3 000
Rent and rates	Area	11 550	8 400	210	840
Machinery insurance	Cost of machinery	16 200	540		
Premises insurance	Area	3 850	2 800	70	280
Depreciation	Cost of machinery	40 500	1 350		
Total maintenance				3 420	
Maintenance apportioned		2 223	855	(3 420)	342
Total canteen					5 022
Canteen apportioned		1 255	3 767		(5 022)
Total production depts		141 778	74 812		

The seven overhead costs are apportioned according to appropriate bases as shown. The maintenance department is totalled and this figure is re-allocated to the other three departments in accordance with the percentages given in the question. The same is then done for the canteen but leaving out the maintenance department. The machining and assembly departments are then totalled.

(b) The overhead absorption rate for each production department should be calculated in accordance with machine hours for the machining department and with direct labour hours for the assembly department, since the former is capital intensive and the latter is labour intensive.

Overhead absorption rate for the machining department = £141 778 ÷ 30 000 machine hours = £4.72

Overhead absorption rate for the assembly department = £74 812 ÷ 105 000 labour hours = £0.71

(c) and (d) See text.

Question 17.2

(a)

John Barber
Overhead Allocation and Apportionment Statement

Cost	Basis	Sauna	Squash courts	Gym	Bar	Admin
		£	£	£	£	£
Staffing	Allocation	12 500	12 500	12 500	8 000	15 000
General running costs	Allocation	12 300	18 400	31 300	3 400	11 600
Building depreciation	Area	1 200	3 200	1 600	1 200	800
Equipment depreciation	Customer capacity*	5 882	9 412	4 706		
Total bar					12 600	
Bar re-apportioned	Customer capacity	3 706	5 929	2 965	(12 600)	
Total canteen						27 400
Canteen re-apportioned	Customer capacity	8 059	12 894	6 477		(27 400)
Totals		43 647	62 335	59 548		

*Equipment depreciation would normally be apportioned according to cost but we do not have this information.

(b) Pricing Strategy A: (90 + 50 + 90) customer hours × £4 each per day

= 230 × £4 = £920 per day
£920 × 360 days = £331 200 income per annum

Pricing Strategy B: (80 + 50+ 70) customer hours × £2 each per day
= 200 × £2 = £400 per day
= 400 × 360 days = £144 000 per annum + membership fees
= £144 000 + (1 200 members x £150 annual fee)
= £144 000 + £180 000
= £324 000 income per annum

Pricing Strategy C: 1 000 members × £300 annual fee = £300 000

Pricing strategy A maximises income but John would run less risk by charging an annual fee at the beginning of the year as this income would be sure. Charging on a variable basis means that there is more chance of an income variance – this could be adverse or favourable.

(c) (i) Occupancy rate means at what percentage of capacity his equipment is being used. For example, if on average the equipment is lying idle for 6 hours per day, the occupancy rate is 50%.

(ii) John could improve the occupancy rate by allowing a discount on the hourly rate to customers who use the equipment for a second or a third hour. He could also offer a discount or gift to any members who introduce new members.

(a) To improve demand for the services of the club as a whole, John could:

(i)   advertise in the local press and on local radio;

(ii)   work in cooperation with the local hospital and specialist doctors to offer orthopaedic therapy etc;

(iii)   run promotional evenings with guest sporting celebrities;

(iv)   offer special package deals for fitness clubs etc to use his premises.

Question 17.3

(a) It is first necessary to prepare an Overhead Analysis Sheet.

Item	Basis	Total £	Machine shop A £	Machine shop B £	Assembly £	Canteen £	Maintenance £
Indirect wages	Actual	78 560	8 586	9 190	15 674	29 650	15 460
Consumables	Actual	16 900	6 400	8 700	1 200	600	
Rent and rates	Area	16 700					
Insurance	Area	2 400	5 000	6 000	7 500	3 000	1 000
Heat and light	Area	3 400					
Power	Usage	8 600	4 730	3 440	258		172
Depreciation	Value	40 200	20 100	17 900	2 200		
		166 760	44 816	45 230	26 832	33 250	16 632
Re-apportionment:							
Maintenance	Machine		4 752	11 880			(16 632)
Canteen	Labour hours*		7 600	5 890	19 760	(33 250)	
		166 760	57 168	63 000	46 592	0	0

* Ideally it would be best to use number of employees but in the absence of this
information, direct labour hours seems the best alternative.

We can now calculate the overhead absorption rates for jobs passing through the
production departments. The following methods have been chosen:

Department	Method	Reason
Machine Shop A	Machine hour rate	Capital-intensive
Machine Shop B	Machine hour rate	Capital-intensive
Assembly	Direct labour hour rate	Labour-intensive

Machine shop A: £57 168 ÷ 7 200 = £7.94 per machine hour

Machine shop B: £63 000 ÷ 1 800 = £3.50 per machine hour

Assembly: £46 592 ÷ 20 800 = £2.24 per direct labour hour

(b)

Production Overhead Control Account

	£		£
Overhead expenditure incurred	176 533	Overheads absorbed:	
		Machine A, 7 300 hours @ £7.94	57 962
		Machine B, 18 700 hours @ £3.50	65 450
		Assembly, 21 900 hours @ £2.24	49 056
		Unabsorbed to P & L	4 065
	176 533		176 533

(c) The word 'control' suggests that it is a Total Account and not part of the double-
entry system but representing the aggregate of entries in the cost ledger of overheads
incurred and absorbed. The control account is useful as a checking device. The total of
the individual accounts should be equal to the single entries in the control account. If it
is not, the cost clerk is alerted to errors in the cost ledger.

Control accounts are also used in financial accounting such as the sales ledger
control account for the individual entries in the sales ledger and purchase ledger
control account for the purchase ledger (see Chapter 2).

Question 17.4

(a)

G Locks Ltd
Overhead Allocation and Apportionment Statement

Cost	Basis	Raps	Taps	Baps	Stores	Repairs
		£	£	£	£	£
Indirect labour	Allocation	153 000	190 000	240 100	42 000	68 000
Indirect overheads	Allocation	105 000	80 000	125 000	78 000	92 000
Total stores					120 000	
Stores	Units produced	42 000	30 000	48 000	(120 000)	
Total repairs						160 000
Repairs	Machine hours	40 000	48 000	72 000		(160 000)
Totals		340 000	348 000	485 100	0	0

Overhead absorption rates:

Raps: 340 000 ÷ 40 000 = £8.50

Taps: 348 000 ÷ 60 000 = £5.80

Baps: 485 100 ÷ 45 000 = £10.78

(b) When selecting the labour hour rate, the company must ensure that the time
    booking system is good so that the number used accurately reflects the amount of
    labour time actually spent in production. When selecting the machine hour rate,
    the company must again ensure that the figure for the number of hours is accurate;
    computerised equipment will log its own time but this does not apply to older
    machinery.

(c) Two of: direct wages, number of staff, direct materials.

(d) An unsatisfactory method of overhead absorption will not affect overall profits but
    it will make a difference to the amount of profit or loss calculated on each
    product. This is turn will affect decisions on whether to increase or decrease the
    production of individual products.

Chapter 18

Question 18.1

(a)

T Eddy Printing Ltd
Job Costing Statement for Job 5/207

	£	£
Materials:		
Paper: 30 boxes @ £26 per box less 10% discount	702	
Ink: 12 litres @ £50 per litre less 15% discount	510	
Binders: 200 @ £1.50 each less 10% discount	270	
		1 482
Direct labour:		
Printing department: 120 hours @ £6 per hour	720	
Printing bonus: 50% of (144 – 120) × £6	72	
Colour department: 40 hours @ £6 per hour	240	
Colour bonus: 50% of (50 – 40) × £6	30	
Binding department: 20 hours @ £4 per hour	80	
Binding bonus: 50% of (22 – 20) × £4	4	
		1 146
Prime cost		2 628
Production overheads:		
Printing: 200% of 792	1 584	
Colour: 200% of 270	540	
Binding: £5.40 × 20 hours	108	
		2 232
Total production cost		4 860
Administration overheads: 20% of production cost		972
Total job cost		£5 832

Note that the overheads are absorbed in the Printing and Colour departments on the basis of actual labour costs incurred (i.e. including the bonus) but in the Binding department on the basis of actual time taken (i.e. excluding the bonus).

(b)

If the selling price is based on a 10% net profit margin this means that the net profit made (after all costs) is 10% of the selling price. Since we have only the cost price we have to work it out as follows:

If 5 832 = 90% then what is 100%?

$$100\% = 5\,832 \times \frac{100}{90}$$

= 6 480

We can check that this is correct:
The net profit is £6 480 – 5 832 = £648
This is 10% of £6 480

(c) The answer to this section can be found in the text of Chapter 20.

(d) See text of this chapter.

Question 18.2

(a)

Jetprint Limited
Costing Statement for Batch of 10 000 leaflets

	£	£
Materials:		
Paper: £12.50 × 10 (10 000 ÷ 1 000)	125	
Ink and consumables	40	
		165
Direct labour: 4 hours @ £8 per hour		32
Prime cost		197
Artwork	65	
Machine setting: 4 hours @ £22 per hour	88	
Fixed overheads per hour × 4 hours (W_1)	100	
		253
Total cost of batch		450
Add 30% profit mark-up		135
Selling price of batch of 10 000		£585

Costing Statement for Batch of 20 000 leaflets

	£	£
Materials:		
Paper: £12.50 × 20 (20 000 ÷ 1 000)	250	
Ink and consumables	80	
		330
Direct labour: 8 hours @ £8 per hour		64
Prime cost		394
Artwork	65	
Machine setting: 4 hours @ £22 per hour	88	
Fixed overheads per hour × 8 hours (W_1)	200	
		353
Total cost of batch		747
Add 30% profit mark-up		224
Selling price of batch of 20 000		£971

Workings

W_1

Fixed overheads: £15 000 ÷ 600 labour hours = £25 per labour hour. Notice that, although these costs are fixed, they have been calculated on an hourly basis so the figure must be adjusted for the number of hours worked on each batch.

(b)

Profit and Loss Account for period

	£	£
Sales:		
64 batches of 10 000 @ £585	37 440	
36 batches of 20 000 @ £971	34 956	
		72 396
Less: cost of 64 batches of 10 000 @ £450	28 800	
cost of 36 batches of 20 000 @ £747	26 892	
Cost of sales		(55 692)
Profit		£16 704

(c) The profit margin is $\dfrac{16\,704}{72\,396} \times 100 = 23\%$

This seems to be a good return. Fixed overheads per hour are high but this is probably explained by the fact that the firm has a lot of expensive equipment.

Question 18.3

(a)

Shorter plc
Contract Account

	£		£
Surplus material transferred b/f	6 300	Materials returned to suppliers	3 400
Plant transferred b/f	8 000	Materials on site not yet used c/f	21 600
Materials purchased	726 000	Value of plant c/f ($\mathbf{W_1}$)	34 000
Direct wages	290 000	Cost of work not certified c/f	110 000
Administration expenses charged	103 500	Cost of work certified (balance)	1 174 000
Allocated overheads	65 000		
New plant delivered to site	44 000		
Plant hire	3 100		
Paid to sub-contractors	68 000		
Architects' fees	10 300		
Direct wages accrued c/f	10 200		
Owing to sub-contractors c/f	8 600		
	1 343 000		1 343 000
Cost of work certified b/f	1 174 000	Architect's certificate	1 500 000
Profit and loss – profit taken ($\mathbf{W_2}$)	173 867		
Profit not taken (balance) c/f	152 133		
	1 500 000		1 500 000

1 April 1998		1 April 1998	
Materials b/f	21 600	Wages accrued b/f	10 200
Plant b/f	34 000	Owing to sub-contractors b/f	8 600
Cost of work not certified b/f	110 000	Profit not taken b/f	152 133

Workings

$\mathbf{W_1}$ Depreciation on new plant = £(44 000 – 4000) ÷ 4 = £10 000 per year.
The plant is thus worth £44 000 – £10 000 = £34 000 at the end of the first year.

$\mathbf{W_2}$ Profit taken = Apparent profit $\times \dfrac{2}{3} \times \dfrac{\text{cash received}}{\text{work certified}}$

$\qquad = £(1\,500\,000 - 1\,174\,000) \times \dfrac{2}{3} \times \dfrac{4}{5}$ (20% retention)

$\qquad = £326\,000 \times \dfrac{2}{3} \times \dfrac{4}{5} = £173\,867$

Valuation of year-end Work in Progress

	£
Cost of work certified to date	1 174 000
Cost of work not certified	110 000
Add profit taken to date	173 867
	1 457 867
Less progress payments received (80% of 1 500 000)	(1 200 000)
Work in progress	257 867

(b) See text.

Chapter 19

Question 19.1

(a)

Second Process Account

	Units	Unit price £	Total £		Units	Unit price £	Total £
Balances b/f:							
In WIP b/f							
Direct materials	1 200		10 800	Normal loss	520		
Direct wages			6 840	To finished goods (W₁)	3 200	29.45	94 240
Production overhead			7 200	Completed units not yet	500	29.45	14 725
				transferred c/f			
Finished goods b/f	4 000	7.50	30 000	Closing WIP c/f:			
Second process costs:				Direct materials	980	9.75	9 555
Direct materials			4 830	Direct wages (W₂)			4 655
Direct wages			32 965	Production overhead (W₃)			4 998
Production overhead			35 538				
	5 200		128 173		5 200		128 173

Workings

W₁

	Direct materials	Direct wages	Production overhead
Opening WIP			
10 800 + 30 000 =	40 800	6 840	7 200
Second process costs	4 830	32 965	35 538
Total cost	45 630	39 805	42 738
Completed units	3 700	3 700	3 700
Closing WIP equivalent units *	980	490	490
Total equivalent units	4 680	4 190	4 190
	£45 630	£39 805	£42 738

Unit costs:

Direct materials: £45 630 ÷ 4 680 = £9.75
Direct wages: £39 805 ÷ 4 190 = £9.50
Production overheads: £42 738 ÷ 4 190 = £10.20
Total unit cost = £9.75 + 9.50 + 10.20 = £29.45

*

		Units
WIP units b/f		1 200
Finished units b/f		4 000
Total units in process		5 200
Normal loss	(520)	
Completed units transferred	(3 200)	
Not yet transferred	(500)	
Total units accounted for		(4 220)
Balance (= unfinished units)		980

W_2 Direct wages   490 units × £9.50 = £4 655

W_3 Production overhead   490 units × £10.20 = £4 998

(b)

Statement of Cost of Second Process

(i)

	£
Direct materials	9.75
Direct wages	9.50
Production overhead	10.20
Total	29.45

(ii) Cost of production transferred to finished goods
    3 200 units × £29.45   = £94 240

(iii) Cost of production awaiting transfer
    500 units × £29.45   = £14 725

(iv) Cost of closing work in progress:

Direct materials	980 units × £9.75	= £9 555
Direct wages	490 units × £9.50	= £4 655
Production overhead	490 units × £10.20	= £4 998
Total		£19 208

Question 19.2

(a)

Process Account

	Kg	Unit price £	£		Kg	Unit price £	£
Materials	16 000	1.60	25 600	Normal loss	2 400	0.40	960
Labour			4 800	Output	14 000	2.50	35 000
Overheads			4 560				
Abnormal gain	400	2.50	1 000				
			35 960				35 960

Unit cost = Total costs ÷ number of units of output
Total costs = £25 600 + 4 800 + 4 560 = £34 960
£34 960 ÷ 14 000 = £2.50 per unit

(b) See text.

Question 19.3
Frameit plc
(a)

Heating Process Account

	Kg	Unit price £	£		Kg	Uni price £	£
Material X	1 250	9.72	12 150	Normal loss	50		0
Direct labour			16 250	Moulding process	1 000		32 000
Overheads			10 000	Stock	210		6 720
Abnormal gain	10	32	320				
			38 720				38 720

Unit price: Total cost ÷ normal production
Total cost = £12 150 + 16 250 + 10 000 = £38 400
Normal production = 1 250 kg introduced – normal loss of 4%
i.e. 1 250 – 50 kg = £1 200 kg
Unit price = £38 400 ÷ 1 200 = £32

We shall not include an amount for the normal loss since the 4% is taken into account when calculating the unit price of £32.

(b)

Moulding Process Account

	Kg	Unit price £	£		Kg	Unit price £	£
Heating process	1 000	32	32 000	Normal loss	75	4	300
Material Y	500	26.90	13 450	Abnormal loss	50	38	1 900
Labour			3 000	Good output	1 375	38	52 250
Overheads			6 000				
			54 450				54 450

Unit price: Total cost ÷ normal production
Total cost = £32 000 + 13 450 + 3 000 + 6 000 – 300 = £54 150
Normal production = 1 500 kg introduced – normal loss of 5%
i.e. 1 500 – 75 kg = 1 425 kg
Unit price = £54 150 ÷ 1 425 = £38

(c)

Abnormal Gain Account

	Kg	Unit price £	£		Kg	Unit price £	£
Profit and loss			320	Heating	10	32	320

(d)

Abnormal Loss Account

	Kg	Unit price £	£		Kg	Unit price £	£
Moulding	50	38	1 900	Bank	50	4	200
				Profit and loss			1 700
			1 900				1 900

Chapter 20

Question 20.1

(a)

	1998	1999
Opening stock (units)	450	300
Production (in units)	8 000	7 000
Less closing stock (in units)	(300)	(600)
Number of units sold	8 150	6 700
Total sales value (number of units × £72)	586 800	482 400

(b)

	Cost per unit
	£
Direct materials	22
Direct labour	4
Variable overheads	14
Total variable cost	40

1998: 8 000 units × total variable cost of £40 = total variable costs of £320 000

1999: 7 000 units × total variable cost of £40 = total variable costs of £280 000

(c)

(i)   Fixed overhead absorption rate $= \dfrac{\text{Fixed costs of production}}{\text{Normal level of activity}}$

$= \dfrac{£90\,000}{7\,500 \text{ units}}$

$= £12$

(ii)   Total fixed overheads charged to production:
1998: 8 000 units × £12 = £96 000
1999: 7 000 units × £12 = £84 000

(iii)   1998: (8 000 units – 7 500 units) × £12
= 500 × £12 = £6 000 over-absorption
1999: (7 000 units – 7 500 units) × £12
= – 500 × 12 = – £6 000 under-absorption

(d)

(i)   Marginal costing:
Multiply by total variable costs per unit (£22 + £4 + £14) = £40
1998: Opening stock = 450 units × £40 = £18 000
1998: Closing stock = 300 units × £40 = £12 000
1999: Opening stock = 300 units × £40 = £12 000
1999: Closing stock = 600 units × £40 = £24 000

(ii)   Absorption costing:
        Multiply by total costs per unit (£40 + £12 absorption rate) = £52
        1998: Opening stock = 450 units × £52 = £23 400
        1998: Closing stock = 300 units × £52 = £15 600
        1999: Opening stock = 300 units × £52 = £15 600
        1999: Closing stock = 600 units × £52 = £31 200

(e)

	£	£	£	£
(i) Marginal costing				
Sales		586 800		482 400
Opening stock	18 000		12 000	
Variable costs	320 000		280 000	
Less closing stock	(12 000)		(24 000)	
		(326 000)		(268 000)
Contribution		260 800		214 400
Fixed costs		(90 000)		(90 000)
Profit		£170 800		£124 400
(ii) Absorption costing				
Sales		586 800		482 400
Opening stock	23 400		15 600	
Variable costs	320 000		280 000	
Fixed costs	96 000		84 000	
Less closing stock	(15 600)		(31 200)	
		(423 800)		(348 400)
		163 000		134 000
Adjustment for over/under absorption		6 000		(6 000)
Profit		£169 000		£128 000

Question 20.2

(a)

Monteplana Ltd
Income Statement for the year ended 31 December 1994 under Absorption Costing

	£	£
Sales (130 000 × £3)		390 000
Less		
Direct materials	130 000	
Direct labour	52 000	
Variable factory overhead	13 000	
Fixed factory overhead	100 000	
	295 000	
Less closing stock (W₁)	(103 250)	
Cost of goods sold		(191 750)
Gross profit		198 250
Selling and distribution expenses	70 000	
Administration expenses	30 000	
		(100 000)
Net profit		£98 250

$$\mathbf{W}_1 \text{ Unit production cost} = \frac{£295}{200} = £1.475$$

Value of closing stock = 70 000 units @ £1.475
= £103 250

(b)

Monteplana Ltd

Income Statement for the year ended 31 December 1994 under Variable Costing

	£	£
Sales		390 000
Less		
Direct materials	130 000	
Direct labour	52 000	
Variable factory overhead	13 000	
	195 000	
Less closing stock ($\mathbf{W}_2$)	(68 250)	
Total variable cost		(126 750)
Contribution		263 250
Fixed factory overhead	100 000	
Selling and distribution expenses	70 000	
Administration expenses	30 000	
		(200 000)
Net profit		£63 250

$$\mathbf{W}_2 \text{ Unit production cost} = \frac{£195}{200} = £0.975$$

Value of closing stock = 70 000 units @ £0.975
= £68 250

Question 20.3

Duo Limited

(a)

Profit and Loss Accounts for Period 1 using marginal costing

	Alpha		Beta	
	£	£	£	£
Sales		207 000		120 000
Opening stock				
Direct materials	34 500		19 200	
Direct labour	41 400		19 200	
Variable overheads	27 600		12 800	
Less closing stock	(9 000)		(4 500)	
		(94 500)		(46 700)
Contribution		112 500		73 300
Fixed costs		(75 000)		(35 000)
Profit		£37 500		£38 300

Profit and Loss Accounts for Period 2 using marginal costing

	Alpha		Beta	
	£	£	£	£
Sales		171 000		93 750
Opening stock	9 000		4 500	
Direct materials	28 500		15 000	
Direct labour	34 200		15 000	
Variable overheads	22 800		10 000	
Less closing stock	(18 000)		(4 500)	
		(76 500)		(40 000)
Contribution		94 500		53 750
Fixed costs		(57 000)		(25 000)
Profit		£37 500		£28 750

(b)

Profit and Loss Accounts for Period 1 using absorption costing

	Alpha		Beta	
	£	£	£	£
Sales		207 000		120 000
Opening stock				
Direct materials	34 500		19 200	
Direct labour	41 400		19 200	
Variable overheads	27 600		12 800	
Fixed costs	75 000		35 000	
Less closing stock	(15 000)		(7 500)	
		(163 500)		(78 700)
Profit		£43 500		£41 300

Profit and Loss Accounts for Period 2 using absorption costing

	Alpha		Beta	
	£	£	£	£
Sales		171 000		93 750
Opening stock	15 000		7 500	
Direct materials	28 500		15 000	
Direct labour	34 200		15 000	
Variable overheads	22 800		10 000	
Fixed costs	57 000		25 000	
Less closing stock	(30 000)		(7 500)	
		(127 500)		(65 000)
Profit		£43 500		£28 750

Workings for Period 1:

Sales:
Alpha = 2 300 units × £90 = £207 000
Beta = 1 600 units × £75 = £120 000

Direct materials:
Alpha = 2 300 units × £15 = £34 500
Beta = 1 600 units × £12 = £19 200

Direct labour:
Alpha = 2 300 units × £18 = £41 400
Beta   = 1 600 units × £12 = £19 200

Variable production overheads:
Alpha = 2 300 units × £12 = £27 600
Beta   = 1 600 units × £8 = £12 800

Closing stock under marginal cost: multiply by total variable cost per unit.
Alpha: Units produced – units sold
= 2 500 – 2 300 = 200 units
 200 × (15 + 18 + 12) = 200 × 45 = 9 000

Beta: = 1 750 – 1 600 = 150 units
150 × (12 + 12 + 8)
= 150 × 30 = 4 500

Closing stock under absorption cost: multiply by total variable cost per unit + fixed
cost recovery rate per hour per unit.
Alpha: 200 units × variable cost per unit + (£10 per labour hour × 3 labour hours)
= 200 × (45 + 30)
= 200 × 75 = 15 000
Beta: 150 units × variable cost per unit + (£10 per labour hour × 2 labour hours)
= 150 × (30 + 20)
= 150 × 50 = £7 500

Fixed costs are recovered on direct labour hours
Alpha: £18 direct labour cost per unit ÷ £6 per hour = 3 labour hours
Beta: £12 direct labour cost per unit ÷ £6 per hour = 2 labour hours

Total labour hours:
Alpha: 3 hours × 2 500 units = 7 500 hours
Beta: 2 hours × 1 750 units = 3 500 hours
i.e. a total of 11 000 labour hours
Recovery rate per hour = £110 000 total fixed cost ÷ 11 000 labour hours
= £10 per labour hour

Alpha: 7 500 hours × £10 = £75 000 fixed cost
Beta: 3 500 hours × £10 = £35 000 fixed cost

Workings for Period 2:

Sales:
Alpha = 1 900 units × £90 = £171 000
Beta   = 1 250 units × £75 = £93 750

Opening stock is the closing stock from Period 1.

Direct materials:
Alpha = 1 900 units × £15 = £28 500
Beta   = 1 250 units × £12 = £15 000

Direct labour:
Alpha = 1 900 units × £18 = £34 200
Beta   = 1 250 units × £12 = £15 000

Variable production overheads:
Alpha = 1 900 units × £12 = £22 800
Beta   = 1 250 units × £8 = £10 000

Closing stock valued under marginal cost:
Alpha: Opening stock + units produced − units sold
= 200 + 1 900 − 1 700 = 400 units
400 × (15 + 18 + 12) = 400 × 45 = 18 000

Beta: = 150 + 1 250 − 1 250 = 150 units
150 × (12 +12 + 8)
= 150 × (30) = 4 500

Closing stock valued under absorption cost:
Alpha: 400 units × 75 = 30 000
Beta: 150 units × 50 =   7 500

Fixed costs are recovered on the same basis as in Period 1.

Alpha: 3 hours × 1 900 units = 5 700 hours
Beta: 2 hours × 1 250 units = 2 500 hours
i.e. a total of 8 200 labour hours
Recovery rate per hour = £82 000 total fixed cost ÷ 8 200 labour hours
= £10 per labour hour

Alpha: 5 700 hours × £10 = £57 000 fixed cost
Beta: 2 500 hours × £10 = £25 000 fixed cost

Chapter 21

Question 21.1

(a)

Bell Manufacturing Ltd

Profit and Loss Accounts for the year ended 31 March 1998

	Product X		*Product Y*		*Product Z*	
	£	£	£	£	£	£
Sales		90 000		130 000		200 000
Direct materials	60 000		80 000		100 000	
Direct labour	20 000		22 000		25 000	
Variable overheads	12 000		16 000		20 000	
		(92 000)		(118 000)		(145 000)
Contribution		(2 000)		12 000		55 000
Fixed costs		(20 000)		(20 000)		(20 000)
Profit / loss		£(22 000)		£(8 000)		£35 000

Total profit for the year = £(22 000) + (8 000) + 35 000 = £5 000

(b)

	Product Y		*Product Z*	
	£	£	£	£
Sales		130 000		200 000
Direct materials	80 000		100 000	
Direct labour	22 000		25 000	
Variable overheads	16 000		20 000	
		(118 000)		(145 000)
Contribution		12 000		55 000
Fixed costs		(30 000)		(30 000)
Profit / loss		£(18 000)		£25 000

Discontinuing Product X would lead to an increased overall profit of:
£(18 000) + 25 000 = £7 000

	Product Z	
	£	£
Sales		200 000
Direct materials	100 000	
Direct labour	25 000	
Variable overheads	20 000	
		(145 000)
Contribution		55 000
Fixed costs		(60 000)
Profit / loss		£(5 000)

Discontinuing both Product X and Product Y would lead to an overall loss on
Product Z alone of £5 000.

(c)

The company should concentrate on both products which have a positive contribution. Even though a loss is made on Product Y, it does make a contribution to the fixed costs. Product Z on its own cannot absorb all the fixed costs and still make a profit.

Another suggestion is to concentrate only on Product Z but to reduce the fixed costs. Having only one product to manufacture might mean that the firm could manage with a smaller premises and less machinery.

Question 21.2

(a)

Eagle Ltd
Trading and Profit and Loss Account for Proposal 1

	£000	£000	£000
Product X			
Sales (80% of 650)		520	
Cost of sales (80% of 520)		(416)	
Profit on X			104
Product Y			
Sales (80% of 480)		384	
Cost of sales:			
Hire of machinery	24		
Variable costs	240		
Profit on Y		(264)	120
			224
Less general administration expenses			(108)
Overall net profit			£116

(b)

Eagle Ltd
Trading and Profit and Loss Account for Proposal 2

	£000	£000	£000
Product X			
Sales (unchanged from 1997)		650	
Cost of sales (unchanged from 1997)		(520)	
Profit on X			130
Product Y			
Sales (unchanged from 1997)		480	
Cost of sales:			
Hire of machinery	29		
Rent on premises	48		
Variable costs	360		
		(437)	
Profit on Y			43
			173
Less general administration expenses			126
Overall net profit			£47

(c)

An extra £1 000 of sales on an original £480 000 will involve only an increase in the variable costs (all other costs are fixed).

i.e. £360 000 + (1/480th of £360 000)

= £750

The contribution is 25%.

i.e. there will be an extra profit of £1 000 – 750 = £250

(d)

The existing system gives an overall profit of £82 000

Proposal 1 gives an overall profit of £116 000

Proposal 2 gives an overall profit of £47 000

Proposal 1 gives the biggest profit but sales of Y would be lost and the supplier can enter the market.

Proposal 2 gives the firm the capacity to produce 50% more of Y.

This would give 50% extra sales i.e. £240 000 which gives an additional contribution of £60 000 (25%) and an overall profit of £107 000. This is still not as good as the profit from Proposal 1.

Continuing with the existing system gives a medium-level profit and is less risky as it does not involve any investment in fixed assets.

Question 21.3

(a)

Twister Ltd

Revised Forecast Profit

	Depts A + C £000	A under Plan 2 £000	A under Plan 3 £000
Sales	4000	1 080	1 200
Cost of goods sold (variable cost)	2 050	720	600
Gross profit	1 950	360	600
Direct departmental costs	700	190	190
	1 250	170	410
Administration costs (all fixed)	640	320	320
Net profit (loss)	£610	£(150)	£90

Course of action 1:

Existing profit from all three departments – contribution previously made by Department A

i.e. £500 – 210 = £290

Course of action 2:

Sales = £1000 × 9/10 x 120%

= £1 080

Cost of goods sold = £600 × 120%

= £720

Total profit = £(150) from A, £130 from B and £480 from C = £460

Course of action 3:
The margin is the same as in Dept B i.e. 50% so cost of sales = £600
Total profit = £90 + 130 + 480 = £700

(b)

	Original forecast	Course of action 2	Course of action 3
	%	%	%
Gross profit %	40 (400 / 1000 × 100)	33.3 (360 / 1 080 × 100)	50 (600 / 1 200 × 100)
Net profit %	−11% (−110 / 1000 × 100)	− 4% (−150 / 1 080 × 100)	× 100)

(a) This should be in report form and should make the following points:

Course of action 1 appears to cut a loss, but closing Department A results in a fall in overall profit since the positive contribution of £210 000 previously made by Department A is now lost.

Course of action 2 results in an increased sales volume but it reduces the margin. The result is a greater loss.

Course of action 3 results in increased sales and an improved margin and is the best plan to choose.

Chapter 22

Question 22.1

(a)

W Ltd
Flexible Marketing Budget for 1997

	£	£	£
Sales levels (£m)	9	10	11.5
Fixed costs			
Salaries – sales representatives	200 000	200 000	200 000
– sales office	60 000	60 000	60 000
Salary-related costs	32 000	32 000	32 000
Rent	100 000	100 000	100 000
Depreciation of furniture	5 000	5 000	5 000
Depreciation of cars	67 000	67 000	67 000
Insurance	20 000	20 000	20 000
Advertising	250 000	250 000	250 000
Telephone rentals	2 000	2 000	2 000
Sales representatives' car expenses	7 000	7 000	7 000
Sales promotions (W_1)	300 000	300 000	300 000
	1 043 000	1 043 000	1 043 000
Variable costs			
Sales representatives' commission	57 600	64 000	73 600
Salary-related costs	7 200	8 000	9 200
Sales representatives' ordinary expenses	22 500	25 000	28 750
Bad debts	90 000	100 000	115 000
Stationery and postage	45 000	50 000	57 500
Agency fees	72 000	80 000	92 000
Telephone, metered calls	12 600	14 000	16 100
Sales representatives' car expenses	43 200	48 000	55 200
Sales promotions (W_2)	180 000	200 000	230 000
	530 100	589 000	677 350
Total marketing budget (fixed + variable)	1 573 100	1 632 000	1 720 350

Workings

W_1

To find the fixed element in the sale promotions costs:

At a sales level of £8.9m

	£000
Total cost	478
of which the variable element is 8.9×20	(178)
Fixed element is therefore	300

Check:

Sales level	£3.4m	£7.5m
	£000	£000
Total cost	368	450
Variable element	$3.4 \times 20 = 68$	$7.5 \times 20 = 150$
Fixed	300	300

W$_2$

Sales promotion: We can find the variable element of this semi-variable cost by noting the change in the cost as the activity level changes. As sales fall from the maximum of £8.9m to the minimum of £3.4m, cost falls from £478 000 to £368 000.

The variable element therefore = $\dfrac{£478\ 000 - 368\ 000}{£8.9\ -\ 3.4}$

$=\ \dfrac{£110\ 000}{£5.5}\ = £20\ 000$ per £1m of sales

From this we can work out the variable element of this cost at the different activity levels.

Sales	Variable element
£m	£000
9	180
10	200
11.5	230

(b) At a sales level of £10.75 million:

	£
Fixed cost	1 043 000
* Variable cost : $\dfrac{589\ 000 \times 10.75}{10}$	633 175
Total marketing cost allowance	1 676 175

* or $\dfrac{677\ 350 \times 10.75}{11.5}$

Question 22.2

(a)

Hilda Cannon

Cash Budget for the three months ending 31 August 1999

	June	July	August
	£	£	£
Receipts			
Receipts from credit sales	10 400	10 000	12 000
Receipts from cash sales (20%)	2 500	3 000	3 300
Total receipts	12 900	13 000	15 300
Expenditure			
Purchases	6 560	6 300	7 570
Rent	6 000		
Expenses	1 800	1 800	1 800
Purchase of van		7 700	
Drawings	1 200	1 200	1 200
Total expenditure	15 560	17 000	10 570
Opening bank balance	700	(1 960)	(5 960)
Add receipts	12 900	13 000	15 300
Less expenditure	(15 560)	(17 000)	(10 570)
Closing bank balance	£(1 960)	£(5 960)	£(1 230)

(b)

Forecast trading and profit and loss account for the three months ending 31 August 1999

	£	£
Sales		44 000
Opening stock	4 700	
Purchases	22 170	
Less closing stock	(5 010)	
Cost of sales		(21 860)
Gross profit		22 140
Rent	3000	
Expenses	5 400	
Depreciation on van [1/6 of (14 700 × 20%)]	490	
Depreciation on fixtures (1/4 of 26 000 × 10%)	650	
		(9 540)
Net profit		£12 600

(c)

Forecast balance sheet as at 31 August 1999

	£	£	£
Fixed assets			
Fixtures and fittings at cost	26 000		
Less accumulated depreciation	(11 050)		
		14 950	
Van at cost	14 700		
Less depreciation	(490)		
		14 210	
			29 160
Current assets			
Stock	5 010		
Debtors (80% of 16 500)	13 200		
Rent prepaid	3 000		
		21 210	
Current liabilities			
Creditors	8 300		
Garage	7 000		
Bank	1 230		
		(16 530)	
Working capital			4 680
Net assets			£33 840
Capital		24 840	
Net profit		12 600	
Less drawings		(3 600)	
			£33 840

The question asked only for the current assets and current liabilities but the whole balance sheet has been done here to check the accuracy of the calculations. In an examination, never do something you have not been asked for as you will gain no more marks and will waste valuable time.

(a) See text in Chapter 12.

(b) Three reasons why Hilda's forecast profit is £12 600 but her forecast bank balance is an overdraft of £1 230:

   (i) She has paid £3 000 rent in advance.

   (ii) She has paid the first instalment of £7 700 on the van in cash.

   (iii) Her debtors are considerably larger than her creditors.

(c) See text in this chapter.

Question 22.3

(a) (i)

Riley Ltd

Production Budget for Periods 1 – 5

	1	2	3	4	5
	£	£	£	£	£
Sales	3 100	3 300	3 600	3 800	3 300
Less opening stock (W_1)	(620)	(660)	(720)	(760)	(660)
Add closing stock (W_1)	660	720	760	660	640
Units to be produced	3 140	3 360	3 640	3 700	3 280

Workings

W_1

Stock at the end of each period must be 20% of the budgeted sales for the next period i.e. closing stock for period 1 is 20% of £3 300 (budgeted sales for period 2) etc

(ii)

Production capacity = 88 units × 2 machines × 5 days × 4 weeks = 3 520 units per period

A shortfall happens in periods 3 and 4:

Period 3: 3 640 budgeted units – 3 520 capacity = 120 units
Period 4: 3 700 budgeted units – 3 520 capacity = 180 units
This makes a total of 300 units.

(b)

Production Budget for Periods 1 – 5 using Option 1

	1	2	3	4	5
	£	£	£	£	£
Sales	3 100	3 300	3 600	3 800	3 300
Less opening stock	(620)	(800)	(1 020)	(940)	(660)
Add closing stock	800	1 020	940	660	640
Units to be produced	3 280	3 520	3 520	3 520	3 280
Stockpile	140	160			

(c)

Budgeted trading accounts for Options 1 and 2 for periods 1 – 5 inclusive

	Option 1		Option 2	
	£	£	£	£
Sales (17 100 units × £14)		239 400		239 400
Opening stock (620 units × £8)	4 960		4 960	
Manufacturing cost:				
Option 1: (17 120 units × £8)	136 960			
Option 2: (16 820 units* × £8)			134 560	
Buying in (300 units × £13)			3 900	
Less closing stock (640 units × £8)	(5 120)		(5 120)	
Cost of sales		(136 800)		(138 300)
Gross profit		£102 600		£101 100

* 17 120 units – the shortfall

(d) (i)

The report should recommend option 1 as it gives a greater profit and does not include the risk of reliance on an outside supplier for supplies. However it will have the disadvantages of greater storage costs and the possibility of a breakdown in the machinery.

(ii) Alternative courses of action could be:

introducing weekend working or overtime hours during the week in order to produce the shortfall, but this will involve paying overtime labour rates and extra factory overheads.

purchase a third machine as long as there is enough space and labour. Financing might be a problem, especially if interest rates are high.

Question 22.4

(a) See text

(b) (i)

Projected sales:
July: 20 000 units
August: 20 000 units + 6% = 21 200 units
September: 21 200 units + 6% = 22 472 units

Required production over three-month period:
Closing stock + July sales + August sales + September sales – opening stock
= 10 000 units + 20 000 units + 21 200 units + 22 472 units – 8 344 units
= 65 328 units in total to be split evenly over three months
= 65 328 ÷ 3 = 21 776 units per month.

Budget for Stocks of Finished Goods

	July	August	September
	Units	Units	Units
Opening stock	8 344	10 120	10 696
Production	21 776	21 776	21 776
Less sales	(20 000)	(21 200)	(22 472)
Closing stock	10 120	10 696	10 000

(ii)

Material cost per unit = £25 ÷ 2 = £12.50

The materials are purchased in the first month, used in the second month and paid for in the third or fourth month, depending on the credit arrangement. This can be tricky so it is a good idea to incorporate the time sequence into the table.

Budget for Creditors

	July £	*August* £	*September* £
Purchased in May, used in June (41 600 units x £12.50) paid for in July	520 000		
Purchased in June, used in July (21 776 units x £12.50) and split evenly between July and August	136 100	136 100	
Purchased in July, used in August (21 776 x £12.50) and split between August and September 80:20		217 760	54 440
Purchased in August, used in September (21 776 x £12.50) and paid for in September			272 200
Total creditors	656 100	353 860	326 640

(ii)

Budget for Debtors

	July £	*August* £	*September* £
June: credit sales (80% of [20 000 x 30])	480 000		
July: cash (20% of [20 000 x 30])	120 000		
July: credit (80% of [20 000 x 30])		480 000	
August: cash (20% of [21 200 x 30])		127 200	
August: credit (80% of [21 200 x 30])			508 800
September: cash (20% of [22 472 x 30])			134 832
Total debtors	600 000	607 200	643 632

Question 22.5

See text

Question 22.6

See text

Chapter 23

Question 23.1
Sun plc
Variance Report for May

To: Mr Ray

Calculation of variances

Material variances:

	£
Standard price 241 000 kilos × £0.18	43 380
Actual price	43 300
Price variance	80 F

Price variance:

Standard usage = 4 800 units × 50 kilos
       = 240 000 units

Usage variance = (standard quantity – actual quantity) × standard price
      = (240 000 – 241 000) × £0.18 = (180) A

Labour variances

	£
Standard cost for actual time 3 400 hours × £1.60	5 440
Actual cost	5 500
Rate variance	(60) A

Rate variance

Standard time = 4 800 Beams × 45/60 = 3 600 hours

Efficiency variance = (standard time – actual time) × standard rate
        = (3 600 – 3 400) × £1.60 = 320 F

Fixed overhead variances

	£
Budgeted 5 000 units × £0.80	4 000
Actual	4 140
Expenditure variance	(140) A

	£
Budgeted	4 000
Standard cost absorbed 4 800 units × £0.80	3 840
Volume variance	(160) A

For causes of variances, see text.

Question 23.2

Dash Ltd

(a)

(i) Material price variances:
   (Standard price – actual price) × actual quantity
   Ammonia: $(1.10 - 0.9) \times 240 = 48.00$ F
   Colouring: $(0.1 - 0.09) \times 950 = 9.50$ F
   Fragrance: $(14.20 - 15) \times 11 = (8.80)$ A

(ii) Material usage variances:
   (Standard quantity – actual quantity) × standard price
   Ammonia: $(200 - 240) \times 1.10 = (44.00)$ A
   Colouring: $(1\,000 - 950) \times 0.10 = 5.00$ F
   Fragrance: $(10 - 11) \times 14.20 = (14.20)$ A

(iii) Total direct material cost variance:
   (standard units × standard price) – (actual units × actual price)
   $[(200 \times 1.10) + (1\,000 \times 0.10) + (10 \times 14.20)] - [(240 \times 0.90) + (950 \times 0.09) + (11 \times 15)]$

   $= (220 + 100 + 142) - (216 + 85.50 + 165)$

   $= 462 - 466.50$

   $= (4.50)$ A

Check that the results of the sub-variances equal the overall materials variance:

48.00 F + 9.50 F – 8.80 A – 44.00 A + 5.00 F – 14.20 A = (4.50) A

(iv) Labour rate variance:
   (standard rate – actual rate) × actual hours
   Blending: $(12 - 13) \times 11 = (11)$ A
   Mixing: $(8 - 9) \times 10 = (10)$ A

(v) Labour efficiency variance:
   (standard hours – actual hours) × standard rate
   $(8 - 11) \times 12 = (36)$ A
   $(12 - 10) \times 8 = (16)$ F

(vi) Total direct labour cost variance:
   (standard hours × standard rate) – (actual hours × actual rate)
   $[(8 \times 12) + (12 \times 8)] - [(11 \times 13) + (10 \times 9)]$
   $(96 \times 96) - (143 \times 90)$
   $192 - 233$
   (41) A

Check that the results of the sub-variances equal the overall labour variance:
–11 A – 10 A – 36 A + 16 F = (41) A

(b) and (c) See text.

Question 23.3

(a) See text in Chapter 15.

(b)

Standard Cost Card

	£	£
Materials Cost Centre A:		
3 kilos × £5 per kilo	15	
Materials Cost Centre B:		
1 kilo × £6 per kilo	6	
Total material cost		21
Labour Cost Centre A:		
1.5 hours × £3	4.50	
1.75 hours × £4	7.00	
Total labour cost		11.50
Overheads		
Cost Centre A: 40 000 ÷ 50 000	0.80	
Cost Centre B: 60 000 ÷ 50 000	1.20	
Total overheads		2.00
Total standard cost		£34.50

(c) Variances:

(i) Material Price Variance for Cost Centre A:
(standard price – actual price) × actual quantity
$(5 - 4.51935) \times 15\,500 = 7\,450$ F

Material Price Variance for Cost Centre B:
$(6 - 5.9) \times 5\,100 = 510$ F

(ii) Material Usage Variance for Cost Centre A:
(standard quantity – actual quantity) × standard price
$(3 - 3.1) \times 5 \times 5\,000 = (2\,500)$ A

Material Usage Variance for Cost Centre B:
$(1 - 1.02) \times 6 \times 5\,000 = (600)$ A

Check with the overall materials variance:
(standard units × standard price) – (actual units × actual price)
Cost Centre A = $[(3 \times 5) \times 5\,000] - 70\,050 = 4\,950$ F
Cost Centre B = $[(1 \times 6) \times 5\,000] - 30\,090 = (90)$ A
$4\,950$ F + (90) A = $4\,860$ F

$7\,450$ F + 510 F + $(2\,500)$ A + (600) A = $4\,860$ F

(iii) Labour Efficiency Variance Cost Centre A:
(standard hours – actual hours) x standard rate
$= (1.5 - 1.44) \times 3 \times 5\,000 = 900$ F

Labour Efficiency Variance Cost Centre B:
$= (1.75 - 1.76) \times 4 \times 5\,000 = (200)$ A

(iv) Labour Rate Variance Cost Centre A:
   (standard rate – actual rate) × actual hours
   = (3 – 3.15) × 7 200 = (1 080) A

   Labour Rate Variance Cost Centre B:
   = (4 – 3.8) × 8 800 = 1 760 F

Check with overall labour variance:
(standard quantity × standard rate) – (actual quantity × actual rate)
Cost Centre A = [(1.5 x 3) × 5000] – 22 680 = (180) A
Cost Centre B = [1.75 x 4) × 5000] – 33 440 = 1 560 F
(180) A + 1 560 F = 1 380 F

900 F + (200) A + (1 080) A + 1 760 F = 1 380 F

Question 23.4

(a) (i)

Sales variance = (2 000 × 20) – (1 800 × 22)
= 40 000 – 39 600
= £(400) adverse

This is broken down into:

Price variance = 1 800 (20 – 22)
= £3 600 favourable

Volume variance = 20 (2 000 – 1 800)
= £4 000 adverse

(ii)
Materials variance = (1 800 × 2) – (3 718)
= £(118) adverse

This is broken down into:

Price variance = 880 (4 – 4.225)
= £(198) adverse

Usage variance = 4 (900 – 880)
= £80 favourable

(iii)
Labour variance = (1 800 × 12) – 23 985
= 21 600 – 23 985
= £(2 385) adverse

This is broken down into:

Labour rate variance = 3 900 (6 – 6.15)
= £(585) adverse

Efficiency variance = 6 (3 600 – 3 900)
= £(1 800) adverse

(b)

Statement Reconciling Budged Profit to Actual Profit for May 1998

	£
Standard profit (2 000 x £6)	12 000
Less profit on actual sales at standard price	(1 200)
	10 800
+ Favourable selling price variance (1 800 x £2)	3 600
– Adverse materials variance	(118)
– Adverse labour variance	(2 385)
Actual profit	£11 897

(c)

Actual contribution per unit:

	£
Selling price per unit	22.00
Material cost per unit (3 718 ÷ 1 800)	(2.066)
Labour cost per unit (23 985 ÷ 1 800)	(13.325)
Contribution per unit	£6.609

(d) The report should be in report format.

    (i) The adverse sales variance means that the price was higher and less units were sold (the overall effect will depend on the elasticity of demand for the product). The materials variance was adverse, which means that more was paid for them but less material was used as perhaps it was of a better quality and there was less wastage. The labour variance is adverse, meaning that the workers were paid more and needed more time to produce a unit.

    (ii) Actual profit is less than the budget – this was due to labour inefficiencies. Labour could be paid more to attract more skilled people whose productivity will be higher. Alternatively machines could be substituted for labour. As far as materials are concerned, the firm should find a cheaper supplier but should not buy inferior quality. The selling price of the product could also be reduced to attract a larger market, although this will depend on the price elasticity of demand (availability of substitutes etc).

Chapter 24

Question 24.1

(a)

(i) Contribution = Selling price – variable cost
     Selling price = £1 450/20 = £72.50 per unit
     Variable cost = £500 + 300 + 150 = £950
     Variable cost per unit = £950 / 20 = £47.50
     Contribution = £72.50 – 47.50 = £25

(ii)

	£000	£000
Sales		1 450
Less		
Direct labour (£25 per unit)	500	
Direct material	300	
Variable production overheads (£7.50 per unit)	150	
Fixed overheads	300	
		(1 250)
Profit		£200

(iii) Break-even point in units = Fixed costs / Contribution
      = 300 000 / 25 = 12 000 units

Break-even point in sales value = 12 000 units × selling price of £72.50
= £870 000

(b) Total profit Option 1

	£000	£000
Sales		1 450
Less		
Direct labour (£20 per unit)	400	
Direct material	300	
Variable production overheads (£6 per unit)	120	
Fixed overheads	350	
		(1 170)
Profit		£280

Total profit Option 2

	£000	£000
Sales (23 000 units × £80.50 per unit)		1 851.50
Less		
Direct labour (£25 per unit)	500	
Direct material	300	
Variable production overheads (£7.50 per unit)	150	
Fixed overheads (including advertising)	400	
Sales commission (23 000 × £4)	92	
		(1 442)
Profit		£409.50

Total profit Option 3

	£000	£000
Sales (20 000 units × £87.50 per unit)		1 750
Less		
Direct labour [500 + (25% of 500)]	625	
Direct material [300 + (25% of 300)]	375	
Variable production overheads (£7.50 per unit)	150	
Fixed overheads	300	
		(1 450)
Profit		£300

(c) Break-even point for option 3 = 300 000 ÷ [87.50 − (31.25 + 18.75 + 7.50)]
   = 300 000 ÷ 30 = 10 000 units
   In sales value this is 10 000 × £87.50 = £875 000

   The margin of safety = Sales beyond the break-even point / break-even units
   = (20 000 − 10 000) / 10 000
   = 10 000 / 10 000 = 100% i.e. the firm is selling twice its break-even level.

   In sales value this is equal to £875 000.

(d) See text.

(e) If Lonard plc undertakes option (iii), workers will have to be trained in more efficient techniques. Although there will be no extra production, more time will be spent making each unit and there may be the chance of overtime work for the employees.

Question 24.2

(a) This statement is untrue since there can be changes in costs and revenues at all levels of output. Changes in selling price and in variable costs change the break-even point itself and changes in fixed costs affect the amount of profit made.

(b) Special Occasions Restaurant

    (i) Contribution = Selling price − variable costs
               = 12 − 4 = 8
    Fixed costs = 2 salaries + depreciation on assets + fixed overheads
               = £20 000 + 4 000 + 10 000 + 16 000
               = £50 000
    Break-even point = 50 000 / 8 = 6 250 meals

    (ii)

	£	£
Sales (£12 × 25 customers × 300 days)		90 000
Less		
Raw materials (1/3 of 90 000)	30 000	
Salaries (10 000 × 2)	20 000	
Depreciation on premises (2% of 200 000)	4 000	
Depreciation on fixtures and fittings (20% of 50 000)	10 000	
Fixed overheads	16 000	
		(80 000)
Profit		£10 000

(iii) Margin of safety:
Break-even point = 6 250 meals
Actual sales = 7 500 (25 customers × 300 days)
(1 250 / 6 250) × 100 = 20%
This is not a very large margin of safety and assumes capacity. The number of customers has to fall off by only a small amount and the business will be making a loss.

(c) Expansion of premises

(i) Contribution is the same.
Fixed costs = 5 salaries + depreciation on old assets + depreciation on new
assets + new fixed costs
£(50 000 + 4 000 + 10 000 + 6 000 + 10 000 + 50 000) = £130 000
130 000 / 8 = 16 250 break-even number of meals

(ii)

	£	£
Sales (90 000 × 2)		180 000
Less		
Raw materials (1/3 of 180 000)	60 000	
Salaries (10 000 × 5)	50 000	
Depreciation on premises (2% of 500 000)	10 000	
Depreciation on fixtures and fittings (20% of 100 000)	20 000	
Fixed overheads	50 000	
		(190 000)
Loss		£(10 000)

(iii) The break-even point has risen from 6 250 to 16 250 with the doubling of the number of customers. This is because, apart from the raw materials, other costs have more than doubled.

Question 24.3

(a)

Armagh Ltd
Net Profit Forecast for the year to 31 May 1999

	£	£
Sales (W_1)		46 800
Less		
Direct material (£5 per unit × 3 600 units)	18 000	
Direct labour (£2 per unit × 3 600 units) (W_2)	7 200	
Variable overheads (W_3)	3 600	
Fixed overheads	3 400	
Advertising	5 000	
		(37 200)
Profit		£9 600

Workings

W₁

Sales: Last year's selling price = £20 – 30% trade discount = £14

    Total sales ÷ selling price = number of units sold

     33 600 ÷ 14 = 2 400 radios sold

    Forecast = 2 400 units + 50% = 3 600 units

    Forecast selling price = £14 – £1 = £13

    Forecast sales = £13 × 3 600 units = £46 800

W₂ Labour: Last year's unit price = £4 800 ÷ 2 400 units = £2 per unit

W₃ Variable overheads: Total overheads = variable overheads + fixed overheads

  Last year: 5 800 = 2 400 + 3 400

  Variable overheads per unit = £2 400 ÷ 2 400 units = £1 per unit

  Forecast variable overheads = £1 × 3 600 = £3 600

(b) (i) Break-even units:

    1998: Contribution = 14 – (6 + 2 + 1) = 5

    Break-even point = 3 400 ÷ 5 = 680 units

    1999: Contribution = 13 – (5 + 2 + 1) = 5

    Break-even point = 8 400 ÷ 5 = 1 680 units

  (ii) Margin of safety units:

    1998: 2 400 – 680 = 1 720

    1 720 / 680 = 253%

    1999: 3 600 – 1 680 = 1 920

    1 920 / 1 680 = 114%

(c) The margin of safety is twice as big in the year just gone than in the forecast. The fall in material cost compensates for the increase in trade discount allowed but the advertising budget is very big for a small company and increases the fixed costs to a point where the break-even point becomes very large. A 50% increase in sales is very ambitious and may not happen.

Question 24.4

(i) The break-even point = Fixed costs / (Selling price – variable cost)

    Perth = 42 000 / (60 – 45)

      = 2 800 units

   Sales value = 2 800 × £60 = £168 000

   Inverness = 67 000 / (60 – 40)

      = 3 350 units

   Sales value = 3 350 × £60 = £201 000

(ii) Perth: (Profit / loss) at sales of 4 000 units:
$$= (4\ 000 \times 60) - (4\ 000 \times 45) - 42\ 000$$
$$= \text{a profit of £18 000}$$

Profit / loss at sales of 2 500 units:
$$= (2\ 500 \times 60) - (2\ 500 \times 45) - 42\ 000$$
$$= \text{a loss of £4 500}$$

Inverness: (Profit / loss) at sales of 4 000 units
$$= (4\ 000 \times 60) - (4\ 000 \times 40) - 67\ 000$$
$$= \text{a profit of £13 000}$$

(Profit / loss) at sales of 2 500 units
$$= (2\ 500 \times 60) - (2\ 500 \times 40) - 67\ 000$$
$$= \text{a loss of £17 000}$$

(iii) An after-tax profit of £48 000 with a tax rate of 20% gives a before-tax profit of:
$$= 48\ 000 \times (100 / 80)$$
$$= £60\ 000$$

Perth $= (42\ 000 + 60\ 000) / (60 - 45)$
$$= 6\ 800 \text{ units} \times £60$$
$$= £408\ 000$$

Inverness $= (67\ 000 + 60\ 000) / (60 - 40)$
$$= 6\ 350 \text{ units} \times £60$$
$$= £381\ 000$$

(iv) The margin of safety is the amount of sales above and beyond the break-even point

Perth: 7 500 units – 2 800 units = 4 700 units
              4 700 units × £60 = £282 000 sales value

Inverness: 7 500 units – 3 350 units = 4 150 units
              4 150 units × £60 = £249 000 sales value

(v) The Profit / Volume Ratio is the same as the Contribution / Sales Ratio

Perth: (15 / 60) × 100 = 25%

Inverness: (20 / 60) × 100 = 33%

(b)

The difference between the fixed costs of Perth and Inverness is

67 000 – 42 000 = 25 000

The difference between the variable costs per unit of Perth and Inverness is

40 – 45 = –5

The variance needed to absorb the fixed cost variance is

25 000 ÷ 5 = 5 000 units

5 000 units × £60 per unit = £300 000 sales

Chapter 25

Question 25.1

(a)

Darton plc

Calculation of Net Cash Revenue Receipts for Proposal 1

	Year 1 £000	Year 2 £000	Year 3 £000	Year 4 £000
Sales	320	320	352	422.4
Materials	(160)	(176)	(193.6)	(193.6)
Labour	(22)	(24)	(28.6)	(30.8)
Net revenue receipts	138	120	129.8	198

Calculation of Net Cash Revenue Receipts for Proposal 2

	Year 1 £000	Year 2 £000	Year 3 £000	Year 4 £000
Net receipts as Proposal 1	138	120	129.8	198
Repairs, maintenance etc	(16)	(16)	(16)	(16)
Net revenue receipts	122	104	113.8	182

(b)

Net Present Value Table

Year	Discount factor	Proposal 1 Net receipts £000	Present value £000	Proposal 2 Net receipts £000	Present value £000
0	1	(420)	(420)	(300)	(300)
1	0.909	138	125.442	122	110.898
2	0.826	120	99.120	104	85.904
3	0.751	129.8	97.480	113.8	85.464
4	0.683	198	135.234	182	124.306
			37.276		106.572

(c)

The answer should be set out in report format and should contain the following points:

Both proposals give a reasonable return. The repairs and maintenance on proposal 2 make its net receipts lower over the four-year period (£585 800 as opposed to £521 800), but the net present value of proposal 2 is greater than that of proposal 1.

Buying the new machine is a longer-term prospect than repairing the existing machine; the latter will have to be replaced at the end of the four years. If funding is available now at low interest rates, it might be good to take advantage of this; credit might be tighter and more expensive in four years' time.

The new machine gives the firm a spare capacity of 2 100 doors on the demand in years 3 and 4. The existing machine has a spare capacity of only 100 doors and, if demand increases during the four-year period, it will not be possible to satisfy this.

Both proposals have advantages and disadvantages but the question requires you to indicate which should be implemented. This means that you must choose one or the other. In most questions of this kind, there is no right or wrong answer and you will be given marks for stating which you recommend and for developing this recommendation by backing up your selection with reasons.

Question 25.2

See text in chapter.

Question 25.3

(a)

Lakeside plc
Calculation of Net Cash Revenue Receipts for Take-over of Turner Ltd

	Year 1	Year 2	Year 3	Year 4
	£000	£000	£000	£000
Sales (80 000 units)	1 200	1 200	1 200	1 200
Sales (20 000 units)	280	280	300	320
Operating costs	(690)	(690)	(740)	(740)
Depreciation	(60)	(60)	(60)	(60)
Net revenue receipts	730	730	700	720

Calculation of Net Cash Revenue Receipts for Take-over of Paxton Ltd

	Year 1	Year 2	Year 3	Year 4
	£000	£000	£000	£000
Sales	2 600	2 600	2 800	3 000
Operating costs	(1 110)	(1 210)	(1 410)	(1 610)
Depreciation	(90)	(90)	(90)	(90)
Net revenue receipts	1 400	1 300	1 300	1 300

Net Present Value Table

		Turner Ltd		Paxton Ltd	
Year	Discount factor	Net receipts	Present value	Net receipts	Present value
		£000	£000	£000	£000
0	1	(2 150)	(2 150)	(3 500)	(3 500)
1	0.893	730	651.89	1 400	1 250.2
2	0.797	730	581.81	1 300	1 036.1
3	0.712	700	498.40	1 300	925.6
4	0.636	720	457.92	1 300	826.8
			£40.02		£538.7

(b) The net present value of the investment in Paxton Ltd is more than ten times the size of that of Turner Ltd. However, Paxton's sales depend upon the existing contract which may lapse at the end of the four years. Although 80% of Turner's sales depend upon a similar contract, 20% are done on the open market, thus expanding the customer book. You should at this point recommend one or the other.

Question 25.4

Year	Cash inflow £000	Cash outflow £0000	Net cash flow £000	Discount factor at 12%	Present value £
Jimmy Jam					
0		200	(200)	1.000	(200 000)
1	200	50	150	0.893	133 950
2	200	50	150	0.797	119 550
3	200	50	150	0.712	106 800
4	200	50	150	0.636	95 400
5	200	50	150	0.507	76 050
					£331 750
Johnny Star					
0		100	(100)	1.000	(100 000)
1	400	200	200	0.893	178 600
2	400	200	200	0.797	159 400
					£238 000

It is worth acquiring both players but, since only one can be purchased, the projected future cash flows favour the younger man, Jimmy Jam, largely because his positive net cash flows benefit the club for five years compared with Johnny Star's two years. Another benefit of buying Jam is that, when his contract expires, it will be possible to sell him for a considerable fee as his potential is realised (at that time he will be aged 26, in the prime of his playing career). There is no such residual capital value attached to Star.

Other non-financial factors that should be considered:

Position and styles of the two players. The team manager and coach should be consulted on which player they would prefer in their team. Do they want to strengthen the defence, midfield or attack?

The age of the current team would also influence the investment decision. If the average age is young, buying Johnny Star might help to develop the younger players more quickly than if Jimmy Jam is purchased. If, on the other hand, the team already has a number of old heads, introducing a keen young player might be better.

Chapter 26

Question 26.1

Report

To: The Directors of Eurasifrac

(a) Coal Mine

It is necessary to know the variable cost of coal mined. If this is less than the market price of £80, it may be worth keeping the mine open in the hope that the geological difficulties are overcome or that the price of coal increases.

The social effects of closure must be considered. If the mine is in a town where other industries are expanding, it will be easier to stop operations and make redundancies than if the town is heavily dependent on coal for jobs. The effect of any redundancy payments on the firm's finances must also be considered before a decision is reached.

(b) Pollution of River

Your claim that the factory is not profitable is not borne out by the figures. Excluding the £3 million allocated overheads from the parent company, the true profit of the factory was £4 million in year 1, £4.2 million in year 2, rising to £4.8 million in year 3. Sales have also increased. There seems to be a strong case for the instalment of a pollution-reducing device. Not only can the company afford it but it is also worthwhile in terms of the benefit to the local environment. The company has no right to pollute the river, kill fish and damage nearby land, and if you shirk your responsibility on this, you risk the escalation of local protest with the adverse publicity which accompanies it.

(c) Igoxi

(i) Stock should be valued at the lower of cost and net realisable value, in line with SSAP 9, i.e. at £6.50 per lb.

(ii) The stock should be charged to the income statement at historic cost i.e. at £6.50. The current market price of £10 represents the opportunity cost of use but the historic cost concept prevents it from being entered anywhere in the books.

Question 26.2

See text.

Extra Questions

Question E.1

(a)

The adjusted cash book balance is the balance given minus the bank charges and the returned cheque not recorded in the cash book.
= £6 000 – 4 000 – 3 000 = £(1 000)

Bank Reconciliation Statement at 30 June 1996

	£000
Balance as per bank statement	5
Add lodgements not yet entered	6
Less outstanding cheques	(12)
Cash book balance	(1)

(b)

Revised Balance Sheet at 30 June 1996

	£000	£000
Fixed assets at cost		500
Less accumulated depreciation (**W₁**)		(240)
		260
Current assets		
Stock (69 + 5 – 1) (**W₂**)	73	
Debtors (87 + 3 – 7) (**W₃**)	83	
	156	
Current liabilities		
Bank overdraft	1	
Trade creditors	90	
	(91)	
		65
		£325
Financed by		
Ordinary shares of £1 each		195
Profit and loss account (**W₄**)		130
		£325

W₁

The correct depreciation figure is:
$(500 – 100) ÷ 10 = 40$
The figure used for the year was 10% of 500 = 50, so the depreciation figure must be reduced by 10 000. The profit will be increased by this amount.

W₂

The stock figure must be reduced by 1 000, as the net realisable value is less than the cost and the lower figure must be used. Profit will fall by 1 000.
The goods sent out on sale or return must be added to the stock at their cost price (5 000) as they still belong to the company. The profit will also increase by this amount.

W₃

The debtors figure must be reduced by the goods on sale or return at their selling price of 7 000, since this is not yet a sale. Profit must also be reduced by this amount. The cheque which was returned means that the 3 000 paid by a debtor is still owing and this must be added on. It does not affect the profit.

W₄

The profit figure must be adjusted for the items mentioned above. In addition the provision for bad debts of 2 000 is to be removed – this increases profit. The bank charges which were not recorded must be deducted from profit.

(c) The realisation concept requires that profit should not be recognised until goods have been sold.

(d) The prudence concept requires that unrealised losses be recognised as soon as they become apparent.

Question E.2

(a)

Amount paid to Rain:

	£000
Capital account balance	300
Share of asset revaluation (1/2 of 120 000)	60
Current account balance	10
Total due to Rain	370

(b)

	Squall £000	Deluge £000
Opening capital balances	250	200
Share of asset revaluation (1/3 and 1/6 of 120 000)	40	20
Balances at 30 June 1995	290	220

(c)

Appropriation Account for the year ended 30 June 1996

	£000	£000
Profit		180
Interest on capital		
Squall (10% of 290 000)	29	
Deluge (10% of 220 000)	22	
		(51)
Salaries:		
Squall	20	
Deluge	31	
		(51)
Share of profits:		
Squall (50%)	39	
Deluge (50%)	39	
		(78)
		0

Partners' Current Accounts for the year ended 30 June 1996

	Squall	*Deluge*
	£000	£000
Opening current balances	15	20
Interest on capital	29	22
Salary	20	31
Share of profits	39	39
Less drawings	(25)	(35)
Closing current balance	78	77

(d)

Under the Partnership Act 1890, in the absence of any agreement to the contrary, the profit would be divided equally between the partners. In this case each partner would receive £90 000 (half of £180 000).

(e)

Advantages of becoming a limited liability company:

    (i)   limited liability for the company's debts – owners' personal assets would be protected in the event of liquidation or bankruptcy.

    (ii) separate legal entity

    (iii) easier to raise new capital by selling shares

Disadvantages:

    (i)   lack of privacy of financial affairs as accounts have to be published

    (ii) more costly and complex to set up

    (iii) access to profit and capital is regulated by law

Question E.3

(a) A majority shareholder is an individual or company who owns more than 50% of the shares in a limited company. This shareholder has effectual control of the company, having the ability to outvote all of the other shareholders at the Annual General Meeting on the election of directors; the policies of the company can then be controlled through the directors.

(b)

Patmann plc
Balance Sheet as at 10 October 1997

	£000	£000
Authorised share capital		
600 000 ordinary shares of £1 each		600
720 000 ordinary share of 25p each		
200 000 8% preference shares of 50p each		100
Issued Share Capital and reserves		
320 000 ordinary shares of £1 each, fully paid		320
120 000 8% preference shares of 50p each, fully paid		60
Share premium account **(W₃)**		210
Profit and loss account		340
		£930

Fixed assets		570
Investment in Quinoxite plc at cost (**W₁**)		314
Current assets (**W₂**)	286	
Creditors: Amounts falling due within one year	(190)	
Net current assets (liabilities)		96
		980
Creditors: Amounts falling due after more than one year		
10% debenture stock		(50)
		£930

Workings

W₁

Patmann's investment in Quinoxite is now the original 80 000 plus the new shareholding:
Patmann has purchased an extra 65% of the 720 000 shares
i.e. 468 000 shares at 50p each = 234 000
234 000 + 80 000 = 314 000

W₂

Current assets = original figure of 280 + the proceeds of the rights issue – the cost of the new shareholding in Quinoxite.
The rights issue is 80 000 shares (1 in 3 of 240 000) at £3 each = 240 000
The cost of the shares in Quinoxite is 234 000, as calculated above.
i.e. current assets = 280 000 + 240 000 – 234 000 = 286 000

W₃

The share premium is the original 50 000 plus the premium on the new rights issue,
i.e. 80 000 shares at £2 (the difference between the nominal value of £1 and the price paid of £3) = 160 000
i.e. 50 000 + 160 000 = 210 000

(c) (i)
Gearing is the relationship between debt and equity, i.e. it shows the percentages of the total capital comprised by long-term debt, which pays a fixed interest, and by share capital, which does not have a fixed return commitment.

(ii)
The gearing ratio is found by the following formula:

$$\frac{\text{Preference shares} + \text{long} - \text{term liabilities}}{\text{Shareholders' funds} + \text{long - term liabilities}} \times 100$$

Patmann's gearing ratio at 30 September is:

$$\frac{60 + 50}{690 + 50} \times 100 = 14.86\%$$

and at 10 October:

$$\frac{60 = 50}{930 + 50} \times 100 = 11.22\%$$

(iii) The gearing has decreased as there has been an increase in the amount of ordinary
       shares and share premium. A low gearing is safer for the company as there is a
       smaller fixed return commitment each year. For the shareholder, a change in
       profits will have less of an effect on dividends paid when the gearing is low as,
       although there is more profit available to be distributed, there are also more
       shareholders for it to be distributed between.

(d) (i)
     A 'wholly-owned subsidiary' company is a company whose ordinary shares are
     all in the hands of one shareholder (holding company). The holding company has
     total control over the subsidiary.

     (ii) To obtain total control over Quinoxite, Patmann would have to purchase the
          remaining 90% of its shares.
          90% of 720 000 shares = 648 000 shares at 50p each
          = £324 000 extra to pay on top of the 10% already held.
          If we add the £80 000 which the original 10% of the shares cost, we have a
          total bill of 80 000 + 324 000 = £404 000.

     (iii) The cost of the 90% shareholding of £324 000 would have been partly
           financed by the rights issue, which raised £240 000. This leaves a shortfall of
           324 000 – 240 000 = 84 000 to be financed by the issue of the remaining
           preference shares available.
           120 000 preference shares have been issued out of an authorised 200 000
           i.e. another 80 000 can be issued.
           The issue price must therefore be 84 000 / 80 000 = £1.05p each.

Question E.4

Bashmetal Ltd

Manufacturing, Trading and Profit and Loss Account for the year ended 31 October 1995

	£	£	£
Raw materials			
Opening stock			18 260
Purchases			49 770
Carriage inwards (190 + 90)			280
			68 310
Less closing stock			(19 460)
Cost of materials consumed			48 850
Production wages			71 940
Prime cost			120 790
Factory overheads			
Wages		21 450	
Depreciation on buildings		840	
Depreciation on plant and machinery		5 684	
Rent, rates and insurance ([3 650 – 150] x 3/5)		2 100	
Light, heat and power (2 200 x ½)		1 100	
			31 174
			151 964
Add work in progress at 1 November 1994			12 480
			164 444
Less work in progress at 31 October 1995			(14 444)
Factory cost of finished production			£150 000

Sales			300 000
Less cost of goods sold:			
Opening stock of finished goods		18 060	
Factory cost of finished production		150 000	
		168 060	
Less closing stock of finished goods		(24 215)	
			(143 845)
Gross profit			156 155
Selling expenses			
Carriage outwards	2 840		
Light, heat and power (1/4)	550		
Advertising	1 350		
		4 740	
Administration expenses			
Depreciation on fixtures and fittings	1 920		
Bad debts	460		
Light, heat and power (1/4)	550		
Rent, rates and insurance (2/5)	1 400		
Directors' salaries	41 205		
Audit fee	1 600		
Administration expenses	18 230		
		65 365	
Financial costs			
Bank charges	1 400		
Debenture interest (600 + 600)	1 200		
		2 600	
			(72 705)
Net profit			83 450
Less provision for tax			(30 000)
Profit after tax			53 450
Profit and loss account b/f			18 550
Profits available for distribution			72 000
Proposed dividend			(12 000)
Retained profit c/f			£60 000

Balance Sheet as at 31 October 1995

	£	£	£
Fixed assets	*Cost*	*Depreciation*	*Net Value*
Factory buildings	42 000	(5 040)	36 960
Plant and machinery	28 420	(22 736)	5 684
Fixtures and fittings	9 600	(5 760)	3 840
	80 020	(33 536)	46 484
Current assets			
Stocks: raw materials		19 460	
work in progress		14 444	
finished goods		24 215	
Debtors		64 947	
Prepayment		150	
Bank		38 400	
		161 616	

Less current liabilities

Creditors	20 260		
Accruals (150 + 90)	240		
Proposed dividend	12 000		
Debenture interest accrued	600		
Provision for tax	30 000		
		(63 100)	
			98 516
Net assets			£145 000

Financed by:

Share capital (authorised and issued)	
240 000 ordinary shares of 25p each	60 000
Share premium	5 000
Profit and loss account	60 000
	125 000
6% debentures	20 000
Capital employed	£145 000

Question E.5

Aristo

	1991	1992	1993
	£000	£000	£000
Sales (number of units x £9)	270	360	450
Material (number of units x £1.80)	(54)	(72)	(90)
Labour (number of units x £2.2)	(66)	(88)	(110)
Depreciation (900 000 ÷ 10)	(90)	(90)	(90)
Fixed costs	(100)	(100)	(100)
	(310)	(350)	(390)
Profit (loss)	(40)	10	60

Tottle

	1991	1992	1993
	£000	£000	£000
Sales (number of units x £9.50)	190	285	380
Material (number of units x £1.60)	(32)	(48)	(64)
Labour (number of units x £0.90)	(18)	(27)	(36)
Depreciation (200 000 ÷ 10)	(20)	(20)	(20)
Fixed costs	(92)	(92)	(92)
	(162)	(187)	(212)
Profit (loss)	28	98	168

(b)

Break-even point = Fixed cost / Contribution
Aristo: 190 000 / (9 – 4) = 38 000 units
Tottle: 112 000 / (9.5 – 2.5) = 16 000 units

(c)

The profits earned by Tottle are higher than those of Aristo in each of the three years. The contribution earned is higher and the fixed costs are lower so its break-even point is lower.

(d)

If the firm buys from Hume Ltd, the contribution would be $9 - 8 = £1$. There are no extra fixed costs to be paid and, if 10 000 units were sold, the profit would increase by £10 000.

If the firm buys additional plant, the contribution from each unit will be £5, as shown above, but there will be extra fixed costs in the form of depreciation. This will be £90 000 and extra sales of 10 000 units will give a loss of £40 000 (50 000 – 90 000). Buying the product from Hume is a better choice.

Question E.6

(a)

(Worksheets follow after this question)

(b)

Job 2019:
Cost of material Prolux = 7 140 + 7 500 = 14 640

(c)

Job 2019

	£
Prolux	14 640
Other material	1 500
Direct labour	2 640
Variable overheads	5 280
Fixed factory overheads	1 408
Total cost	25 468

Solutions

(a) (i) LIFO

Blank Stock Record Card (to be filled in)

Date	Description	RECEIPTS			ISSUES			BALANCE		
		Quantity	Unit Price £	Value £	Quantity	Unit price £	Value £	Quantity	Unit Price £	Value £
March										
1	Balance							500	20	10 000
8	Supplier	500	....	....				....		....
9	....				500			....		....
14	Supplier	500	....	....				....		....
16	Supplier				100	25.60	....	....		....
17	....				300	....	....	....		....
21	Supplier	500	....	....				....		....
26	....				400	....	....	....		....
					100					....
30	....				100	....		....		....
					100					

(a) (ii) AVCO

Blank Stock Record Card (to be filled in)

Date	Description	RECEIPTS			ISSUES			BALANCE		
		Quantity	Unit Price £	Value £	Quantity	Unit price £	Value £	Quantity	Unit Price £	Value £
March										
1	Balance							500	20	10 000
8	Supplier	500	....	....				....	....	....
9	....				600	....	....	....	....	....
14	Supplier	500	....	....				....	....	....
16	Supplier				100	25.60	....	....	....	....
17	....				300	....	....	....	....	....
21	Supplier	500	....	....				....	....	....
26	....				400	....	....	....	....	....
30	....				300	....	....	....	....	....

Solutions

500

Answer

(a) (i) LIFO

Stock Record Card

Date	Description	RECEIPTS Quantity	RECEIPTS Unit Price £	RECEIPTS Value £	ISSUES Quantity	ISSUES Unit price £	ISSUES Value £	BALANCE Quantity	BALANCE Unit Price £	BALANCE Value £
March										
1	Balance							500	20	10 000
8	Supplier	500	24.00	12 000				1 000		22 000
9	Job 2018				500	24.00	12 000	500		10 000
					100	20.00	2 000	400		8 000
14	Supplier	500	25.60	12 800				900		20 800
16	Supplier				100	25.60	2 560	800		18 240
17	Job 2019				300	25 60	7 680	500		10 560
21	Supplier	500	26.20	13 100				1000		23 660
26	Job 2018				400	26.20	10 480	600		13 180
					100	26.20	2 620	500		10 560
					100	25.60	2 560	400		8 000
30	Job 2019				100	20.00	2 000	300		6 000

Answer

(a) (ii) AVCO

Stock Record Card

Date	Description	RECEIPTS			ISSUES			BALANCE		
		Quantity	Unit Price £	Value £	Quantity	Unit price £	Value £	Quantity	Unit Price £	Value £
March										
1	Balance							500	20	10 000
8	Supplier	500	24.00	12 000				1 000	22.00	22 000
9	Job 2018				600	22.00	13 200	400	22.00	8 800
14	Supplier	500	25.60	12 800				900	24.00	21 600
16	Supplier				100	25.60	2 560	800	23.80	19 040
17	Job 2019				300	23.80	7 140	500	23.80	11 900
21	Supplier	500	26.20	13 100				1 000	25.00	25 000
26	Job 2018				400	25.00	10 000	600	25.00	25 000
30	Job 2019				300	25.00	7 500	300	25.00	7 500

Index